THE REV ELEAZAR WILLIAMS.

*From a Portrait by the Chevalier Fagnani.*

G.P. PUTNAM &Co. N.Y.

# The Lost Prince:

FACTS TENDING TO PROVE

THE IDENTITY OF

## LOUIS THE SEVENTEENTH, OF FRANCE,

AND THE

## REV. ELEAZAR WILLIAMS,

MISSIONARY AMONG THE INDIANS OF NORTH AMERICA.

BY

JOHN H. HANSON.

THERE is no historical truth against which obstinacy cannot raise many objections. Many people think themselves justified in asserting against an alleged historical fact its improbability, without considering that nothing is true or untrue in the eye of history because it is probable or improbable, but simply because assuming its general logical possibility, it can be proved to be or not to be a fact.—BUNSEN.

ON applying, after a number of years, to the evidence of facts, it will always be found, in the end, that probability is in all things the best symptom of truth—LAMARTINE.

NEW YORK:
G. P. PUTNAM & CO., 10 PARK PLACE.
1854.

W. H. Tinson, Stereotyper, &c.,
22 Spruce Street, New York.

TO

THE REV. FRANCIS L. HAWKS, D.D., LL.D.,

AT WHOSE SUGGESTION THE INVESTIGATION

INTO

THE HISTORY OF THE REV. ELEAZAR WILLIAMS,

WAS FIRST UNDERTAKEN,

This Volume,

WHICH EXHIBITS AN OUTLINE OF ITS RESULTS,

Is Respectfully Dedicated,

ALIKE AS A TOKEN OF ADMIRATION FOR HIS GENIUS, ESTEEM FOR HIS VIRTUES, AND GRATITUDE FOR HIS KINDNESS

BY

HIS AFFECTIONATE FRIEND AND BROTHER IN THE MINISTRY,

THE AUTHOR.

# PREFACE.

THE public, I trust, is sensible by this time, that in this investigation there has been no attempt to impose on its credulity. If there be aught I hate, next to injustice, and against which I would stoutly contend, it is what Carlyle calls *shams*. The chief interest in this discussion is its intense reality. With Mr. Williams, as a clergyman, it has become a vital question of veracity; and I would not have published one word on the subject, had I not been morally convinced of his truthfulness, since I would not, for the sake of any temporary, but worthless literary *éclat*, trifle with the fortunes of a suffering brother in the ministry. He is no claimant for royal name, any more than he is an aspirant for political elevation. He stands in the position of one who asserts facts, the confirmation of which is derived, without his aid, from the most widely different sources. Even with respect to his journals and the events of his life, the use I have made of them in the argument, is as novel to him as it is to others. And for myself, I seek only to establish a historical fact, and let that fact take care of itself.

I received, this morning, a call from a gentleman, who represented himself to be a friend of M. de Beauchesne, whose curiosity, I find, is roused by the circumstances of Mr. Williams's life, though it would appear from the statements of this gentleman, M. de Beauchesne knew much of his history many years before I heard of his existence. Long before the conclusion of the reign of Louis Philippe, I learn that M. de Beauchesne had his name registered, among some thirty others, of whom it had been asserted that they were Louis XVII. This fact is of high importance, for, as M. de Beauchesne, if he did not write under the command of the French government, did so with its knowledge, it affords evidence, that in France, the name of Mr. Williams was associated with the history of the Dauphin, and, therefore, renders more equivocal the conduct of the Prince de Joinville, in professing ignorance of the name of Mr. Williams. Where so much deception has been practised, it is difficult to distinguish between the innocent and the guilty, and, although the motives which animated the composition of the work of M. de Beauchesne remain yet a mystery, it will afford me great pleasure to find he is no partizan, bent on the falsification of history, but is honestly devoted to the discovery of truth. By chronicling facts which came under his knowledge, he has rendered great service. A fact, however trivial, is inestimable—even a fact concerning falsehood—and, in due time, finds its place in a chain of evidence. M. de Beauchesne is seeking to obtain from the imperial government permission to examine the cemetery of St. Marguerite, and will, I hope, succeed; for, though the result would throw no light on the question of identity, it might aid in developing some details of the history.

I would take this opportunity of acknowledging many favors received, during this investigation, from the Hon. Hamilton Fish, the Hon. J. C. Spencer, the Provisional Bishop of New York, the Bishop of California, the Rev. Dr. Vinton, of Brooklyn, Dr. J. W. Francis, Mr. John Jay, Mr. Beach, of the Sun, the Chevalier Fagnani, Mr. Bogle, Mr. G. Genet, Mr. E. Genet, the Rev. Dr. Leacock, and the Clergy generally of New Orleans, Mr. Bradford, of that city, the Rev. Mr. Wells, of Boston, the Rev. Mr. Denroche, of Brockville, C. W., the Hon. Phineas Attwater, and many others. But more especially would I return thanks to the Rev. Dr. Hawks, and Mr. A. Fleming. in whom I have always found firm and judicious friends. With the one, long known, long loved, and long honored, this investigation has only served as a cement of friendship, and with the other, it will be, I trust, a bond of affection, lasting as life, since I can never forget the generous spirit he has manifested throughout.

*Hoboken*, *N. J.*, *November* 22, 1853,

# CONTENTS.

# PART I.

## THE PALACE AND THE PRISON.

THE

# LOST PRINCE.

---

## CHAPTER I.

### PRINCIPLES.

My object, in the following pages, is simply to group together for historic reference, the circumstances which tend to prove that in the person of a venerable clergyman of the Protestant Episcopal Church, there is still living, in America, the representative of the ancient glories of the French Monarchy.

The interest which this subject has excited, and the deep conviction entertained by those who have had the best opportunity of judging of the truth of many of the facts upon which this opinion is based, together with the inherent importance of the question, in a historic point of view, must form my apology for again appearing before the public in connexion with it.

I have hesitated as to the precise form into which I should throw this little work. At first, my design did not extend beyond a reprint, with notes, of the original articles in which a portion of the evidence is contained, together with an Appendix furnishing the testimony which has since come to light. I was inclined to pursue this course because the easiest for a person whose time is already fully occupied with professional duties, and also because anxious to exhibit in this way the gradual manner in which facts have been developed, as the investigation has proceeded. But, apart from the dislike of mere verbal repetition, there are many points of importance to the general understanding of the subject, and a correct estimate of the evidence, which I have either not alluded to, or but slightly touched upon, and which it is necessary to include, when throwing the matter into a permanent form. I have, therefore, determined to rewrite the whole, adopting the simplest and most natural plan, viz. to give a narrative of the main circumstances in what seem to be two lives spent in different hemispheres, and in forms of society the most widely different, but which, if there be truth in circumstantial evidence, blend harmoniously into one, conducting the same individual from the palace and the prison to the wigwam, the camp, and the church.

I shall begin by a cursory review of the events which led to the subversion of the French Monarchy, towards the conclusion of the last century; of the imprisonment of the royal family; of the tragical death of several of its members; and of the mysterious disappearance of the child whose strange after history forms, it is my belief, the principal portion of the following pages. As it is necessary to keep distinctly in view the thread of events on both sides of the Atlantic, as far as they have any bearing on the historic problem at issue, I shall next consider some of the subsequent changes in France, with especial reference to the history and movements of the members of the Bourbon family, and also give a summary account of the pretensions and life of Herr Naundorf, all of which are deserving close attention.

From Europe we shall next be carried by the necessities of the case to this country, and, after briefly tracing the romantic history of the family, in one of whose supposed members the lost Prince appears to be discovered, I will furnish from the most authentic sources all that is worthy of note, or has a bearing on the subject of our investigation, in the life of the Rev. Eleazar Williams, up to the period of his interview with the Prince de Joinville. Here we enter on the great debateable ground, and must introduce, in substance, the matter which has already appeared, bringing up the testimony to the time of publication.

The introduction of many of the circumstances of Mr. Williams's private life, which would otherwise have been omitted, has been forced upon me by others, and is necessary to clear away the obscurity which hangs over a chequered and sorrowful career. His journals and papers might never have seen the light but for the present discussion; and it is with reluctance that he has permitted what was intended merely for his own eye, and which from early boyhood has been kept in secrecy, to be made public. But everything which I shall produce weaves itself into the chain of evidence, or is necessary for his vindication.

That discussion of a somewhat exciting nature has been caused by what I have already written, is not surprising; for the question at issue is likely to awaken the most different feelings, according to the natural disposition of men, their power of weighing evidence, and estimating character, the social influences by which they are affected, and the direction from which they contemplate the subject. Society is pretty equally divided between two classes of men, the generous and enthusiastic, and the cold and sceptical. The first are, perhaps, too ready to adopt, without sufficient examination, whatever appeals to their sympathies, and addresses itself to their imagination—and the other are equally prone to form hasty conclusions against everything which seems strange and marvellous. It requires time to adjust these states of mind to each other, and to attain among masses of men to the true critical temper, which I conceive to be as far from precipitate incredulity, as it is from precipitate belief—a happy compound of what is noble in sentiment and cool in judgment, and which as little mistakes ridicule for argument, as it does feeling for proof. It was to this temper that I have sought—it is to this that I still seek to address myself; and however those who have neither understood my motives nor weighed my words, may have accused me of special pleading, or of jumping at conclusions, I can honestly say, that I have never knowingly strained a point of evidence beyond its just extent, or indicated a conclusion which facts did not seem fairly to warrant. Had the opposition I have met been merely the result of natural incredulity respecting the marvellous, the imperfection of the testimony adduced, or my own inability in handling the subject according to its merits, to which no one would more willingly subscribe than myself, I should have had neither room nor desire to complain. But in many quarters, and from various motives, there have been attempts to put down discussion. Such attempts will never succeed in cases like this, where people have to deal with a man of ordinary firmness, convinced alike of the rectitude of his intentions and the power of his position. I have no desire, however, to perpetuate strife, and shall be silent concerning much which deserves animadversion.

Before I plunge into the stream of rapidly shifting events, let me say a few words as to the nature of the evidence which it is reasonable to expect can be produced in a case like this, granting the supposed identity actually to exist. This is the natural point from which any candid mind will approach the subject. He will not ask impossibilities or improbabilities, and sneer because his demands are not complied with; but being satisfied that a position is taken by its advocate in good faith, will expect him to produce only such evidence as under given circumstances it is rational to look for; neither will he say that evidence is no evidence, because not of one particular kind, viz. demonstrative.

There are comparatively only a few things—and those not affecting our highest interests or appealing to our noblest faculties—which admit of demonstration. In all that is most important, morally, intellectually, historically, "probability is the very guide of life." Not, however, such probability or improbability as Bunsen refers to in the passage placed on the title page—the mere coinage of the fancy, apart from or in defect of evidence—the familiar "it is likely or unlikely" of conversation—but probability based on the critical survey of varied fact and extensive data—such as Lamartine refers to when he says, "On applying after a number of years to the evidence of facts, it will always be found in the end that probability is in all things the best symptom of truth." In ascertaining a disputed historic fact, the probabilities of every kind must be reckoned in as parts of the evidence determining its value; but the conclusion finally arrived at, if investigation be rightly conducted on sufficient data, is something more than mere probability, something upon which we can rest as fact.

"Probable evidence," says Bishop Butler, "is essentially distinguished from demonstrative by this, that it admits of degrees, and of all variety of them, from the highest moral certainty to the very lowest presumption. We cannot, indeed, say a thing is probably true upon one very slight presumption of it; because, as there may be probabilities on both sides of a question, there may be some against it, and though there be not, yet a slight presumption does not beget that degree of conviction which is implied in saying a thing is probably true, but that the slightest possible presumption is of the nature of a probability appears from hence, that such low presumption often repeated will amount even to moral certainty." "In questions of difficulty, or such as are thought so, where more satisfactory evidence cannot be had, or is not seen, if the result of examination be that there appears upon the whole, any the lowest presumption on one side, and none on the other, or a greater presumption on one side, though in the lowest degree greater, this determines the question even in matters of speculation." The question under consideration is one of probabilities, and I shall neither insult the understanding of the reader by denying, nor do I weaken my cause by confessing, that the probabilities prior to examination against the conclusion to which I arrive are very strong; only I contend that the probabilities in its favor are far stronger, and that to an extent which can leave little doubt to an impartial and reasoning mind of its truth, or, in other words, which carries moral conviction very nearly to its fullest height.

Now, granting that the supposed personal identity is actual, what kind of probable evidence is it likely can at this time and place be adduced in proof of it? There is a great state secret affecting vitally the interests and the honor of some of the most distinguished persons in Europe, and which has done so for more than half a century. The parties interested in keeping it will, it is probable, both use every effort to suppress whatever evidence exists, and hold in their own hands all correspondence between themselves on the subject, and all communications proceeding from agents who from time to time they may have found it necessary to employ. In the absence, therefore, of original evidence of this description, the only conceivable means by which the secret can come to light is the want of prudence in some of the parties concerned, or of fidelity in some of their agents, affording a clue or indication of its existence, and leading thoughtful minds to review carefully the whole field of the past, and gather into one focus all those tokens which an extraordinary event can scarcely fail to leave behind in its progress, and which, like foot prints and down-trodden grass and broken branches to the Indian in the forest, imperceptible or disregarded by the careless observer, conduct the diligent investigator directly and inevitably, with a precision like fate, to the very root and heart of the mystery.

I should like to have seen one of a certain class of our modern newspaper critics and philosophers with eyes that never look beyond the police intelligence and party politics of the day, and who has grown mole-sighted in falsifying the appearance of everything to suit the passions and prejudices to which he professionally panders, standing beside a quick-witted savage on the trail, whose only aim was to find his way by aid of the faculties which God gave him. How acute would be his sagacity of denial! How potent his sceptical profundity! What pointed paragraphs would he enter on his note book concerning the folly which saw a sign-post in a broken twig—a pathway in a bent reed, and followed the guiding of these in preference to verbal reports which he has no discernment to see are incongruous or false. There are many ways of arriving at truth, and we live in times when History is written backward, and the wisely doubting Niebuhr of to-day is more to be trusted than the annalist who was two thousand years nearer the facts which they relate in common.

The simple historic question under discussion is, whether a person known in this country as the Rev. Eleazar Williams be the son of Louis XVI. of France, who it has been asserted died in the Temple in the year 1795. The negative of this can be shown clearly in either of three ways. 1. By proving that the son of Louis XVI. in question died at the time and place mentioned. 2. By proving that the Rev. Eleazar Williams is an Indian. 3. By establishing as a fact, that although the Dauphin may not have died as reported, and Eleazar Williams is not an Indian as reported—there is nothing to prove a personal identity between them, or that the evidence adduced for this purpose is not reliable. The affirmative of the question on the contrary requires me to show that there is no reliance to be placed on the accounts given of the death of the royal child—that Eleazar Williams is not an Indian, and that the circumstantial identifying testimony is multifarious, strong, reliable and to the point. Here is the issue, and I meet it with no purpose or design, but to argue it on its merits. The audience in the presence of which I speak is in itself a guarantee that I shall deal fairly with the subject. Besides which, belonging to a profession happily standing aloof from secular strife, and constitutionally inclined in all things to seek for truth, I have neither the art of the special pleader nor the disposition of the sophist. If there be strength in my argument it is simply because facts clearly stated and logically reasoned from make it strong.

It is beyond the wit of man to coin a chain of circumstantial evidence upon a great historic question like this which will bear examination. Various attempts have been made to do so, in all quarters by those to whom I stand opposed, but I regard them all as signal failures. By some loophole or other the true state of the case will leak out. Whoever examines with candid and unprejudiced mind the facts I have to present, instead of ridiculing any lack of evidence will, I think, express surprise that Providence has preserved, and rendered available here, so much testimony bearing on a remote point of European history. To those who meet the investigation with the query, cui bono? I have only to say, it will be very unfortunate for mankind, morally and intellectually, when they find themselves in the majority—and where there is nothing in historic truth to awaken the curiosity, or in great reverses to excite the sympathy, of men. To me it seems a moral lesson, not unimportant for the world's welfare, if it can be shown in so striking an instance, that wrong, however carefully concealed, can scarcely hope to escape ultimate detection even on earth—and that, though it be through chinks and crevices, truth buried, like a plant immured in darkness, will grope its way by strange avenues to the light.

## CHAPTER II.

### REVOLUTION.

A PASSENGER, miraculously rescued from a late terrible railroad accident, describes the scene of unexpected and irremediable ruin by saying, that while the train was dashing on in apparent safety, the car in which he was sitting, broke, without visible cause, into a thousand fragments, and disappeared, while a motley group of legs and arms and heads came flying in the air towards him. He witnessed on a small scale what was seen in a large one in the disastrous era of the Revolution. When all is over we can philosophize upon it, trace its causes, remote and immediate, and show how it might have been avoided. But to the majority of its spectators it was as sudden and inexplicable, as the death crash of the flying train against the abutment of the open drawbridge. "A frightful gulf," says a French writer, "opens on a sudden beneath the feet of Louis XVI. He is irresistibly swallowed up—he, his throne, his power, and his family. The effects of the lightning are not more terrible or more swift. In an instant all has disappeared, and the affrighted spirit seeks in vain some vestige of so many grandeurs." In moments and scenes like these, all ordinary calculations are at fault, and facts can alone determine what is possible or probable, who shall rise and who shall fall, where and in what condition they shall alight. Whatever can happen, may happen, and the same apparent freaks of destiny which elevated persons from the lowest ranks of society to be generals, princes, and monarchs, may as easily cast the descendant of a hundred kings like sea weed to the remotest shores.

In reviewing the history of France from the beginning of the reign of Louis XVI. to the present time, I shall not enter further into details than is necessary for the clear presentation of the evidence I have to lay before the reader. I aim at no originality either of thought or statement, but simply desire to recall, in connection and for a definite end, facts well known to every general reader.

Louis XIII. died in 1643, leaving two sons, Louis XIV. who ascended the throne at the age of five years, and Philip Duke of Orleans, great-grandfather of Philip Egalité. Under the regency of Anne of Austria and the able ministry of Cardinal Mazarin, the power of the French Monarchy, and the subjection of the people of France, were carried to their greatest extent, and what was wanting was supplied under the sovereignty of Louis XIV. and the ministry of Colbert. Prerogative was at its height. But so were the glory, power, wealth and intellect of France, and in a social atmosphere, impregnated with the slavish maxims of a gorgeous superstition, and not yet disturbed, though voluptuously illuminated with the nascent brightness of an epicurean philosophy, the gilded yoke of despotism was borne proudly by both nobles and people.

But the clouds which gathered round the declining years of the Grande Monarch, and dimmed the military splendors of the early portion of his reign, were fit precursors of the convulsion whose elements were fermenting in concealment beneath the corruption, infidelity, and intellectual activity of the age. It required the regency of Orleans, the impure reign of Louis XV. and the infidel intoxication produced by the writings of Voltaire and Rousseau to bring the nation to that maturity of evil which issued in the French Revolution. Yet never did the French Monarchy seem to stand on a firmer basis of national consent and popular favor than on the 10th May, 1774, when the courtiers of France, rushing, with "a terrible noise like thunder," from the room wherein lay the disfigured remains of Louis XV. paid their first heartless service to Louis XVI. and his queen. Dissolved in tears, and on their knees, the youthful pair besought of heaven the wisdom and the strength they needed.

In the midst of a licentious court, compared with which the seraglio of the sultan is as the purity of heaven, Louis XVI. had received a careful education, which gave him the morals of an anchorite, the implicit faith of a devotee, the fortitude of a martyr, and the bashfulness of a rustic. He would have formed the happiness of a domestic circle, or been the beau ideal of an English clergyman—for he had all virtues under heaven but those which he most needed,—self-reliance, energy, promptitude, and decision. He could be the father of his people—he could not be their ruler; and sacrificed the lives of thousands who loved him and deserved his love, because unable to speak the kingly word which should crush anarchy and punish murder. There was many a crisis in the Revolution, when a word, a look, a gesture of the hand, such as duty demands from all who govern, would have rolled back the tide of revolt and rallied a million swords around the throne. But while he diligently educated himself, as the dangers of the social fermentation increased, to play, with dignity and self approval, his part in the judgment hall and on the scaffold, he neglected, with a weakness which Christianity may pardon, but which Christian wisdom cannot justify, the active heroism which makes a great ruler, entrusted with the guardianship of social order, as prompt to do as he is ready to suffer. He was but twenty years of age when called to the most arduous political position which the world has yet offered to ambition.

Born on the very day on which the towers and temples of Lisbon reeled beneath the throes of an earthquake, which was felt by half the world, Providence seemed to afford, at the moment in which Marie Antoinette entered on the theatre she was to adorn and sadden, some prognostic of the moral and political convulsion in the midst of which she was to expire. Possessed of natural abilities, in every way answerable to the aërial beauty and queenly majesty of her person, her education was deficient in those solid mental acquirements which are the chief ornament and safeguard, next to moral principle, of a woman in high station. When a child, the present Queen of England was seen diligently studying Blackstone. Marie Antoinette carried to the court of Versailles an absolute ignorance, not of law merely, but of history. A complete familiarity with Italian, the conversational mastery of French, a little music, great skill in needle-work, beauty made perfect by grace, an understanding ready to grasp whatever it grappled with, and a tongue fluent to express in words most appropriate every varying emotion of the soul, childlike simplicity, a contempt for etiquette, and a love of nature, but, above all, a spirit warm, gentle, affectionate, and true, form the sum of what she brought to Louis; enough, indeed, to make home happy in private station, or to shine foremost in courtly circle, but inadequate to render woman the Mentor of a man in times when thrones reel and nations are convulsed. It is impossible to read the domestic history of this true hearted woman in the pages of a faithful chronicler like Madame Campan, and gaze upon some portrait which truly reflects her image, without feeling for her, even apart from the mighty griefs and the unparalleled tragedy of her closing life, love, pity, admiration, and respect, which may teach even republican hearts what loyalty is towards an object morally worthy of it. It is the misery of high station, that it hides from the multitude all that would most create love. It is hardly too much to say, that had even revolutionary

France known its king and queen, as we now know them, the tribune would have been silent, the tricolor unraised, the Marseillaise unsung, and the scaffold unstained.

Louis Stanislaus, Count de Provence, the eldest brother of the king, the Monsieur of the Revolution, had acuter intellect, bolder character, more cultivated mind, better knowledge of what is bad in men, and greater capacity for governing them than his unfortunate brother; but his superiority was only in the understanding. He was inferior to Louis in religious faith and moral principle. In creed a philosopher of the school of Voltaire, in disposition an intriguer, in politics an innovator with an eye to self, he regarded himself, even from early life, as the most considerable person, in all but the accident of birth, of his family; and, though not destitute of affection for his brother, habitually looked down upon him, and loved the flattery which drew a contrast in his favor. Eastern despotism may have had its reasons for liking no brother near the throne. Height is apt to produce high thoughts, and the latitude of future possibilities afford perilous scope for the imagination. There is no greater temptation than that which may be, but is not. The Count de Provence was among the foremost to give the first impulse to the Revolution. His object may be questioned—the fact is beyond dispute.*

The Count D'Artois, afterwards Charles X., though destitute of personal daring, had the high bearing and the chivalric accomplishments which are the pride and ornament of a court; together with the mediocral abilities which are moral blessings to a younger brother of regal family, in times when circumstances foster ambition in the naturally aspiring. There seemed no probability of his ever mounting the throne; his pride was to be what he was, high among the highest, enjoying all the pleasures without any of the responsibilities of royalty. But the tendency of events was to foster a prospective ambition for his posterity, which he had too much

* Alison, Hist. Europe, vol. i. 63. Lamartine, Hist. Rest., vol. i, 254.

good sense and proper feeling to entertain for himself. His creed was what was established—his philosophy courtly conservatism, which views the world as a theatre for the privileged classes, and the utility of the people as confined to uttering bravos, trimming the lights, and paying the orchestra. A beautiful illusion, but destined to vanish like fairy scenery under the hands of the scene-shifter. As the tragic drama of the Revolution advanced to its *dénoûment*, and the political position of Louis XVI. grew hopeless, his interests became identified with those of the Count de Provence. The brothers were drawn closer together by their marriage to two daughters of the King of Sardinia; and as for many years it seemed likely that, either from the coldness and indifference of the king, or other more insuperable causes, Marie Antoinette would have no issue, the hopes of succession appeared to rest with the Countess D'Artois, who, in 1778, had already two children—the Duc D'Angoulême and the Duc de Berri. But this family distinction, diminished at the close of that year, when the queen gave birth to a daughter, was entirely done away by the birth of the first Dauphin in 1781—and of the Duke of Normandy in 1785.

There is a mysterious story* connected with the birth of the first Dauphin, which, resting entirely on the authority of Louis XVIII., is important in the light of a personal confession, and confirms all that history has asserted of his ambition. He states that on the evening of the 22d October, 1781, the birthday of the prince, on retiring to rest, he found on a table near his bed a letter addressed, "for Monsieur only." In answer to his inquiries, his attendants professed ignorance of the source from whence it came, when he directed one of them to open it. When the envelope was removed, another was discovered with a similar superscription. He then took it into his own hands; and, as he represents, with a presentiment that he was going to read something unusual, turned from his attendants, that no one but himself

* Filia Dolorosa, p. 8. De Quincey's Autobiographical Sketches, vol. 1. p. 330.

might see the contents. The second envelope contained a sheet of black paper inscribed with white characters. Having dismissed his suite, he retired to bed, and by the light of his night lamp read as follows:—

"Be comforted; I have just drawn the horoscope of the new-born prince; he will not deprive you of the crown; he will cease to live when his father ceases to reign. Another besides yourself will, however, succeed to Louis XVI., but you will, nevertheless, be one day king of France. He who becomes your successor will be most unfortunate. Rejoice greatly that you are without progeny—the existence of your sons would be menaced by too many evils—for your family is destined to drink to the very dregs of the bitterest draught contained in the cup of Fate.

"Adieu, tremble for your life should you seek to know me.

"I am, DEATH!!!"

At this period the political atmosphere already began to exhibit signs of the approaching storm. To the views of the theorists of whom France was full, the American Revolution had given a deceptive impetus; deceptive, because if ever there were countries dissimilar in every particular on which sound calculations of political expediency can be based, they were the United States of America and the kingdom of France. It was not merely that one country was crowded with a dense and fermenting population, and the other, in its vast outstretched expanse of unreclaimed wilderness, afforded ample latitude for the peaceful growth of a mighty people for centuries to come, but that the genius, the character, the intelligence of the two nations placed them mutually in the most antipodal position which civilization can allow. In America liberty was a principle—in France it was the passionate dream of a people constitutionally in love with despotism—in America it was but another name for law—in France it meant the disruption of all legal restraint. When America revolted she stood in a conservative attitude—pleading precedent, upholding law, protesting against innovation; but France did what no nation can do and live—torė herself violently from the past, and disregarded everything chartered and prescriptive. The new country was in truth the old—the old country a political infant. Anglo Saxon law, reformed religion, English literature, and colonial life republican in essence, all combined to make America emphatically the land of self-government. In France, superstition dead even to rottenness, and giving birth only to the efflorescent but deadly fungi of infidelity, ignorance of law, save that of caste and prerogative, and utter incapacity to keep down brute force and the upheavings of a physical hell, but by the compulsion of grape shot, all rendered the establishment of republican freedom as chimerical as the return to patriarchal simplicity and nomadic life. Louis and his ministers had not discernment to perceive that the era of mere rival nationalities was for the present over, and that what might have been policy in the reign of Louis XIV., was the height of folly in 1777. Chatham could afford to applaud the sturdy colonists, for their spirit was the spirit of Englishmen—but Louis brought the inflamable mind of France in contact with a flame which burnt healthily enough where it was native, and the very vital spirit of the body whose iron enginery was of calibre to bear it, but which exploded to the four winds of Heaven the rust-eaten constitution of an efféte despotism.

The Count de Provence, sitting on nearly the highest step which led to the throne, had long made himself the centre of theoretic schemes of public reformation, the object of which was to ingratiate himself with the party of movement, increase his own popularity; and, in the event of a convulsion, supplant his brother and his family.* Louis had begun his reign by a prudent system of retrenchments, which if persisted in throughout, might have warded off the dangers of revolution until the advent of some less cautious monarch; but war induced expenditure, expenditure recklessness, recklessness ruin. His brother perceived his difficulties,

* Lamartine, Hist. Rest., vol. i. p. 253.

and took advantage of them. He had gone so far as to devise a new constitution of which he should be the head. Religious principle could not restrain him, for he had none; and a creedless man has no compass but self-interest. Even natural affection could be reconciled by an easy philosophy to the dictates of ambition. Believing his brother incompetent for the crisis which he saw approaching, and which he did his utmost to hasten, he fraternally consulted his happiness, as well as the welfare of the kingdom, in an imagined abdication, which should place the crown on his own head, and hand over the conduct of the revolution to one capable by nerve, and philosophy, and intellect, to control its forces, and reconstruct society in harmony with principles of which Voltaire could approve. "He surrounded himself," says an indulgent historian, "with philosophers, theorists, and censors of government and religion. He allowed them to divulge in public his criticisms on the ministry, his ideas for reforming the kingdom, his accordance in heart and soul with the general spirit of the nation, which was evincing itself in complaints against the government, and in outbursts of enthusiasm, the precursors of revolution. But he never permitted these murmurs and this enthusiasm to pass the bounds of external respect for religion and the throne. Although a sceptic in religion and revolutionary, he regarded the church and monarchy as two popular idols, whose divinity might be contested without removing their images from before the eyes of the people. There was etiquette and ceremony even in his convictions, for he believed in the Divine right of established custom; and all reform which extended to *his own* dynasty, appeared to him sacrilegious. *He foresaw a revolution*, and thinking *his brother* unequal to the struggle of the times, *believed his weakness would drive him to abdication;* that the Count D'Artois would lose himself in vain resistance to the progress of the world; *and that France, reconstituted on a new monarchical plan, would take refuge under his own government.* He did not conspire to obtain, nor even desire this consummation; but he expected all. Nevertheless, he loved the king—his brother—*as much as he was capable of loving any one ranking above him.*"*

There is one clause in this passage which contradicts all the rest, and which cannot, if the rest be true, be true itself:—"He did not conspire to obtain—he did not even desire, this consummation." He did not openly, it is true, conspire and say to the nation—'Dethrone Louis XVI., set aside his descendants—and make me king instead'—for this would have been to defeat his own object, and de Provence was too wise, and had too much sense of propriety to act thus; but he who could precipitate a revolution, which he foresaw must end in the dethronement of the existing monarch, and which he imagined would lead to his own elevation; who placed himself knowingly in the path of convulsion, as its termination, and took care that his creatures should publish his schemes and principles of reform, to the evident prejudice of his brother, and the acceleration of the crisis which must cause his downfall, did conspire, as effectually as a man in his position could conspire, against the throne of Louis XVI., and did desire to possess that for which he so conspired. He even predicted the king's death.†

We must judge men in such periods by their actions, and those of the Count de Provence neither showed the brother nor the loyal subject. It is remarkable how entirely, in his visionary schemes for the future, the right of inheritance, vested by the immemorial laws of France in the male descendants of the king, were set aside. He did not, according to the plain statement of Lamartine, contemplate merely an abdication and a regency in his person, during the minority of the young Prince, but an actual transference of kingly power intact to him and his heirs; in other words, a Provence dynasty. And if so, it follows that, ere one single stone was removed from the ancient structure of the monarchy, the mind of the Count de Provence was occupied with the problem of his nephew's fate. It was an element in the future which could not be overlooked by an acute and circumspect intellect like his. The

* Lamartine, Hist. Rest. Book x. sec. v. † Lamartine, Girondists, vol i. p. 454.

incident of the mysterious letter is a proof that it was not. When the leprous distillment of revolutionary principle had removed the old Hamlet, there would still remain the young one; and there was no widowed majesty of Denmark, by wedding which he could safely permit the scion of an elder house to wander fetterless through the land; and if there had been, the young man's sword might have smelt in due time a rat behind the arras, without there being any Polonius for a scapegoat; or in a domestic feud, as in the classic example, both uncle and nephew might lose their lives.

These were contingencies which the Count de Provence could not but foresee, for they were all inseparaby included in the idea prophetic of a throne. How he purposed to deal with these difficulties it is not for me to determine. Suffice it to show that they must have been before his mind even prior to the outbreak of the Revolution. He may have trusted to accident for some pathway out of the labyrinth. He might propose to reconcile all difficulties by adopting as his successor one who had legal rights before him; or, education, controlled by him in the principles of his proposed philosophic monarchy, might make the facile intellect of youth a convert to the laws of his regenerated constitution. This was afterwards the republican plan—it may have been that of De Provence. But there was a far darker mode of escape from all perplexity, which there are strong reasons for supposing he resorted to. It was by impeaching the legitimacy of the children of Marie Antoinette, for which the long period which elapsed between her marriage with the king and the birth of her first child, together with the scandal her enemies had for many years industriously circulated, afforded some coloring of probability. At the meeting of the Assembly of Notables in 1787, Monsieur appeared for the first time publicly in his character of reformer, and by throwing the whole weight of his influence against the aristocracy, and in favor of the masses, and proposing sweeping schemes of constitutional amendment, gained an amount of popularity which for awhile intoxicated him, and which he never ceased to strive after by the same means, until the revolutionary tide, which he had put in motion, threatened to sweep him away.

While he was thus seeking to accomplish two portions of his general design, viz. to shake the throne of his brother, and in so doing attract the popular favor to himself, attempts were made in the same Assembly to set aside the royal children, by the introduction of documents denying their legitimacy, by the Duke Fitz James, of which Monsieur was openly declared to be the author.*

Letters, said to be written by the Count de Provence to Fitz James, have been published. That they express his sentiments I have no doubt. As to their authenticity I know nothing. The only thing suspicious about them is, that documents so damnatory should ever see the light. A knowledge of their history would however be requisite to decide this point—for when a letter once gets out of a man's hand there is no telling into whose it may fall. [A.]

But, Monsieur, like all persons endowed with similar powers of foresight, read the future only through the medium of his personal interests, and imagined that events would take the course which he desired. Every one at that time was willing to revolutionize to his own level, and vainly imagined that the downward tendency of things would be arrested just where he stood. A truly honest and unselfish mind, which had no bad ambition to gratify, would never have been so blinded.

It is conclusive evidence against the moral integrity of Monsieur, that he could weakly dream of a revolution potent enough to compel abdication on the part of the reigning sovereign, but whose waves should subside in admiring murmurs beneath his own feet. Such a revolution was the vain chimera of that ambition which o'erleaps itself. Monsieur made two miscalculations. He underestimated both his brother's powers of endurance and the intensity and scope of the revolutionary forces.

* Moniteur, 20 Germinal, year 6. Ireland's France, p. 286.

Louis XVI. had the passive heroism of the martyr, if he had not the active heroism of the king. The last of his thoughts would have been abdication, which should compromise the interests of his son. In the midst of his most trying difficulties, the idea that he could retire from the contest with his people seems never to have crossed his mind. But both he and the queen were almost as much disturbed by the fear of royalist movements without the kingdom, having for their object the transference of sovereignty to some other hand, as they were by the present dangers of an insurgent populace. And as for the Revolution itself, when once set in motion it must run its course. It was beyond the control of court intrigue. It was a whirlwind which could be ridden [illegible] those bold enough to mount it, but which could not be individually directed or allayed.

The States General were summoned to provide means for liquidating the public debts contracted by the war. They did not even consider the question. To relieve the king from his embarrassment was not their desire. They resolved themselves into a single chamber. The Tiers Etats swallowed up the clergy and nobility. Individuals hesitated, struggled, and deserted, but the tide of innovation swept on without impediment. The National Assembly, declared permanent, set to work under the inspiration of its master-spirit, Mirabeau, to reform the Constitution. The king gave in his adherence to the project. He was no longer king. Concession only created the appetite for demand. From the senate chamber the revolution descended into the streets. There were conflicts between the royal troops and the populace. The Bastile was besieged and taken. The struggle every day displayed more visibly its deadly nature. Too late the high nobility perceived their error. In despair they began precipitately to fly from danger self-invoked. Emigration disintegrated the vital forces of the nation.

Foremost among the emigrants, were the Count D'Artois and the Prince de Condé. Monsieur, in no personal danger, remained in Paris; supposing, that though the reformation was more radical than he had imagined, things were yet taking the course which he desired. Like a philosopher, he watched his time, and in loving intercourse with the brother whom he imagined himself destined to supplant, abided the moment when the pressure of revolution should render his throne no longer tenable. D'Artois removed, and placed in opposition to the reforming nation, left no alternative in case of regal vacancy but himself. The popularity derived from his early advocacy of reform, and his connexion with Mirabeau, still continued; and having the art to remain on good terms alike with the king and people, he occupied for a considerable time the very position most favorable for the accomplishment of his views. But, as months passed on, and though the revolutionary movement continued unabated, gathering strength as it proceeded, Louis XVI. showed no signs of weakly flinching from personal danger by abdication, Monsieur seems to have grown impatient; and, standing between both parties, to have hoped by a *coup d'état* to render himself master of both. The conspiracy of which the Marquis de Favras was the ostensible agent, had for its object no less bold and sweeping measures than the destruction of Lafayette, Neckar, and Bailley, the abduction of the king to Perone, the proclamation of the Count de Provence as Regent, and the denial of the legitimacy of the Dauphin and Madame Royale, on the evidence of the documents formerly presented to the Assembly of Notables; from all which, if successful, there would have been but a short cut to the actual possession of monarchical power by the Regent.* Now, the evidence connecting Monsieur with this conspiracy is all but conclusive. In the first place, the Marquis de Favras had been an officer in the household of the Count de Provence; and, as the whole scope of the conspiracy was to exalt the latter at the expense of the most eminent men in the kingdom, it does not seem in any

* Moniteur, 20 Germinal, year 6. Ireland's, France, p. 287.
Lamartine Hist. Rest. vol. i. p. 255.

way likely, that a person in the subordinate position of Favras would have undertaken a project of such magnitude, without the knowledge and consent of the party chiefly interested, and with whom he stood at the time, as his agent, in the most intimate relation.

At the very moment in which Favras was preparing to carry his project into execution, he was engaged—on the confessed authority of the Count de Provence, for the fact was proved, and could not be denied—to negotiate the loan of large sums of money. Favras confessed his guilt, but refused to tell the names of his instigators and accomplices; hoping, as it would seem to the last, that those who involved him in danger, would do what he felt they had the power to do—extricate him from it. But, finding himself disappointed in his just expectations, he broke out as the guillotine was about to descend, in "muttered curses" on some powerful accomplice who had thus left him to perish.* Posterity will incline to the belief, that the astute philosopher who had the audacity to ask of the tribunal the pardon of Favras, perhaps the better to keep him silent, at the very moment that he denied all knowledge of his plot, though he admitted having employed him to negotiate a loan, was not as innocent as he asserted, and as the judges, before whom he voluntarily went with an imposing retinue, declared him to be.

Lamartine attributes the acquittal of Monsieur at this critical moment less to his innocence than to the pride of the people and the tribunal, at the unusual spectacle of a prince royal condescending to plead his cause before them, and profess his adherence to democratic principles. One thing is clear—if history has not the power of absolutely condemning him in this affair—she is equally powerless to acquit him, for probabilities are all against him. He was unprincipled enough for anything, and had only one purpose in life—self-aggrandisement. In June, 1791, the royal cause in France had grown hopeless, and the transfer of authority from one member of the Bourbon family to another, impossible. Monsieur,

* Lamartine, Hist. Rest., vol. i. p. 255.

therefore, determined on emigration, which afforded the best chance for the accomplishment of his designs. On the night in which his brother set out on the fatal journey to Varennes, the Count de Provence, leaving his wife to encounter all dangers unprotected, fled from Paris, joined his mistress, the Countess de Balbi, and with her hastened to Coblentz, the head-quarters of the royalists,* which thenceforth became the centre of opposition to the authority of Louis XVI., as uncompromising as that shown by the republicans. Deplorable was the position of the king, after his return from Varennes. A prisoner in his own palace, insulted and trampled on by his subjects, he beheld his brothers on a foreign soil collecting round them the ancient loyalty and chivalry of the kingdom, but, without consulting even his privately expressed wishes, or regarding him as still invested with kingly authority. The Count D'Artois had attempted to foment an European crusade against republican France; but, though he received promises from various courts, no active measures were taken; and he had finally established himself at Coblentz, to which place the princes and nobility of France thronged from all quarters. Even before the arrival of the Count de Provence, it had been proposed to establish a regency, without the King's consent, in the person of one of the emigrant princes; and this may have accelerated his movements to prevent the choice falling in his absence on his younger brother. No sooner had he arrived, than he took on himself the control of everything, and established a royal court surpassing in magnificence those of the monarchs who visited Coblentz. Without proclaiming himself Regent he acted as king, distributed among the emigrants, as the true source and fountain of honor, crosses and military commissions, borrowed money from all who had any, sent letters throughout France to the nobility who yet remained, urging emigration, and threatened with forfeiture those who hesitated to join his standard; thus depriving his brother of

* Lamartine, Hist. Rest., vol. i. p. 259.

the countenance and presence of all who might aid him, and leaving him in helpless solitude among his enemies. But, there was no class of men whom he more courted than the clergy, not because he had any respect for religion—for his infidel principles are well-known—but because he could use them as instruments.* The bait which he held out was the promise of the restoration of all confiscated ecclesiastical property. He also established a system of agencies throughout the whole of Europe, by means of which he had his creatures everywhere; and, in proportion as the power of the king declined at home, his grew abroad, and even spread in secret throughout France, and in Paris itself, where he held, or imagined himself to hold, from a safe distance, communication with the revolutionary chiefs, and especially with Robespierre, who, there is strong reason to believe, was often his unconscious instrument. That he corresponded personally with Robespierre is most certain, since the late M. Genet saw a letter written by him to the latter. "There is a time," said a writer of the period, "prescribed by experience, when truth must be brought to light upon all occurrences; awaiting which period we can, nevertheless, pronounce from proofs collected in various directions, this truth: that it was from the exterior that Robespierre acted. He was surrounded by the agents of Monsieur, who successively pointed out to him the persons whose remorse of conscience gave that Prince cause of fear; those who had penetrated his projects, and such as were not favorable to his views." There were many, indeed, in all directions, who perceived the tendency which Monsieur was thus giving to affairs.† The unfortunate Louis and his queen were tormented with apprehensions that their wily brother—whose character they well knew—would take advantage of their condition,‡ to set them entirely aside; and the tenor of his communications to them was such as to show that he regarded himself as the centre of all hope and power. They were to trust no one in France, but to rely

* Ireland's France, p. 290. † Lamartine, Girondists, vol. i. p. 194; Ireland, p. 291.
‡ Lamartine, Girondists, vol. i. pp. 154, 457.

implicitly on him, and on the foreign aid which he would bring, and hence it was evident that in case of a restoration, as the convulsions which had occurred would be attributed to the imbecility of the king, so the revival of order would be placed to the account of his brother, who, with popular consent, might retain the throne instead of handing it back to its owner. And many of the emigrants themselves, though compelled by circumstances to act in concert with Monsieur, yet feared, hated, and mistrusted him. They knew him to be undoubtedly ambitious and intensely selfish. "*The only thing*," says Lamartine, "*in which he profoundly believed was himself, his blood, his tradition, his right, his necessity. He adopted everything which could serve him.*" And if this be not the character of a man ripe for all iniquity, I have learnt language and read history in vain.

But the interests of the great majority of emigrants—bishops, princes, nobility, officers, inferior clergy, philosophers, political theorists, and writers—were so clearly bound up with those of the Count de Provence, who seemed alone able to conduct the wrecked vessel of their fortunes into a safe harbor, that, although there were not wanting those who openly accused him as being the author of every misfortune, yet the general feeling among them at this period was, that the king had proved himself unfit for the crown, that a regency was necessary, and that Monsieur was the only person to whom the regal authority should be delegated. The idea of personal legitimacy was subordinated, among royalists of eminence, to that of proved capacity to reign, and they were willing to sacrifice the letter of regality, provided they could insure the substance, and regain their own footing and prerogative. Monsieur was at this time proclaimed Regent, but the project was, through policy, abandoned, and he contented himself, for the present, with exercising the power without continuing the name. "Louis XVI.," says Lamartine, "disapproved of emigration, and was not without a feeling of offence at his brother's intriguing abroad, sometimes in his name, but without his wishes. He shrank from the idea of passing in the eyes of Europe for *a prince in leading-strings, whose ambitious brothers seized upon his rights in adopting his cause*, and stipulated for his interest without his intervention.

"At Coblentz a regency was openly spoken of, and bestowed upon the Count de Provence, and this regency, which had devolved on a prince of the blood of emigration, whilst the king maintained a struggle at Paris, greatly humiliated Louis XVI. and the queen. This usurpation of their rights, although clothed in the dress of devotion and tenderness, was even more bitter to them than the outrages of the Assembly and the people. We always dread most that which is nearest to us, and the triumph of the emigration only promised them a throne disputed by the Regent who had restored it."

Until the acceptation of the new constitution, the king continued a prisoner of state in the Tuileries, enjoying the mockery of respect under the control of Lafayette. Barnarve, like Mirabeau at a former period, too late endeavored to repair the evils he had done, but the clandestine meetings between him and his sovereigns may have lent a merciful illusion to the dreary interval. The new constitution adopted and sworn to by the king, it seemed for a time as if the bottom of the precipice had been safely reached, and the surrender of ancient prerogative might restore the king to the affection of his people. The dissolution of the Constituent Assembly, composed of men ripe in age and competent by experience for the task of legislation, without capacity in its members for re-election, from which, with Quixotic self-denial, they had debarred themselves, handed over the task of government, or rather gave the power of social demolition, to the Legislative Assembly, who, with the rashness of youth, and the enthusiasm of theorists, proceeded to undo all that their predecessors had, not without wisdom, accomplished. Meanwhile the Clubs surpassing the Assembly in audacity, and the brute masses exceeding the Clubs in violence, ushered in the reign of anarchy, until, at length, on the arrival of the ferocious Marseillais in Paris, on the 30th July, 1792, the hydra of ultra democracy gathered its strength for a last assault on everything which legislation had sanctioned, and on the 10th of the following month, the painted skeleton of royalty, crumbled, at its first deadly touch, into dust.

Falling dynasties, to expire with honor, should have heroes at their head. Louis should have died in the Tuileries, but in those corridors and courtyards the blood of the slaughtered Swiss, loyal in vain and martyrs to honor, finds a voice which, but for the sight of a mother and her children, would bid us suspend our sympathy for the fall of unheroic greatness in the presence of a more costly sacrifice.

The imprisonment of Louis threw all the remains of royal power into the hands of his brother. As time advances, and the annals and secret underplots of the Revolution are more thoroughly understood, the character of De Provence will loom up into an evil eminence, and History, in her classification of monarchs, will place him on the same page which holds John and Richard of England.

## CHAPTER III.

### CHILDHOOD.

Louis Charles, the second son of Louis XVI. and Marie Antoinette, was born at Versailles, March 27, 1785. It had formerly been the practice of the French court that the delivery of the queen should take place in public, but this needless cruelty had been abolished in consequence of the danger incurred at the birth of Madame Royale, and only the royal family and the chief officers of state were present on the occasion—witnesses enough to testify that a prospective heir to the throne had entered the world. But alas! how needless the precaution! By a singular fatality, at the very moment when the accoucheur proclaimed aloud the birth of the Prince, a crown which ornamented the canopy of the queen's bedstead fell suddenly from its place, and rolled shattered towards Marie Antoinette. Though little noticed at the time, subsequent events caused this incident to be viewed as a vivid prognostic of the fate of the French monarchy under him who should be inheritor of its phantom royalty and broken crown.*

The child was baptized the same day by the Cardinal de Rohan. The Count de Provence stood godfather and Madame Elizabeth was the representative, as sponsor, of the queen of the Two Sicilies. He received the title of the Duke of Normandy, was decorated with the insignia of the order of the Holy Ghost, and fireworks, illuminations, popular acclamations, and royal bounties testified the national joy.

The republican element was already fermenting, and, nine days after the birth of the child, a paper was read, before the royal academy in Paris, advocating the novel idea that the title to the throne rested on the will of the people. On the 24th May, Marie Antoinette returned public thanks to God for her safe delivery. The next year was signalized by the journey to Cherbourg. The infant duke accompanied his father, and shared with him the popular acclamations which hailed his progress through his dominions, and especially through the province from which he took his title. "Come, my little Normandy," exclaimed the enraptured king, "thy name brings happiness."†

Amid the increasing difficulties of the kingdom, two years of domestic felicity succeeded—when, in the year 1788, the infant princess Sophie died, a calamity which the queen always looked upon as the first drop of the thunder shower. The opening of the States General took place—and, on the eve of fresh domestic sorrow, and yet darker political troubles, superstition, by strange coincidence, contributed to cast its cloud over the future. Four wax candles were burning on the toilette table of the queen as she was sitting one evening, towards the end of May, conversing with

* Memoirs of the Duchess D'Angoulême, p. 10.

† Beauchesne, vol. I. p. 21.

her ladies respecting the incidents of the day, and indulging in mournful prognostications, when in succession the lights began of themselves to go out. When the third was extinguished "Misfortune," said the queen, "has the power to make us superstitious; if the fourth taper go out like the rest, nothing can prevent my looking upon it as a fatal omen." It went out—and though simple natural causes were suggested to the queen, the unusual incident rested on her spirits.

The Dauphin had for a long time been in a rickety and scrofulous condition. Public opinion, always unjust to Marie Antoinette, attributed the maternal affection with which she kept the child from injurious indulgences and amusements, to superior affection for the robust, healthy and lovely little Duke of Normandy. On the 4th June, 1789, the young prince died at Meudon, only too happy to escape thus early the troubles of his family. The death of the child was however made an occasion by the Tiers Etats for exhibiting their disrespect for the king, and their growing encroachments on the royal prerogative. The President of the Assembly intruded almost forcibly into the apartment where the king was weeping over the remains, to ascertain the Prince's death. "Are there no parents in the Tiers Etats?" said the indignant king. The anxiety of the Assembly on this occasion strangely contrasts with the apathy of the Convention in 1795, when informed of the asserted death of the succeeding Dauphin.* This child, now in the fourth year of his age, was too young to have much sense of the calamities which crowded on his parents—and, together with the apparent title to a succession he was destined never to enjoy, was made, by the death of his brother, the owner of a little pet dog called Moufflet. The Bastile fell on the 14th June. On the succeeding day the Dauphin made his first appearance, amid the stormy scenes of the Revolution, in the balcony of the courtyard of Versailles, where the queen presented him to the people in her arms in

* Campan, vol. ii. p. 37.

obedience to the popular clamor, and in the hope to still the tempest of democracy by the presence of childhood. Vain hope! "Here is that throne," said one of the creatures of the Duc d'Orleans, as he looked up into the state room of the castle—"Here is that throne, the vestiges of which will soon be sought in vain."

The personal appearance of the young Prince at this time is described by historians as of the most captivating character—and in the pictures taken of him after his imprisonment in the Temple, when confinement and disease had produced their terrible ravages on his constitution and intellect, it is not easy to trace the infantine beauty he possessed, when as yet the personal attractions, derived from the combined blood of many kingly races, had only been fostered by association since infancy with the most refined court in Europe, and all the ease and splendor of Versailles. It must, indeed, have been an incomprehensible scene to the child as for the first time he gazed upon the demoniac heavings of the wild tempest of democracy, and felt—but knew not why—that those he most loved, and of whom he knew nothing but what could awaken love, were the objects on whom fell its concentrated rage.

His blonde flowing hair, fair open physiognomy, full of sense and innocence, and finely-proportioned form, gave promise of both beauty and vigor. One feature I must not overlook. There is a marked discrepancy between the color of his eyes as described by many historians, and as represented in the pictures which have come down to us. The first say they were of a brilliant blue—whereas the latter, the most trustworthy witnesses, especially where the artist is of the literal and unimaginative school, show them to have been of a clear hazel—tinted perhaps slightly at the edges with a bluish coloring, but having nothing of the deep clear azure which enhance the aërial beauty of Marie Antoinette by recalling the hues of a southern sky. How far confinement and disease* may

* Beauchesne, vol. ii. p. 252.

have contributed to modify the color of the eyes, is a question for physicians to determine.

If the sayings and doings of most children in cultivated ranks of society were carefully recorded, they would, I suppose, present about the same level of intellect. Those which are handed down concerning the Dauphin are in no way remarkable. Their interest consists in the picture they present of the opening aspect of a life so soon to be obscured by clouds. The queen was in the habit of playing little airs upon the harp or guitar, as he lay amid the happy group at evening by her side, and, on one occasion, she accompanied the music with the words—

"Sleep, my child, and close thine eyelids,
For thy cries disturb my heart,
Sleep, my child, for thy poor mother
Feels affliction's keenest dart."

At the words, "thy poor mother," and the allusion to sorrow, he seemed touched; and, reclining on the couch, gazed silently and intently on the queen. Madame Elizabeth, misled by his silence, cried out, "the best of it is, that Charles is sleeping."

"Ah, my dear aunt," was the reply, "how can I sleep when listening to Mama Reine?"*

What a contrast between the peaceful evenings at St. Cloud and the long, dark nights of solitude and affliction in the Temple.

There is more point in another anecdote. One day, in the garden at Bagatelle, he threw himself, with the waywardness of a child, into the midst of a rose-bush, and, on an attendant warning him of the danger he ran of tearing out his eyes, he exclaimed, "thorny paths lead to glory!"

"My child," said the queen, when she heard his reply, "the maxim you have cited is true, but your application of it is not just. There is no glory in tearing your eyes out. Were you to

* Beauchesne, vol. i. p. 26.

expose yourself to destroy some pernicious animal, or protect some fellow creature from danger, that might be called glory. But, before you again speak of glory, wait till you have read the histories of Du Guesclin, Bayard, and Turenne, who shed their blood for France."

Blushing for his folly, he kissed her hand, and said, "Dear mamma, it shall be my glory to obey you."*

On another occasion, having hidden a flute belonging to one of the pages in a chink in the terrace, the queen, to punish him, confined his dog, Moufflet, as his accomplice. Distressed by the cries of the animal, he implored his release. "It is not Moufflet who did it. It is not Moufflet who should suffer." At his own request he was confined and the dog liberated; and, when again set free, immediately restored the flute with apologies to the owner.

The following incident occurred after the flight to Varennes, but may be mentioned here. Before going to his little garden at the Tuileries, he exercised himself in the management of a light gun. At the moment of departure, the officer of the National Guard on service said to him, "Monsiegneur, before you go out give up your gun." He stoutly refused, and on being reproved by his governess, replied, "If monsieur had asked me to give him my gun, it would have been well. But, he said, give it up." "Always quick and blunt," said the king—"but I am glad to perceive that he knows the value of words and feels the propriety of terms."†

These anecdotes may serve to give some idea of the natural disposition of the child during his happiest days, and show a character which, under proper culture, promised to manifest the best fruits. He appears to have been affectionate, thoughtful, bold, and endowed with a quick sense of his own rights, and what justice demanded in respect of others.

His chief employment, during his brief space of happiness at Versailles, was in the cultivation of his flower garden, that he might be able to present bouquets to "Mama Reine." But the time had

* Beauchesne, vol. i. p. 29. † Beauchesne, vol. i, p. 60.

arrived when these delights of childhood were to be surrendered. The 2d Oct., 1789, is memorable for the entertainment imprudently given to the body-guard at Versailles. The heart-intoxication of the royalist chivalry was at its height, and the Dauphin as he entered the festal chamber, holding his mother's hand, was greeted with the wildest acclamations of delight—and there can be no better proof of the insane joy of the assembled soldiers, than the suicide of one of the body-guard out of remorse for previous feelings of disloyalty.

A different scene did the Chateau of Versailles present to the eyes of the child, who must have been bewildered by these inexplicable changes, when the brute rabble assailed the ancient dwelling of their kings, and his mother narrowly escaped the knives plunged into her just vacated bed. Then came the hideous journey to Paris amid troops and sans-culottes, and women, and cannon, and dust, and blood, and gory heads, and curses, and insults. The Tuileries had been uninhabited for more than a century, and presented a desolate and dismantled appearance to the Prince, accustomed to the freshness and splendor of Versailles. "How ugly everything is here, mamma," he said, as they entered. To which the afflicted mother replied—"Louis XIV. lodged here, my son, and was well satisfied. We should not be more difficult to accommodate than he."

Notwithstanding the rapid increase of political troubles, the king and queen were diligent in the oversight of their children's education—and the Dauphin, by this time, had made considerable progress in his studies. He was still under the care of a governess—but the Abbé Davaux, of whom he was very fond, acted as his private tutor. No sooner were they settled in their new abode, than the routine of careful study was recommenced, and the marks of thought and proficiency exhibited by the Prince, afforded his parents some consolation under the pressure of political troubles. The day after the arrival in Paris, hearing a noise in the court-yard—and, afraid of another popular outbreak—he exclaimed, "Good God, mamma, has yesterday come again?"

A few days after, his father, perceiving that he looked very thoughtful, inquired what occupied him?—on which he asked, in a serious and affectionate manner, why the people of France, who formerly loved him so well, were now so exasperated against him? The reply of the king is memorable, affording a happy instance of the manner in which the most complicated events can be conveyed to childish apprehension, and also exhibiting the simple view which the king himself took of the Revolution. "I wished, my child, to render the people still happier than they were. I wanted money to pay the expenses occasioned by wars. I asked my people for money, as my predecessors had always done. Magistrates composing the parliament opposed it, and said that the people alone had a right to consent to it. I assembled the principal inhabitants of every town, whether distinguished by birth, talents, or fortune, at Versailles. That is what is called the States General. When they were assembled, they required concessions of me, which I could not make, either with due respect for myself, or with justice to you, who will be my successor. Wicked men, inducing the people to rise, have occasioned the excesses of the last few days. The people must not be blamed for them."* He was easily made to see the necessity of showing an obliging spirit to all the public officers with whom he came in contact, and after conversing with any of them, would say to his mother, "Was that right?"

The people in general—and even the members of the Assembly—entertained respect and love for the child, the danger and difficulties of whose position none could fail to perceive, and few could refrain from pitying. Never were the popular acclamations, during temporary lulls in the tempest, more heartfelt and sincere, than when the royal parents presented themselves in company with their child. Then, whether in the presence of the Assembly or the mob, the air was rent with the cries of "Vive le Roi!—Vive la Reine!—Vive M. le Dauphin!" O, France! France! thou art a

* Campan, vol. ii. p. 72.

strange land—variable as the sky or sea, and presenting some features of the angel when most the demon.

Deprived of his recreation in the spacious gardens of Versailles, he had given to him as a substitute a little spot of ground near the Tuileries. "It is this same garden," says Beauchesne, "changed, renewed, enlarged, that at a later period Napoleon consecrated to the King of Rome, Charles X. to the Duke of Bordeaux, and Louis Philippe to the Count de Paris. How many thoughts are awakened by this little spot of ground, so soon abandoned by its young proprietors." There is indeed a melancholy interest attached to it. Here the Dauphin amused himself with raising flowers to present as of old to his mother—and as, in his visits to the garden he was usually accompanied by a detachment of the National Guard, he himself assumed their uniform. It was this which probably led to the formation of a little regiment of boys, which gloried in the title of the "Royal Dauphin," of which the Prince was appointed honorary colonel. The design of the king in giving his consent to this scheme, was to take advantage of the popular feeling in favor of the Dauphin, and in this he for a time succeeded.

"The Royal Dauphin" became a general favorite. Recruits were readily obtained, and after a few weeks' drilling, they took their place among the troops of the line and acquired a semi-political importance. Parisian wit indeed not inappropriately dubbed it "The Royal Bonbon"—but it survived the satire—though at length disbanded on account of difficulties which arose from the formation of similar corps leading to jealousies, conflicts, duels and wounds—until parents protested against so serious an amusement, and "The Royal Dauphin" was seen no more—having however taken part in the funeral solemnities of Mirabeau and joined with its little tambourins in beating the "générale."*

The year 1790 was spent by the royal family between the Tuileries and the palace at St. Cloud—and during this period of

Beauchesne, vol. i. p. 64.

domestic quiet the advancement of the Dauphin was rapid in his different branches of study, and the healthfulness of his constitution, and the robustness of his form, were daily on the increase. He presented no sign of the scrofulous disease of which his brother had died, and never at any period had more than an incipient tendency to it.

The next important incident in his life was the flight to Varennes on the 21st June, 1791. For many months projects of escape had been agitated among the royal family and their friends, but in agreement with the fatality and fatuity which seemed to attend all their plans, the favorable period of escape was allowed to pass, and the time chosen when all France was alive with suspicion.

Let us look at this event in the point of view in which it appeared to the Dauphin himself. Roused out of sleep in the middle of the night, he found himself dressed in girl's clothes—and all the family were in some masquerade disguise. "What do you think of all this?" said his sister as she equipped him. "I suppose we are all going to the theatre."—He was carried down a secret stairway into the street. It was midnight. The party separated into twos and threes. He was put into a carriage, and fell asleep amid the mutual congratulations of the family. The morning broke, the weather was fine, the country lovely, and all the party in good spirits. The comedy was complete. The king was a valet, the queen a governess, and the Dauphin transformed into the daughter of the Baroness de Koff, and rejoiced in the name of Aglæ.

But it was again night, and there was difficulty and danger. They had lost their way. They descended from the carriage and wandered about by the light of a lantern—returned to the vehicle, drove on, were stopped, questioned, forced to alight—then there were crowds, confusion, altercation and dismay, in the midst of which the poor child dropped asleep in a strange dark room. When he again awoke his sister said to him, "O, Charles—you have deceived yourself—this is no comedy!" "I have seen that for a long time," he replied.

Again he was in a carriage, and two strange gentlemen were added to the company. One was kind and polite, and protected them from insult and abuse, and the child in gratitude clambered upon his knees.—He was once more in Paris, in his old apartment in the Tuileries—And such, to the Dauphin, was the flight to, and return from, Varennes. Merciful ignorance of reality, which hides from childhood the calamities of life. Worth a thousand pages of philosophising is the following from Bertrand de Molleville, relative to a period not long posterior to this:—

"While the queen spoke to me, the little Dauphin, beautiful as an angel, amused himself with singing and dancing in the apartment, with a little sabre of wood and a buckler, which he held on his arm. They came to call him to supper, and in two bounds he was at the door.

"'My son,' said the queen, 'do you go out without bowing to M. Bertrand?'

"'O, mamma,' said the child, continuing to dance, 'M. Bertrand is one of our best friends, good evening, M. Bertrand,' and he sprang out of the apartment.

"'Is he not handsome?' said the queen, when he had gone out.

"'He is very happy,' I added, 'to be so young. He feels none of our sorrows, and his happiness does us good."'

During the fourteen months which intervened between the return from Varennes and the final catastrophe at the Tuileries, there is little particularly deserving of record in this brilliant but hapless childhood. When the mob defiled through the palace on the 20th June, the Prince, seated on a table in front of his mother, and half smothered with a red cap, served, as a safeguard for her in the perils of the hour.

But, with the exception of such occasional inconveniences, whilst the faintest shadow of royalty remained, it was to the children of the king as if his power stood on a base like the Pyramids. Sheltered from the mental anxiety which wrung the hearts of his parents, and which in one hour at Varennes had bleached the hair of Marie Antoinette into the whiteness of snow, the Prince continued to enjoy all the happiness which his age permitted, and to develope alike in strength and mental activity. Under the care of the Abbé Davaux he made great progress, and wrote a good hand. The life he led was calculated to expand his faculties, and impart an unusual facility of acquirement. One example of depth of thought remarkable in a child will serve to close the record of his happiest days. While reading in the fifth book of Telemachus, the questions proposed by the Cretans to the candidates for the throne, when electing a king, he came to the second question, "Who is the most unfortunate of men?" "Let me," he said, "reply to this question, as if I were Telemachus. The most unhappy of men is a king who has the misfortune to see that his subjects do not obey his laws."

The 10th of August came at last, and all was dismay and anguish in the Tuileries. The Prince, in company with the king, queen, Madame Elizabeth, and his sister, passed through the ranks of the National Guard, and then the whole party returned into the palace, where the chambers were filled with military, and looked from the windows upon the mingled throng of soldiers and people in the gardens and streets below. Then there was confusion and alarm, women hurrying hither and thither in helpless dismay—sounds of conflict, rage, despair, in the midst of which the Prince was led by his parents, through the ranks of the grenadiers, into the chamber of the Assembly. He was no longer heir to a throne. The next change was to a little green-papered cell in the monastery of the Feuillans, where the royal family awaited transmission to their memorable prison with which we are chiefly concerned—the Temple.

# CHAPTER IV.

## THE ORPHANS.

On the 10th August, 1792, the king and royal family took refuge from the violence of the mob in the chamber of the National Assembly. They were placed in the reporters' box—a small enclosure, exposed to the burning heat of the sun. During the exciting sitting they remained without refreshment, while the work of carnage went on without. The Dauphin fell asleep on his mother's lap. Late in the night they were transferred to the monastery of the Feuillans. Destitute of everything, linen was supplied to them by their friends—and the wife of the English ambassador, Lady Gower Sutherland—sent, for the use of the Dauphin, the clothes of her son, who was a child of about the same age. They continued at the monastery until 13th August, when, by the order of the Commune, they were transferred to the Temple. They were at first taken to the portion of it called the palace, formerly inhabited by the Count D'Artois. At night they were transferred to their final prison in the Tower. "Your master," said a municipal officer to one of the king's attendants, "was used to gilt ceilings—he shall now see how the assassins of the people are lodged."

The following brief outline of the imprisonment of the royal family divides itself into three parts:

1. From 13th August, 1792, to the execution of Louis XVI., on 21st January, 1793.

2. From thence to the execution of Marie Antoinette, October 16, 1793.

3. From the death of the queen to June 8, 1795, when the Dauphin disappeared from the Tower, and was asserted to have died.

The present chapter will contain a brief examination of the first two periods, in which I shall confine myself to those points which enter into the general argument.

The Tower of the Temple—one of the most ancient and remarkable buildings in Paris—was erected by the Knights Templar, about the year 1200, and was designed as the treasury and arsenal of the order. It consisted of a massive square tower one hundred and fifty feet high, the walls of which were more than nine feet thick. It was flanked at the angles by four circular turrets, and had on the north side a small stone building—attached to it, but without internal communication—called the little tower, having similar turrets of lesser dimensions at the angles—while the whole series of compacted structures were crowned with conical caps, and presented an appearance of stern gloomy strength in keeping with the men and times that reared them.

This building had been the theatre of much of the heroism, crime, magnificence, luxury, and tragic suffering which are blended in the history of the priestly knights of Jerusalem. It was now dismantled and desolate, and converted into the sepulchre of a dynasty. During the repair of the principal tower, the royal family were temporarily placed in the little tower—the queen and ladies occupying the second story, and the king and his attendants the third.*

The fall from the height of royalty had been sudden and terrible. But it found the king, formed by nature and education to act the martyr, prepared to meet it with calmness and dignity. He experienced some little regret at having made no effort to suppress the insurrection, but solaced himself with the thought that he was not responsible for the blood that had been shed. He knew there was now no escape from death. The policy pursued by the Count de Provence had left him alone in the midst of his enemies. The royalists were all gathered round his brother at Coblentz. From the moment of entering the Temple, he began his preparation for

* Clery,

death. The name of Charles I. was frequently on his lips. There was providentially a library of some fifteen hundred volumes in the tower, which formed a solace for his captivity, but he kept his eye chiefly on the record of the sufferings of the martyr king.

The queen, but for her children, would, without a sigh, have died in the Tuileries. She likewise was well aware that death awaited her, and, though hope might occasionally revive, looked steadily to this as the consummation.

The fate of their children after their own decease, must have both occupied the thoughts of the unfortunate pair and formed the subject of conversation between them. The Dauphin was necessarily the chief object of their anxiety. Madame Royale was shielded by her sex and the salique law. The king did not for a moment contemplate the forfeiture of his son's right to the throne. To the last he aimed at transmitting the princely inheritance to him with all its dangers, and trained his mind for this end, looking forward to the hour when France would right itself.

It is remarkable that, on the 10th August, he did not adopt so obvious an expedient for personal escape as abdication. Had he retired into private station, even at that late hour, he might have been saved. But he could not do this without sacrificing the future interests of his son. The nation would have required of him a dynastic surrender—and, on the other hand, the effect of abdication would have been to throw all power into the hands of his brother, whose ambition he well knew, and whose designs he distrusted. He chose rather to run all hazards, and permit power to be wrested from him with life, than to jeopard the succession of his son.

Freed from the cares of government, he applied himself religiously to the task of educating his child. From the moment the royal family entered the Temp[illegible] outine of life was established, which, occasionally inter[illegible] kness or unusual calamity, continued to be observed [illegible] emained together. Particular seasons were set apart for devotion, study, rest, and recreation. From ten till one was given by the king and queen to the education of their children. The Dauphin possessed intelligence precociously developed, great facility of acquisition, and a remarkably retentive memory. History and geography formed his principal studies—and the latter was taught him according to the new division of France. In the evening, the instruction of the Dauphin was continued.

The massacres of September broke in upon their calm and not unhappy life, but the usual routine was soon resumed. At the latter end of that month they were removed to the great tower, and as this was the scene of the Dauphin's long confinement, we must enter into the details of the arrangements.

The enormous and massive pile was divided into four stories, having a large central pillar mounting as high as the floor of the fourth story, which rested on its supreme capital. The walls were between nine and ten feet thick, and the space which they enclosed nearly thirty-six feet square. The ground floor presented bare walls, and was devoid of all ornament, except the elegant carving of the capital, arches, and columns. It was devoted—together with the apartments in three of the turrets—to the municipal officers on service in the Temple.

In the fourth turret was a spiral staircase, which ran uninterruptedly to the top of the building—and, at each of the landings, were two doors, one of oak and one of iron. The relative position of this staircase and the different suites of apartments must be borne in mind, as it shows how communication could be held with the upper stories without the knowledge or suspicion of persons occupying the other chambers. The first story resembled the ground floor, and was occupied by the guard, who stacked their arms around the central column. Provided the sentry was gained over, any changes could be effected by the municipal officers without the knowledge of the soldiers, when confined within the massive walls of the guard-room. The second story was divided into four chambers, and was devoted to the king, the Dauphin, and their attendants. The apartments were warmed in winter by a central stove.

In the third story, similarly divided, resided the queen, and the other female members of her household. The fourth story, destitute of the pillar which ran through all the others, presented a vast open hall, and was used, together with the gallery opening from it, and running round the exterior of the building, for exercise —although the spaces in the battlements were filled up with close lattice-work, to prevent any communication by signals between the captives and persons outside.

During all the trials to which the royal family had for years been subjected, the health of the Dauphin had remained unimpaired, and at the time of going to the Temple he was in the very height of his beauty, strength, and elastic vigor. But long confinement, notwithstanding all the precautions taken by his parents to keep him in exercise, began now sensibly to wear upon his spirits.

In the beginning of December it was determined to bring the king to trial—but as yet the royal family were kept in suspense concerning the time and method of proceeding. With a patient heroism above praise, they continued to the last the routine which they had established at the beginning of their captivity. On the 11th, the king and Dauphin went as usual at nine o'clock to breakfast with the queen, and though various indications showed that a crisis was approaching, Louis, with calm demeanor, retired with his son to his apartment. They amused themselves for awhile with a game of chance. The number sixteen was invariably unfortunate with the Dauphin. "I cannot" he exclaimed, "get beyond sixteen."* The coincidence seemed sensibly to affect the king. He was hearing him read when the commissioners entered to take the boy away. Louis tenderly embraced him and they parted. The child had

* Clery.

repeated the last lesson to the father. Cut to the heart, the unfortunate man continued for half an hour leaning his head on his hand in speechless dejection.

At one o'clock on the same day he was brought to trial at the bar of the Convention. Into the particulars of this long and memorable process, the end of which was determined from the beginning, I will not enter. For the second time in history a sovereign stood for judgment at the bar of his people. The most innocent of rulers was offered as a sacrifice for the sins of generations. The trial was still in progress, on Christmas day, when Louis shut himself up in his cabinet, and wrote his will. It is a document which must claim a place even in this brief summary, for it affords evidence of the mind of the king, in reference to his brothers, than which no direct accusation could speak more eloquently at the bar of posterity.

I give it for brevity's sake in the abridged shape in which it appears in the pages of Lamartine—nothing being omitted but some unimportant formalities of expression. It ran thus:

"I, Louis, XVI. of that name, king of France. confined for four months with my family in the tower of the Temple, at Paris, by those who were my subjects. and deprived during eleven days, of all communication with even my family, and moreover implicated in a trial, the issue of which it is impossible to foresee, on account of the passions of men, having no one save God as a witness of my thoughts, or to whom I can address myself—declare here in His presence my last wishes and sentiments. I bequeath my soul to God my Creator, and pray He may receive it into His mercy for Christ's sake. I die in the faith of the Church, and obedience to its decisions. I pray God to forgive me all my sins. I have striven to remember and detest them, and to humble myself before Him. I beg all those whom I have involuntarily injured (for I do not remember ever having wilfully injured any one) to forgive me the evil they believe I have done them. I request all men who have any charity, to unite their prayers to mine. I pardon, from the bottom of my heart, all those who have become my enemies without my ever giving them any motive, and I pray God to pardon them, as well as those who, from a false or mistaken zeal, have done me much harm I recommend to God my wife and children, my brothers, and all those attached to me by ties of blood, or any other manner. I pray God to look with compassion on my wife, children, and sister, who for a long time have suffered with me, and to support them if they lose me, and so long as they remain in this world. I recommend my children to my wife, whose affection for them I have never doubted. I also pray her to teach them to look upon the grandeurs of the world, if they should be condemned to suffer them, only as dangerous and temporary possessions, and to turn their thoughts to the only real and durable glories of eternity. I pray my sister to continue to show the same tenderness to my children, and to replace their mother should they have the misfortune to lose her. I pray my wife to forgive me all the misfortunes she suffers on my account, and the sorrow I may have caused her in the course of my life, as she may be certain that I forgive her all, if she fancied she had anything wherewith to reproach herself. I recommend my children, after their duty to God—which is before all, to remain always united among themselves, to obey their mother, grateful for all the care she has taken of them, and in memory of myself. I pray them to look upon my sister as a second mother. I recommend my son, if he has the misfortune to become king, to remember that he owes himself to the happiness of his fellow citizens, to forget all hatred and resentment, and especially that which relates to the misfortunes and sorrows I now undergo. Let him remember that he can only make his subjects happy by reigning according to the laws—but that a king can only cause the laws to be respected, and do all the good he wishes, so long as he possesses the necessary power; but that when the contrary occurs, being thwarted in his actions, and inspiring no respect, he is more injurious than useful. I conclude by declaring before God, and ready to appear in His presence, that I am innocent of all the crimes laid to my charge.

"Written in duplicate at the Tower of the Temple, December, 25th, 1752.

"Louis."

At the moment the king penned this sublime and touching testament, the Count de Provence and the Count D'Artois at the head of their respective courts, were maintaining the splendor and exercising the functions of royalty among their adherents. In appearance, as well as by the ties of blood, they were the props on which the youthful Prince would seem compelled to lean. But though the king includes his brothers in the general prayer for all those united to him by kindred, or in any other way, he pointedly omits their names from all those portions of his will where it would have been natural to mention them. At the beginning of the document he shows, by retaining the title of Louis XVI., that he has not relinquished his own claim to the throne. But instead of commending his son to the care of his uncles, as guardians of his rights, he pointedly passes them by, and entrusts him solely to the imprisoned queen, assigning emphatically as a reason, that he had never doubted her affection—and in case of the queen's death, he commits the guardianship of his children to his sister. But there is no intimation that in any event he expects anything from his brothers.

So marked an omission, under such circumstances, cannot be explained on any probable ground but this, that he distrusted them, and knew, from past experience, that their efforts, for the restoration of monarchy in France, were designed for their own benefit, and not for that of him and his family He had no confidence that they would respect the rights of his child, and therefore committed him to the care of two feeble, imprisoned women. The substitution of the Princess Elizabeth as guardian for his son in case of the queen's death, is most marked and emphatic.

The last days of Louis XVI. have been chronicled by the ablest pens of France and England. It does not enter into the scope of my design to speak of them in detail. The historic drama is one which holds us breathless though read a hundred times. We know full well the tragic truth—yet scarcely can we refrain indulging a fleeting hope as we mingle in fancy with the pale and weeping group in the Temple—or picture the majestic martyr nightly conferring with his heroic counsel, or exchanging, with the fondness of a lover, clandestine letters with those whom he is only to meet once more before the long, long parting of death. We can sympathize with the emotions in the chamber where the dread struggle is going on—we can enter into the deep scorn of Robespierre as Verniaud belies by his vote the eloquence still reverberating in the air, and hear him hiss to his neighbor, "These are your orators"—or feel the dead chill silence, of horror and disgust, as Phillip of Orleans gives his voice for death.

But the saddest and the most heart-rending scene of all is that with which the painter's art has made us most familiar—the separation of the dying king and his family. And this, too, was the first deep sorrow of the Dauphin's life. Children do not grieve at the exchange from palaces to poverty. His health might suffer from confinement, but the happiest place on earth for him was the prison chamber of his parents. In the midst of the terror of the 10th of August, the queen had made the little fellow happy by promising, as a reward for his presence of mind, that he should sleep in her room. It was when he hung in agony to the venerated form of his father, while his other relatives were fainting or weeping around, that the Dauphin first entered into the shadow of the cloud which was to go on increasing in darkness until it finally left him in the merciful midnight of prostrated intellect.

At this time he was sufficiently old and intelligent to feel the full bitterness of a bereavement which has had few parallels on earth—and his acutely sensitive nature, at that tender age must have received a severe shock by the loss of his parent, his preceptor, his friend, his companion. Terrible was the tension of feeling with which the bereaved family waited the next morning for the promised interview, at the moment of death, which Louis, with a loving self-denial, forbore to grant. Charles the First, by his calm heroism on the scaffold, assured the restoration of his family to the throne of England—and Louis, treading with equal fortitude in his steps, would have achieved the same end in respect to the sovereignty of France, but for the brutality which first bereft his child of reason, and the dark intrigue which, under the show of kindness, removed him, as probability indicates, from the country he would otherwise have governed.

I have no doubt, that Lamartine's judgment of the Count de Provence, is correct—that he loved his brother as much as it was possible for him to love any one ranking above him—and can easily conceive, that the blow which laid the discrowned head of Louis in the dust, occasioned him as much sorrow as it was possible for him to feel for any event, which removed the chief apparent obstacle between him and the throne. But, that he dreamed of permitting a helpless child to remain a perpetual barrier between him and the prize so long coveted, and so nearly his, is an idea which cannot be entertained by any fair estimate of the probable motives and aims of such a character.

Hitherto, the royalist party, notwithstanding the efforts of De Provence and his adherents, had steadily resisted his assuming the title of Regent—and the pity with which the tragic death of the king had filled all hearts, forbade any attempt to do more than adopt that dignity now. Had Monsieur, in the face of the indignant sorrow of Europe, dared to assail, openly, the title of the young Prince to a throne that lay in ruins, it would have for ever defeated his ambitious designs. No course remained for him but to acquiesce nominally in the general sentiment, and seek to accomplish his wishes in a more covert manner. So soon, therefore, as he received tidings of the execution of his brother, and while still at Ham, in Westphalia, he issued the following proclamation. This was on the 28th January, 1792:—

"Louis Stanislaus Xavier de France, son of France, uncle of the king, Regent of the kingdom, to all those to whom these letters shall come, greeting:—

"Penetrated with horror, on learning that the most criminal of men have crowned their numerous outrages, by the greatest offence, we have first implored heaven to obtain his assistance to surmount the sentiments of a profound grief, and the movements of our indignation; so that we may be able to deliver ourselves to the accomplishment of the duties which, in circumstances so grave, are the first in the order of those which *the immutable laws of the French monarchy impose upon us.*

"Our most dear, and most honored brother and sovereign lord, the King, Louis XVI., of that name, having died on the 21st of the present month of January, under the parricidal steel which the ferocious usurpers of the sovereign authority in France have brought upon his august person :—

"We declare, that the Dauphin, Louis Charles, born 27th March, 1785, is King of France and Navarre, under the name of Louis XVII., and that, *by the right of birth, as well as by the disposition of the fundamental laws of the kingdom, we are and will be Regent of France, during the minority of the king, our nephew*, and lord.

"Invested in this quality, with the exercise of the rights and powers of sovereignty, and of the superior ministry of royal justice, we, in taking charge, being bound to acquit our obligations and duties, to the effect of employing, with the aid of God, the assistance of the good and loyal French of all orders of the kingdom, and of the recognized power of the sovereign allies of the crown of France, do pledge themselves,

"1st. To the liberation of the king, Louis XVII., our nephew. 2d. Of the queen, his august mother and nurse; of the princess, his sister, our very dear niece; of the Princess Elizabeth his aunt, our very dear sister; all detained in the severest captivity by the chiefs of faction, and, simultaneously, to the re-establishment of the monarchy upon the unalterable bases of the Constitution; to the reformation of abuses introduced into the regimen of the public administration; to the restoration of the religion of our fathers in the purity of its worship and canonical discipline; to the re-establishment of the magistracy for the maintenance of order and the disposition of justice; to the re-establishment of the French of all orders in the exercise of their legitimate rights, and in the enjoyment of all their property usurped and alienated; to the severe and exemplary punishment of crimes; to the re-establishment of the laws of peace; and, in fine, to the accomplishment of the solemn engagements which we have taken, conjointly with our very dear brother Charles Philip, of France, Count D'Artois, to whom are united our very dear nephews, grandsons of France, Louis Antoine, Duc de Angoulême, and Charles Ferdinand, Duc de Berri, and our cousins, princes of the blood royal, Louis Joseph of Bourbon,

Prince of Conde, Louis Henry Joseph de Bourbon, Duc of Bourbon, and Louis Antoine Henri de Bourbon, Duc d'Enghien, by our deliberations addressed to our brother the king, 11th September, 1791, and other acts emanating from us, in which acts we persist and shall invariably persist.

"To which end we command and ordain to all French and subjects of the king, to obey the commandments which they shall receive from us on account of the king, and the commandments of our very dear brother Charles Philip, of France, Count D'Artois, whom we have nominated and instituted lieutenant-general of the kingdom, when our said brother and lieutenant-general shall ordain anything on account of the king and the Regent of France. * * * * * *

"Given at Ham, in Westphalia, under our sign and seal ordinary, of which we shall make use for the acts of governing, until the seals of the kingdom, destroyed by the factions, shall have been re-established—and under the countersign of the ministers of state, the Marshals de Broglie and de Castries.

"Signed,

"Louis Stanislaus Xvaier,

"By the Regent of France,

"The Marshal Duc de Broglie.

"The Marshal de Castries."

Now, on this proclamation I may remark, that neither by the right of birth, nor by the disposition of the fundamental laws of the kingdom, was the Count de Provence necessarily Regent on the demise of his brother. Precedency was in favor of the regency of the queen-mother, and a proposition that Marie Antoinette should be appointed regent had actually been made prior to the imprisonment of the royal family, but was strenuously opposed by the adherents of Monsieur. During the minority of Louis XIII., the Queen-mother, Marie de Médicis, became regent, although an uncle of the king, Gaston, Duke of Orleans, was alive. And so also on the accession of Louis XIV., Anne of Austria, as queen-mother, was nominated, notwithstanding the imaginary "rights of birth and fundamental laws," which should have given this office to the brother of the late king, Philip, Duke of Orleans. He had as little in the will of

Louis XVI. to rest on, as in the customs and laws of the kingdom. But to believe in his own rights and necessity was part of the fundamental creed of De Provence. He accordingly issued another proclamation to the French refugees, in which the same idea is repeated. "I have taken the title of Regent of the kingdom, which the right of my birth, gives during the minority of the king, Louis XVII., my nephew."

But, another remarkable portion of the first of these documents, is the pledge given by the Regent, that he would seek to accomplish the liberation of Louis XVII. from the Temple. We must expect, therefore, to find the young Prince surrounded in prison by the secret emissaries of the Regent, whose character leaves no doubt that he would not undertake the project without turning it to his own advantage. Copies of the Regent's proclamations were printed and spread through France by millions, showing the vast system of agencies under his control. The Vendéean army, under La Rochejaquelin, proclaimed Louis XVII. king—but without any recognition of the authority of the Count de Provence—which was, however, proclaimed, together with the accession of the young king, by the Prince de Condé, in Swabia. Among the European governments there was a general acknowledgment of the Dauphin as king.

The hapless survivors in the Temple were, for a time, sunk in the lowest abyss of despondency. But, necessity roused them to action, and the queen entertained the hope of escape in company with her children. One plot was so ingenious that it would probably have succeeded, had it been put into immediate execution. But, delay was fatal—and the increased severity with which the young king was watched, rendered it impossible to effect his escape —while Marie Antoinette refused to avail herself of a personal deliverance which would be attended with the abandonment of her son.

In the spring of 1792, the health of the child began visibly to decline. He suffered much from fever, pain in the side, and general debility—occasioned in a great measure by confinement, but more by mental exhaustion. It was impossible that one so young could live in the centre of the most terrific alarms and extreme revulsions, without being weakened both in mind and body—and the murder of his father broke down completely the elasticity of his natural disposition.

While he remained under his mother's care everything was done for his relief. But the moment came when he was to be for ever separated from all that made his young life happy. On June 3, the Convention decreed that he should be taken from his mother. The queen resisted desperately. But his life was threatened unless she complied, and she resigned him. For several days both mother and child remained inconsolable in their separation. But, thenceforth, the current of their lives was to flow on apart, and each had soon their peculiar sorrows.

While she remained in the Temple, the queen occasionally saw her son on the top of the tower, through a chink in the wall, but she was soon deprived even of this consolation. On 2d August, she was conducted to the Conciergerie to await her trial. Her relatives never saw or heard from her again, except when she sent to obtain worsted to knit some stockings for her son. The last letter of the queen to the Princess Elizabeth, in which she committed to her the care of her children, seems never to have reached its destination. In this letter, the same omission is observable which we have remarked in the will of Louis XVI. She mentions her brothers in the same brief manner with the king, but, in compliance with the wishes of her deceased husband, commits the care of her children, solely and entirely, to the Princess Elizabeth. M. Beauchesne, indeed, attempts to show the affectionate and confidential footing on which Marie Antoinette stood with the Count de Provence and the Count D'Artois, by inserting a few lines, said to be written by the queen, to each of them, immediately after the execution of Louis XVI. If these documents are authentic, it is not surprising that at such a dreadful moment, she should write half a dozen lines in a tone of affection and kindness to the brothers of her deceased husband. I am inclined to look on them as forgeries of Louis XVIII., because the signature of the Dauphin, appended to the one written to the king, a fac simile of which is given at the end of the first edition of "Clery's Memoirs," does not correspond with his handwriting at the time, but seems to belong to an earlier period. Louis the XVIII., who showed the documents to Clery in a very dramatic manner, evidently, got him to publish them to create an idea that he had been on the best footing with the queen, which every one who knows their mutual relations during late years, must be satisfied, was not the case. But, be this as it may, acts speak more plainly than words; and the distrust with which both the king and queen regarded their ambitious and scheming brothers is shown by their committing at death the heir of their throne and their misfortunes to an unprotected and imprisoned woman.

But the foresight of the dying queen seems to have extended yet further. She anticipated that efforts would be made to keep her children separate, and by so doing lessen their mutual attachment, and destroy the power they would possess so long as they continued united. It was not difficult for the keen perception of a woman like Marie Antoinette, thoroughly acquainted with all the persons, elements, and interests at work, to decipher the combinations which would probably be attempted after her decease, and events show that she did not err in her calculations. "I hope," she writes to her sister, "*that when they are older they will be reunited with you*"—and then, using language as explicit as prudence would permit, she begs her to remind her children, "that their friendship and mutual confidence will be their happiness,"—and, "that in whatsoever position they may find themselves, they will be only truly happy by their union." It was evidently her desire, that, avoiding all entangling connections with the families of the Count de Provence and the Count D'Artois, her children should, for their mutual interest, remain together under the sole care and guardianship of the Princess Elizabeth.

But few were the thoughts which the dying queen could give to this world. Her trial was the burlesque preliminary to the judical murder, which on 16th October, 1793, left the Dauphin and his sister orphans, unconscious of their loss. She died on the scaffold, with the dignity and courage befitting her race and station; and fulfilled her dying wish, to show the same firmness which had distinguished her husband in his last moments, and the calmness of one whose conscience was at peace.

## CHAPTER V.

### SIMON.

In the Revolution all parties deceived themselves, and every individual miscalculated his interests. The king trusted in the love of his people—they brought him to the scaffold. Monsieur fostered convulsion in the hope that it would unseat his brother and enthrone himself—he was twenty years an exile. Egalité looked for an Orleans, instead of a Bourbon dynasty—the same blade that decapitated the king dissipated the illusion. The ambition of Lafayette was to be the Washington of America—to save life he had to abandon politics. The Royalists fell before the Constitutionalists—the Constitutionalists before the Girondists—the Girondists before the Mountain—the Mountain before men as base as themselves, but less bloody because less bold.

On the 3d July, 1793, when the young Prince found himself separated from his relatives, the party of Marat and Robespierre was in full and apparently stable power. They were cruel on principle. They shed blood to cement institutions. It is probable, they sincerely contemplated a time when the Reign of Terror should cease; but it was when the guillotine had left no more aristocrats in France. To them the death of Marie Antoinette seemed necessary to widen the breach between republican France and its enemies, and render a return to royalty impossible. They would have killed the Dauphin to eradicate the race, if they could have found any justification for the act. The weakness of childhood was its defence.

Simon was a shoemaker, who lived next door to Marat, in the Rue de Cordeliers—and it is, perhaps, to this circumstance that history owes its acquaintance with this interesting personage. He was about fifty-seven years of age, short, robust, and square, with features of sinister and repulsive deformity—coarse black hair, thick eyebrows—and eyes which, could they have been prolonged at their inner extremities, would have met in a sharp angle about the top of the forehead. His wife was a person of similar age; short, fat, brown, and ugly.

This respectable pair might have passed quietly through life but for the Revolution, which dislocated all conditions, and afforded, like all drunkenness, an admirable facility for the display of character. To be coarse, brutal, and unfeeling, was Simon's nature—fortune set him on a pinnacle, to exhibit to generations a specimen of the domestic ruffian. The first effect of the Revolution, had been to make him an orator in his section, and the eloquence which might else have been confined to bestowing curses on Marie Jeane, was soon exerted, under the shade of the trees in the Rue de Cordeliers, in denouncing kings, and instructing sans-culottes in the science of self-government.

Marat, eminently qualified to act as professor and confer degrees in the college of rascality, into which revolutionary France had rapidly resolved itself, partly, out of neighborly feeling, that lingering vestige of amiability in rogues, and partly out of a just appreciation of the latent genius for low evil in his friend, pitched upon Simon as the best person within the range of his acquaintance, to give a democratic education to the young descendant of St. Louis, and destroy him if necessary, both in soul and body. Robespierre approved of the nomination, well knowing the pliant rascality of the man, his revolutionary enthusiasm, and his fidelity in evil.

His patrons must have been pleased with their discernment, when they heard the celebrated conversation between Simon and the deputation from the Committee of General Safety. "Citizens, what is to be done with this young wolf? He is insolent. I will tame him—but what, after all, is desired? Carry him away?" "No." "Kill him?" "No." "Poison him?" "No." "What then?" "Get rid of him."

This was a refinement beyond the intellectual ability of Simon to originate, but he was just the person to carry it into effect. He failed indeed—but it was through lack of time, and the baffling strength of his victim's constitution.

Behold then the child in company with Simon. He had been, up to that moment, accustomed to all ennobling sentiments and all endearing treatment. Torn from the embrace of his mother, he was conducted to the chamber where he had parted from his father on the eve of his execution, and where he had, for many weeks, enjoyed his unremitting attention as his instructor. The memories of the past must have returned with overpowering violence. What a change of tutors, from Louis XVI. to Simon!

His jailer, being yet in ignorance of the designs of the revolutionary chiefs, did not, at first, treat him with full severity. He taunted, but did not beat him. Grief kept the weeping child silent for a time. He declined food. Then, a sense of wrong inflamed him to demand, indignantly, by what law he was separated from his mother; but obtaining no reply, he resigned himself in apathy to his fate.

After two days, Simon, beginning to enter into the spirit of his employment, attempted to teach him to chant the Carmagnole and cry, "Vive la Republique." Being unsuccessful, he gave him a hurdy-gurdy. "Thy wolf of a mother, and thy dog of an aunt, play on the harpsichord. You must accompany them. It will make a nice hurly burly." The child refused, because he would not insult his mother—and received his first blow as a punishment. Similar scenes occurred, and being still strong, he resisted with spirit. "Animal," said Simon, in reply to his expostulations against corporeal punishment, "I am here to command you, and can do what I please. Liberty and equality for ever!"

As soon as he learned definitely the indefinite powers conferred on him, he began, in earnest, his system of brutalization, and did everything to corrupt the morals, and break down the constitution of his victim. "He has no children," cried the agonized Macduff, when informed of the pillage of his castle, and the slaughter of his wife and little ones; and the inhumanity of the childless Simon is a good commentary on the fidelity to nature of the poet.

A few days after his entry on his employment, the news arrived of the capture of Condé by the Austrian army—"Damned wolf's cub," said Simon to the child, "you are half Austrian—you deserve to be half-killed." The 14th July, was the anniversary of the taking of the Bastile, but the popular joy on the occasion was maddened into frenzy, by the assassination of Marat on the previous evening.

When this news reached the apartment of Simon and his pupil, as soon as the first outburst of grief and rage was over, the jailer determined to celebrate the combined feast and fast of revolution in a characteristic manner. He obtained wine, brandy, and pipes, and carried his wife and the child to the platform of the Tower. The mingled sounds of merriment and mourning from the city below ascended to their ears—and, as the drunken revel on the Tower increased, Simon amused himself by puffing tobacco-smoke in the Prince's face, and telling him that the mourning which he still wore for his father, was only retained for the sake of Marat. "Ah, ha, Capet is in mourning for Marat." It was thus that every public event which happened in those exciting times—every reverse of the republican arms—every disaster in the city was made an occasion of ill-treating the unfortunate child—of dragging him about by the hair—lifting him by his ears—dashing his head against the wall—stifling him with smoke—taunting him with the misfortunes and asserted crimes of his family—and telling him revolting stories of his mother and other female relatives.

His beautiful hair and his mourning were offensive to his jailer, who despoiled him of both—put the red cap on his head, compelled him to drink to intoxication, and, in this state, taught him to swear, to sing revolutionary songs, and repeat odious tales concerning his mother, which he afterwards adduced as evidence against her.

Before the removal of Marie Antoinette from the Tower, she had the misfortune to see the wretched child in company with his jailer in one of his fiercest paroxysms of rage—and to find him fast becoming a wreck in body and in mind. To enter into all the revolting details, which M. Beauchesne has carefully collected, is not necessary for my purpose in this chapter. I simply wish to show the gradual manner in which the constitution of the child was broken, and his mind destroyed. His beauty began to desert him; the alternate flush and pallor of drunkenness succeeded to the rich hue of health. The knowledge he had acquired under the teaching of his father and his successive tutors was soon lost—his proficiency in writing, which had been remarkable in a child of his age, was changed into a slow, painful, and almost illegible scrawl, scarcely sufficient to sign his name—and the rapid progress of demoralization and imbecility cannot be better shown than by the hideous accusations he was compelled to make against the mother he had loved so much.

The day of the execution of Marie Antoinette at length arrived. The princesses were entirely ignorant of what was going forward. Simon himself, who, devoted entirely to his charge, lived in great isolation, suspecting the truth from the unusual stir in the city—but, not certain that it was the case, carried, as was his wont on all public occasions, his wife and the Prince to the platform of the Tower—and, in consideration of the occasion, permitted the child to play at ball while the procession was marching to the scaffold. He then made a bet with his wife, that it was the moment of the queen's execution—and amused himself in the evening by making the poor child drink some of the brandy which his wager purchased.

For somewhat more than six months this fearful tyranny continued. Simon confined himself in the strictest manner, and with conscientious fidelity, to the limits of his assigned duty. He would have been ready at any moment, had the command been issued, to put the child to death—but his commission did not extend beyond the slow process of demoralization and domestic ill-treatment, by which murder might ape the appearance of natural decay.

Of all the crimes with which the Revolution is stained, there is not one which in demoniac atrocity can be compared to this. The drunken assassins of September are innocent to those who, in cool blood, could conceive such a project for ridding themselves of a child whose only crime was the misfortune of his birth.

Simon set himself to his task with scientific zest, patience, and perseverance. He had no idea of hurrying a work which, to be done well, must be done with the forbearance of death in its most insidious advances. It was sufficient that, every hour made the child a hair's breadth worse in mind or body than he was the preceding—that no petty irritation—no insult—no wrong which the ingenuity of malice could suggest was omitted—that no opportunity was passed by to impair a virtue or to implant a vice, to take away a grace or add a vulgarity. He was agent at once for death and hell.

The care and affection by which the tenderest of mother's seeks to foster all that is good, and beautiful, and healthful, in her only child, were outdone by the demoniac devotion of Simon to the task of breaking down the constitution, deforming the appearance, corrupting the morals, and weakening the mind of his pupil. If he eat, it was to be driven from the half-finished meal weeping, and, perhaps, bleeding. On one occasion, he narrowly escaped the destruction of his eye by a blow inflicted at dinner.

If he called the child kindly to him, it was to spurn him with his foot to the other side of the apartment. If amusement was permitted or encouraged, it was to mock his misery, to abuse his parents, to caricature the downfall of his house, to stupefy him by inebriation, to make him sing obscene songs, to teach him to curse, blaspheme and lie—and the child was praised and encouraged in proportion as he cöoperated in the work of murder and demoralization of which he was the victim. If his health was broken down too rapidly, a physician was sent for to lengthen out his misery, and give to murder the aspect of tenderness. If he revived more than was desirable, some new brutality speedily reduced him to the required level. If a day had passed without something being done to injure him, Simon would have regretted it, like Titus, as a lost day. When he had been peculiarly happy in his combinations, he retired to rest with the self-satisfaction of a man who has performed his duty—and then arranged beforehand some new mortification, hardship, indignity, or immorality for the ensuing day.

In all this he was strictly conscientious. He believed himself engaged in a work for which the Republic owed him gratitude, and to which there was dignity attached. He was the representative of the French nation, performing an act of retributive justice on the offspring of a race of tyrants, and deserving the praise of posterity by destroying the last link in the succession. He had arrived at that depth of iniquity in which evil is a man's good, and to fail in crime is to fail in duty.

"The Republic is eternal," he said to the child, one day. "There is nothing eternal," was the reply, and then, as if struck with remorse for the mistake, "there is nothing eternal but God." Even Simon's tyranny was to come to an end. A more lucrative office was offered him. He could not retain the two. He resigned, not without regret, his unfinished task in the Temple, but before he left, called the child up to him, and then felled him to the floor with his fist. Such was the parting between the Prince and his jailer.

While this scene of terror was enacting in the Temple, the Count de Provence was exercising, with all the pomp which, in his idea, the situation demanded, his office of Regent of the kingdom. The miseries which his nephew was suffering could not be unknown to him. But while they were at their height he was plotting, through his agents, for the establishment of his own power upon the ruins of the fallen monarchy. It is highly probable that these emissaries deceived him, and for their own purposes reported interviews and correspondence with Danton and Robespierre, which had no foundation but in their misrepresentations.

But, however, this might be, the Regent himself wrote to the revolutionary chiefs, and imagined that he had possession of the clue to a counter revolution in his own favor, in Paris, and that the troubles would terminate by proclaiming him king. "He acknowledged," says Lamartine, "as king, the child then a captive, who was being slowly immolated in the Temple. He gratified the friends of his brother, the Count D'Artois, by appointing him Lieutenant-General of the kingdom—a painful but politic division of that ideal authority which these two princes were going to exercise in exile. Recognised by the army of Condé and by the Empress of Russia, he addressed solemn proclamations to Europe and to the army of Condé at each tragic blow struck by the Convention against the members of the royal family. He fomented, with all his efforts, the troubles, the insurrections, the civil wars of the South and La Vendée. He received all the distinguished negotiators from France, and all the political adventurers who throw themselves between two causes, less to serve them than to serve themselves.

"His court and his council were the perpetual focus of plans, of chimeras, of conspiracies, real or imaginary, of the corruption of generals, of the venality of the Tribune, and movements of the people, with which the men of intrigue amused the idleness or flattered the importance of the exiled courts. He there imbibed the feeling and the taste for those secret reports, for that confidence in underlings, for those intrigues of diplomacy, of police, of government, for that domestic favoritism and that personal labor which afterwards distinguished him on the throne. He there maintained that royal attitude, and that distance between him and the crowd which he never allowed to be violated, except by a few confidants. He knew the prestige of distance for men and for things, and constantly withdrew from events and from observation, to maintain a more imposing attitude. He assiduously studied there the history of his country and his race, in order to personify in himself the power, the kings, and the grandeur of his house, and to recall some day in himself alone, all the illustrious men, or at least all the mementos of his race. He prepared himself incessantly for the throne, never doubting that he would be recalled to it by the vicissitudes of human affairs, and not wishing that his reign should find him for a single day deficient in dignity. Little sought after, and less beloved, he commanded respect from others by the respect which he affected for himself."

And here I would repeat my conviction, that such a man ever seriously designed to permit the infant son of Louis XVI. to mount the throne to his prejudice—is contrary to every probability which knowledge of human character could lead us to entertain. He knew the child to be possessed of a strong constitution and of excellent natural abilities—and that, in bringing him publicly forward, he would be taking the most effectual step to prevent his ever being king himself—more especially, as the feelings of loyalty which the Revolution had outraged, and the regret and veneration which the memory of the martyred king and queen inspired, would naturally centre on the object that inherited their name and rights, and recalled their virtues and their sorrows. The man who, when the monarchy of France stood erect in all the hereditary prestige and potency of centuries, could deliberately contemplate its overthrow, and lay his plans for the humiliation of his brother, to effect his own elevation, was not the person to be thus thwarted in his ambition by a feeble child in prison. I could as soon believe in the sincerity of the kiss of Judas as in the loyalty of Louis XVIII. to Louis XVII.

His acknowledgment of him as king proceeded from the same policy which dictated the appointment of his brother as Lieutenant-Governor of France. This very division of authority has in it something suspicious—for the Count de Provence was not a man to weaken his power in this manner, but through the compulsion of political motive. And had his own right stood on a strong foundation, had there been no necessity for cultivating the good will of the Count D'Artois, to cover sinister designs and support dubious claims, and give him an interest in concealing crimes committed for the advantage of another—he would have kept the reins of government in his own hands.

But leaving the Regent to his plots and his ambition, let us return to the little sufferer in the Temple, the most fearful portion of whose existence was now beginning.

It was a mistake in Marat and Robespierre, not to stipulate that Simon should leave his wife behind when he undertook the tutorship of the Prince. Madame Simon, though not remarkable for sweetness of disposition, was still a *woman*, and did much to soften the severity of her husband's conduct. The beauty and innocence of the boy won from the first upon her heart. She regretted that she had no children herself, and would have gladly been kind to the little captive. Not unfrequently she interposed to check the brutality of Simon, and paid all those nameless little attentions to a child's comfort which only a woman can do.

But, when the child got rid of Simon's ill-treatment, he lost his wife's care. The authorities had lately grown economical, and curtailed in every way the expenses of the prisoners—and now thought it a useless outlay to keep a tutor for the Prince. They therefore determined he should for the future live alone.

He was, consequently, transferred from the apartment he had hitherto occupied to a smaller one, which had been used by Clery, his father's valet. It had only one window, fastened by padlocks. Besides which, it stood in a very deep recess, and the light was obscured by immense iron bars.

It was on the 19th January, 1794, that Simon left him, and from that time till the 27th July, more than six months, he remained in solitude. His food was handed to him through a revolving aperture, which did not permit him even to see the person who delivered it. During the whole period the door of his apartment was never opened. No gleam of sunlight—no breath of fresh air—came to the little victim. To sweep his apartment, while strength permitted him, was merely to transfer the filth from one place to another.

A gruff voice, bidding him at evening go to bed, or calling him at dead of night to present himself for inspection at an iron grating, through which the light of a lanthorn was thrown upon his person, was his whole intercourse with the human species.

It is difficult to conceive the physical condition to which a child would be reduced by such confinement. But, his mental state surpasses imagination. He no longer had liquor to inebriate him. For awhile he must have pondered in silence over the mingled and inexplicable past, the magnificence, the power, the dreamy tenderness, the beauty, the terror, the tears, the strife, the humiliation, the heart-rending separations, and the systematic brutalization, succeeded by blank solitude, silence, and breathless suffocation—and then—having no clue through the labyrinth—intense feeling and agonising thought, would gradually yield to apathy. Thus, in loneliness, and darkness, and filth, and intolerable stench, devoured by vermin, and sharing his food with rats, all consciousness would cease, and mechanical, vegetable life, devoid of memory, and destitute of hope, would alone remain.

But while all was dead silent misery in the apartment of the child, the Revolution was advancing to its goal, with giant strides.

The 5th March saw the downfall of Marat and Desmoulins, the last of the fierce enthusiasts, who, too late, regretting the excesses into which they had fallen, attempted to atone for the past, by stemming the torrent of blood, and perished, tardy advocates of humanity. Then, succeeded the reign of death, when blood drenched the soil of France, like a hot thunder shower. On the 10th May, Madame Elizabeth, the sister of Louis XVI., poured from her veins the purest libation which had yet fallen on the scaffold. The children were now, doubly orphans, but they knew it not. At length, came 27th July—and Robespierre, who, a little more than a month previously, had proclaimed the existence of God, fell beneath his retributive power. Many a prison door was then thrown open—and among them, that of the apartment of the young Prince, whose sufferings were ameliorated at nearly the same time when Simon accompanied his master, Robespierre, to the scaffold.

Baras, commandant of the National Guard, appointed a man named, Laurent, keeper of the Temple. But his powers, in respect to the prisoners, were of a very limited character, and liable, in all things, to be controlled by the acting commissary, who visited the prison daily. As soon, however, as Laurent entered on his employment, he, naturally, visited the different chambers of the Temple, to see the condition of the prisoners.

It was night-time when he first came to the door of the young Prince. The lanthorn was applied as usual to the grating, and the child summoned to the door. But no reply was made to the loud and repeated calls on him, to rise and show himself. He had, in fact, now, lost the power of motion as well as of mental consciousness. A feeble sound, showing he was still alive, was all that came from the suffocating stench of the dungeon.

The barricaded door was, at last, broken open, and Laurent and his associates made their way as well as they could, to the bed-side of the captive. The chamber smelt like the grave, and was hideous as gloom, filth, and pestilential air could make it. The last food received by the child was untouched. He was worn to a skeleton. His livid skin was scarcely visible for dirt. He was covered with vermin. There was vermin everywhere—on the bed, on the floor, on the walls, in every fold of the rags which hung about him. They were matted in his hair, and knitted in every hollow of his body. The noise around him made him tremble—but he did not stir. He answered to no question. He was conscious of nothing. He breathed. His open eyes had no expression. *Their color had changed. He had the look not of a fool, but of an idiot.** His bones seemed protruding angularly from his skin—for he had no flesh to conceal them. Both his knees and his elbows were covered with tumors, the result of long confinement, bad usage, and depression of spirits.

A few hours more of such solitude would have ended his career. God willed otherwise, and he survived. He was to enter on a new stage of his chequered existence, under altered circumstances, which we will pause to review.

## CHAPTER VI.

### INTRIGUE.

"The Republic," said Robespierre, "falls with me." The prophecy was true, and based on a profound insight into the elements at work in France. The Revolution had spared no one capable of conducting it to a successful issue, and of founding a stable and compact structure on the bloody pedestal. To do so, required incorruptible honesty and single-minded devotion to an idea. The race of unselfish, albeit, bloody devotees to principle was fast disappearing. The great revolutionary chiefs had successively fallen —all with whom the Revolution from its earliest stages had been identified—and he was the only person who inherited the memories of the past. To strike at him was to repudiate that past, to stigmatize its deeds as crimes, and say—France has awoke from her dream of blood, and will no more of it. She sought liberty, but

* Beauchesne, vol. ii. p. 253.

she found hell, and cannot love institutions which entwine themselves with a name she abhors. The jubilant crowds who attended Robespierre to the scaffold, chanted the requiem of the Revolution.

From that moment began a new era. Its ultimate form was all uncertain. But full scope was open for speculation, for ambition, for intrigue, for plots and counterplots, and every evil work which shuns the light. Bold, avowed action was over. The dominant party—more sanguinary than Robespierre—were compelled to lean to the side of mercy, and pursue a course of moderation abhorrent to their principles, but in keeping with their mediocrity. Everything took a milder tone. More external decency prevailed, prisons were emptied, tribunals were more cautious, jailers less severe.

With respect to the captive, the republican policy, as well as the republican interest, was unchanged. But, another Simon was not to be found, and had there been, the times would have repudiated him. The condition of the child was, therefore, alleviated, but contrary to the wish of those in power. They admitted the perplexity his life occasioned them, their unwillingness to abate the rigor of his confinement, and their fear of attempts to seat him on the throne. But they shrank from the responsibility of extreme measures, and restricted themselves to such a measure of neglect as the newly-awakened sense of decency rendered safe.

From this point we need a critical examination of the proofs adduced by M. Beauchesne of the death of Louis XVII.; and it is, therefore, necessary to inquire into the general nature of his work. It was published in Paris at the latter end of 1852, and the reasons which induced its publication are thus stated in the preface:—

"We have understood from the beginning of our researches how it has happened that *public opinion has never been definitely settled* on a point imp rceptible in appearance, but, nevertheless, considerable—the death of a ci d. France and Europe have only assisted from afar in the drama of the emple—they have not seen all the scenes—they have only learned the lamentable *dénoûment* in such a manner that *room was still left open for doubt* Before the veil which has enveloped the tragical end of the son of Louis XVI., one is not astonished to hear it said, with *the warmth of a profound conviction*, that the young victim went out living from his prison It is conceded that a child really died in the Temple, but it is added, that if it was the offspring of our kings, no one could affirm it—that the physicians have certified to his death, but not to his identity—that it is not known how the man in the iron mask came on earth—that it is equally uncertain how the infant was taken from the Temple, and that the tomb of the one remains as mysterious as the cradle of the other."

Let me here call attention to the admission of M. Beauchesne. He confesses that, up to the time of the publication of his work, no proof had been adduced of the death of the child. Since the agitation of the subject in this country, some who profess to be profoundly versed in questions of French history and opinion, have assured us that the death of Louis XVII. is as well authenticated as that of Napoleon. Let them listen to M. Beauchesne. Had there been proof of the fact, his work would not have appeared. It was published to supply a felt deficiency. He tells us, that up to November, 1852, "room was still open for doubt," and that, in fact, there was in France "a profound conviction" of the Prince's existence.

"It was natural," he continues, "after this, that impostors should think they were authorized to impose themselves on the world as the inheritors of a glorious name." "The conviction of his death has for me the character of a certainty, authentically demonstrated—a curse on me, if my mind, in possession of the truth, should suffer my pen to lie. I have spared neither care, nor research, nor study to arrive at this truth—I have particularly known Lasne and Gomin, the two last jailers of the Tower, in whose arms Louis XVII. died." "We hope that we bring to this history not only the certitude, but the material authentic proof that the Dauphin of France, the son of Louis XVI. really died in the Temple. I have not raked among these ruins, nor built this edifice to give food to the passions of the day. I have still less the pretension of pleading a cause."

It will be seen that *all the fresh evidence* on which he relies to settle the question, consists simply of *the testimony of Lasne and Gomin*, which, strangely enough, is not ushered before the world until after their death. M. Beauchesne has built a very imposing structure on narrow and infirm foundations. No one who looked, for the first time, upon his portly volumes, containing each their five hundred pages, would be apt to imagine that all the solemnly heralded evidence, which was to lift up for ever the veil from a hitherto impenetrable mystery, dwindled into this.

He spent, we are told, twenty years upon the work—as much as Gibbon spent on the Decline and Fall—and there is something awful in the literary labor of a mature intellect for twenty years upon a single historic point. Either M. Beauchesne's habits of composition are very slow, or he must have found he had a hard task. For there is nothing novel in the bulk of his work. Whole pages of it are transcribed verbatim from such well known writers as Hue and Clery. The novelty and the point of his book consist entirely in the autograph testimony of Lasne and Gomin, taken from his album. Here is what Johnson's ghost calls "the muscipular abortion" of the "parturient mountain."

But how is it, that for fifty seven years, it never entered into the human brain to substantiate the fact of the Dauphin's death in the Temple, by the production of the testimony of these men? How came there such a lack of discernment in the French nation? Because there was evident folly in the attempt. If the Dauphin escaped, it must have been with the connivance of these very officials. With the same plausibility might a counsel for the defence produce two men, accused of stealing some article from their master's shop, to prove that it was not stolen. Fifty-seven years work wonderful revolutions—but cannot make testimony, which has been worthless all that time, worth anything now.

Concerning M. Beauchesne and his motives, I know nothing, and will not trouble myself with conjecturing. I will take his narrative as it stands. The renewed attention I have given to his work has not lessened, but confirmed my conviction of the insufficiency of his testimony, and of the weakness of his position. So far from allaying doubt, his narrative more completely throws the question open—and the nearer we approach the heart of the mystery, the more profound is the conviction that, whether Louis XVII. be now alive or not—which is a question for after-consideration, there is no proof that he died in the Temple—nay, no probability—and, further still, no possibility—if the inquiry be limited to the question, whether the body represented as his was really so or not. And this is the issue. It is not pretended that he died at any other time than the 8th June, 1795—nor under any other circumstances than those specified by Beauchesne. Whoever, therefore, desires to *prove the death*, must first show that *under the circumstances it was physically possible.* And here, I apprehend, will be an insuperable bar.

Laurent who was appointed, on the fall of Robespierre, guardian of the children of Louis XVI. was a man of private property, not devoid of taste, information, and good feeling, but a zealous republican, and devoted to the interests of his party. His appointment was an index of the times. From him, nothing unworthy could be asked—but care was taken that his appointment, which gave dignity to the position of the Convention, should be of as little service to the child as possible. He was permitted to visit the captive only at particular periods, and then but for a short time.

To the child, however, in the vegetable condition of life to which he was now reduced, solitude was no longer a hardship. He had now fallen into that listless apathy which distinguished him, as far as we have any reliable accounts, to the last moment spent in the Temple. He had sense enough to play mechanically with a toy or a flower, but felt no want of companionship.

I have mentioned that, on the opening of his chamber, his knees and elbows were covered with swellings, the result of filth and confined air. The location of these swellings is not only a means of distinguishing the Prince from the substitute who died in the

Temple, on the 8th June, but of establishing the identity of the child at this period, in the Temple, with the one seen and reported on, by Harmand. He also suffered from a continual pain in the head, which was so extreme that the slightest touch made him groan; and he could neither endure a comb to be passed through his matted hair, nor even the gentle friction attending the application of ointment. But change of air, cleanliness, plain wholesome food, the absence of all irritation, and profound repose, gradually revived his corporeal strength, though his mind continued prostrate and unobservant.

But while he was thus slowly recovering, the name of Louis XVII. was the rallying point of hope to tens of thousands in France, and the perplexities of the Convention daily increased. It seemed alike dangerous to keep him in the heart and centre of political intrigue, or to banish him from the country.

The position of the royalist refugees, at this period, was peculiar. The Count de Provence, who had usurped the title of Regent, held his court at Verona—and the Count D'Artois, at Arnheim, while the Prince de Condé, with his army, was actively engaged on the Rhine. The Regent had little power over the other two, and his position, so long as the Prince was known to survive, was embarrassing in the extreme.

At first, the brothers had hoped for assistance from foreign courts, but, with the exception of Russia, none officially acknowledged them, though they clandestinely received and corresponded with their agents. The war in La Vendée promised no profitable results; mainly because the two princes would not risk themselves on the scene of action. Disappointed, however, in his expectations of foreign aid, the principal trust of the Regent was, nevertheless, in La Vendée, and on his agents and intrigues in France.

In La Vendée, and especially among its chiefs and generals, loyalty was a religion and a passion—no thought, unworthy the hero, the martyr, or the patriot, burned in the bosoms of the peasant warriors or their glorious leaders. Unstained by corrupt intrigue, unwarped by selfish ambition, they fought and bled for what they deemed the right.

But they distrusted the Regent, and unfurled their banner solely for the captive monarch of the Temple. To obtain possession of him was their great object, and it may be easily seen, that while nothing could be more detrimental to the ambitious designs of the Regent, than to permit them to do so, his agents could only approach them successfully by feigning an interest in the Prince, and promising to procure his escape, and his surrender to them.

From these agents in the interior, the Count de Provence derived hopes of a speedy movement in his favor—and held intercourse, real or imaginary, with the heads of the French government.* There is far more probability, that the men now in power would intrigue with him, than those in previous periods. The principal royalist agents, were the Count D'Entraignes, Lemaître, Laville Heurnois, and the Marquis de Fenouil. They assumed the appearance of republicans, and often deceived the French government, making their way into places least to have been expected. They swarmed in Paris, and availed themselves of the wide-spread sympathy in favor of the children of Louis XVI. to increase the popular dissatisfaction with the Republic, and the desire to return to monarchy. In addition, royalist journals began openly to advocate a counter-revolution, and though prosecuted, the editors escaped with impunity. Thus, while there was much to discourage the Regent in the apathy shown by European courts, there was everything in the internal condition of France, evidently in a transition state, to promise the fulfilment of his original expectation—that, his nephew being removed, the Revolution would terminate by elevating him to the throne.

After being guardian to the Prince for some months, Laurent, a man of social habits, felt wearied with the incessant servitude, and applied to the Committe of General Safety for a colleague. On the

* Thiers, vol. iii. p. 281.

8th November, a man named Gomin, was appointed to assist him. In this nomination we find the first traces of the influence of the Regent in the Temple, on which, according to his proclamation, his eye had been long fixed with the design of removing the king.

Hitherto, his agents had been unable to gain any footing there, but, under the altered condition of things, the case was different. "M. le Marquis de Fenouil, who knew Gomin intimately," says Beauchesne, an unimpeachable witness on such a point, "had, thanks to certain soi-distant patriotic intrigues, which he knew how to manage and employ with art, contributed powerfully to a nomination, which was a guarantee for the royalist party." In other words, Gomin was placed in the Temple by one of the creatures of the Count de Provence, to act according to instructions. We may be certain, that the pretended republican intrigues—the nature of which Beauchesne is careful not to mention—had relation to Louis XVII., both because by virtue of them he gained the power of nominating his keeper, and also, because when he had placed Gomin in the Temple, he kept up a constant correspondence with him, by means of Doisy, his valet de chambre, who, under pretext of being a relative, went frequently to visit him, and converse respecting La Vendée and the Prince.*

There was also another royalist, named Debierne, who, being appointed acting commissary, opened instant communication with Gomin concerning the escape of the Prince, and received the promise of his co-operation.† Gomin and Debierne were in the habit of holding stealthy interviews in the apartment of the steward, Lienard, who also acted as a sentinel. Debierne, as well as Doisy, falsely represented himself as a relative of Gomin, and under this pretext came frequently to see him. He brought, at first, playthings for the Prince, then showed Gomin some assignats issued in the name of Louis XVII., and made payable on the Restoration. He also informed the keeper of a design for carrying the young king into La Vendée. "The good heart of Gomin," says Beauchesne,

* Beauchesne, vol. ii., p. 298. † Ibid.

"opened itself to this hope with a lively joy." Here, then, we find evidence that the agents of the Regent were playing with both parties—the Convention and the Vendéeans—and that Gomin entered fully into the scheme for the removal of the captive. On another occasion, when Debierne came to see "his accomplice" —the word accomplice is that used by Beauchesne—he brought concealed under his cloak a dove or pigeon. The sight of it occasioned Gomin some anxiety—as it was, in truth, a very suspicious present—and, if discovered, likely to compromise him with the acting commissaries. But, he concealed it under his cloak, and carried it into the Tower.

In all this we may see the way slowly paved for future action. Here, without controversy, is proof that the royalist agents were plotting, in the end of the year 1794, to remove the Prince—that Fenouil, Doisy, Debierne, Gomin, and probably Lienard, were in the plot—that meetings were held for consultation in the apartments of one of the sentinels, who had the responsible post of steward, and all they waited for was the formation of some definite plan to carry their design into execution. And, now let us turn to the state of feeling in the Convention, and to the action of the government respecting the Prince, and see if we can discover anything which corresponds with the events going on within and around the Tower, and any clue to the intrigues of the Marquis de Fenouil, and to the meaning of the project to carry the child into La Vendée.

There had been frequent and fierce debating as to what should be done with the Prince, when, on the 28th December, Leguinio argued, that as there was no hope of quelling the royalists while he remained in Paris, "measures should be taken to purge the soil of the sole vestige of tyranny that remained," and moved, that he should be exiled. But, on the 22d January, Cambaceres, on the part of the government committees, made a report unfavorable to his proposition, taking the ground that the expulsion of tyrants had always prepared the way for their restoration. The Convention was greatly divided in opinion; but, as the view expressed by Cambaceres seemed the wisest, the question was dropped.

It is not, however, from open action that the designs of such a government as the one then ruling France can be derived. Only eight days previous to the report of Cambaceres, a treaty had been made with Charette, at Nantes, in one of the secret clauses of which the government stipulated to put the young Prince and his sister into the hands of the Vendéean leader, on condition that the surrender should be delayed until June 13, 1795.*

If the reader will connect this with the "certaines intrigues soi-disant patriotiques," of Fenouil, and the plot for the young king's removal into La Vendée—he will scarcely have the discernment I would wish to attribute to him, if he does not perceive the gradual working and development of a deep laid scheme, worthy of the intriguing genius of Louis XVIII., a very master piece of Machiavellian policy, to deceive and overreach both parties. It is not improbable that Cambaceres and others may have secretly lent their aid in carrying out his design.

We now come to a portion of this history of utmost importance in many respects. I allude to the visit of three members of the Committee of General Safety, to the Tower, to ascertain the state of the child's health. Before, however, we enter on it, let me call attention to one of the most important considerations it involves, viz. the mental condition of the Prince at the time.

M. Beauchesne, without formally raising the question or throwing the subject into the shape of argument—a thing he carefully avoids throughout—labors to prove that the mind of the captive was not impaired. This position is necessary to give any weight to the evidence he adduces of his death. If his reason was alienated,

* "Charette, avait signé, le 17 Janvier, dans le petit château de la Jaunaie, près de Nantes, un traite, dont les clauses secrétes stipulaient la remise entre ses mains du jeune Roi et de la Princesse, sa sœur. Le gouvernement républicain avait feint d'acquiescer à ces conditions, en demandant seulement que la remise des enfans de Louis XVI., ne fût effectuée que le 13 Juin, 1795."—*Beauchesne*, vol. ii. p. 416.

then every word which Lasne and Gomin have put into his mouth is proof of their falsehood. They represent him as not only retaining his senses, but manifesting to the last the most sprightly and vivid intelligence, in conjunction with a fixed heroic determination, which savors of the miraculous.

The Duchess D'Angoulême, who derived her knowledge from Gomin, says her brother's mind "suffered from the effects of the cruel treatment that had so long been exercised towards him, and showed symptoms of increasing weakness;" and again, that "the horrible treatment of which he was the victim gradually affected his mind, and even had he lived, it is probable he would never have recovered from the effects of it." Lamartine says—"They had brutalized him not only to dethrone him, but to deprive him even of his childish innocence and *human intelligence*."*

On the 26th February, 1794, the commissaries of the Temple, Laurent and Gomin, reported to the Committee of General Safety, that the life of the prisoner was in imminent danger—and, on being asked, "What was the nature of the danger?" they replied, "that the little Capet had tumors on *all the articulations, and particularly at the knees*—that it was *impossible to obtain from him a single word*—and that always, whether sitting or laying down, he refused all kinds of exercise." When questioned as to the period from whence this obstinate silence and systematic immobility dated, they said it was since the 6th October, 1793, the day on which he had been made to sign a charge of incest against his mother. Here let me remark, that Gomin stands directly opposed to himself. As one of the commissaries, he affirmed that it was impossible to get a word from him, and, in fact, that he had never heard him speak; and yet, through M. Beauchesne, he has favored us with particular accounts of his conversations.

A committee, consisting of MM. Harmand, Matthieu, and Reverchon, were appointed to visit the prisoner. They found him in a clean and well-lighted room, having no furniture but a bedstead, a

* Lamartine's Girondists, vol. i. p. 300.

table, and earthen stove. "The Prince," says Harmand, "was sitting before a little square table, on which were scattered some playing-cards, some bent into the form of boxes and little chests, others piled up in castles. He was amusing himself with these cards when we entered, but he did not give up his play. He was dressed in a sailor's jacket of slate-colored cloth—his head was bare." Harmand approached him, but he took no notice. He spoke to him, but he looked steadily forward without any change in his position. He promised him toys, but he stared with steady and vacant indifference. To all questions, he answered neither by gesture, expression, nor word. Baffled in all attempts, Harmand now tried peremptory command, which succeeded a little better. "Monsieur, have the goodness to give me your hand. He presented it, and I felt, in prolonging my movement up to the arm-pit, a tumor at the wrist, and another at the elbow, like knots. The tumors were not painful, for the Prince showed no sign of their being so. The other hand, Monsieur. He presented it also. There was nothing. Permit me, sir, to touch your legs and your knees. He raised himself up. I felt the same swellings at the two knees under the joint." This mechanical movement of his limbs at command was the only indication of sense he showed during the whole interview. "He remained on his seat—his look did not change a single instant, by the least apparent emotion, by the least astonishment in the eyes—he acted as if we were not there and I had said nothing."

His dinner was now brought. He eat without saying anything. They threatened if he did not speak, to remove the commissaries (Laurent and Gomin), who were kind to him, and send him others who might be more disagreeable to him. He neither changed his look, nor gave an answer. "Do you wish," inquired Harmand "that we should go away?" There was no reply.

The deputies began now to question the commissaries, *i. e.*, Laurent, Gomin, and the acting commissioner for the day, as to the cause of this. "We demanded, if this obstinate silence had been really preserved since the day when that monstrous deposition against his mother had been violently forced from him. They assured us, that ever since that day, the poor child had ceased to speak. *Remorse had prostrated his understanding*."* These words, preserved by Lamartine, are omitted by M. Beauchesne, who inserts three points in their stead, though he pretends to give the narrative of Harmand entire. He well knew that a prostration of the child's understanding would be fatal to all the accounts of pointed remarks, and interesting conversations, between the Prince and his jailers, which give so much particularity to their narrative of the last days and hours of his life; and, not content with omitting the testimony in respect to his aberration of mind, accuses Harmand of having exaggerated in his statement concerning the child's silence.

Now, it is undeniable that the commissaries, in their first report to the Committee of General Safety, acknowledged that the Prince never spoke even to them—that Harmand and his colleagues could obtain from him, no reply or token of sense—that Laurent and Gomin acknowledged a second time to them, that he never spoke, and had not done so for months—that the deputation justly concluded, that his understanding was prostrated—that his sister believed him to be incurably insane, and that Lamartine represents him as deprived of "human intelligence." Of what value, then, let me ask, is testimony which proceeds upon an entirely different hypothesis, and which represents him indulging to the last in a lavish garrulity?

On the 29th March, 1795, Laurent left the Temple. He was tired of his employment, and wished to return to his family, and to the care of his private affairs. He parted with affection from the prisoner, whom he had always kindly treated, and in two days afterwards, the vacancy was filled by the appointment of Etienne Lasne. Lasne, had formerly been a soldier in the Garde Française; in 1789, he entered the National Guard; and in 1791,

* Lamartine, Hist. Restoration, vol. i. p. 308. Beauchesne, vol. ii. p. 309.

was made captain of grenadiers. "Revolutionary influences," says Beauchesne, "had nominated Lasne, as royalist influences had nominated Gomin, but they both belonged to the moderate party." As the Marquis de Fenouil, Gomin, and Debierne, are proofs that it was no unusual thing for royalists to appear in republican garb—and as M. Lasne's republicanism was confessedly of a moderate character, being, probably, of that convenient quality which enables a man to do whatever seems best for his pecuniary interests—his practical principles must be estimated by his actions.

His republicanism yielded to time, for he was a very loyal subject at the Restoration, and, when Mr. Beauchesne first visited him, in 1837, had, in his room, many portraits of the royal family, including some of the Dauphin. He had sufficient influence with Louis XVIII. to induce him to discredit the word of an eminent physician like Pelletan.

As soon as Lasne entered on office, we find indications of a disposition to aid in the escape of the Prince. The keys made a great noise in turning in the locks, and he accordingly had them carefully oiled. He also denied the necessity of the doors being closed on the landings, and ordered them to be left open. There can be no question that these are the very things which would be done by a person in his position, anxious to facilitate escape.

The acting commissaries, however, objected to the doors being left open, as they said they were put there to be shut; and Lasne, "*knowing that all resistance would be untimely, and could only bring suspicion on him*," acceded in silence. There was a perfect understanding between Lasne and Gomin, and they continued to act from beginning to end in entire harmony. They made mutual arrangements to give each other the fullest liberty, and broke up every established usage which interfered with this. Hitherto the keys could only be used in the presence of both the keepers. They were now placed at the disposal of either of them, at any time. Instead of the previous severe and silent discipline, they introduced music into the tower, and, though unskilled, Gomin played on the violin, and Lasne accompanied him with his voice; all which was well calculated to distract attention, and accustom all who might entertain suspicion, to noise and commotion in the hitherto quiet and monotonous prison.

We are here reminded, by M. Beauchesne, that the silence of the Prince was only relative—in other words, that he could talk when and to whom he pleased—and are informed that although he observed, for three weeks, an obstinate silence towards Lasne, he, at length, yielded to the kindness of his keeper, and, during the rest of his life, took pleasure in chatting with him, especially respecting the events of his early childhood, before the Revolution, of which he retained a distinct and clear remembrance. "*Contrary to his habit*," this is admitting something, "he theed and thoud him and treated him, with familiarity."

For reasons already given, and for others which will appear as we advance, I can yield no credence to these long jocose conversations, and shall, therefore, merely allude to them for the purpose of denying in the strongest manner their probability. They militate with everything recorded of the captive, by those whose testimony can be credited—they indicate a state of mind entirely different from what his physical condition would require—they are confessed to be exceptions to his usual conduct—and unless, therefore, they rest on evidence, itself above dispute, they deserve to have no place in history.

But as their improbability, though great, is far exceeded by what we shall be asked to believe hereafter, I must beg the reader to observe that it was three full weeks before Lasne, by dint of the most assiduous and unremitting care, could get even a look of recognition, or the slightest intimation that his attention was appreciated.

Never since the beginning of the Revolution was the prospect of the royalist party so bright in France as in the spring of the year 1795. The strife between the two extreme factions in the state, the

It was with difficulty the child could be induced to take the medicine prescribed. The government refused to comply with the physician's request for his removal, and hop tea and sal-volatile frictions constituted, let me repeat, the whole treatment the child received at the hands of Desault. The frictions had no effect in diminishing the swellings, and there can be little doubt that continued confinement, but not scrofula, would soon have deprived the child of life. The only evidence of immediate danger adduced, is the testimony of Lasne and Gomin, who are themselves on trial. Both M. Hue and Madame Royale were forbidden to see him, so that we have none but most suspicious witnesses to prove his condition—for no record of Desault's opinion remains.

We are told that the child gradually became attached to his physician, and, towards the last, before he left his apartment, would timidly detain him by the skirt of his coat. This incident seems, under the circumstances, characteristic and natural. If he had any sense at this time, it was just in such acts of shy, sensitive gratitude that he would show it.

We now come to the point of mystery.* Up to the 30th May,

* "On the 11th Prairial (30th May), le Sieur Brieullard, the acting commissary for the day, who accompanied Desault, said to him, in going down the staircase, 'The child will die—will he not?' 'I fear it; but there are, perhaps, those persons in the world who hope it,' replied Desault, the last words which he pronounced in the Tower of the Temple, and which, though spoken in a low voice, were heard by Gomin, who walked behind Brieullard.

"On the 12th Prairial (31st May), the acting commissary, on his arrival, at nine o'clock, said he would wait for the Doctor in the chamber of the child, to which he caused himself to be introduced. This commissary was M. Bellanger, painter and designer of the cabinet of *Monsieur* (the Count de Provence, afterwards Louis XVIII.) who lived No. 21 Rue Poissonnière. He was an honest man; *the misfortune of his benefactor*—alas, in those sad times he was almost an exception—had not dried up *the devotion of his heart.* M. Desault did not come.

"M. Bellanger, who had brought a portfolio filled with his drawings, asked the Prince if he liked painting; and, without waiting for an answer, which did not come, the artist opened his portfolio, and put it under the eyes of the child. He turned it over, at first with indifference, afterwards with interest, dwelt a long time on each page, and when he had finished, began again. This long examination seemed to give some solace to his sufferings, and some relief to the chagrin which was caused by the

Navarre. On the other hand, it was said that the courts of Vienna, Petersburg, and Berlin designed to place him on the throne of Poland. There was a general public belief that attempts were on the eve of execution to carry him from the Tower. He was an object of universal conversation, and everything betokened a crisis. Never, perhaps, in the history of the world, was there a child on whom so many expectations and fears were centered—who stood in the path of so many ambitions, who had so many potent rivals, anxious to remove him out of their way, or who was exposed in such perfect helplessness to his enemies. It seems inexplicable, that in those times of blood, no one was found to deprive him of life. Before the downfall of Robespierre, it might have been effected without leaving a trace behind. Providence, it is all that we can say, destined he should survive.

At this critical moment, we find him in the hands of a royalist keeper, placed in his position by an intriguing agent of the Count de Provence, who, to effect this end had, with Jesuit policy, feigned to be a republican. We see this keeper closeted with royalists, and are permitted to hear enough of their conversations to know that they contemplate his removal from the tower in which he is confined. We next find another keeper added to the previous one, who, though nominally republican, does everything which would be politic were he preparing for his liberation. In the French government we perceive men ready to lend themselves to anything—anxious, if the Republic survive, to remove the child—but equally willing, should there be a change in the tide, to court the favor of an usurper.

Such is the situation of affairs, when the curtain lifts upon the scene of mystery, in which the Prince disappears from our sight.

## CHAPTER VII.

### DISAPPEARANCE.

The thirteenth of June, on which day the Convention had covenanted to deliver the royal children into the hands of Charette, rapidly approached. The Marquis de Fenouil, though endeavoring to outwit the republican government, was possessed of its confidence, and ostensibly acting with it, to overreach the Vendéeans. Between him and his creatures in the Temple, there was, doubtless, a complete understanding and a concerted plan of operations. They could act with greater freedom, because plotting against the government under its shadow, with its sanction, and, perhaps, with the secret co-operation of some of its members. The lax discipline which prevailed in the Temple; the good-natured, easy, and unsuspicious course of the keepers towards each other and the guard; the boisterous fiddling and singing, which made the stern old walls and vaulted staircase ring with unwonted merriment;—were all admirably contrived to lull watchfulness to sleep. "Like master, like men," is a homely but true proverb, and if the principal officials in the Temple led a careless, jovial life, it is not probable that those on whom less responsibility rested, were a whit more alert. The only real difficulty in the way of an escape, consisted in the vigilance of the acting commissaries—officers, whose term of duty lasted only for a single day, and who, on that very account, were apt to be strict and watchful.

But this was an obstacle easily evaded. The Marquis, who had secured the appointment of permanent officials in his interest, could easily, when the proper moment arrived, obtain the nomination of a royalist acting commissary. That he could do so, is evident from the case of Debierne. In agreement, doubtless, with a concerted scheme, the keepers were only obeying their instructions when, in the beginning of May, 1795, they wrote upon the

Register of the Tower, "The little Capet is indisposed"—and the next day, "The little Capet is dangerously ill, and there is fear of his death." It was necessary to go through the formality of an especial sickness, in order to arrive at the formality of a pretended death. On the 6th May, 1795, they were informed that, M. Desault, the chief surgeon in France, a man of world-wide renown in his profession, had been appointed to take care of the Prince.

There is no evidence that the physician considered his young charge in any danger, from which there was not an easy escape. He examined him long, with great attention, and questioned him, without being able to obtain an answer. He expressed in the prison, no opinion of his condition, but ordered merely, a decoction of hops; and on his visit the next day, directed, in addition, that his tumors should be rubbed with volatile salts. These prescriptions are as simple as can well be imagined. They indicate no anxiety—and this quiet, easy course—hop tea and gentle frictions, was continued by Desault to the very last. In his conversations abroad, we are told by M. Beauchesne, that he said, that the Prince "had the germ of the scrofulous affection of which his brother had died, at Meudon; but this malady had scarcely imprinted its seal on his constitution, nor manifested itself with any violent symptom; neither vast ulcers, nor rebellious ophthalmia, nor chronic swellings of the joints." In the opinion of Desault, and his opinion cannot be rejected, the swellings on the articulations of the Prince's body were *not* scrofulous. They had been in existence ever since his solitary imprisonment; and, if they were scrofulous tumors, the disease must, already, have been of long standing, and firmly seated in his constitution. Instead of suffering from scrofula, Desault said, he was sinking under decline, occasioned by confinement, and proposed an immediate transportation to the country, hoping that good air, careful treatment, and constant attention, would restore him. In a word, "He undertook," says the Duchess D'Angoulême, "to cure him.*

* Filia Dolorosa, p. 245.

It was with difficulty the child could be induced to take the medicine prescribed. The government refused to comply with the physician's request for his removal, and hop tea and sal-volatile frictions constituted, let me repeat, the whole treatment the child received at the hands of Desault. The frictions had no effect in diminishing the swellings, and there can be little doubt that continued confinement, but not scrofula, would soon have deprived the child of life. The only evidence of immediate danger adduced, is the testimony of Lasne and Gomin, who are themselves on trial. Both M. Hue and Madame Royale were forbidden to see him, so that we have none but most suspicious witnesses to prove his condition—for no record of Desault's opinion remains.

We are told that the child gradually became attached to his physician, and, towards the last, before he left his apartment, would timidly detain him by the skirt of his coat. This incident seems, under the circumstances, characteristic and natural. If he had any sense at this time, it was just in such acts of shy, sensitive gratitude that he would show it.

We now come to the point of mystery.* Up to the 30th May,

* "On the 11th Prairial (30th May), le Sieur Brieullard, the acting commissary for the day, who accompanied Desault, said to him, in going down the staircase, 'The child will die—will he not?' 'I fear it; but there are, perhaps, those persons in the world who hope it,' replied Desault, the last words which he pronounced in the Tower of the Temple, and which, though spoken in a low voice, were heard by Gomin, who walked behind Brieullard.

"On the 12th Prairial (31st May), the acting commissary, on his arrival, at nine o'clock, said he would wait for the Doctor in the chamber of the child, to which he caused himself to be introduced. This commissary was M. Bellanger, painter and designer of the cabinet of *Monsieur* (the Count de Provence, afterwards Louis XVIII.) who lived No. 21 Rue Poissonnière. He was an honest man; *the misfortune of his benefactor*—alas, in those sad times he was almost an exception—had not dried up *the devotion of his heart.* M. Desault did not come.

"M. Bellanger, who had brought a portfolio filled with his drawings, asked the Prince if he liked painting; and, without waiting for an answer, which did not come, the artist opened his portfolio, and put it under the eyes of the child. He turned it over, at first with indifference, afterwards with interest, dwelt a long time on each page, and when he had finished, began again. This long examination seemed to give some solace to his sufferings, and some relief to the chagrin which was caused by the

Desault paid his visits regularly, at nine o'clock, without any change, either in the patient or in his treatment. On that day, it is asserted, on the authority of Gomin, he expressed, in a low voice, fears for the child's life, when going down stairs, never to return. The next day, a new actor appears upon the scene under most suspicious circumstances. Already, the child was surrounded within and without the Temple by royalist agents, who were plotting to effect his removal. There now entered another, *who was a creature and confidant of the Regent, and devoted to the cause of his patron*

absence of his physician. The artist often gave him explanations of the different subjects of his collection. The child had at first kept silence, but, little by little, he listened to M. Bellanger with marked attention, and finished by answering his questions.

"In taking the portfolio from his hands, M. Bellanger said to him, 'I much desire, sir, to take away one drawing more, but I will not do it if you object.' 'What drawing?' said the Dauphin. 'That of your countenance; it will give much pleasure, if it will not cause you pain.' 'Will it give you pleasure?' said the child, and the most gracious smile completed his sentence and the mute approbation which he gave to the desire of the artist. M. Bellanger traced in crayon the profile of the young king, and it is from this profile, that, some days after, M. Beaumont, the sculptor, and, twenty years after, manufacturer of Sèvres porcelain, executed the bust of Louis XVII.

"The 13th Prairial (1st June), M. Desault did not come again. The keepers were astonished at his absence, and the child regretted it. The acting commissary, M. Benoist, Faubourg St. Denis, 4, was of opinion that word should be sent to the house of the physician, to inquire the cause of so prolonged an absence. Gomin and Lasne had not yet dared to act according to this advice, when the next day M. Bedault Rue de Bondi, 17, who relieved M. Benoist, hearing him on his arrival pronounce the name of M. Desault, said immediately, 'Don't wait for him any longer, he died yesterday.'

"This sudden death, under such circumstances, opened a vast field of conjecture There is one, which must astonish by its boldness, let us say more justly, by its infamy. They dare assert that M. Desault, after having administered a slow poison to his patient, had been himself poisoned by those who had commanded the crime. But the noble life of M. Desault protects him, without any doubt, against such a calumny. Other inventors have not feared to say, that M. Desault did not recognise in the poor, sickly one in the Tower of the Temple, the child so full of strength and grace whom he had admired more than once, and in a happier dwelling; and that it was because he showed an intention of revealing to the government this substitution, that the doctor had been poisoned. This supposition is equally true with the first. M. Desault, who had been physician to the royal children, never doubted that his young patient was the Dauphin."—*Beauchesne*, vol. ii. 349.

*and benefactor*—M. Bellanger, painter and designer of the cabinet of Monsieur. It cannot, with semblance of reason, be denied that this man was there as agent of the Regent. And now, let us watch his actions. It was usual for the acting commissary to wait the arrival of the physician, and go with him and the two guardians —who were also styled commissaries of the Committee of General Safety—into the chamber of the patient; but M. Bellanger, though he arrived precisely at the hour when M. Desault was expected, said that he would go up at once to the Prince's room, and stay there till the physician came. The discipline of the prison was relaxed, so that this infraction of rule would occasion no particular remark. The physician did not come, and the creature of the Regent remained with the child the whole day. He had come prepared to stay, and try to gain the affections of the captive. He amused him with pictures, and concluded by taking a sketch of him. When he went away, or how, we are not informed. What was done in the prison that day, besides, has no record. But, there was time enough to effect any change, and there were hands enough within and without the prison ready to co-operate in removing the young captive. There was no spy on their operations—no inconvenient physician—no harsh republican commissary. All were agreed, keepers, commissary, steward, probably sentinel, within—Fenouil, Doisy, Debierne, and who else, we know not, without. The child, conciliated and pleased with pictures, and dosed for a month with decoction of hops, which I very much question whether Desault ever ordered, would offer no opposition to accompanying a stranger. If ever there were a conjunction of men and circumstances favorable to the easy and unobserved removal of a prisoner, we have them here. But we are left to imagine what happened, with probability only for our guide.

The next day comes, and no physician appears. The guardians, according to their testimony, are very much astonished, and the child very sad. On the 2d June, the news arrives that Desault had died the previous day. Even before the event of the Dauphin's illness is known, the sudden death of such a man, at such a time, throws all Paris into bewilderment. The public mind feels that there is a mystery transacting. It conjectures this, and it conjectures that; but though its surmises take different shapes, there is a rooted suspicion of foul play, and a firm belief that, for some reason, Desault has been poisoned. It can scarcely be imagined that a careful and skilful practitioner, like Desault, would keep no record of his visits to the Prince—no description of his case, his symptoms, and the probabilities of his recovery or death. But, no such record is found, which creates another strong suspicion that his papers were tampered with, and all traces of an inconvenient character removed. Had his memoranda been preserved, it would, probably, have appeared that the Dauphin was in no immediate danger. Desault did not act as if he imagined him to be in any. Physicians do not like to assume sole responsibility in such cases. The moment that Pelletan was called to the Tower, he asked for a colleague. Desault continued to treat the case, quietly, by himself, making no extraordinary visits, giving no unusual remedies. He was taken sick, we are told, by M. Beauchesne, in explanation of his death, with ataxique fever, on the night of the 29th May. M. Abeillé, his medical pupil, who, probably, understood his symptoms better than any one else, has declared, both in Europe and America, that he was poisoned.* But, notwithstanding his asserted sickness on the 29th May, the 30th found him well enough to visit his patient, as usual, without exhibiting any signs of indisposition. Had he been suffering, at his last visit to the Temple, under a fever, which in a few hours would bring him to the grave, he would have shown some indication of his condition; but, the veracious witness, Gomin, observed none, and was at a loss to imagine the reason of his absence the next day.

If his illness increased so much during the 29th that he found himself unable to make his usual visit to the Prince, he would, *in*

* Percival, p. 165.

*all human probability, have sent some substitute, had the child, in his opinion, been in immediate danger.* A great physician is the most faithful of mortals; and the sense of duty and the *esprit du corps* operate, as in the soldier's or the sailor's heart, to the last beat of life. That Desault, even on his death-bed, would voluntarily allow the dying Prince, if such he deemed him, to be neglected for forty-eight hours, is impossible. Let the profession say whether I am right. In short, the conduct, as well as the death, of Desault, are wrapped in impenetrable mystery, and do not, in any way, coincide with the hypothesis that he regarded his patient in extreme danger.

At this point there occurs an entire break in the narrative of M. Beauchesne. From the time that Bellanger left the Tower, on 31st May, until June 5, there is no record of anything that transpired in the sick chamber, except a remark, requiring no great stretch of intellect to coin, that the child felt sad on June 1st. The space left, at this most critical period, affords ample room and verge enough for any new arrangements, and we are not to suppose the ingenuity of our friend the marquis, and his accomplices within and without the Temple, was at fault.

Pelletan, receiving his appointment from the Committee of General Safety, on the morning of June 5, went to visit his patient at five in the afternoon. He was entirely unacquainted with the Prince, and had never seen him. "I found the child," he says, "in so sad a state that I demanded instantly that another professional person should be joined with me, to relieve me from a burden I did not wish to bear alone." The instinctive feeling and the ordinary practice of the medical profession immediately displayed themselves, in a case fraught with real danger. No sooner did Pelletan cast his eyes upon the child he was called on to attend, than he cried, "Give me a colleague." Desault convinced, as the Duchess D'Angoulême acknowledges, that he could cure the Prince, made no allusion to the subject.

The sick child in the Temple was now in the hands of a perfect stranger. Of such a person the Prince was, according to every account, most shy. His timid recognition of Desault, after the lapse of some weeks' acquaintance, we have seen, as well as the difficulty experienced by every one in obtaining, by the most winning arts, the slightest attention. But, if the authorities on whom M. Beauchesne relies are to be trusted, an entire change now came over his feelings and conduct. Instead of waiting to be spoken to, he began to converse with the strange physician, and displayed every sign of a mind thoroughly alive to all that was going on.

Rogues have seldom the genius of Shakespeare, and truth, therefore, has little to fear from the combinations of falsehood. They outrage nature and probability in their attempts to make a plausible case, and though they may deceive some, cannot deceive all. The physician, it is said, on entering the apartment, found fault with the confined air, and, in a loud tone, proposed to the municipal officer on duty, that the child should be carried into another room, on which he immediately beckoned M. Pelletan to approach, and said, "Speak lower, I pray you; I fear they will hear you above, and I should be very sorry they should learn that I am sick, for it would give them much pain." He was removed to another room, and during all the time the preparations were being made, his eyes followed every motion.

So many asserted details respecting his feelings, which must be purely imaginary, are given, that it is folly to notice them. As even M. Beauchesne could perceive the necessity of accounting for the remarkable change which is henceforth visible, he ascribed it to the sunny room. "He found himself in an airy chamber, without bars, and ornamented with great white curtains, which permitted him to see the sky and the sun. The gay sun of June entering by the open window—what a spectacle for a child so long shut up in a dungeon!"

There is some inconsistency in this, for the sky and the sun were not such strangers to the eyes of the child who had been for months accustomed to a daily walk on the Tower, and the deputation who visited him in February, represented his room as agreeable and well lighted. "Are you pleased with this chamber?" said Pelletan. "Oh, yes! very much pleased," was the ready and animated reply. His heroic resolution of never speaking again, must have been long abandoned. On 7th June, M. Dumangin, chief physician of the Hospital of the Unity, was added to Pelletan, and both of them came immediately to visit the child, who, at all convenient occasions, continued to talk and chat, with unabated interest, respecting all that was going on around him.

But we are not left without other testimony of the real scenes which the interior of the Temple, at this time, presented.

"A very respectable tradesman," says Ireland,* in stating the prevalent disbelief in Paris at the Restoration, concerning the Dauphin's death, "is my authority for the following narrative, who has heard his father, to whom the circumstance occurred, repeat it in society fifty times. I shall now give it as nearly as possible, in his own words, or, rather, as if the father himself were repeating the facts:—

"'As I was then a resident in that quarter of Paris where the Temple was situated, in my capacity as a National Guard, it became my turn to attend there as sentry; when having seen the Dauphin about six months before, and being anxious, if possible, to behold him again, prior to his death, as the current report was his being in a very dangerous state; I, in consequence, applied to the jailer to know whether I might be permitted to occupy the post of the guard, destined to keep watch on the Dauphin's apartment, there being always one stationed there. To this request, after regarding me with an air of doubt, which the frankness of my manner dispelled, he acceded under one proviso, that I was not to exchange a single syllable with citizen Capet in case he addressed me, as the infringement of such order would be attended with the loss of my head. I promised strict obedience to these commands, and immediately entered upon my duty, being forthwith introduced into the chamber, where I relieved a brother guard. In this

* Ireland's France, p. 27. London, 1822.

apartment there were three common chairs, a table, and a low bedstead, whereon the Dauphin was lying, but from the position of the bed clothes I could not perceive his countenance, and thus I continued nearly the space of an hour, only observing, at intervals, a motion beneath the covering; at length, however, he pushed away the sheet from his head, when I was enabled to consider a countenance squalid in the extreme, partially covered with blotches, and disfigured by one or two sores; as he perceived in me a stranger, he inquired, in a faint voice, who I was, but the peremptory order received, and the heavy price set upon a breach of my faith, sealed my lips, upon which I placed my finger, thereby indicating the prohibition under which I lay.

" 'At this he appeared displeased, and after turning about, I beheld his body rise until he sat upright in the bed, when nothing could exceed my astonishment, on viewing a figure much taller, from the head to the bottom of the back, than the Dauphin could possibly have displayed from what I had seen of him only six months before; my wonder, however, increased on beholding him thrust his legs from beneath the covering, from which I was enabled to form an estimate of the height of the figure before me, if standing erect, when I felt an inward conviction, that however extraordinary the efforts of nature may be in some instances, no such change could have taken place in the growth of a youth in the half a year, as must have been the case, supposing the object before me to have been the Dauphin. With respect to the physiognomy it was impossible to identify from thence anything for a certainty, as the frightful effects of disease, with blotches and sores, had so disfigured the countenance, that no conjecture could be hazarded as to what its appearance might be in a healthful state; the lips, like the face, were also covered with livid spots, and it appeared to me that there were also scabs on the hinder part of the head; in short, a more pitiable object never met the human sight, whosoever it may have been, for as to the Dauphin, *I am fully convinced it was not him.* After remaining some minutes with the legs exposed, and seated in a kind of stupefied position, he again replaced them beneath the clothes, and covered himself as high as the neck, leaving the face exposed, and turned towards me, the eyes being sometimes shut for a few minutes, which, when re-opened, were always bent upon me, and, in two or three instances, I saw the lips move, and heard a faint articulation, but nothing was distinguishable. In this manner the allotted period of my attendance elapsed, upon which I was relieved by another National Guard from the melancholy duty, and descended to the chamber adjoining the grand entrance of the Temple, where I found the jailer, who inquired of me how I had left the citizen Capet, upon which, after expressing my opinion that his death must soon take place, I very foolishly remarked that, I thought the youth by far too tall for the Dauphin —when he hastily demanded my reason for harboring such a doubt. I then explained my having seen the youth six months before, and the absolute impossibility of such a change in stature taking place within so short a period. To which remark I received the following singular reply, "Sick children, citizen, will sometimes shoot up very fast; but I advise you to go home and keep a still tongue in your mouth, lest you should grow shorter by the head." I immediately left the prison and profited by this advice, as I never opened my lips upon the subject until the settled state of affairs in France, left me at liberty to do so without any apprehension of danger.' "

I give this narrative as I find it in the pages of Ireland. It is simple and natural. The time and place at which the work in which it occurs was published, and the absence of design in the writer to connect it with any theory on the subject, simply recording it as an isolated fact, which had come to his knowledge, entitle it to weight, and will not justify its omission, when presenting the evidence of the Dauphin's having survived his captivity. I may observe, further, that the external condition of the body, as described above, corresponds well with the account of its internal state given in the procès verbal, and is quite agreeable to an advanced stage of scrofulous disease.

The last night of the child's life is thus described by De Beauchesne:—

"'How unhappy am I to see you suffer so much,' said Gomin. 'Console yourself,' replied the child, 'I shall not suffer always.' Gomin placed himself on his knees to be near him. The child took his hand, and carried it to his lips. The religious heart of Gomin (Gomin, of course, is the authority) breathed forth an ardent prayer, one of those prayers which sorrow wrings from men, and love sends to God. The child did not quit the faithful hand which remained with him; he lifted his eyes to Heaven, while Gomin prayed for him. It is impossible to describe all that is holy and angelic in this last look of the child. You will ask without doubt, what were the last words of the dying child? You have heard those of his father, who, from the height of the scaffold, which his virtue had made a throne, sent pardon to his assassins. You have heard those of his mother, that heroic queen, who, impatient to quit the earth where she had suffered so much, prayed the executioner to make haste. You have known those of his aunt, of that Christian virgin, who, with supplicating eye, when they removed her dress, to strike her better, asked, in the name of modesty, that they would cover her bosom.

"And, now, shall I dare to repeat the last words of the orphan? Those who received his last sigh have related them to me—and I come faithfully to inscribe them on the royal martyrology. Gomin, seeing the infant calm, immovable, and mute, said to him, 'I hope you do not suffer at this moment?' 'Oh, yes, I suffer still, but much less, the music is so fine.' Now, there was no music in the Tower or its neighborhood; no noise from without came into the Tower where the young martyr lay. Gomin, astonished, said to him, 'In what quarter do you hear this music?' 'From above.' 'Have you heard it a long time?' 'Since you have been on your knees;' and the child raised by a nervous movement his falling hand, and opened his great illuminated eyes in ecstasy. His poor guardian, not wishing to destroy this last and sweet illusion, set himself also to listen, with the pious desire to hear that which could not be heard. After some moments of attention, the child was again agitated, his eyes flashed, and he cried in indescribable transport, 'In the midst of all the voices, I have heard that of my mother.' This name falling from the lips of the child, seemed to take from him all pain. His contracted eyebrows distended, and his look was illumined with that serene ray which gives the certainty of deliverance or of victory. His eye fixed on an invisible spectacle—his ear open to the far-off sound of one of those concerts which the human ear has never heard—his young soul seemed to blaze out with a new existence. Lasne came up to relieve Gomin, who went away with a broken heart, but not more unquiet than the evening before, for he did not foresee an approaching end. Lasne seated himself near to the bed. The Prince looked at him, for a long time, with an eye fixed and dreamy. Lasne asked him how he was, and what he wanted? The child said, 'do you think that my sister could have heard the music? What good it would have done her.' Lasne could not reply. A look, full of anguish, from the dying child, darted—earnest and piercing—towards the window—an exclamation of happiness escaped his lips—then, looking at his guardian—'I have something to tell you.' Lasne approached, and took his hand—the little head of the prisoner fell on the breast of his guardian, who listened, but in vain—God had spared the young martyr the hour of the death rattle—God had preserved for himself alone the confidence of his last thought. Lasne put his hand upon the heart of the child. The heart of Louis XVII. had ceased to beat. It was *two hours and a quarter after mid-day*."

As every striking discrepancy between the statements of those connected with this affair should be brought out, I will here refer to a curious question of time. At half-past two o'clock on the afternoon of the 20th Prairial (8th June), according to the statement of Lasne, the prisoner died. When he had drawn his last breath, Lasne went to inform Gomin, and Damont, the acting commissary, who went up into the room. Some time was spent in arranging the clothes on the bed, in opening the windows, and in making the ordinary changes in a chamber of death. After all this, Gomin set off to the Tuileries, in a distant part of the city, to inform the Committee of General Safety of the event. But, he found the session for the day was over. "La séance est levée."

It was, consequently, impossible for him to make his report to the committee. He met, however, in the Tuileries, one of the members, who said to him, "*Keep the secret until to-morrow*," which he accordingly did. Now, the next day after the procès verbal had been made out, Sevestre, one of the Committee of General Safety, reported to the Convention the death of the Prince, from "*a swelling in the right knee and the left wrist*," adding, that the Committee of General Safety "received the news of the death of Capet's son at a quarter past two the previous afternoon."

How it was possible for them to do this, when the sitting was closed before Gomin got to the Tuileries, which must have been at least an hour after the death of the Prince, is more than I can conceive. In the procès verbal, the decease is said to have occurred about three o'clock; in Gomin's certificate of death, exactly at three ;and yet the Committee of General Safety heard of it at a quarter past two. As in those days there were no electric telegraphs to antedate time, the reader must frame the best explanation he can for these facts.*

But, it now comes out that, on the 8th June, the Committee of General Safety were engaged in business of another kind, which may serve to explain this difficulty as to time. On the very day on which the tragic death-scene of the Prince—so graphically and lugubriously chronicled by Beauchesne—occurred, the Committee made no less a discovery than that they had been overreached, and that he had escaped. "The great fact of the escape of the Dauphin from the Temple," writes the Paris correspondent of the "London Atlas," quoted in the "New York Tribune," of September 19, "is well established by the archives of the police, where is still preserved the order sent out to the departments to arrest on every high road in France any travellers bearing with them a child of eight years or thereabouts, as there had been an escape of royalists from the Temple. This order bears date June 8, 1795—the very day of the death of the child in the Temple." That this

* Sevestre also informs us that Desault died on the 4th June—Beauchesne says he died on the 1st. When did he die?

order was rigorously acted on, and that the police over the whole of France were on the alert, the reader will hereafter see, when he comes to the statement of M. Guérwiére, of Paris, who was arrested, shortly after, when travelling in the carriage of the Prince de Condé, under the suspicion that he, then a child of ten years, was the Dauphin.*

At the very sitting, therefore, of the Committee of General Safety, to which Sevestre affirms that the death of the Dauphin was reported by Gomin, who did not arrive until the hour after the session was closed—this very police order must have been prepared. The fact is acknowledged by the historian of the Duchess D'Angoulême.†

But, to proceed with the solemn farce. In the morning of the 21st Prairial (9th June), two members of the Committee came, at eight o'clock, to verify the decease of the Prince. But they made no examination of the body, and treated the matter as a thing of no moment. "The event," they said, "is a matter of no importance. The Commissary of Police in the section will come and receive the declaration of the decease—he will certify it, and proceed to the inhumation without any ceremony. The Committee will give the necessary orders."

Four surgeons were appointed to open the body, and visited the Temple for this purpose. I give the procès verbal, but it is worthy of remark, as indicating the nervous haste with which the affair was hurried through, that the year is omitted from the date entirely, and that, although, at the conclusion, reference is made to a day and year on which the instrument was written, there are none given.

"PROCES VERBAL of the opening of the body of the son of the deceased Louis Capet, drawn up at the Tower of the Temple, at eleven o'clock in the morning of the 21st Prairial :—

"We, the undersigned, Jean Baptiste Eugène Dumangin, Physician-in Chief of the Hospital of the Unity, and Philippe-Jean Pelletan, Surgeon-in-Chief of the Grand Hospital of Humanity, accompanied by the citizens

* Percival, p. 170. † Filia Dolorosa, p. 476.

Nicholas Jeanroy, Professor in the Schools of Medicine at Paris, and Pierre Lassus, Professor of Legal Medicine in the School of Health at Paris; whom we have joined to ourselves in virtue of a decree of the Committee of General Safety of the National Convention, dated yesterday, and signed Bergoing, President, Courtois, Gauthier, Pierre Guyomard, to the effect that we should proceed together to the opening of the body of the son of the deceased Louis Capet, to declare the condition in which we have found it, have proceeded as follows :—

"'All four of us having arrived at eleven o'clock in the morning at the outer gate of the Temple, we were received by the Commissaries, who introduced us into the Tower. We proceeded to the second story into an apartment, in the second division of which we found upon a bed the body of a child, who appeared to us about ten years of age, which the Commissaries told us was that of the son of the deceased Louis Capet, and which two among us recognised to be the child of whom they had taken care for some days past. The said Commissaries declared to us that the child died the day before, about three o'clock in the afternoon, upon which we sought to verify the signs of death, which we found characterized by an universal paleness, the coldness of the whole habit of the body, the stiffness of the limbs, the dullness of the eyes, the violet spots common to the skin of a corpse, and, above all, by an incipient putrefaction of the stomach, the scrotum, and between the thighs.

"'We remarked before proceeding to the opening of the body, a general leanness, which was that of marasmus. The stomach was extremely swollen and puffed with air. On the inner side of the right knee we remarked a tumor without change of color to the skin; and another tumor, less voluminous, upon the os radius near the wrist of the left side. The tumor of the knee contained about two ounces of a greyish matter, pussy and lymphatic, situated between the periosteum and the muscles; and that of the wrist contained matter of the same kind, but thicker.

"'At the opening of the stomach, there flowed out about a pint of purulent serum, yellow and very offensive; the intestines were swollen, pale, and adhering one to another, and also to the sides of the cavity; they were covered with a great quantity of tubercles of different sizes, and which presented, when opened, the same matter that was contained in the exterior deposits of the knee and of the wrist,

"'The intestines, open throughout their whole extent, were very healthy inwardly, and contained but a small quantity of bilious matter. The stomach presented to us the same condition—it adhered to all the surrounding parts, was pale outside, covered with small lymphatic tubercles, like those on the surface of the intestines; its inner membrane was sound, also the pilorus and the omentum; the liver adhered by its convexity to the diaphragm, and by its concavity to the viscera which it covered, its substance was healthy, its volume ordinary, the vessel of the gall bladder was moderately filled with bile of a yellowish green color. The spleen, the pancreas, the reins, and the bladder were sound, the epiploon and mesentery covered with fat, were filled with lymphatic tubercles, similar to those of which we have spoken. Similar tumors were scattered over the thickness of the peritoneum, covering the inward face of the diaphragm. This muscle was sound.

"'The lungs adhered by their whole surface to the pleura, to the diaphragm, and to the pericardium; their substance was sound, and without tubercles; there were only some near the tracheal artery and the omentum. The pericardium contained the ordinary quantity of serosity—the heart was pale, but in its natural state. The brain and its dependencies were in their most perfect integrity.

"'All the disorders of which we have given the detail, are evidently the effect of a scrofulous disease of a long standing, and to which the death of the child should be attributed.

"'The present procès verbal has been made and signed at Paris, at the said place, by the undersigned, at four hours and a half, in the morning of the day and year below written.

"'J. B. E. Dumangin.
"'P. J. Pelletan.
"'Pierre Lassus.
"'N. Jeanroy.'

"This procès verbal was completed in 1817, by M. Pelletan, who made the following declaration:—

"'I, the undersigned, Chevalier of the Order of the Legion of Honor, member of the Royal Academy of Science, professor of the Faculty of

Medicine, certify moreover, that after having cut the cranium transversely, on a level with the orbits, to make the anatomy of the brain in the opening of the body of the son of Louis XVI., which had been assigned to me, I replaced the skull-cap of the cranium, and covered it with four strips of skin which I had separated, and which I sewed together; and that, finally, I covered the head with a linen handkerchief, or perhaps with a cotton cap, fastened below the chin, or at the nape, as is practised in similar cases. This dressing will be found, if it be true that corruption has not destroyed it; but certainly the skull-cap of the cranium still exists enveloped in the remains of those linens, or the cotton cap.

'" Signed,

"' PELLETAN.

"' PARIS, *17th August*, 1817.'"

M. Pelletan declared still later, that he had set apart the heart of the Dauphin in the operation of the autopsy, and had carried it away, so as to be able to offer to the royal family this sad and mournful relic of the infant king.

Beside the procès verbal, the documentary proofs of the death of Louis XVII., are the official declaration of Lasne and Gomin, and Bigot, a royalist, and certificates written by the said Lasne and Gomin for M. Beauchesne in 1837 and 1840; that of Lasne being confided to the scented pages of our author's album. Lasne asserts "on his honor, and before God, that the young prince died in his arms," at the time and place officially specified, and tells us that, having all his life told the truth, he will not lie at its conclusion. Both of the keepers unite in affirming the scrupulous exactness of our author. That these authentic testimonials of asserted facts may make the deepest impression, they are given in the form of fac-similes, after which M. Beauchesne states that Providence preserved the lives of the two old men to give light to his researches, and present, hour by hour, the bulletins of the dying agony. He then carries us to the grave in the cemetery of l'Eglise Ste. Marguerite, expresses "painful perplexity" as to whether the body was interred by itself or in a common sepulchre, indicates on a map the exact spot of interment, relates all the efforts which Louis XVIII. made to obtain certainty as to the place of burial, and of a certain monument which he intended to erect to the memory of the royal martyr, but which "n'a point été exécuté," and ends with the Latin epitaph which was to have been inscribed on the said Mausoleum, "Memoriæ et cineribus Ludovici XVII."

I would here call attention to one or two singular and suspicious facts, which in a subsequent chapter I will consider at greater length. The royal ordinance, issued in 1816, for the disinterment of the body of Louis XVII., was without any sufficient reason, revoked, as if it were a matter the king was afraid to meddle with. Again, orders were issued for the removal of the heart, asserted to be in the possession of Pelletan, to St. Denis; but, according to Beauchesne (see Appendix), Lasne, who was present at the autopsy, declared that he never left the surgeons for a minute, and that Pelletan did not take the heart out; consequently, he was left in possession of the sacred and precious relic, which the royal family did not deign to receive. Now, it is obvious that either Pelletan or Lasne must have lied, and thus either the procès verbal is discredited, or the testimony of Lasne; and the whole affair is left in uncertainty. For myself, I believe the statement of Pelletan. And here, too, the reader is requested to mark that *the whole testimony, as to identity, resolves itself into the truth or falsehood of declarations made by Lasne and Gomin.* To this, we have only to add that, according to Beauchesne, the testimony as to the place of interment is equally contradictory; and that, to say the least, it is singular, that in 1817, *after* Louis XVIII. was on the throne, he should have thought it necessary to call in the aid of Pelletan, to make a further statement, had it not been felt that the procès verbal was transparently defective.

We are now prepared to consider the authentic demonstration of M. Beauchesne.

He has proved undoubtedly, that a child died in the Temple, 8th June, 1795, and was buried somewhere in the cemetery of l'Eglise

Ste. Marguerite, on the 10th June, and we will not dispute the assertion that at nine o'clock that night, "the air was pure, and the aureola of luminous vapor which crowned that fine evening seemed to retain and to prolong the adieu of the sun." But I give the following reasons for denying entirely that it was Louis XVII. who then and there died, and was buried.

I. The surgeons do not testify that it was the body of the Dauphin which they opened.

II. Louis XVII. had tumors at *all* the joints, and particularly at the *knees*. This is a fact, so positively stated by the French officials, as to stand beyond reach of contradiction. The tumors were not scrofulous, but the result of confinement, and were in the shape of knots.

The procès verbal speaks of only *two* tumors, one on the inner side of the right knee, and the other near the left wrist.

III. M. Desault, on 6th May, testified that scrofula had scarcely imprinted its seal on the constitution of the Dauphin, and that he had merely the germ of a scrofulous affection.

MM. Dumangin, Pelletan, Lassus, and Jeanroy, certify that the death of the child, whose body they examined, was the effect of a scrofulous disease, *which had existed for a long time*, and the internal condition of the body, so minutely specified by them, shows how deeply seated the disease was in the constitution, so that the whole stomach and intestines were covered with a great quantity of tubercles, and all the other organs, where the disease could manifest itself, were in the state which showed the ripeness of the malady unto death.

IV. All testimony, except that of Lasne and Gomin, *nay*, *that of Gomin also*, *in* 1795, proves that, mentally, the Dauphin was in a condition of imbecility, coincident with his physical prostration, lethargic, timid, mute, difficult of access, shy of strangers.

The boy who died, if the whole account is not false, was exactly the contrary, forward, talkative, animated, imaginative.

V. Again, let any physician say whether a child in the mental condition in which Desault found the Dauphin, could have had not only the brain, but all its dependencies, perfectly healthy, or whether its vessels would not have been in a state of temporary derangement. The examining physicians say, "Le cerveau et ses dépendances étaient dans leur plus parfaite intégrité.

VI. The police records prove the fact of escape.

Now, unless M. Beauchesne can demonstrate that a body having tumors at both knees, both wrists, and both elbows, is the same with a body having only two tumors in all, and leaving one knee, two elbows, and one wrist, without them; that a child who, on the 8th of May, had scarcely a taint of scrofula, but whose diseases were caused by confinement, could, on the 8th of the next month, die of scrofulous disease of long standing; that mental characteristics the most opposite, are the same, and all the dependencies of an enfeebled brain can be in the most perfect integrity, his certificates, and his witnesses, and his sentimentality, his tears, unbuilt cenotaph, and Latin epitaph, and even "le cœur de l'enfant," of which M. Pelletan says, "je l'enveloppais en linge, et je le mit dans ma poche," and which he afterwards touched and examined, "avec attention, plus de mille fois," will be of no avail, and he must be forced to confess that a fact may be authentically demonstrated, and yet physically and morally disproved.

The certificates of our author may be correctly copied—his reports of conversations, as Lasne testifies, of the most "scrupuleuse exactitude"—but certificates are pieces of paper with ink upon them, and words spoken are sounding breath, and there their worth begins and ends, in times and cases on which great issues hang, unless consistent with confessed facts, and we have moral confidence in those who spoke and wrote.

But some possible objections may be made to this conclusion. It may be said that the number of the swellings was decreased by the frictions and applications made by order of Desault, and that he may have been mistaken in his opinion as to the nature of the Dauphin's malady, or that it increased with an unusual rapidity during the last month of his life. Such objections can never be made by medical men, but it is necessary to guard against the possible difficulties of others. If the disease were scrofulous, all diminution of the tumors would imply diminution of the disease, unless it manifested itself in some other place, of which there is no intimation, and thus the first and the last supposition would be at entire variance. Again, Desault was the most celebrated surgeon of the time in France, and it is not conceivable that he could have erred in opinion in a case of such importance; and, if his opinion were correct, that, in the beginning of May, scrofula had scarcely imprinted its seal on the constitution of the Dauphin, then it is a physical impossibility that it should attain its most advanced stage in a month; for scrofula, as I am professionally advised, is a disease most slow in its progress, beginning in the glands, progressing to the skin and articulations, and gradually taking possession of the intestines and vital organs, nor does it destroy life until the mastery over the last is complete. It would require years to bring about the state of things described, in the procès verbal, as being presented at the autopsy of the asserted Dauphin, and the declaration of the physicians that the disease was of long standing concedes this.

Now, against evidence of this character, proving by undeniable physical differences the non-identity of two bodies, no official recognition of identity based on mere casual observation, however positively declared, and however formally certified, can be of any avail. Bodies change so much after death, in many cases, that nothing but the closest examination, with the desire to ascertain the truth, can afford grounds for certain, or even a probable opinion. Four members of the Committee of General Safety came to verify the death of the Prince, but they showed the greatest indifference. The officers and sub-officers of the guard of the Temple were, we are told, afterwards admitted, but no documentary evidence is afforded of the fact. Some of them, *it is said* by Beauchesne, without proof, recognized the body of the Prince.

How they could have done so, when the police were hunting him all over France, is somewhat difficult to understand.

But I am able to neutralize such testimony, if any should be inclined to attach importance to it, by proof at least of equal weight. Mr. H. B. Muller, of Howard street, New York, an eminent artist, and who authorizes me to refer to him, assured me, in the presence of Mr. A. Fleming, that he was well acquainted with a person named Auvray, formerly an officer in the household of Louis XVI.—and who, though afterwards a republican, still retained his attachment for the royal family, and frequently saw the Prince in the Temple, both in a civil and military capacity, having previously known him well at the Tuileries; and that the said Auvray declared to the said Muller that he was present when the body was exhibited to the officers of the Garde National, and that *it was not the body of the Dauphin.*

In the "New Jersey State Gazette," of February 11th, 1800, published at Trenton, N. J. there occurs the following paragraph: "It is stated in political circles as a fact, that about two years ago, a Frenchman who had left his country on account of his principles, and resided at Philadelphia, affirmed that he was on the Committee of Surgeons who examined the body of the child said to be the Dauphin, and to have died of scrofula, in the Temple, but having known the Prince while alive, in examining the face of the corpse (*contrary to positive instructions*) he perceived no resemblance, and was convinced that some artifice had been used *to preserve* the life of the young Prince.

"This circumstance is related by gentlemen of credit, who received it two years ago from the surgeon who was present at the dissection, and is therefore highly confirmatory of the recent rumor that, Louis XVII. was really saved from the prisons of the National Convention by an artifice of Sieyes."

There are several discrepancies in this statement, though it is probably substantially true. I have never heard that either of the four physicians officially employed at the autopsy were in this country. But M. Abeillé, the pupil of Desault, who would be likely, as well as his master, to know the Dauphin, was in America, and declared openly his belief in the Dauphin's existence, and in the murder of Desault. He probably may have been admitted to the apartment under the circumstances described, though not in an official capacity.*

It may, however, be mentioned in this place, that Charles Lafond de Savines—ex-Bishop of Viviers, a man of learning, honesty, and ability, though he had embraced French revolutionary principles, till convinced, by the events, of their pernicious consequences, and who became the chief advocate of Hervagault, the first of the Pretenders, was mainly influenced by what he heard from the four physicians, "He was more convinced that the alleged Dauphin was really the brother of the Duchess of Angoulême from the fact that he, the bishop, *had conversed* with the surgeons who had been summoned to open the body of a child, but that they had not recognized it, nor were able to pronounce upon it as that of the Son of Louis XVI."†

I therefore meet hearsay with hearsay, neither being legal evidence, and one just as good as the other.

The evidence adduced renders it, I think, certain that Louis XVII. was removed from the Temple after his last interview with Desault—and another boy of about the same age, in the most advanced stage of scrofula, introduced in his stead—while Desault himself was murdered.

Between May 30th and June 1st, there were only four persons who are said to have had any intercourse with the Prince, Desault, Bellanger, Lasne, and Gomin. The first, who knew the Dauphin intimately, and, as a noble and good man, could never have been brought to testify that he was dead when he knew him to be alive, died suddenly, as all Paris suspected, of poison, on 1st June. Bellanger was alone in the Prince's room for hours on 31st May, under circumstances which show that he was seeking to gain the

* Percival, p. 165.

† Memoirs of the Duchess D'Angoulême, p. 389.

affections of the child. The keepers in the prison, placed there by an emissary of Louis XVIII., present us with the very combination of instruments necessary for the removal of the child.

The precise mode by which the death of Desault was accomplished, or the agents, may never be known, but I think there will be few to deny the extreme probability that he was poisoned.* Certainly, death never occurred more opportunely. He knew the Dauphin well, and was convinced of the identity of the patient he was attending with the son of Louis XVI.

Had he visited the Temple after M. Bellanger had removed the Prince, he would have at once detected and exposed the imposition that had been practised. It would have been impossible to obtain from him a procès verbal, stating that Louis XVII. was dead when he knew him to be alive, or even an indefinite document, of the character furnished by Pelletan and his colleagues, which would, in fact, from him have been worthless. They might shelter themselves under the plea of personal ignorance. He could not do so; and had he violated the principles of his moral nature, and disgraced himself in the eyes of the profession and the world, by the lame non-committalism that the commissaries assured him, that the dead body was that of the Dauphin, no one would have believed him, and the deception would have immediately recoiled on the heads of its contrivers. Nor would it have answered to have dismissed him and appointed other examining physicians in his place, for the world would immediately have asked, Why is this? Why keep away from the body the man who knows the Dauphin, and substitute others who do not know him? A crisis had evidently

* De Quincey, who has pronounced in the first volume of his autobiographical sketches, a favorable opinion of the evidence adduced in my articles, in "Putnam's Magazine," expresses some hesitation on this point. I am inclined to think, that further reflection will induce him to change his opinion. It is, indeed, an act abhorrent to the thought—but the times of the Revolution were not ordinary times, and men were so accustomed to bloodshed, out of mere caprice, that I cannot conceive they would find any difficulty in murdering even "a celebrated physician," when the crown and destinies of France were at stake.—*Vide Appendix B.*

arrived in those unscrupulous and bloody days, when either Desault must die, or the combined treachery of two hostile factions must be exposed, and all their plans and contrivances, and hopes for the future, come to naught. Can we think the moving agents in this dark drama would hesitate a moment between murder and utter discomfiture, or that they would lack the instruments to accomplish their resolves.

As to Lasne and Gomin, if my reasoning on the evidence be sustained, no other sentence can be passed on them than that they lied knowingly to the end, and the solemnity of their falsehood is on a par with the credulity of M. Beauchesne. Perhaps they were taught to regard it as a religious duty thus to act, and superstition was strengthened by habit, worldly interest, and the too natural desire to preserve consistency to the last. It is not improbable also, that while they found silence or falsehood lucrative, they knew that truth would be attended with the forfeiture of life. (Appendix C.)

Let me say a few words, before I conclude this chapter, as to the treaty with Charette. It seems evident that, in the contest of chicanery, the republicans were outwitted by the Regent and his agents—as the Vendéeans were duped by both. The Convention never designed to fulfil their stipulation, but merely to gain time; and a pretended death was necessary to cloak their breach of faith. What they intended to do with the Prince, is beyond conjecture. Certainly they had no expectation that he would escape their hands. The Vendéean treaty was just the thing to afford scope for every species of intrigue. The agents of the Regent in Paris were corresponding at the same time both with Charette and the government, and got the better of both—forwarding the ratification of the treaty to please the Vendéeans, countermining it to gratify the Convention; and, in the confusion into which everything was finally thrown, they advanced the ambitious designs of their master, by removing the lad from the clutches of both parties. In days when life was so rapidly sacrificed, and many of the royalist intriguers perished in the midst of successive conspiracies, it may have easily happened that most of the prominent actors in the removal of the Prince died upon the scaffold.

On the whole, the matter stands thus :—

1st. There is no shadow of pretence that Louis XVII. died in the Temple, at any other time than June 8, 1795, or that any other body was the body of Louis XVII. than that opened by M. Pelletan, and described in the procès verbal. If he did not die at this time, and if the body in question was not his, then it is conceded that he did not die in the Temple.

2d. The only evidence adduced to prove his death is that of Lasne and Gomin. If that fail, there is utter absence of proof. But, their testimony is not reliable, 1st. Because they were interested parties. 2d. Because a great portion of their statement is evidently false—inasmuch as they represent a person to have talked and been in his senses, who is known to have been devoid of reason, and from whom one of them acknowledged it was impossible to extract a word.* Probability is, therefore, against their credibility—and there only remains a naked possibility, that they spoke the truth in this instance. Such is one side of the question.

3d. As it is conceded, in the premises, that the body described in the procès verbal is that of the boy who died on the 8th June, 1795, it is physically impossible—as explained in this chapter—that this individual could have been Louis XVII.; and, therefore, the possibility in favor of the truthfulness of Lasne and Gomin is annihilated, and it is evidently demonstrated that Louis XVII. did not die in the Temple. In addition, there are a cloud of collateral circumstances, all tending to establish the same result, the half of which are not yet exhibited.

What is remarkable, in this case, is that, circumstantial evidence breaks down and brings to naught seemingly direct testimony, and shows that those do not widely err who attribute to circumstances, undoubtedly proved, a greater power in the development of

* Ces officiers municipaux (Laurent and Gomin) repondent—*qu'il était impossible de lui arracher une parole.*—*Beauchesne*, vol. ii. p. 299.

truth, than to verbal testimony. Facts cannot lie. Interested men may. In this instance, you might bring a thousand witnesses to swear to the identity of the dead body with that of Louis XVII., without affecting my conclusion, because, while their testimony, if unimpeachable on the ground of veracity and sincerity, might be resolved into mistake arising from physiognomical resemblance, it could with irresistible cogency be said to them—you swear that two bodies are identical, but they are known to be in entirely different conditions; and, therefore, you must speak false or be in error, unless you can prove that different things can yet be the same. In a celebrated criminal case, witnesses swore they saw a person walking in the street who was at that moment a dismembered corpse. It is easy to multiply proofs that Louis XVII. did not die in the Temple; but, I need nothing more than a comparison of Desault's opinion with the procès verbal, to satisfy my own mind. Those who do will find it in the police records and the acknowledgment of the French government.

## CHAPTER VIII.

### FUNERAL SOLEMNITIES AND DRIED HEART.

The death of Louis XVII. was officially declared. The procès verbal of the autopsy was published. His death was inscribed on the minutes of the Convention, and on the register of the section. The room in which he had been confined was empty. A funeral, said to be his, had taken place. Still the public mind was not satisfied. There was a general belief that the Prince was not dead. The mystery and contradiction, which hung over everything connected with the alleged event, created an impression of foul play never removed.

One thing alone was certain. He was not to be found. He had disappeared. He had been *got rid of*. The desire of the Convention was accomplished. The treaty with Charette was evaded.

The long ambitious dream of the Count de Provence seemed also nearly realized. He was now Louis XVIII. Between him and the throne there was now no known barrier of prior hereditary right. The nominal monarchy was vested in him, and the times appeared peculiarly favorable for the restoration of royalty. The excesses of the Revolution had produced disgust, and there was an ardent desire for the establishment of a more stable government than the Republic could offer.

On his accession, Louis XVIII. issued a proclamation to the people of France. It is a curious document, and well deserves attention. Its length prevents my giving it entire, but in the present historical inquiry it cannot be passed without notice. In it the long repressed impatience of an ambitious mind, chafing under a sense of its own importance, breaks out in despite of all politic considerations.

"LOUIS, BY THE GRACE OF GOD, KING OF FRANCE AND NAVARRE.

"*To all our subjects, greeting:—*

"In depriving you of a king, whose whole reign was passed in captivity, but whose infancy, even, afforded sufficient grounds for believing that he would prove a worthy successor to the best of kings, the impenetrable decrees of Providence, at the same time that they have transmitted his crown to us, have imposed on us the necessity of tearing it from the hands of revolt, and the duty of saving the country, reduced by a disastrous revolution to the brink of ruin.

"*Long, too long, have we had to deplore those fatal circumstances which imperiously prescribed the necessity of silence; but now that we are allowed to exert our voice, attend to it.*"

This is a strange sentence. What fatal circumstances had imperiously prescribed the necessity of silence? The existence of Louis XVII., and the limited, uncertain, and unacknowledged powers of the Count de Provence. He could only speak as Regent. In that capacity he had found his voice was but little heeded by those who knew his ambition, and disliked or feared him, or who had ambitious designs of their own. He could not address France from the position of self-inherent authority which belongs to one who stands in unquestioned possession of hereditary right, wherever that right is acknowledged to reside in any one. He had been a self-appointed regent, not nominated by the late king's will, not elected by the royalist party—and the adherents of the monarchy could all take their own stand, and make their own terms, independently of him. Condé could manage his forces as he pleased, without consulting the Regent. The Count D'Artois, at the British camp, paid him but a nominal submission, followed his own plans, and intrigued for his own interests. Charette and the Vendéans did not acknowledge him as Regent. The royalist leader fought in the name, and for the sake of the legitimate king, Louis XVII. And could he have obtained, in accordance with the treaty, possession of the person of his sovereign, what would he have cared for the Regent Provence? He would have struggled for the restoration of monarchy on his own terms, and in his own way. The head-quarters of the royalists would have been transferred from Verona, or wherever the Count de Provence held his court, to the camp at La Vendée; and the Regent, if he desired to exercise any control, must have appeared, as a subordinate, in the midst of a fierce insurgent army, and complied with the wishes of its chief.

All this was, to the last degree, galling to the proud mind of Louis XVIII. And now he breaks out with the confession, "Long, too long, have we had to deplore." Deplore what? I can see but one answer. The continued existence of Louis XVII., who obstinately persisted in dragging out an imprisoned life in the Temple, to the detriment and impediment of his successor. "But now that we are allowed to exert our voice, attend to it." Allowed, by what? By the death of that infant king, whose crown, by the impenetrable decrees of Providence, had been transferred to the Regent.

Had the proclamation of Louis XVIII. been the composition of a friend, or a minister, no sentence of this kind would have laid bare his heart. It was profound policy in Talleyrand to commit to a secretary the composition of his despatches, that his judgment might not be swayed by the natural egotism of an author. But Louis XVIII., vain of his literary acquirements, prided himself, in every crisis of his fate, in penning every important document himself; and, on this occasion, joy at deliverance from the embarrassments of a regency was too great not to find vent in words.

In a subsequent part of the proclamation, he expresses a somewhat similar feeling. "In those empires," he says, "which have attained the highest pitch of glory and prosperity, abuses most generally prevail; because, in such states, they are the least likely to attract the attention of those who govern. Some abuses had, therefore, crept into the government of France, which were not only felt by the lower class of the people, but by every order of the State. The deceased monarch, our brother, and sovereign lord and master, had perceived and was anxious to remove them. What Louis XVI. could not effect, we will accomplish."

Here again he involuntarily gives expression, in the midst of words of loyalty and affection for his brother, to feelings which had long engrossed his mind—and justifies all that history says of his brother's incompetency, fostering expectation of his own elevation. Had he tried, he could scarcely have more effectually disclosed, than in this proclamation, his sentiments towards the unfortunate princes whose fatal dignity descended on him.

This document, however, as a whole, though labored and pompous, like everything else which proceeded from his pen, was not unsuited to the occasion. He depicts in strong colors the miseries of revolutionary France, the social advantages which the country would derive from a return to her ancient institutions, admits the necessity of reform, to adapt the institutions of the country to the intelligence and wants of the age, promises reward to the royalists, mercy to the republicans—denies, in strange inconsistency with his known sentiments and previous expressions, all feelings of ambition, and ends by declaring his hopes for the future, and lavishing praise on the army of Condé.

One of the closing sentences shows the strong expectations he cherished of effecting a restoration. "Misfortune has removed the veil which was placed before your eyes, the harsh lessons of experience have taught you to regret the advantages you have lost. Already do the sentiments of religion, which show themselves, with eclat, in all the provinces of the kingdom, present to our sight the image of the glorious ages of the church; already does the impulse of your hearts, which brings you back to your king, declare that *you feel the want of being governed by a father*." Louis XVIII. could readily apply balms to any feelings of remorse which might at times disturb him, and believe that the end sanctified the means—that the weakness pertaining to a contested regency, in troublous times, and the dissipation of authority, consequent on the absence of one acknowledged head, imperatively demanded the politic usurpation of authority by one competent to govern. The French nation needed *a father*. Could it find one in the embecile captive of the Temple?—and though, both by his age and inability, the practical duties of sovereignty must devolve on some one else, a regency would leave the door open for perpetual resistance to authority and the strivings of ambition. The shortest and easiest way for the Regent was to cut the Gordian knot—and by making himself the sole source and fountain of legitimacy and right in the kingdom, to consult the common weal, while he advanced his own individual power.

The asserted death of Louis XVII. led necessarily to the liberation of Madame Royale, his sister. There was no longer any object or policy in retaining her as a captive. The press took up the unfinished work of Charette. Petitions and addresses poured into the Convention on all sides. Deputations from distant parts of the country presented themselves in Paris, to pray for the release of the last remnant of the unfortunate family of Louis XVI Concession to public opinion cost nothing, and was an escape from embarrassment. But a pecuniary ransom offered by Austria was rejected, and the more popular measure adopted of exchanging the Princess for certain representatives and other official persons, whom the fortune of war had thrown into the hands of that power.

Previous to her release, however, care was taken to communicate the intelligence that she was now alone on earth, and Madame de Chanteraine was commissioned to perform the task. "Madame," she said, "has no parents." "And my brother?" was the immediate question. "No brother." "And my aunt?" "No aunt." "All is finished!" was her pathetic exclamation. Her situation was gradually ameliorated. Madame de Mackau and the former governess of the Dauphin, Madame de Tourzel, were permitted to visit her, with Madame de Chanteraine.

Louis XVIII. employed M. Hue to communicate his wishes to the Princess. "He hired," says Lamartine, "one of the windows which overlooked the garden, where he used to sing like Blondel, the servant of another royal captive, consolatory lays to the daughter of his sovereign. By means of signals, he succeeded in putting her in possession of a letter from her uncle, to which the princess sent a reply by the connivance of the commissioners (*i. e.* Lasne and Gomin), who shut their eyes on the occasion. Charette also transmitted to her, through this medium, the wishes and devotion of the army."

We here still find the agents of Louis XVIII. holding communication with the inmates of the Temple, through the connivance of the *soi-disant* republican jailers, and, at the same time, maintaining intercourse with Charette. Some time elapsed before the necessary negotiations for the exchange with Austria were concluded, and it was not until the night of December 18th, that the princess left the Temple. Gomin accompanied her—and from him she derived confirmation of her brother's death. Surrounded by such influences she had composed, in the tower of the Temple, previous to her release, the account of the captivity of her family and the death of Louis XVII., so frequently appealed to as direct evidence, whereas her testimony, at this time, simply resolves itself into that of Louis XVIII., Lasne, and Gomin.

At a subsequent period, as I will hereafter show, the true secret of his fate was communicated to her, and she was made acquainted with the fact that, instead of having expired in the Temple, her brother was living in America. On 25th December, the exchange was consummated at Huningue, and on 9th January, 1796, she arrived at Vienna, where she remained for some time in the enjoyment of the hospitalities of the imperial court. Her travelling companion had been Madame de Soucy, a confidante of Louis XVIII., but, who, in consequence of the rivalry which arose between the house of Austria and the exiled Bourbons, in seeking her hand, was compelled to leave her. The emperor, anxious to unite the daughter of Marie Antoinette to the Archduke Charles, viewed with suspicion the appointment of Madame de Soucy. Her dismissal, however, was attended with no beneficial result to his wishes, and Madame Royale evinced her preferences for the Duke D'Angoulême, to whom it was the policy of Louis XVIII. that she should be united. "I am, before all things, French," she said to the emperor, "and consequently in entire subjection to the laws of France, which, from my childhood have rendered me alternately the suject of the king, my father; the king, my brother; and the king, my uncle; *and I will yield obedience to the latter whatever be the nature of his commands.*" "I remained inflexible," she says, "constantly making reference to the will of the king, my uncle."*

Louis XVIII. was, at that time, sojourning at Mittau, where the Czar Paul had afforded him a refuge. Through the intercession of the latter with the court of Vienna, the princess was released, and arrived at Mittau, on 4th June, 1799. On the 10th of the same month she was married to the Duke D'Angoulême. "The affianced pair," says the historian of the daughter of Louis XVI., "were calmly happy, and yet there had been no wooing. The

* Memoirs of the Duchess D'Angoulême, p. 263.

ceremony was the result of a political combination."* In all his wanderings, the king kept by him the prospective successors to his throne, whose affections, feelings, interests, and views became naturally identified with his own. Over the duchess he exercised an almost despotic control.

The industry and zeal of the agents and intriguers of Louis XVIII., who assumed also the title of the Count de Lisle, were only increased by his nominal accession to the crown. The whole of their plots, conspiracies, and correspondence is wrapt in such mystery, that it seems impossible to distinguish clearly the true from the false—what they did, from what they only pretended to do. But from first to last, they were thoroughly unprincipled.

In La Vendée, the contest for the Restoration was the result of an heroic passion. A species of religion pervaded all ranks, prompting a willing surrender of property and life for the sake of a beloved cause. But the partizans of Louis XVIII., with few exceptions, were actuated by purely mercenary motives, and continued their conspiracies against the internal peace of France, that they might draw their accustomed stipend.

The year 1796 witnessed the death of Charette, who was taken prisoner and shot—manifesting to the last a heroism worthy of his name and cause.

From the suppression of the war in La Vendée, all interest in counter-revolution ceases. It is impossible to respect those whose object is money—whose weapons are intrigue—and who work in the dark. It is equally foreign to my purpose to chronicle the successive efforts and systematic chicanery, through a series of years, by which they sought to impose upon France a government daily becoming more distasteful to the people, as the military triumphs of Bonaparte gave a new object to the popular enthusiasm.

France was now under the power of the Directory, which was a gradual preparation for still more concentrated authority; and the certainty that the government of five was only an introduction,

* Memoirs of the Duchess D'Angoulême, p. 273.

in some shape, for the government of one, gave an impetus to the intrigues of the royalists, which sometimes were on the brink of success. Under the protecting shadow of the Directory, the Empire grew gradually up, in the person of the victorious chief, who gave the principal eclat to the Republic in its final forms. With superstitious confidence in his destiny, he steadily and sternly resisted all overtures to cast his sword into the scale of royalty—while Pichegru, and, perhaps, Moreau, listened to offers tempting to all ambitions but the highest.

The 18th Fructidor (September 4, 1797) witnessed, however, the death-blow to the present hopes of the royalists; when the Directory, by a bold *coup d'état*, excluded from the legislature the deputies of forty-eight departments—banished forty-three members of the Council of Five Hundred, and eleven of the Council of Ancients. Deprived of all influence in the government of the Republic, the royalists sank into an insignificant faction. By petty conspiracies they might give work to the police—or, by pretended or exaggerated intrigues, draw subsidies from England—but were utterly powerless to disturb the country, in the presence of the gigantic influence and reputation of Bonaparte. His course of empire must be run before a sane word could be lisped for the dethroned Bourbons. Rising first into power soon after the disappearance of the child, he seems, like a gigantic storm cloud, thrust between Louis and the crown.

The Count D'Artois retired to Great Britain, and divided his time between the Palace at Holyrood, and his residence in London —except when absent, on brief intriguing excursions, to the continent. He had become far less obsequious to Louis XVIII., and his plots and manœuvres had an individual bearing. He designed, if an opportunity offered, favorable to the restoration of royalty, to throw himself into France and forestall his brother in the race of popular favor.

In the meantime, the king, driven from one place to another, by the current of events, still preserved, under every mutation of fortune, the mock majesty of external state, which, but for his ultimate elevation to the throne, would have shown him to posterity in the light of a monomaniac.* His court was transferred successively

* "Surrounded by his two young nephews, the Dukes D'Angoulême and Berry, his niece, his ministers, his great officers, his courtiers, his friends, his captain of the guards, the Dukes de Villeguier and Fleury, Count D'Avary, Count de Cossé, Commandant of his Swiss Guard, the Marquis de Jancourt, the Duke de Vanguyon, Marshal de Castres, by his gentlemen, his almoners, and by all the appendages of the Church and the Court which he included in his suite, he still represented in miniature the showy royalty of Versailles. Differing from Dionysius of Syracuse, who taught children at Corinth, he only knew the business of a king, which he exercised even among the peasants of Brunswick. It might be said that this long exile was only the rehearsal of a reign. The same solemnity presided at every act and every step he made. The ceremonies of worship, the levees, the councils, the public dinners, the assemblies, the play, were all assigned to their respective hours, with the uniform etiquette of the palace. From thence he conferred powers on his commissioners in the provinces, and withdrew them, as he thought fit, reigning, in idea, over the map of his dominions, which always lay open before him. He encouraged the armies at a distance by proclamations, and the chiefs by a smart saying. He wrote to Marshal Broglie in a style full of epic allusions about his son, who had distinguished himself on the Rhine:—'Ancient chroniclers inform us that the Cid was the last of the sons of Don Diego de Bivar, and that he surpassed him, in the opinion of all Spain. Adieu, my marshal.' His costume was that of the old regimé, absurdly modified by the alterations which time had introduced in the habits of men. He wore velvet boots, reaching up above the knees, that the rubbing of the leather should not hurt his legs, and to preserve, at the same time, the military costume of kings on horseback. His sword never left his side, even when sitting in his easy chair—a sign of the nobility and superiority of arms, which he wished always to present to the notice of the gentlemen of his kingdom. His orders of chivalry covered his breast, and were suspended with broad blue ribbons over his white waistcoat. His coat, of blue cloth, participated by its cut in the two epochs whose costumes were united in him. Two little gold epaulettes shone upon his shoulders, to recall the general, by birth, in the king. His hair, artistically turned up, and curled by the hairdresser on his temples, was tied behind with a black silk ribbon, floating on his collar. It was powdered, in the old fashion, and thus concealed the whiteness of age under the artificial show of the toilet. A three-cornered hat, decorated with a cockade and a white plume, reposed on his knees or in his hand. He seemed desirous that ceremonial should command respect through astonishment. He generally continued in a sitting posture, supported on the arm of a courtier or a servant."—*Lamartine.*

from Verona to Blankenbourg, Mittau, Warsaw, and, a second time, to Mittau. Finally, in 1807, he took refuge in England.

For a long time he retained the chimerical hope of reducing Napoleon to be the architect of his throne. But the great captain —though he justly despised him—to rid himself of the continual conspiracies of the royalists, made overtures to the king for the renunciation of his title to the crown—a proposition which, with verbal dignity that never failed him, he declined. The theatrical pomp and circumstance of his life were somewhat modified by the bracing republican air of England, and he gradually abated the mimicry of inexistent power, in which his puerile mind delighted. With the ken of a political prophet, and the patient, egotistic arrogance of a fatalist, he looked forward, even under the empire, against which he, as usual, protested, for the restoration of the kingdom.

The climax of Napoleon's power came at length—and then its descent and obscuration. Disaster followed disaster. The image which had filled the world, stricken on its feet of clay, at length grovelled in the dust. Napoleon was no founder of a dynasty.* Had he died in the Tuileries, and been succeeded by his son, loyalty—like a plant growing on the grave of the Bourbons, and bearing old heroic fruit—would have twined around the column of the empire, and rendered glorious, and venerable, and stable, the stately, but newly erected structure. But it was otherwise ordained. As the long anticipated moment for the Bourbons came more distinctly in view, the rivalry of the brothers increased in a manner which shows that D'Artois felt he had as much right to the throne as Louis XVIII. "My brother," said the latter, "contests and almost devours me for the attainment of this reign before it is assured to either."

Let us now pass rapidly over the interval. In the early part of the year 1814 the Count D'Artois entered France, and assuming the

* Inaugural Address of Napoleon III.

title of Lieutenant-General of the kingdom, took measures for the restoration of the Bourbons on the downfall of Napoleon, which appeared certain. He was strongly inclined to negotiate for himself. Great mistrust existed between him and Louis XVIII., not compatible with an assured hereditary title in the king; and I shall hereafter show that the Count D'Artois was well acquainted with the existence of his nephew. Feeling, therefore, that, in point of fact, the legitimate claim to the throne was vested in neither, he would be naturally inclined to dispute a possession which, if hereditary, could only be achieved by his brother as an act of usurpation. The force of events, the influence of family, prudence, and a thousand motives—personal and political—may have contributed to quell the temptation.

The treaty of Fontainbleau, between Napoleon and the allied sovereigns, was signed on the 11th April. But, on the 6th, the Senate had already acknowledged Louis XVIII. as king. He left Hartwell on the 18th April—entered London in state on the 23d, and, the next day, sailed from Dover for his long anticipated dominion.

With all the intricate combinations of political events to which the Restoration gave rise, we have nothing to do. But much that transpired of a more private nature in Paris, is so intimately connected with the historic problem before us, that I must consider it in detail.

Soon after the re-establishment of the royal family in the capital, arrangements, of various kinds, were made to pay due honors to the memory of all the Bourbons who had perished since the beginning of the Revolution. Here we evidently tread on ground which must present some strong indications of the truth in respect to the death or preservation of Louis XVII. Were he dead, nothing was more easy and simple than the course to be pursued. If alive, and the fact known to all the members of the Bourbon family, nothing could be more perplexing, or more likely to lead to those inconsistencies of conduct and contradictions in policy, which mark the era, and which constitute a labyrinth inexplicable on any other ground. But, let the reader judge when he has the whole before him.

The first act in the funereal drama, was the exhumation of the remains of the unfortunate Duc D'Enghein from the moat in the Château of Vincennes, where they had been deposited after the inhuman murder, perpetrated by order of Napoleon, the most damning deed in his career of blood.

The Duchess D'Angoulême played the most prominent part in the funeral pageant. She caused a chapel to be fitted up in the château, draped in black, rendered entirely dark, and lighted only by feeble tapers. Here the corpse of her murdered cousin was placed, and hither she repaired, once a week, to pray for the repose of his soul.* At the same time efforts were made to discover the remains of Louis XVI., Marie Antoinette, and the Princess Elizabeth. There was the greatest improbability that any vestige of their bodies remained—and certainly no means of identification. They had been buried in the churchyard of the cemetery of the Madeleine, and every care taken to destroy them, and prevent their being afterwards disinterred, as relics, to the prejudice of the Republic.† The bodies had been deposited in beds of quick lime, cartloads of which had been afterwards heaped on them, and, to aid in their rapid and effectual decomposition, immense quantities of water had been poured upon the whole. Hundreds, or rather thousands of bodies, aristocratic and plebeian, royalist and revolutionary, had been heaped pell-mell in the narrow ground—the royal dust lay in the very midst of the five hundred Swiss;‡ interments, of all kinds, had been purposely and recklessly made to defeat identification, and no wonder then that "the thermometer of sentiment descended below freezing point as soon as the royal conclusion was published, that the ashes of the illustrious dead should be publicly and solemnly transferred to St. Denis."§

* Ireland, p. 23.

† Alison, vol. i. p. 155. Memoirs of the Duchess D'Angoulême, p. 326. Ireland, p. 26.

‡ Memoirs of the Duchess D'Angoulême, p. 321. § Ibid, p. 325

Paris stood laughing by as the mock pageant swept along, in funereal pomp and heraldic blazonry, bearing to the royal mausoleum "the *bodies* of the most high, most powerful, and most excellent Prince, Louis XVI. by name, and by the grace of God, King of France and Navarre; and of the very high, very powerful, and very excellent Princess, Marie Antoinette Joseph Jeane, of Loraine, Archduchess of Austria, wife of the very high, very powerful, and very excellent Prince Louis, XVI. of the name, King of France and Navarre.* But, while the transaction was ridiculed, attention tion was drawn to the significant fact, that there were no funera. solemnities for Louis XVII. Attempts, I know, are sometimes made to explain this, by saying that, the Roman Church offers no prayers for the souls of children, who are not supposed to need them.† But this is an evasion, and by no means meets the difficulty. The Roman Church buries children, and relatives, in Romish countries, respect the remains of those members of their family who die in youth. Louis XVII., if dead, was buried in a spot, well-known—no quick lime had been cast, as in the other cases, on the corpse—an indication, by the by, that it was not deemed worth while to destroy inexistent relics. The Duchess D'Angoulême, who showed such marked respect and affection for the dust of the Duc D'Enghien, a distant relative, would be likely to pay equal regard for the memory and remains of a brother, who shared her captivity, and with whom the most mournful memories of her life were connected. If she did not pray for his soul—for that is not the point—she would assuredly gather his remains, to be deposited beside those of his august parents, or would at least take care that a monument was erected to perpetuate his name, his virtues, and his sufferings.

The omission, therefore, of *all respect* to Louis XVII., at such a moment, occasioned, in every place where the circumstances were known, surprise and suspicion, which revived all the doubts con-

* Memoirs of the Duchess D'Angoulême, p. 325.

† Le Phare de New York, February, 1853.

cerning the death of the Prince which had so long slept in the oblivion of the Bourbons and the martial splendors of the empire.

But all speculation on the subject was cut short by the spectral revivification of the power of Napoleon, in 1815. Again were the Bourbons scattered to the four winds, flying, fighting, or intriguing —and the valor and determination of the Duchess D'Angoulême drew from Napoleon the celebrated remark, that she was the only man of her family. But the bloody drama of the Hundred Days soon came to an end, and Louis XVIII., a second time, entered the Tuileries in triumph, at the very moment when Napoleon quitted France for ever.

The perplexities attending the second restoration, for some months, so exclusively occupied the national mind, that the question of the death of Louis XVII. was not again revived, until affairs assumed a sufficiently settled state, to allow the public to see that if the predecessor of the reigning sovereign was indeed no more, common decency required that some respect should be paid to his memory. Public opinion imperatively demanded action of some sort, and Louis XVIII. felt compelled to humor it to a certain extent—or rather to play with and lull it to sleep by promises never fulfilled.

In January, 1816, a law was passed, by the two Chambers, commanding a monument to be erected at the expense and in the name of the French nation, to the memory of Louis XVII. The king, as if designing to put this law in immediate execution, issued a royal ordinance for the erection of the monument in the church of the Madeleine, and gave directions to Lemot, a Parisian sculptor, to execute it. M. Belloc was also employed to write an epitaph to be inscribed on the mausoleum of the infant king.

All this looks well. But after all this show of regard, the law remained a dead letter. The ordinance was never carried into effect—the monument was never erected, and the epitaph has no place but among the curiosities of literature, the Limbo of all lost and all abortive things. I give the proposed epitaph and a translation below.* Facts are more satiric than Juvenal.

The next official action taken in the matter was on 1st March, 1816, when the Count Decazes, Minister of Police, addressed the following letter to the Count Anglès, Prefect of Police:—

"PARIS, *March 1st*, 1816,

"*Monsieur le Comte:*

"His majesty has deternuned by his ordinance of 14th February, the place to be occupied by the religious monument, to be erected to the memory of Louis XVII. It is really necessary, and I have already called your attention to this subject, to discover the precious remains of this illustrious victim of the Revolution. It is known that the young king was interred in the Cemetery of St. Marguerite, in the Faubourg St. Antoine, in the presence of two civil commissioners, and of the commissary of police, of the section of the Temple, 8th June, 1795.

"The young king should be placed in St. Denis.

"I request you to render me an account of the precise measures which you have prescribed to attain this end, and of their probable result. It

| * Memoriæ et cineribus | To the memory and ashes |
|---|---|
| Ludovici XVII., | of Louis XVII., |
| quem | whom, |
| parentibus sanctissimis | from his sacrcd parents |
| infando funere orbatum | separated by a mournful fate, |
| nullas non ærumnas perpessum | and stricken with every sorrow, |
| in ipso fere vitæ limine mors sustulit | on the very threshold of life, death removed |
| die VIII. junii an. MDCCXCV. | on the 8th day of June, 1795. |
| Vixit Annis X. Mensibus II. diebus XII. | He lived 10 years, 2 months, 10 days. |
| Ludovicus XVIII. | Louis XVIII. |
| fecit | hath erected this |
| fratris filio dulcissimo | to his nephew most lovely, |
| ac supra ætatis modum, pietissimo | and, beyond the measure of his age, religious, |
| salve anima innocens | Hail innocent soul, |
| quæ ceu aureum Galliæ sidus | who, like a glittering star of France, |
| beato spatiaris polo | walkest in the blessed skies; |
| volens hanc patriam domum que Borboni- | auspiciously, this country and the House |
| dum placido lumine intuetor. | of Bourbon, with placid eye, behold, |

will be essential, if this precaution has not been taken, to call the commissaries, and other persons who assisted at the inhumation.

"The Minister of General Police,

"COMTE DECAZES."

To this letter M. Anglès returned the following answer:—

"PARIS, *1st June*, 1816.

"*Monsieur le Comte:*

"On the reception of your excellency's letter, I appointed two commissaries of police to obtain from the Sieur Dusser—formerly commissary of police of the section of the Temple, who in this quality must have assisted at the interment of the young monarch—all the information which he could furnish on this subject. It results from the information that the commissaries obtained, that the Sieur Voisin, aged, at present, sixty-five years, and retired to the hospital of Bicêtre—was, at the period of the death of Louis XVII., conductor of funeral processions, in the parish of St. Marguerite, in the cemetery of which the Prince was interred, and that they could, in consequence, obtain all the information on the very spot of the inhumation.

"The Sieurs Simon and Petit have obtained from him many details which have put them in the way of establishing a system of positive information. He has assured them that he dug, in the morning of the day of this sad ceremony, a particular grave, in which the body of the king was placed, and going to the cemetery with the commissaries, Simon and Petit, he traced for them an extent of ground, within the limits of which should be found, according to him, at the depth of six feet, the coffin of the king, made of white wood, and having at the head and at the feet, a D, written by himself with charcoal.

"The commissaries have also seen the Sieur Bureau, keeper of the cemetery for twenty years, who affirms that Voisin asked of him, on the morning of 12th June, 1795, a coffin for a little girl, and that he understood, during the day, that it was for the Prince whom they then called the Dauphin. He pretends that Voisin did not dig a particular grave, and that the procès verbal of the inhumation in the common grave was drawn up in the parsonage house. Following their inquiry, the commissaries have learned from the present curé of St. Marguerite, that a grave-digger named Bétrancourt, called Valentine, whose wife still lived, had taken away the body of the young Prince from the common grave, and had interred it in a separate place. On inquiring of the widow of this man, if she could give any information as to the precise place of burial, she indicated a friend of her deceased husband, named Decouflet, Beadle of the Parish des Quinze Vingts, who informed them that Bétrancourt, called Valentine, in digging a grave in the cemetery of St. Maguerite, in 1802, pointed out a place near a pilaster, on the left of the church, from whence he raised about two feet of earth, and disclosed a stone of the foundation of the church, upon which was a cross. Bétrancourt added, that they would one day make a monument there: for beneath that, he added, is the coffin of the Dauphin.

"From all the information obtained from these different persons, follows, that on 12th June, 1795, the mortal remains of his Majesty, Louis XVII., enclosed in a coffin of white wood, four feet and a half in length, was carried from the Temple to the cemetery of St. Marguerite, about nine o'clock in the evening; that the procès verbal of this ceremony was drawn up in the parsonage house, by the Sieur Gille, then commissary of police: that it appears probable that the body was taken from the common grave; that this operation was executed in secret, and during the same or the following night, by Voisin or Valentine; that, if it was by the last, the place where the ashes of the young king repose, is near the pilaster, on the left side of the gate of the church, on entering the cemetery; that, if it was by the former, the particular grave can be found, within the space which Voisin has designated, to the left of the cross raised in the middle of the cemetery, in going round the back of the church, &c.

"I pray your Excellency, &c.,

"C. Anglès."

Here, certainly, was information, which, though differing in details, was sufficiently precise to found an *investigation* upon. Two places were indicated—in one of which there was every reason to suppose the body would be found. And, to avoid all possibility of being deceived as to the remains, M. Pelletan certified to the condition in which the body buried as the Dauphin would be found; viz. that the skull was divided in a particular manner, which he minutely described, together with the dressing in which it was enveloped, portions of which he said "certainly existed," as means of identification. But there the matter ended. No attempt was made to discover the asserted remains of the Prince. The skeletons of Louis XVI. and his queen, buried in quick lime for twenty years, and mixed up indistinguishably in a common revolutionary sepulchre, were infallibly discovered, by an instinct peculiar to some classes of men. But, notwithstanding the passage of laws and ordinances, the employment of sculptors and epitaph writers, the very first effort was not made to recover a body, whose place of interment was indicated, and which could be submitted to a certain and definite process of identification. Beauchesne, himself, has to acknowledge that he cannot account for the annulling of the royal ordinance, and declares that the place where the body was buried is demonstrably certain. "As I have proved," he says, "that the royal infant died in the Temple, it is to me equally demonstrated that his corpse, wrapped in a winding-sheet, was placed in a coffin, which has neither been opened nor changed; that it was, with the remains which it contained, buried in the cemetery of St. Marguerite, and in the place indicated." Now, if M. Beauchesne's enthusiasm be not all assumed, and, if he, indeed, feels the affection and reverence for the memory of Louis XVII. which he asserts, I cannot doubt that he would most gladly, were he permitted, even at this late day, undertake the search for the royal remains, which he believes to exist. How then, on any principle of natural affection or probability, can it be imagined that the sister of the Prince, subjected to the same imprisonment with him, and the uncle who sat on his throne, would neglect such plain and simple means to gather, from their neglected and dishonored grave, the bones of the young martyr king?

But this is not all. We come now to the controversy concerning the heart of the captive Prince, which affords moral evidence, of precisely the same nature, that the royal family did not believe in the death of their relative in the Temple. At least, if they did, their conduct is the strangest and most unaccountable that the world has ever seen.

What, then, are the facts in the premises? M. Pelletan, one of the surgeons charged with opening the asserted body of Louis XVII.—a man of high character, socially and professionally, whose testimony we are bound to receive, unless we cast aside all reliance on direct evidence—communicated to Louis XVIII., through the Minister of the Interior, the startling information that *he was in possession of the heart of his predecessor*, and gave a minute history of the interesting relic.

Now, the existence of the heart of Louis XVII., if true, was a fact doubly important, in case of there being some insuperable bar to the discovery of his grave, or the identification of his remains; and it would be natural to expect that the royal family would manifest a deep interest in the subject, and not lightly reject the respectable evidence adduced to identify the relic.

Pelletan stated, that being specially charged with conducting the post-mortem, and finding himself, for a few minutes, left alone by his associates, who had retired into the embrasure of the window, to converse, the idea occurred to him of possessing the heart of his patient. Watching a moment when entirely unobserved, and entertaining no fear of being searched, he covered it with bran, wrapt it in linen, and put it in his pocket. On his return home, he deposited the relic in spirits of wine, and concealed it on a lofty beam in his library. During ten years, he replenished the spirits of wine many times—but, at last, it entirely evaporated, leaving the heart dried and shrivelled. There was now no necessity for further precaution, and he placed it in a drawer of his secretary, where he saw and examined it a thousand times.

It, however, happened that he communicated the fact to a pupil, who, when the period of his professional study was over, surreptitiously took it away, and it was some time before he discovered the theft. Being on intimate terms with him, he hesitated to charge him with dishonesty. But when, on his death-bed, his friend confessed the larceny to his family, and commissioned his wife to return him the relic; he received it from her hand—and, as she and other members of the family were witnesses to the confession, we have proof not only of the identity of the heart recovered, but of Pelletan's truthfulness. But, in addition, M. Dumangin, his colleague, testified that, at the close of the operation, he saw him wrap something up carefully, and put it in his pocket. Although he did not at the time know that it was the heart, he declared that, "in his soul and in his conscience he was morally convinced of the fact" stated by M. Pelletan. On the communication of this important information, the following royal order was issued, after full examination of testimony:—

"PARIS, 3*d September*, 1817.

"MINISTRY OF THE INTERIOR.

"*To the Keeper of the Seals, Minister of Justice:*

"MY LORD:—

"I have received the pieces which your highness has done me the honor to communicate, both relative to the preservation of the heart of his Majesty Louis XVII., and as to the place where his body was buried. The intention of the king being that the heart of this Prince, and that of S. A. R. le Dauphin, elder son of his Majesty Louis XVI., which is in possession of the mayor of the 12th arrondisement, be transferred to St. Denis, without pomp, but, nevertheless, with proper ceremonies. I transmit, conformably to the order of his majesty, all the documents to the grand master of the ceremonies.

"THE SECRETARY OF STATE TO THE
"DEPARTMENT OF THE INTERIOR."

Here was the termination of the matter. The order was never carried into effect, as far as the heart of the prisoner of the Temple was concerned. The only plea for not depositing the heart in St. Denis, was the negative testimony of an underling, Lasne, that he had not seen the surgeon put it in his pocket, and although this was in fact confirmatory of Pelletan's statement, yet with an apathy, entirely unaccountable, it was permitted to outweigh the positive and respectable testimony of a man of station and character like Pelletan, confirmed in so many ways. The heart, enclosed in a vase of crystal, remains to this day in the family of the great physician.

In view of all these facts, relative to the funeral solemnities for the departed Bourbons, and the remains of the asserted Dauphin, I do not think there can be any other reasonable conclusion than that the royal family of France knew that the Prince was not dead, and therefore dared not risk the mockery of searching for a corpse that had never been buried—of building a mausoleum for one still alive—of consecrating a relic which they knew, though honestly preserved, had throbbed in no bosom of their race.

I can readily conceive, that state reasons might induce the sister of the Prince to consent that one untrained for political life should continue in obscurity, and not endanger the happiness of France and the peace of Europe by being thrust into a position he was incompetent to fill: but that, while she so far yielded to the sophistry of her uncle and the various influences that surrounded her, she would steadily resist the mockery of rearing a sepulchre to the living.

Throughout this whole transaction the king seems willing to perpetrate the required deceptions, but withheld by some concealed influence.

It is unnecessary to pursue further the history of the Bourbons. Hereafter I may have occasion briefly to refer to some of the subsequent changes in the French government. It is sufficient for the present that I have shown conclusively not only that Louis XVII. did not die in the Temple, but that all the probabilities of history apart from the central chain of evidence, lead to the same conclusion. The review of the French Revolution, and of the history of France up to the period of the second Bourbon Restoration, has opened the various influences, political and domestic, which, from his cradle surrounded the unfortunate Prince. We have seen an ambitious and unprincipled relative scheming to obtain the throne which he inherited, and aiding to produce the convulsion that deluged Europe with blood. We have seen the Prince in person surrounded by the creatures of his uncle, under circumstances which afford the highest probability of their design to remove him. It has been demonstrated on admitted facts that he did not die in the Temple. The data furnished by those who labor to prove his death, establish the contrary. If people cannot be satisfied with abstract physical impossibility, there is no use in reasoning, for, beyond this, argument and evidence cannot go. Finally, although Louis XVII. is, in history, usually numbered among the dead, there is up to this moment no funereal, no monumental recognition of his death, but a mystery, and an inconsistency attending every official effort to pay him the respect which his misfortunes deserve at the hands of the great French nation, and an apathy on the part of his nearest relatives, bound by every principle of religion, morality, and social feeling, as well as by every prescriptive law of custom and decency, to pay some honor to his memory, which carry the historic argument to its climax.

And yet, perhaps, there are those who will tell me, the death of Louis XVII. is an historical fact—the evidence for it direct and positive; and, pointing to some inconsiderate sentence in Scott, or Alison, or Thiers, will sagely assure me that if I deny his death in the Temple, I must also deny that of Napoleon, or of his father and mother, since the testimony for the former was as strong and conclusive as for the latter.* On such persons I do not care to waste a thought or a word. They seem to think that because some man, calling himself a historian, makes a statement, we have no right to question it. *Magister dixit.* Thank Heaven, the age for such mental slavery has passed.

In truth, much that we call history is very loosely written, and the conclusion of most sensible minds will, I think, be, that the historic guides, on whom, in a general way, we are forced to depend, lead us astray as often as they conduct us right; that usually only

* The United States Review. June, 1853, vol. i., No. 6.

Dr. Stephen Williams's Appendix and Notes to the Redeemed Captive, p. 190.

the most superficial aspect of events is presented by the chronicler, and that he who would gain light on material points must search for it himself.

---

## CHAPTER IX.

### NAUNDORFF AND RICHEMONT.

We now approach a portion of our subject, invested with a mystery which may never fully be removed. Many of the attempts to personate Louis XVII., were simply the result of the popular belief in his existence; and, standing entirely apart from the main current of events, do not deserve even a passing attention, except as evidences of that impression in the public mind, out of which they originated, and from which they derived their power of deception. There are others, however, which though equally false in themselves, yet bring us into contact with facts that bear directly on the subject of our investigation. Such, especially, is the claim put forth by Herr Naundorff.

The imposture of Hervagault, 1798, is of no historic importance, except as eliciting, through his zealous partizan, the bishop of Viviers, the fact, that the physicians who opened the body in the Temple, expressed, in conversation, the same uncertainty apparent in the procès verbal, and acknowledged their inability to testify to the death of Louis XVII.*

Marturin Bruneau, the second pretender, after personating the son of a French nobleman, went to America, and on his return to France, in 1815, set up in the new character of the Dauphin. His fictions, concerning his personal history, were so gross and palpable that I need not allude to them. It seems, probable, however, that the idea of his imposture was derived from a report then circulating in France, that Louis XVII. was in the United States. As he

* Memoirs of the Duchess D'Angoulême, p. 389.

had been in this country, this was a sufficient basis for his pretensions. In a letter, addressed by him, from Rouen, in March, 1816, to the Duchess D'Angoulême, he says, "I dispersed the last calumny which perversity had aimed at me, when it declared that, *your brother was still in the United States.* No, I had left it long ago."* However slight be the indication here presented, it is worthy of preservation, as it tallies with the alleged fact that, about this time, a certificate of the death of the Prince, in a foreign land,† was forged by the adherents of Louis XVIII.

## NAUNDORFF.

It was no ordinary imposture which could deceive the class of minds whom Naundorff enlisted in his service, and we cannot dismiss his pretensions without examination, because while they prove their own falsehood, they also establish important historic facts. In 1838, the Hon. and Rev. G. C. Percival published, with notes, an English translation of the evidence adduced by his advocates, M. M. Gruan and Bruquet. In an introduction to the work, he states the grounds of his own belief, which are simply these—that Naundorff had endeavored to procure a legal inquiry into the validity of his claims; that the French government, which had brought other pretenders to trial, had declined to grant him a hearing; and that persons of respectability and credibility imagined that they recognised him.‡ Mr. Percival frankly admits that there are many difficulties attending the pretensions of Naundorff, and that much of his evidence, especially the supernatural portion, is of a questionable character; but perceiving clearly that there was some unexplained connection between the Pretender and the truth, and having no clue, but the statements of Naundorff, to the mystery, appears to have yielded a forced acquiescence. The work of Naundorff's advocates is most

* Memoirs of the Duchess D'Angoulême, p. 417.

† Percival, p. 185.

‡ Percival, Preface, p. xvii.

perplexed in its arrangement, or rather want of arrangement, but I will endeavor to extract from it the evidence which it contains. Falsehood attends truth like its shadow, and undesignedly gives testimony against itself, and in favor of that which it darkly mimics.

In 1833, a stranger arrived in Paris, who represented himself to be the son of Louis XVI. He assumed the name of Louis Charles, Duke of Normandy—introduced himself into legitimist circles, and very soon obtained ardent and highly respectable adherents. Among them were Madame de Rambaud, who had been nurse to the Dauphin from his birth until his confinement in the Temple. M. Marco de St. Hilaire, formerly gentleman usher to Louis XVI., and M. Morel de St. Didier. Of the perfect sincerity and honorable convictions of these persons there can be no question.

The most diligent inquiries respecting Naundorff's past history could only elicit a few leading facts apart from his own account. He arrived in Prussia in 1810, was known by the name of Charles William Naundorff, and followed the trade of a watchmaker. He lived as a citizen of Spandau from 1812 to 1821, having married in 1818, without producing the certificate of his birth. In 1820 he was arrested on a charge of having circulated false coin, and, being found guilty, was sent to the house of correction. In the course of the trial he avowed himself to be a prince, but without stating any name. He was at the same time accused of setting fire to the theatre at Brandenburg, but his accusers were found guilty of perjury, and, on the other charge, the evidence against him was far from satisfactory. He continued in prison until 1828, when he received pardon, and was sent into Silesia. In 1832, he obtained a passport to France, and, passing through Bavaria and Switzerland, arrived in Paris, declared himself to be Duke of Normandy, affirmed that the proofs of his identity were in the hands of the Prussian cabinet, and referred to the inhabitants of Spandau for a vindication of his character.

In support of his pretensions, Naundorff gave the following

account of his early years. His memory, he pretended, extended back, without a break or flaw, until some time prior to the journey from Versailles to Paris, when he was four years of age. From that time he professed the most minute knowledge of places, persons, names, dresses, the situation of furniture, the succession of events, and everything, public and private, which happened to the Dauphin. He was acquainted with all the details of the Temple, the manner in which the rooms were furnished, and the familiar manners and actions of all the members of the royal family, which he described in the style of exact and well-written memoirs, composed when objects and events were fresh before the eye and mind. He, however, evidently overdid the matter, and while he sometimes fell into egregious misstatements,* pretended to be familiar with minute details of transactions occurring in his early childhood, such as no ordinary human memory could have retained, and which were peculiarly inconsistent with the mental condition to which the Prince had been reduced.

In respect to his asserted escape, he said that, some months previous, he was conveyed from his apartment into the large, open room at the top of the Tower, and concealed behind furniture. Prior, however, to his removal, *he had witnessed the substitution of a large wooden doll for him*, which was carved and painted to resemble him, and placed in his bed. This story outraged all probability, and he subsequently modified it. The doll was exchanged for a dumb boy, the person visited and reported upon, by Harmand; Desault was taken out of the way for not recognising in this dumb child the Dauphin—and the dumb child had in turn a rickety child substituted for him, because, though poisoned, he would not die—and then the rickety child was poisoned outright, and the dumb child carried as the Dauphin to Madame Beauharnais. The body of the rickety child was buried in the Temple privately, and he was then brought from the garret and placed in

* "The particulars given respecting the return of the royal family after the ill-fated journey to Varennes, are not in accordance with those mentioned by Madame Campan and others."—*Percival*, p. 88.

the coffin; but a further change was effected in the carriage between him and some stones, which were buried as the Dauphin.* "My friends," says Naundorff, "fearing I might be discovered, disguised me, and sent me in a carriage out of Paris, thinking it expedient to remove me from the capital. At the same time to put my enemies upon a wrong scent, *they sent off a child, a native of Versailles, with his parents, intending to pass him for me.* It was intended to convey me to the Vendéean army." During this jourdey, he says he was taken sick, and remained at a château in the country under the care of a lady, when "one day there came three persons dressed in uniform with which I was unacquainted. I was told they were General Charette and two of his friends." "While at the château, I knew that a Mr. B. was in communication with Madame * * *; he had also another friend, formerly dame du palais to my excellent mother. It was they who then furnished me with all that was necessary. I have seen Mr. B. at a distance, always disguised as an old peasant. I was delivered into the hands of Mr. B., with whom I found a young girl named Marie, and his huntsman Jean, whose real name was Mont Morin.

"These two friends, henceforth, managed my affairs. They sent for a man *and his son, who was about my age.* This man received a sum of money sufficient *to enable him to embark for America,* and when these measures were taken, we set out ourselves for Venice." Here, he asserts, he had a secret interview with the Pope, that he was rejoined by the old man and his son, who again embarked, that he took flight for England;† that Mr. B—— and the young Marie were assassinated, and he himself taken prisoner and carried into France, where he remained in confinement until 1803, when he was liberated by Josephine and Fouché. In 1804,

* This story is very different from one which he told in an earlier period of his career, when he stated that he was removed from the Temple, in a basket, in a state of unconsciousness.—*Vide Filia Doloroso*, p. 475.

† In his earlier narratives, he went himself to America, at this time and "was inclined to think he learned watchmaking there, but could not exactly tell whether he acquired this art in the United States or in Italy."—*Filia Dolorosa*, p. 476.

he was carried by his friends to Strasburg, where he was arrested and confined in the fortress. The description of his sufferings in this prison is so graphic, that it would almost induce me to regard them as real. It strongly contrasts, in its vivid simplicity, with the forced and mystified style of the earlier portions of his narrative, where everything is enveloped in clouds of incongruity. "The light of sun or moon never reached me. All idea of day was effaced from my mind as well as of division of time. I knew every step of my dungeon. With the exception of that of my jailer's feet, I heard no sound but that of the heavy drums, which appeared to me like the rolling of distant thunder. The space in the roof through which the light might have penetrated more freely, gave me the idea of being at the extremity of a long tube, which appeared to terminate in dirty water, through which the sun might shine, or which was covered with cobwebs. The space between the walls formed a square of about twelve feet. My hair became long and curly, my beard had grown, and when I touched my face I could have fancied myself a wild beast. My nails were so long that they broke in bits, and I could only avoid the pain, which was the consequence, by biting them with my teeth. I despaired of again beholding the surface of the earth." In the spring of 1809, he was delivered from this dungeon by his friend, Mont Morin, and the secret aid of Josephine. He was taken to Frankfort. Mont Morin, at this time, he pretends, sewed in the collar of his great-coat, *certain papers, written by Marie Antoinette,* earnestly recommending him never to part with them, as they would prove undeniable proofs of his identity to all the sovereigns of Europe. So that, according to his own statement, the papers which were to establish his claims, did not come into his possession until fourteen years after the escape of the Prince, and would be worthless as evidence, could they be shown, because *they would prove just as much in favor of any person who might chance to hold them.*

Again he led a life of wandering and romantic adventure, the account of which seems, from its raciness and simplicity, to be for the most part, genuine. In January, they obtained from the Duke of Brunswick, letters of recommendation for Prussia, by means of which they were kindly received at Semnicht, by Major de Schill, an officer of the duke's army. In a skirmish Mont Morin was killed, and he himself struck from his horse by a blow from the butt-end of a musket. He was taken prisoner and put in an hospital. While still suffering from the effects of his wound, he was carried to the fortress of Wesel, on the frontier of France, and, mixed up with other prisoners, was transferred from one prison to another. Left behind in consequence of sickness, he regained his liberty, and lived a wretched vagabond life until 1810, when he emerged from the dreamy obscurity which attends him while he has only himself for a historian, to the daylight of a watchmaker's shop, Schutz en Strasse, 52, Berlin. Here, he pretends, he lost his papers, by giving them for the purpose of his identification to Mr. Lecoque, who handed them to the Prince Hartenburg. He now assumed, by compulsion, he asserts, the name of Charles W. Naundorff. From 1812 to 1832, when he appeared in Paris, he was in the habit, at intervals, of writing letters to the Duchess D'Angoulême, the Prince Hartenburg, Louis XVIII., and other eminent persons, but without obtaining any response.

Such was the story which in 1832, '3, Naundorff told to his circle of intimate friends, in Paris; although it was not published in detail until several years after, when he had exhausted, without success, every means of obtaining an interview with the Duchess D'Angoulême, or a hearing of his cause before the French tribunals. His adherents imagined that they recognised in him the Dauphin by his Bourbon physiognomy, by marks upon his person, and by his memory of historic events. But not content with natural means of identification, he resorted to supernatural. There was, at that time, in France, a peasant named Martin, who had the reputation of being inspired. It seems to be historic, that in 1818, he obtained an interview with Louis XVIII., under the plea of having some divine revelation to communicate; and popular rumor declared that it related to the king's nephew, as it undoubtedly exercised a great influence on his mind. In 1825, Martin announced in public, with oracular brevity, the burden of his interview with Louis XVIII. "Louis XVII. exists." Naundorff, who before his coming to Paris, had disbelieved and hated Christianity, was suddenly converted to the Romish faith, and shortly after had an interview with Martin, when it appeared they were old acquaintances, and had long seen each other in visions, except that Martin's ghostly counterpart had white hair; but I may state, on the authority of the curate of St. Arnoult, who relates the story, that the peasant's hair, soon after, miraculously changed from a raven black to a snowy whiteness. After this, apparitions crowded thick upon each other, and the Prince was consoled in his troubles, by spiritual converse with the *protecting angel of France*, and as Martin was also in habits of intimacy with the spirits, they received telegraphic information from the other world of all that was to occur in this. One day, Martin brought the news of his own death, and the Prince became the sole receptacle of ghostly information, and, in a truly Christian spirit, was accustomed to forewarn his enemies, and among them, Louis Phillipe, of the ills that awaited them.

Things stood in this position in the beginning of 1834, when it was determined that M. Morel de St. Didier should visit the Duchess D'Angoulême, then resident at Prague, and by the presentation of evidence, induce her to grant an interview with Naundoff. He carried with him a letter from Madame de Rambaud, in which that lady assured the duchess of her full and entire conviction that Naundorff was her brother, that his personal appearance, their interchange of recollections and especially *an inoculation mark in the form of a crescent* were indisputable proofs to her that he was what he asserted himself to be—"the Prince, the Orphan of the Temple."

Marco de St. Hilaire also stated that, on similar grounds, his conviction was so strong that it was impossible to overthrow it. St. Didier had two interviews with the Duchess, one in February, and the other in September, 1834, in which her words on some occasions were so enigmatical, her conduct so much at variance with her expressions, her anxiety so evident, and her final treatment of St. Didier and Madame de Rambaud so disingenuous, if not insulting, that it seems impossible to explain the affair, except on the score of her knowledge of some secret which entirely undercut the claims of Naundorff, but was of a nature which would not permit her to state her grounds of action. On seeing the portrait of Naundorff, she remarked, after attentive examination, "I do not see *any* resemblance to my family." Subsequently she rejected that of Richemont with an indignant, "No, sir, that is not the thing." While she professed to believe that her brother was dead, "*unless another was substituted in his place*," she evinced, to say the least, her uncertainty on the subject, by saying, "This is too serious a matter to be lightly examined, and of such importance that it will be necessary to devote several days to the consideration of it." As to the evidence adduced she remarked, "If anything could for a moment arrest my attention, it would be Madame de Rambaud's letter, because I remember that she was in fact my brother's attendant, but all that is nothing." When his recollections of the details of early events were mentioned, she replied, "yes, I understand, but all that is not sufficient; I must have other proofs before I can grant the interview—tell him *he must send me by a confidential messenger, and in writing, all that he now refuses to tell me but by word of mouth. Above all, tell him to send me all the details relative to his escape from the Temple; that is absolutely necessary, and I persist particularly on this point.*" And here I may remark that this message argues an acquaintance on the part of the duchess with the fact of her brother's existence, and with the mode of his escape, otherwise she could not have brought Naundorff's statement, however false, to any test—while at the same time the evasive answer, which, as we shall see, the pretender returned, shows, he felt, she had the power of detecting his falsehood. M. de St. Didier departed from Prague to consult with Naundorff. Meanwhile, a remarkable and mysterious interview took place between the duchess and the King of Prussia, in relation to Naundorff. Dresden was the spot first fixed on for the meeting, and the king went there incognito, but not finding her, he followed her first to Pilnitz, and then to Toplitz, where they had a long conference, concerning which, nothing distinct can be ascertained, except that the duchess asked a variety of questions respecting Naundorff, which the king answered. St. Didier again went to Prague in September, carrying with him a letter in relation to the asserted escape of Naundorff, and being accompanied by Madame de Rambaud. He found the manner of the duchess this time, entirely altered. She was cold and reserved, and instead of the interest she had formerly manifested, she now showed perfect indifference and contempt for Naundorff, as if she had fathomed him. As to his recollections, she said all that he had stated had appeared in print, or must have been read by him.

When St. Didier spoke of a recent attempt to assassinate him, though she smiled incredulously at first, yet on being assured it was a fact, she used, in reply to the observation that "*no one would think of assassinating an impostor*," the remarkable words, "*Pardon me, sir*,"—and, then, struggling between affected composure and irritation, exclaimed, "M. de St. Didier, this man is nothing but an impostor, an intriguer, but very clever—*bien habile*—you are under a delusion of which I do not partake." This was all that St. Didier could obtain, except an acknowledgment of the interview with the King of Prussia. The letter, of which he was the bearer, was certainly not calculated to increase the confidence of the duchess. It is remarkable on two accounts. 1. It tells *a different story* from that which Naundorff has elsewhere given. 2d. *It shifts the point of mystery from himself to another.* He begins, "Madame, your royal highness wishes to know in what manner I escaped from the Temple. Three men came to me, among whom was the person who guarded me constantly, and who was also one of those who removed me first out of this room, and soon afterwards out of the Temple. I was put, against my will, into a large kind of wicker basket, from which *a child of about my own age and size had been taken and placed in my bed.*" Here the wooden doll entirely disappears from the narrative, and the substitution of the children is direct. Instead of proceeding to state, as was required of him, how *he* got out of the Temple, he continues, "This, madam, is all the information that I think I ought to give your royal highness *in writing*, *prudence forbidding me to confide to paper the mystery which envelopes*"—what, in the name of consistency, does the reader think?—" *all which relates to the child who was substituted for me.* Nevertheless, I am willing to give to my sister, *to your royal highness, I mean*, but to your royal highness alone, and by word of mouth, indisputable proofs which will remove all your remaining doubts, if any remain; and it is on that account that I firmly believe that an early interview between you and myself is now become indispensable. Admitting, for an instant, that I am not the son of the unfortunate Louis XVI., that I am, in fact, only an impostor," &c., &c., &c. The presentation of this letter, and all St. Didier's entreaties having failed to obtain the consent of the duchess to a personal interview, the following singular scene occurred. "There remained another painful duty for me to fulfil. I was about to wound the heart of the Prince's unfortunate sister in its dearest affections. All the strength of a deep and entire conviction was necessary to determine me to do so. But, fidelity, devotion, and honor, imposed on me this painful duty, and I could not shrink from it. Having gathered all my resolution, I added in a serious tone:

"'My respect for your royal highness is a sacred duty which my heart will never allow me to forget. Your royal highness will, therefore, condescend to appreciate the violence I do to my own feelings in wounding a heart already torn by so many sorrows; but, however, painful the effort, my orders are peremptory, and my obedience to them must be implicit. I am commanded to inform your royal highness, in the name of the Prince, that he has certain knowledge of the two following facts'—

* * * * * * * *

It is not my business to reveal them here. Secresy is commanded by the Prince. I will only say, that I had the honor of informing her royal highness that he had in his possession unanswerable proof of the facts in question. Her royal highness listened to me with great and visible attention; her agitation was extreme, it was in vain that she endeavored to assume an air of calmness, she was unable to recover her composure. Her royal highness denied one of these facts—the other she passed over in silence."

Still, St. Didier did not despair. Having failed himself, he next strove, through the agency of the Viscountess D'Agoult, to obtain an audience for Madame Rambaud, who had gone from Paris to Prague, expressly to see the duchess; but, to his infinite and somewhat ludicrous mortification and surprise, he received from the viscountess the following note: "Sir—I have executed your commission; the answer of the Dauphiness is: that she knew Madame de Rambaud, who, more than forty years ago, was the attendant of the Dauphin: that not thinking it possible that a person of her age should have undertaken so fatiguing a journey, she has no reason for seeing the person of that name whom you have brought hither." They soon received a notification from the police to leave Prague, and the door of all further communication was closed.

The next event which throws any light on the affair, is the account of a conference by M. Lamprade, between him and M. de Rochow, ministers of the interior, at Berlin, in 1836. This seems to admit us to the knowledge of the sentiments of the Prussian court upon the subject, and, consequently, to lift the veil, in part, from the interview between the king and the duchess. Lamprade began by attempting to prove the escape of the Dauphin, when Rochow interrupted him by saying, "Every one knows what to think on that subject, and *I believe with you, the Dauphin did not die in the prison of the Temple*, but how do you prove *the identity?*" and, after admitting there was *a mystery*, referred to the documentary proofs which Naundorff asserted, had been confided by him, in 1811, to the Prince Hartenburg, denied that there were any such in the king's possession, but added "*Even if the papers were in the king's cabinet, what would that prove? Might it not be possible that this man had, in fact, known the real Dauphin?*" We may fairly conclude these words of the Prussian minister to be an indication of more distinct knowledge possessed by his master.

It is not necessary to say much respecting the vain efforts which Naundorff made to bring his claim for adjudication before the tribunals of France. There is no question, that he used every possible exertion to bring the matter to a legal issue, but was denied. Hervagault and Bruneau had long since been tried and condemned. Richemont seems to have been brought forward almost under the patronage of the police, to disconcert Naundorff, for, in his baseless claims, he had none of the enthusiasm of an intriguer, but the placid coolness of an instrument who feels himself safe. But Naundorff was excluded from a hearing. It seems certain, also, that an attempt was made to assassinate him—for the fact does not rest on his own testimony, but on that of the St. Hilaires, who were people of station and character. The evident injustice, in a legal point of view, which was done him, naturally created sympathy, and induced the belief, that since the French government shunned an investigation, they believed him to be what he pretended. In 1838, he was quietly hustled out of France and conveyed to England. He employed himself at first in the manufacture of rockets, and afterwards of bomb-shells. Another attempt at assassination induced him to retire to Delft, in Holland, where he expired in 1844, and was buried with regal honors—an object of sympathy and respect to thousands, who felt that he could not be confounded with the ordinary run of impostors.

The pretensions of Naundorff kept the French government, from

1832 until 1844, in continual uneasiness, because they tended to revive half-buried memories, to excite discussion, and to elicit important evidence upon the general question. Persons in almost every rank of society came forward and threw their contributions upon the accumulating pile. Unfortunately, much fell either into the hands of Naundorff or of the government—by the latter it was concealed for its own purposes, and by the former, mangled and mystified in publication, by the substitution of initials for names, and by being mixed up with documents, undoubtedly forged, or liable to strong suspicion of being so. But there are two species of evidence elicited by the appearance of Naundorff, which have intrinsic value. 1. That which was published by persons of character and standing, challenging denial, and giving authorities of name, time, and place; and, 2, That which, though imperfectly stated in respect to these particulars, by the legal advisers of Naundorff, yet, tended to cast discredit on his individual claims, and was acknowledged by his friends to militate with his story, while it went to establish historical facts independently of him. Such evidence I consider to be historical and just as good now as ever.

Thus M. Morin de Guérivière, an artizan and manufacturer, 2, Rue Chapon, Paris, laid a memorial before the Count D'Artois, in 1823, an account of which was published in the "Quotidienne" of November 6th, of that year, stating that in July, 1795, while travelling in a postchaise, under the protection of M. Jervais Ojardias, agent of the Prince de Condé, he was arrested on his arrival at Thiers, Puy de Dôme, on the charge of being the Dauphin. He was surrounded by gens d'armes, the local authorities summoned, a procès verbal drawn up, and he was only set at liberty after full examination and disproval.*

* He was fortunately able to exhibit the order for his release, which is as follows:

"LIBERTY. "JUSTICE.

"*Du Puy, the* 22 *Messidor*, *year* 3, (10 *July*, 1795).

"EQUALITY. "HUMANITY.

"J. P. Chazel, representative of the people, delegated by the National Convention

In 1832, he published a pamphlet, entitled—"*Recollections to serve as a supplement for the completion of the proofs of the existence of the Duke of Normandy, son of Louis XVI.*," in which, besides stating the above facts, he gives an account of an interview with an agent of Louis XVIII, in 1823, named Desmarres, living in the court of the Palais Royal, who was sent to him, in consequence of the presentation of the memorial to the Count D'Artois, *and stated that he had caused great alarm in the palace, and occasioned the report that Louis XVII. had presented himself there.* After this, another person from the court, who was in close intimacy with the Duchess D'Angoulême, and who went direct from him to her, advised him to preserve the document concerning his arrest with great care, as it would hereafter be of value, adding, "Well, Louis XVII. is living, I know it, but the dearest interests of France forbid that he should now ascend the throne of his ancestors." The Abbé Allègre Tourzel also congratulated him on having been arrested as the son of Louis XVI., and said, "I know from good authority that the Prince is living, and that his health is not at all injured by the dreadful sufferings he endured in the Temple. My conviction, on this subject, is so strong, that I have not feared to declare it openly to the king himself, and to tell him that the crown he wears does not belong to him."

Again, M. Labreli de Fontaine, librarian to the Duchess D'Orleans, in a pamphlet, entitled—"Disclosures respecting the exist-

in the department of Puy-de-dôme, of the Upper Loire, of Cantal of the Aveyron, and Lozère to the Procureur Syndic of the district of Thiers. I have heard Ojardias, he has justified his conduct, the charge made against him is false, I authorize you to rescind the orders which detained the child in Barge Real's house, as also any which may have issued against Ojardias's liberty,

"HEALTH AND FRATERNITY.

"Signed, J. P. Chazel.

"A true copy.

"The Procureur Syndic of the
"District of Thiers.

"Signed, Bruyere Barante."

ence of Louis XVII.," says, "The first article of the secret treaty of Paris, 1814, explains the manner in which the powers of Europe had permitted the Count de Provence to occupy the throne of France; the following is the substance of the article:

"That although the high contracting powers, the Allied Sovereigns, have no certain evidence of the death of the son of Louis XVI., the state of Europe and its political interests, require that they should place at the head of the government in France, Louis Xavier, Count de Provence, ostensibly with the title of king; but, being in fact, considered in their secret transactions only as Regent of the kingdom for the two years next ensuing, reserving to themselves during that period to obtain every possible certainty, concerning a fact which must ultimately determine who shall be the sovereign of France." A person of his position would scarcely make such a statement without good authority. He also asserts, that when he was himself at Venice, in 1812, Signior Erizzo, formerly a senator of Venice, showed him a proclamation of the Count de Provence, dated from Verona, the 14th October, 1797, in which he only assumed the title of Regent of the kingdom, and justly asks, "if Louis XVII. died in the Temple, why did not his uncle assume the title of king." M. Gruau, declares that, "It is known from good authority, that during the reign of Louis XVIII., a court sycophant had a false certificate fabricated of the *death of the Dauphin in foreign lands after his escape*."*

The "Journal of Commerce," 3d December, 1832, in a review of a work, entitled—"Secret History of the Directory," says:—

"It appears certain that the public has been deceived as to the real time and place of the death of Louis XVII. *Cambaceres acknowledges this, but would never reveal what he knew on this point.* We shall be led to believe there was some great mystery concerning it, when we remember with what consideration the

Percival, p. 185

restored Bourbons treated this regicide, and the eagerness with which they took possession of his papers after his death."

In a pamphlet published by M. Bourbon le Blanc, there is an attestation by M. Pezold, notary of Crossen, in which he says: "I have found fifty documents fully substantiating the existence of his majesty; for instance, the manner and by whom he was taken from the Temple. I can prove all that I state; *and there is not a sovereign in Europe who did not in* 1818 *receive letters from me on the subject.* I will always affirm that he was carried off from the Temple by one of my friends.

"Pro vera copia in fidem publicam testatur, a 15 Januar, 1832.
"Signed, "Pezold, Notar."

M. Pezold, it must be remarked, did not pretend to affirm anything concerning identity; his statements respect the fact of escape. He died of poison. There is another important piece of testimony contained in the pamphlet of Labreli de Fontaine.

"M. Abeillé, medical pupil under Dr Desault at the time of his violent death, has declared to whoever would hear it in France and in the United States, where he has since sought refuge, that the murder of the doctor immediately followed the report he made to the effect that the child to whom they had introduced him was not the Dauphin. The 'American Bee,' edited by M. Chandron, mentions this fact in an article inserted in 1817. Madame Delisle, an inhabitant of New York, and now in Paris, has declared that she heard this circumstance mentioned by M. Abeillé himself, and has, moreover, read the above cited article in the American journal."

But, one of the most important items of evidence is, that a boy, purporting to be the Dauphin, was, in 1795, actually delivered into the hands of Charette. The proof of this is partly historic, and partly rests on the testimony adduced by M. Gruau, the advocate of Naundorff; but, as the fact directly overthrows the claims of the latter, and the bearing of it was perceived by M.

Gruau, we may accept his evidence, though unable to fathom the motives which led him to produce it.

1. There is, extant, a proclamation of Charette, cited by Labreli de Fontaine, towards the close of 1795, addressed to his army, in which he speaks of Louis XVII. as being then in his camp, and asks his followers—"Will you abandon to the caprice of fortune, to the uncertainty of events, the royal orphan whom you swore to defend—or, rather, lead him captive in the midst of you, conduct him to the assassins of his father, and cast at their feet the head of your innocent king."

2. A friend of Gruau's, who served in the army of Charette, remembered to have seen a child who was shown to the Vendéean army as Louis XVII.

3. Another royalist, cited by Gruau, declared that he, himself, "delivered Louis XVII. into the hands of Charette;" adding—"By what means General Charette and I obtained possession of him, and where we took him to—this is what I shall not hesitate to prove, when the proper time is come. Till then, a solemn oath binds me to silence." Now Gruau, Naundorff's advocate, states that this testimony does not refer to the real Dauphin. But, look at the position in which it places Naundorff. He says, that, being the true Dauphin, he saw Charette in 1795. Why Charette so easily allowed him to escape his hands, he does not say. Now, either he was, or was not, the child mentioned above, as being in the Vedéean camp. If he was that child, he was not "the real Dauphin," according to the confession of his advocate, and stands also convicted of falsehood, in the details of his story. If he were not, then it will be impossible to explain how Charette, being personally acquainted with the true Prince, should allow himself to be so deceived immediately after, as to receive a pretender into his camp. Percival feels the full difficulty of the case, and confesses that he cannot "satisfy the curiosity which may be felt as to the motives which led" to the production of such testimony.

On reviewing the facts presented in this involved case, the

obscurity clears away sufficiently to enable us to discern distinctly the following truths. It appears :—

I. That, Naundorff was an impostor, because—1. There is a radical discrepancy between the two accounts given by him of his escape from the Temple, in one of which he represents himself to have seen a wooden doll substituted for him before the introduction of the dumb child; and, in the other, to have seen, at the same time and place, the immediate substitution of the child himself.

2. The account, given by him, of his interview with Charette, cannot be made to tally with the evidence adduced and vouched for by his advocate, respecting the presence of a child, supposed to be Louis XVII., in the Vendéean army.

3. The accounts, he gave of his early history, vary so much from each other, at different periods of his life, at one time representing him to have been in America at the moment when, according to another statement, he was on the continent of Europe, that one or the other must be fictitious.

4. His conduct, in the affair of Martin, proves him to have been a *deceiver*. The man who was on such intimate terms with the protecting angel of France, is of veracity too etherial for ordinary credence.

II. That, Naundorff, though an impostor, had facts as the basis of his deception, and was in possession of some state secret, and some documents of importance, which enabled him to carry on the deception, because—

1. He was denied by the French government a legal hearing, which was not only granted to, but forced upon, the other impostors; was subjected to attempts against his life, and compelled by the authorities to leave France to prevent investigation.

2. The conduct of the Duchess D'Angoulême showed his case embarrassed her, and she confessed that though he was an impos-

tor, yet there were circumstances which might, in the eyes of the French government, render his assassination expedient. The interview between her and the King of Prussia, in relation to him, proves the importance attached to his pretensions; and all these things in connection, are only consistent with the idea of dangerous truth lying beneath the falsehood of his individual claim.

3. He undeniably had the means of deceiving persons so competent to judge as Madame de Rambaud, St. Hilaire, St. Didier, and others, and showed an acquaintance with facts, known solely to the initiated, explicable only on the ground that he had been behind the scenes, or obtained authentic information of things hidden from the public eye.

III. That, the secret which gave him political importance as an impostor, did not relate to himself but to some other person, because—

1. He confessed as much in his letter to the Duchess D'Angoulême, when required to give an account of his escape from the Temple, by saying, that prudence forbade him to commit to paper the mystery which enveloped some other child in the Temple, which child, it is every way probable, was Louis XVII.

2. In the opinion of the Prussian court, whom Naundorff acknowledged to be in the secret of his life, the facts in his case only went to show that he knew the true Dauphin.

IV. That, it seems to be a historic fact, that a child purporting to be Louis XVII., was actually in the possession of Charette, in 1795, and afterwards disappeared, no one knows where.

V. That the government was aware of the fact of the Prince's escape, because: 1. the police records of the time show that orders were issued for the arrest of Louis XVII. 2. M. Guérivière was arrested by the police, on the charge of being the Dauphin, while travelling in a carriage with the agent of the Prince de Condé;

and both of these circumstances confirm Naundorff's story, that carriages with children were sent out in different directions, for the purpose of baffling pursuit, and tend to prove that he was, by some means, conversant with the events connected with the escape.

VI. That, Naundorff intimates his knowledge of the fact, that a child, said to be Louis XVII., was sent to America, that a certain Mr. B—— was engaged in the transaction, that he was in concert with a lady, formerly a member of the queen's household, and that they had with them a young girl.

VII. That it is shown by the statement of Madame de Rambaud, that Louis XVII. had on his arm a crescent-shaped scar, the result of inoculation.

The following points, which it is not necessary to specify separately, were also brought out by the discussion of Naundorff's claims—viz. that the existence of Louis XVII. was not only suspected but a well-known fact, admitted in the best informed circles, and by the agents and intimates of Louis XVIII. and the Duchess D'Angoulême; that in 1797, Louis XVIII. signed a proclamation as Regent, which was seen by Labreli de Fontaine, at Venice, that at the Restoration of the Bourbons the allied powers declared there was no proof of the death of Louis XVII.; and that M. Abeillé, pupil of Desault, solemnly declared that that physician had been murdered.

Taking all the circumstances of Naundorff's history into consideration, I do not think that you can harmonize them, and reduce them to their true proportions, but by some theory which will not vary far from the following, which I propose as the most probable view of his life and character, and most consistent with facts which are proved.

I conceive him, then, to have been one of the boys made use of at the time of the Dauphin's escape to personate him, and selected for the purpose on account of his Bourbon features, which may be traceable as a native of Versailles or Paris, to illegitimate Bourbon blood—furnished with credentials and information to enable him to act his part plausibly—conveyed to Charette, and exhibited to his army as the Prince, whom he continued to represent until the trick was discovered, having personally learned the general outline of the real Dauphin's destiny, and the names of the agents by whom he was removed. He was probably imprisoned to conceal his secret—and afterwards reduced to a wandering and necessitous life, but retained documents and letters originally given him to play his part, and which admitted him to the knowledge of many of the incidents of the private life of the royal family.

The journals and papers of Marie Antoinette and the Princess Elizabeth, were taken from them, during their imprisonment in the Temple;* and if any of these, by some of the accidents of the times, fell into his possession, they would sufficiently account for his familiarity with recondite incidents. The documents delivered to Prince Hartenburg probably revealed to the eyes of diplomatists the true nature of his case, and may have induced them to watch him as one who might be dangerous. Meanwhile, his early adventures moulded his mind and destiny—a man of one idea, he prepared himself through life to play his part, so that he became at last "bien habile," and gathered from all available sources all that could give consistency to his pretensions. Possessor of a secret which might shake thrones, he could not rest till he tried its potency in evoking strife. He does not seem to have had any settled plan—but to have shaped his course by circumstances. When he first came to Paris, he is described by St. Didier as very timid and shy—but success soon emboldened him, and he made use, with equal facility, of the fanatic falsehood of Martin and of the sincere and honorable devotion of Madame de Rambaud and M. St. Hilaire. With the talents of a fortune-teller, he might easily draw forth information while

* Clery.

seeming to impart it, and make a conversation with one the source of a revelation to another. He had judgment to perceive the strength of his position, and tact to avail himself of it. He had nothing to hazard. The French authorities had all to lose. He could safely appeal to the tribunals, because he knew that his appeal would never be granted—for his condemnation might have been gained at the expense of political destruction, too dear a price to pay for the suppression of a charlatan. My impression is, that he desired to sell his secret, and bring his adversaries of the two opposite parties to terms. Thus, on the one hand, he offered the Duchess D'Angoulême to make over his rights to the Duc de Bourdeaux, and held up his knowledge of the mystery which hung over the real Dauphin, as an inducement why she should grant an interview—and, on the other, he gave hints and indications of the truth, in some instances puzzling to his own adherents. After all, finding it most for his advantage to retain his secret and maintain his dubious position, he gave vent to the swaggering boast, fully characteristic of the swindler, "I fear nothing, for it is not in the power of any one to prove that I am not the son of the martyr king of France, the true orphan of the Temple."

## RICHEMONT.

A person, named Richemont, who, for years, has been known as one of the most obscure of the Dauphin pretenders, has lately died in France, and, it is said that, now he is dead, an attempt will be made to prove that he was actually the son of Louis XVI. I return my thanks to the "Tribune" for calling my attention to the article in the "London Atlas," on this subject, which otherwise I should not have seen, and hope that it and other papers will advise us of any facts which may transpire on the other side of the Atlantic, or of any suggestions contained in European publications. A great change has come over the Parisian letter writers, within a few months. On the first agitation of this subject, at the beginning of the year, nothing was more certain than the death of Louis XVII., in the

Temple, in 1795. But, now, it is admitted that he did not die, that the Convention was deceived—and that the archives of the police prove he escaped shortly before January 8, 1795. This fact may, therefore, now be considered historically beyond dispute. The existence of the decree of the French government to arrest Louis XVII. after his asserted death, is admitted by Mrs. Romer.*

The story of Richemont is, in some respects, the counterpart of that of Naundorff. Neither of them pretended to be the child who was visited by Desault, and who, up to the 1st of June, was known to be the Prince. But there was this difference between them—Naundorff did not leave the Temple till the day of the burial—Richemont escaped so long ago as the good old times when Madame Simon held sway, and was removed, with her furniture, in a basket of clothes. But how does this story of Richemont tally with the order given to the police, on the 8th of June?

Is it credible that, if Louis XVII. had been a year out of the Temple, the whole police of France would then be set to work to arrest him, just then escaping, in a postchaise; or that, out of the hundreds of acting commissaries and other officials, who had seen the captive, not one had discovered the fraud until this identical 8th June?

I can see no reason for the shadow of a doubt, that the child represented to be Louis XVII. up to the beginning of June, was actually so. His identity is proved—

1. By the marks upon his body.

2. By the recognition of Desault, who knew him, and never expressed a doubt, during the month he attended the child, as to his being the Prince.

3. By the picture of Bellanger, which is confessed to be that of the Dauphin.

But, establish this fact, and the pretensions of both Naundorff and Richemont go to the ground; for each asserts himself to be *not* the child whom Desault visited.

* Filia Dolorosa, p. 476.

Nothing can be more *unnatural and absurd* than the account of the interview between Richemont and the Duchess D'Angoulême; which the correspondent of the "Atlas" says, he himself heard from Madame Chateaubriand, *provided* the words attributed to the duchess, are considered *as referring to one she deemed her brother*. Under such a construction, the story carries falsehood on its face, no matter who tells it—give them a different sense, and I have no objection to it. It is as follows: "Madame Chateaubriand, whose truth has never been questioned, has told me the circumstances of this interview, at which, by virtue of her office, she was present. The duchess was walking on the terrace of Versailles, when the Prince de Condé, coming up the marble steps of the parterre, suddenly appeared before her, leaning on the arm of the Baron de Richemont—the latter fell at the feet of the duchess, who seemed for a moment overcome with emotion. The baron spoke in a low tone, recalling circumstances which had taken place in their early youth, and which were unknown to the world beside. The duchess drew back presently, and, gazing at the baron from head to foot, she exclaimed, "*Go, sir, I cannot call you brother—you are my mother's murderer*." The idea intended to be conveyed, is that, the duchess recognised Richemont as her brother—but would not acknowledge him as such, on account of the paper which he had been compelled to sign in prison, charging Marie Antoinette with incest. The duchess was a woman of too much good sense and right feeling ever to entertain such sentiments—the child was the mere passive instrument of the brutality of others. Her memoirs show that she never dreamed of imputing to him as a crime, what was merely his misfortune. Besides which, the charge of incest did no harm to Marie Antoinette. No one believed it. It rather aided her, and came near causing her acquittal. If the duchess did utter those words, it is most certain they bore no relation to her brother; and that, instead of proving anything in favor of Richemont, they settle the question against him. It is not impossible that he, as well as Naundorff, may have been some child connected with the Temple, and that the duchess did recognize him as one who had been instrumental, on some occasion, in inflicting injury on her mother, perhaps in preventing her escape. This is far the most natural conclusion. The duchess, we have seen, indignantly rejected his portrait, when offered her by St. Didier, saying, "No, sir, that is not the thing."

After the interview was over, she took the arm of Madame Chateaubriand, "and pushed open the glass door of the grand *salon* with such violence, that several panes of glass fell to the ground. She did did not sleep that night, she did not even retire to her own room, but paced the floor of the drawing-room till morning, now and then sinking on her knees in prayer, and often stopping in her restless walk to lean her head against the wall and sob aloud." It seems undeniable that some deep chord of feeling was stirred. Knowing, as I have evidence she did, her brother's existence, in America, but compelled from state motives to conceal the secret, every fresh attempt at imposture was calculated to wound her spirit most acutely; and this, together with memories of the sufferings of departed years, awakened by the incident, is quite sufficient to account for her agony of mind, without attributing to her the absurdity of calling her *brother the murderer of her mother*. There are some things impossible—and this is one of them.

Richemont, like Naundorff, attributed all the assassinations among people of rank in Europe, to acquaintance with his secret, and favor of his pretensions. This is cheap kind of evidence. But it amounts to nothing. Kleber and Pichegru, and the Duc de Berri, and the Prince de Condé might be assassinated, but it proves nothing in favor of the pretensions of either impostor. As to the offer of Louis Philippe, by letter, to give the Princess Louise, afterwards Queen of Belgium, to Richemont, we will wait till the letter is produced. If he had such a thing, he would have shown it during his life-time, and, besides, would scarcely have rejected an offer which would, necessarily, have been accompanied by the public recognition of his claims, *if he were the Dauphin*, and by his ultimate accession to the throne. But I care not what documents may be produced under the circumstances. Such things only prove their own existence, nothing more. So long as Richemont's own story disagrees fundamentally with known facts, all the documents in the world would not prove identity. For this is a case of *alibi*. *Richemont was not in the Temple in June*, 1795. *Louis XVII. was in the Temple until the first week in June*, 1795. No, Richemont was both an impostor, and, in all probability, an instrument of Louis Philippe; and, should the attempt ever be made to silence the truth respecting the living, by setting up the baseless claims of the dead, it will only add a tenfold force to every argument in favor of the former.

Here I must let the curtain fall upon the Old World, leaving everything uncertain, unfinished, mysterious. A great wrong has been done, and we can clearly trace the whole course of motives and events up to a given point, and then there is an abrupt cessation, with only, here and there, an indication of a dark secret, to which the published annals of Europe afford no clue. Like one of those rivers which suddenly lose themselves in the earth, and roll their tide along in subterranean darkness, the fate of Louis XVII. is, for more than half a century, hidden from the eyes of men, and every attempt hitherto made to unriddle the enigma of his destiny, only deepens the mystery, and carries the mind into more inextricable labyrinths, which, like the mazes of some primeval forest, afford no outlet.

END OF THE FIRST PART.

# PART II.

## THE WIGWAM, THE CAMP, AND THE CHURCH.

## CHAPTER X.

### ADOPTION AND EDUCATION.

SCIENCE has remarked mysterious affinities between the Old World and the New, and there are social yearnings, historic ties and sympathies of unearthly brotherhood, which unite hands and hearts across the deep, and make men love each other with an intenser love, because they at once are and are not one. The two continents were made for each other. There is the battle-field—here the asylum from strife—and yet it is from those old ensanguined soils, that the men, the principles, and the faith have been derived, which make the New World glorious and peaceful. It will add another strange link to the chain of union, if it can be shown that, republican America numbers among her citizens, one born to be a monarch, in Europe; and that the Protestant Episcopal church has, in the same individual, a minister and a missionary, who, but for reverses, unparalleled in history, would have wielded the forces of a rival communion.

In the year 1795, a French family, calling themselves De Jardin or De Jourdan, arrived in Albany, direct from France. Refugees were crowding at that time to America, but there were circumstances connected with these persons which attracted unusual attention. The family consisted of a lady, a gentleman, and two children. The two former, though they bore the same name, did not seem to be, nor were considered, as husband and wife. While Madame de Jardin dressed with elegance, Monsieur was very plainly attired, and acted in almost a menial capacity. Much mystery was observed concerning the children under their care, who were never taken out in public. The eldest was a girl, named

Louise, the youngest a boy of nine or ten years of age, who was called, simply, Monsieur Louis. He was scarcely seen, except by a few ladies and children. He did not appear to notice those who saw him. Madame de Jardin, who had in her possession many articles which belonged to the deceased king and queen of France, and among them some gold plate, on which was engraven the royal arms, stated, in familiar conversation, that she had been a maid of honor to Marie Antoinette, and was separated from her on the terrace of the palace, prior to her imprisonment in the Temple. She was in a state of high mental excitement, and while speaking of the events of the Revolution, would wildly play the "Marseillaise," and then burst into tears. The children were considered by those on terms of familiar intercourse with Madame de Jardin, and who had opportunities of judging which others had not, to belong to the royal family of France. The little boy, is said, by a highly respectable and intelligent lady, who saw him under peculiar circumstances, calculated to excite her attention, to resemble, in the general contour of his face, the Rev. Eleazar Williams. The De Jardins, after remaining a short time in Albany, for what purpose was not publicly known, sold most of their effects, some articles of which are still, or recently were, in that city, and then suddenly disappeared, no one knew whither. Conjecture, for a time, aroused and excited, fell at length asleep, for want of material to work on, but the mystery attending these incidents, has caused them to be vividly remembered to the present time.

An interesting letter on this subject from Mrs. Dudley, of Albany, a near connexion of Governor Seymour, whose character and social position place her testimony beyond reach of question, will be found in the Appendix, and repay perusal. (Appendix D.) Learning from a friend that she was in possession of information, which might throw some light on the subject, I called on her, in company with the Rev. Dr. Kip, now Missionary Bishop of California, and Mr. Williams, when she furnished me with the particulars detailed above, and afterwards threw them into a written form.

The reader, as he advances, will be able to judge of the connexion of these facts with the thread of our narrative, but before I leave them, I would call his attention to the coincidence, which, however, can scarcely escape him, between these incidents and the particulars obscurely given by Naundorff.* In both statements occur the lady of Marie Antoinette's household, the gentleman in very plain clothes, and the little girl. These things coupled with the intimation given by the pretender that the Prince was sent to America, and the exact correspondence in time are certainly striking. But from Albany let us now travel, by an obvious route, to Ticonderoga, and observe what happened there in the same year.

There is still living, at about a hundred years of age, a respectable Indian chief, of whose character and veracity I have full assurance from the Hon. B. Skenondogh Smith, of Philadelphia, who has known him upwards of thirty years. His name is John Skenondogh O'Brien, and he is the son of an Irishman and an Oneida woman. He was sent to France for education, and returned to this country during the American Revolution. In the hunting season, he was frequently, with other Indians, in the vicinity of Lake George, and, while at Ticonderaga, in 1795, two Frenchmen, one of them having the appearance of a Romish priest, came there, bringing a weak sickly boy, in a state of mental imbecility, whom they left among the Indians. Being well acquainted with French, O'Brien conversed with the men, and learned from them that the boy was born in France. He was adopted by an Iroquois chief, named Thomas Williams, and O'Brien, who has since repeatedly seen him in youth and manhood, testifies, on oath, that he is the same person with the Rev. Eleazar Williams. (Appendix E.) Now, it is true we have no means of demonstrating that the boy called Monsieur Louis, by Madame de Jardin, at Albany, in 1795, is the boy left at Ticonderoga, in 1795, by the two Frenchmen; but, whoever considers the coincidences of circumstance, time, place, age, mental condition, and bodily resemblance, must admit that

* Vide page 149

apart from all other testimony, it is highly probable. *But, whoever Eleazar Williams be, he is a native of France. This point is established on the threshold.*"

To exhibit the social influences by which he was now surrounded, it will be necessary here to give some account of the origin of the family by whom the child, henceforth known as Eleazar Williams, was adopted.

Among the romantic stories of former days of trial and hardship, which charm the imagination, and, by contrast with present prosperity, gratify the pride of New England, there are few which appeal more strongly to our sympathies, than the sufferings of the family of the Rev. John Williams, at the inroad of the French and Indians on the town of Deerfield, Massachusetts, in 1704. It forms the historic basis of my narrative of events in this country, and is full of the interest which pertains to tales of frontier life in half-rooted colonies. The original settlers of New England looked upon the Indians in much the same light that the children of Israel, under Joshua, viewed the idolatrous Canaanites. In the pages of the inspired warrior, they found a full vindication alike for cruelty and injustice, and the red man repaid at every fit opportunity the injuries he had already received, and avenged, beforehand, the approaching extermination of his race, by ceaseless inroads on the colonists. Deerfield was first settled in 1671, and the Indians treated in the customary manner. The Eastern, or, as they were afterwards called, the St. Francois Indians, had owned the land, and entertained a bitter hostility towards those who had gained possession of their territory. Before the close of the century, they made many attacks upon the place, which, being the most remote settlement on the Connecticut river, was peculiarly exposed to their incursions. In 1697, an attack was made on Deerfield, but was repulsed by the inhabitants, headed by their pastor, the Rev. John Williams. But, though baffled, the Indians did not relinquish their design. In the spring of 1703, some of the "praying" or Christian Mohawks, brought intelligence to Albany, of an intended incursion on Deerfield, and Lord Cornbury, then governor of New York, communicated the tidings to the governor of Massachusetts. A guard of twenty soldiers was sent to the village, and every precaution taken against surprise. But, there was a presentiment in the mind of Williams that the town would be destroyed, and in his sermons he frequently warned the people of the coming calamity.*

The governor of Canada, M. de. Vaudreuil, sent a body of French and Indians into New England, who committed considerable ravages, and slew several hundred men. The New Englanders, in their turn, in the fall of the year, made an incursion into Canada, and killed a great number of the Indians. This was the immediate cause of the attack on Deerfield. The chiefs applied for assistance to M. de Vaudreuil, who sent them two hundred men under the command of Le Sieur Heutel de Rouville, who, accompanied by a large body of Indians, made his way to Deerfield.† John Williams was a man of sincere piety, more than ordinary attainments in literature, a strong mind, and entire devotion to his flock, which, in those days, was like a New England pastor's family. He was in the prime of life, married to an excellent woman, the father of seven or eight children, with a good farm, and every prospect of uninterrupted happiness.

Such was his condition when he retired to rest, on the 28th February, 1704. About daybreak the village was attacked—the sleeping sentinels gave no alarm—the sound of axes and hammers at their doors and windows was the first notification of danger. Williams, who combined the valor of the soldier with the piety of the clergyman, had barely time to seize his pistols from the head of his bed, when the Indians were in his room. He fired, but as he shed no blood, his life was spared. Two of his children were murdered in cold blood, his house set on fire, and himself, his wife, and their remaining children, bound and driven away, in company with about a hundred other captives.

The snow was knee deep when they set out on their journey of

* Hutchinson's Hist. Mass. vol. ii.

† Charlevoix, vol. ii. p. 290.

three hundred miles, towards a "Popish country"—the darkest picture which could be presented to a New England mind. It was not long before Mrs. Williams was murdered. "I overtook her," says her husband, in his simple and touching narrative, "I walked with her to help her on her journey. On the way we discoursed of the happiness of those who had a right to a house not made with hands, and God for a father and friend, as also that it was our reasonable duty, quietly to submit to the will of God, and say, the will of the Lord be done." He was separated from her, and soon heard that, having fallen down in wading through a swift icy stream, her savage captor had buried his hatchet in her head.*

Williams lived now only for his children. But a few hours before, in the enjoyment of happiness, he had nothing but the remnant of a slaughtered and captive family. His wife and two children lay unburied in the snow, and his surviving children were separated from him.

After travelling with tremendous speed, he arrived in the neighborhood of Montreal, and was courteously treated by the French, who, with the ready hospitality of their nation, did everything to alleviate his sorrows. But, in Canada a new series of afflictions began, more trying to the spirit of the Puritan, than even his losses and afflictions. He was compelled to attend mass, and wearied with efforts to convert him. These he could resist himself, but not so his children. His youngest daughter, Eunice, a child of seven, who had been tenderly carried by her captor during the whole journey, was now in the hands of the Jesuits, and though the governor of Montreal used his influence in his behalf, it was with great difficulty that he obtained permission to see her. She had not yet forgotten her catechism, and was anxious to return to her father—but, not long after, he found that, by mixing continually with Indians, she had lost the English language, and had no desire to be redeemed from captivity.

He remained in Canada until 1706, when he was ransomed and

* Redeemed Captive.

carried to Boston, from whence, after an interval, he returned to his old parish of Deerfield, where he spent the rest of his life.

One of his sons in the interval, had embraced the Romish faith, but eventually returned to Protestantism, and all that survived of the family were restored, with the exception of Eunice, who had entirely adopted Indian life and habits, and had no desire to leave her new associations of nation and religion. She married an Indian of the name of Turoges, which is probably a corruption of De Rogers, by whom she had three children, one son and two daughters.

The loss of Eunice and her adoption of Romanism, were calamities from which the afflicted father never recovered. Day and night, in public and in private, she was the object of his prayers. Her conversion to the simple faith of her ancestors, became the passionate desire of the whole community of Deerfield. Those who are acquainted with New England life, can easily understand how it was fanned into an hereditary flame by prayer meetings and sermons, and only glowed more intensely as the lapse of time rendered its accomplishment more hopeless. There is a tenacity in the New England mind which social habits and religious enthusiasm serve alike to encourage, and every effort which persuasion, affection, prayer, and faith could put in operation, was tried, and tried in vain. The friends of the captive had to contend with purpose as determined, and religious zeal as unbending as their own. Mr. Williams died in 1729, but, after his death, the desire for the conversion of Eunice continued as unabated as ever. Before his decease, she had once visited Deerfield, and consented to appear at the meeting house in English dress, but, in the afternoon, she resumed the blanket, and ever after continued inflexible in her attachment to the dress, customs, and religion in which she had been educated. Still her relatives and former neighbors did not despair. In 1740, she was induced again to visit Deerfield. She repeated the visit in 1741. Her voluntary coming caused great hope and excitement among her friends, and a final effort was made for her recovery. A time was set apart "for prayer and for the revival of religion, and on behalf of Mrs. Eunice, the daughter of Rev. John Williams." "Some of you well know," said the preacher, on the occasion, "how long she has been the subject of prayer. What numberless prayers have been put up to God for her by many holy souls now in Heaven, as well as many who yet remain on earth. How many groans and fervent prayers can these ears witness to have been uttered and breathed forth with a sort of burning and unquenchable ardor, from the pious and holy soul of her dear father, now with God. I know not that I ever heard him pray after his own return from captivity without a remembrance of her, that God would return her to his sanctuary. God did not give him leave to see the performance of his wishes and desires for her —but he now encourages us to hope that by the mighty power of his providence and grace, he will give us an extraordinary conviction that he is a God that heareth prayer."*

It was thus in crowded assemblies, and, with all due collateral associations and influences, that the natural desire for the re-conversion of Eunice, was fanned into a flame of enthusiasm, which, bequeathed by one religious gathering to another, was still felt in its effects, when she, herself, was in the grave. All the zeal of her friends was unavailing, and she died as she had lived.

John de Rogers, her son, was killed at Lake George, in 1758, in battle between the English and Indians. Her daughter, Catharine, married an Indian, named Rice. Mary was married to an English physician, named Williams. They had one son, Thomas Williams, who married an Indian woman, named Mary Ann Konwatewenteta, on the 7th January, 1779.

During the Revolutionary War, Thomas Williams fought on the British side, and commanded an Indian detachment. He was present at the naval conflict on Lake Champlain, near Valcour Island, between General Waterbury and Governor Carleton, and operated on the shore, with a body of Indians, intending to surprise the

* Redeemed Captive.

American forces, should they attempt a landing. He accompanied the army of General Burgoyne to Saratoga, and attended the council held by him, at Bouquet river, in August, 1777. After the retreat of the American army, he followed, with his Indians, in pursuit, in company with General Frazer's detachment, and was engaged in the skirmish at Fort Anne, and also in the action at Bennington. The principal service, however, which he rendered to the British, was in the two actions between Burgoyne and Gates, at Saratoga. He escaped from the field, with his detachment, and returned into Canada. In the year 1800, he had eight children, whose names were all registered in the records of the Romish Church at Caughnawaga, and three others were subsequently born, whose names were also found there. The name of Eleazar, the adopted child, is not among them. (Appendix F.) The habits of Thomas Williams were very erratic. Though his usual residence was at Caughnawaga, he paid an annual hunting visit to Lake George, and was often absent from home several years together.

Eleazar was, for a long time, in delicate health, and large quantities of Indian decoctions were given him, by which means his physical condition was much improved, and, though still unsound in mind, he took delight in playing with the other children. He accompanied Thomas Williams to Lake George several years in succession. The Indian hunting grounds were occupied, year after year, by nearly the same persons, and O'Brien remembers that Eleazar, some considerable time after his adoption by the Indians, received a severe fall, from a rock, somewhere in the vicinity of the Old Fort, i. e., Fort William Henry, at the head of the lake. He was taken out of the water with a deep gash on his head, cut by a rock beneath the surface. It is from this time that all distinct recollection begins. Of this fall itself, he has no remembrance, except as told him by others. The first waking image in his mind is the romantic scenery of Lake George. To enable the reader better to understand localities, I give a rude map of the head of the lake, where Thomas Williams was accustomed to encamp.

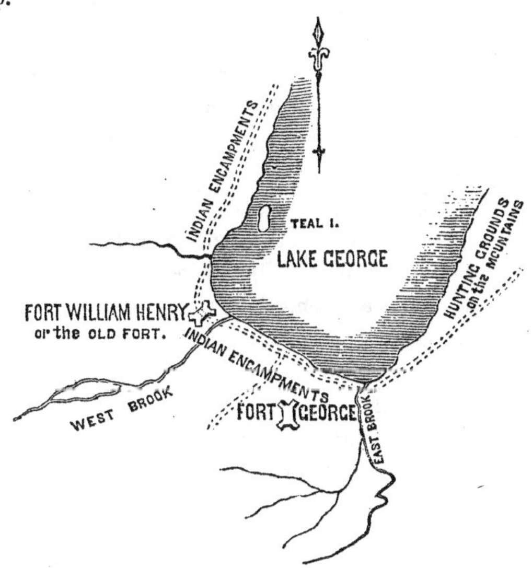


Exquisite, in its own still beauty, is the lake, with its ultramarine waters, locked in by rolling and serrated hills, dyed, at this season, in green and scarlet, purple and gold, the whole scene presenting, under a brilliant sun, that exaggeration of color which, in a painting, would be deemed unnatural. There are few spots which awaken so many sad, yet thrilling, historic recollections. Not far distant, is the rock where the Sachem Hendrick, and Col. Williams, an honored ancestor of the Williams' family, were slain, by Dieskau, in 1755. Then, there is the Bloody Pond, and Fort Gage, and Fort George, and Fort William Henry, each with their own heroic memories. But, if history shall bear me out in the conclusion I would draw from the tale I have to tell, there will be added to them all, a story scarce equalled in the legendary past, and worthy of the scene.

At the end of the last century, there were at the head of the lake no settled habitations. The beach, which had once been alive with armies, was deserted, and the dismantled fortifications were slowly crumbling. But all along the shore, to the West and South, were choice spots for the rude Indian wigwams, under the shade of lofty trees, and on the smooth sloping greensward, cleared of the tangled underbrush. In the fall of the year, there was quite a busy scene where the traders came to barter their goods for furs. The market-ground as we may call it, was on the clearing near the site of Fort William Henry—and it was in the nighborhood of this that Thomas Williams generally encamped. In rowing round the basin, and comparing the statements of Skenondogh with the recollections of Mr. Williams, and the nature of the localities, it seems probable that the spot on which the incident occurred, which led to the restoration of his mind, was in the vicinity of Teal Island, or between that and the old Fort. The purple Sierra, whose lofty peaks shut in the view to the north east, was the first object of which Mr. Williams has any distinct recollection. The gloom that spreads beyond, presents nothing but faint, dreamy, and indistinct remembrances, except in a single instance, in which there is the vivid portraiture of a hideous face, but to which he can attach neither name, nor place. He only knows, that it was connected with feelings of misery. All else is chaotic confusion, in which Indians roasting chestnuts around a fire, are mixed up with dream-like and vague images, which elude the effort to grasp them, as realities, of splendid architecture, of troops exercising in a garden, of being in a room where there were persons magnificently dressed, and of lying on the carpet with his head against the silk dress of a lady, and things of a similar character, but all is indistinct and unconnected, like a phantom of the night, whereas since he was first roused to an apprehension of life, on the shores of Lake George, his mind retains consecutively and with tenacity all that has transpired.

The wigwam of Thomas Williams was a small log house, about twenty feet square, perhaps a little larger, roofed with bark, leaving an opening in the centre to give egress to the smoke from the fire, which blazed beneath it, on the floor, in the middle of the apartment. Around this fire were ranged the beds of the family, composed of hemlock boughs, covered with the skins of animals taken in the chase, bears or deer. As the season closed in, Eleazar, with the other boys, nearly naked, except a check shirt and a handkerchief upon his head, occupied himself in filling up the crevices between the logs with moss plucked from the trees, to keep the wigwam warm; but, sometimes, when the wind was unfavorable, the smoke, unable to ascend through the aperture in the roof, would fill the apartment, and Mrs. Williams, after bearing the annoyance as long as her Indian stoicism permitted, would rush out in her blanket, and destroy the work of the poor boys, by pulling away the moss, to allow passage to the smoke, through the sides of the wigwam. The fare of the family was as simple as their dwelling-place. From cross sticks over the fire, hung a huge kettle in which the squaw made soup of pounded corn, flavored with venison. They purchased their salt and spirits at Fort Edward. The streams, when unfrozen, supplied them with fish, the woods and the mountains with game.

Wigwams, such as I have described, were, in the hunting season, scattered at intervals, all along the shore of the lake, near its head, and it was the habit, when any family got a fresh supply of spirits from the fort, to send round and invite the neighboring Indians. One of these parties, shortly after the recovery of his reason, is vividly remembered by Mr. Williams. The Indians arrived from all directions, bringing in deer and everything necessary for a feast, and waited impatiently for the young men who had been dispatched for that which was the soul of the merry-making. At last, about sunset, the war-whoop was heard over the wooded hills, and responded to and re-responded by the crowd around the wigwam, till the jocund messengers arrived, and the night revel around the forest fires grew fast and furious.

Shortly after this, when Eleazar was one day sporting on the lake near Fort William Henry, in a little wooden canoe, with several other boys, two strange gentlemen came up to the encampment of Thomas Williams, and took their seats with him upon a log at a little distance from the wigwam. With natural curiosity, at a circumstance which broke in upon the usual monotony of Indian life on the hunting grounds, the boys paddled their canoe ashore, and strolled up to the encampment to ascertain who the strangers were, when Thomas Williams called out, "'Lazau, this friend of yours wishes to speak with you." As he approached, one of the gentlemen rose and went off to another Indian encampment. The one who remained with Thomas Williams, had every indication in dress, manners, and language, of being a Frenchman—for Eleazar remembers understanding a few words, sufficient to know that he spoke in French. He had on a ruffled shirt, his hair was powdered, and bore to the child a very splendid appearance. When Eleazar came near, the French gentleman advanced several steps to meet him, embraced him most tenderly, and when he again sat down on the log, made him stand between his legs. In the meantime he shed abundance of tears, said, "Pauvre garçon," and continued to embrace him. Thomas Williams was, soon after, called to a neighboring wigwam, and Eleazar and the Frenchman left alone. The latter continued to kiss him and weep, and spoke a good deal, seeming anxious that he should understand him, which he was unable to do. When Thomas Williams returned to them, he asked Eleazar whether he knew what the gentleman had said to him, and he replied, "No." They both left him, and walked off in the direction in which the other gentleman had gone. The two gentlemen came again the next day, and the Frenchman remained several hours. Thomas Williams took him out in a canoe on the lake; and the last which Eleazer remembers was, their all sitting together on a log, when the Frenchman took hold of his bare feet and dusty legs and examined his knees and ankles closely. Again, the Frenchman shed tears, but young Eleazar was quite indifferent, not knowing what to make of it. Before the gentleman left, he gave him a piece of gold.

After a few days, Thomas Williams, contrary to his usual custom, returned to Caughnawaga, instead of remaining for his winter hunt at Lake George. He had not long returned home, when, one night, Eleazar overheard a conversation between his reputed parents, in whose room he slept. Thomas strongly urged compliance with a request which had been made to them to allow two of their children to go away for education, but his wife objected on religious grounds. But when he persisted in the demand, she said, "If you will do it, you may send away this strange boy; means have been put into your hands for his education, but, John I cannot part with." Her willingness to sacrifice him, and the whole tenor of the conversation, excited suspicions in his mind as to his belonging to them, but they soon passed away.

Though nearly a hundred years had elapsed since the massacre at Deerfield, the memory of it was still fresh in the minds of the descendants of John Williams, and their friends in Massachusetts. Among them was a gentleman named Nathaniel Ely, a deacon in the Congregationalist Church, a worthy and intelligent, though uneducated, man. Until thirty years of age he had worked on his farm, and enjoyed uninterrupted health, when his whole family was attacked with sickness, and his mother and three children swept at once to the grave. During Mr. Ely's illness, he made a vow to God, that if he recovered, "his future life, health, property, and everything dear on earth should be consecrated to God;"* and to the best of his ability he fulfilled his vow. He was a man of sound, clear understanding, and remarkably methodical habits, which latter are evinced by his journal, in which he recorded the principal events of every day. He had warmly at heart the project of converting the aborigines from Paganism and Romanism; and being related, by marriage, to the family of Eunice Wil-

* MS. Sermon by Mr. Storrs, preached at Mr. Ely's funeral.

liams, felt a deep interest in her descendants. He accordingly applied to Thomas Williams for permission to educate two of his children as missionaries; and then the conversation occurred, which I have recorded above, between the reputed parents of Eleazar. Mrs. Williams at last consented that John, one of her own children, who, according to the baptismal register at Caughnawaga, was then seven years old, and Lazar, her adopted child, who was many years older, should be sent to Massachusetts. The name of the latter, according to Mr. Ely's papers now before me, was either Lazar, Lazo, Lazare, Leazer, or Eleazar. It does not occur in the baptismal register.

In regard to his age at this time, there is the same difficulty. In one of Mr. Ely's accounts it is said that he was nineteen years of age in 1800. But this is evidently incorrect. In another, his age, at that time, is stated at thirteen, and in several others, twelve; while a near relative of the family, and a schoolmate of Mr. Williams, Mrs. Mary W. Jewett, now residing at 46 Bank street, New York, testifies that she was then twelve years of age, and that Mr. Williams was about two years her senior. A Romish priest, in an affidavit of his own composition, has made his reputed mother swear that he was then nine years old. This entire discrepancy between all the accounts, shows most conclusively that nothing certain was known on the subject. As to the two extreme statements nine is as absurd as nineteen, nay, more so, as facts, hereafter to be recorded, will show. The truth lies in the medium of between fourteen and fifteen.*

A gentlemen, then residing at Long Meadow, remembers the time when the two supposed brothers entered the village, dressed in their Indian costume, and the entire dissimilarity in their appearance at once excited attention. They became the subject of general conversation and conjecture, and there was something so singular and

* Lazo Williams. Jany. 1800, 19 years of age. In a paper dated December 1802, he is then stated to be 15. Thus, " the two lads, one of whom is in the fifteenth, the other in the tenth year of his age."—*Ely MSS.* (Appendix G.)

mysterious in the difference between them that those who saw them have never forgotten it. (Appendix H.)

Too late to allow of anything more than the insertion of the fact in the text, I have learned that Mr. Ely was, to a great extent, acquainted with the secret of Eleazar's birth. He certainly knew that he was of distinguished origin. Next door to Nathaniel Ely, resided his brother, Ethan Ely, who had charge of a niece by name Urania Stebbins, now Mrs. Smith, and who is still living at an advanced age, at Milwaukee, Wisconsin, with her son, W. E. Smith. She testifies as follows, "Mr. Ely said the names of the boys were Eleazar and John Williams (in English). The Indians, he said, called the former Lazau. Mr. Ely, when remonstrated with concerning the boys being brothers, as they looked not alike, said there was something about it which he should possibly never reveal, but would say this much, that Eleazar Williams was born for a great man, and he intended to give him an education to prepare him for the station."* I have also been informed by Mr. Stanley Smith, of the "Albany Express," who gives me permission to use his name, and has frequently stated the fact in his paper, having learned it from undoubted authority, that money was transmitted from France, to the late John R. Bleeker, and devoted to the support of Eleazar. I have searched the accounts of this gentleman, in a very casual manner, however, but could discover no signs of this transaction. Without some clue to the parties from whom the money was received, it will be next to impossible to trace the affair. Thomas Williams frequently went to Albany, and returned with money in his possession, though without ostensible means of procuring it. It would seem most natural that the funds should be paid over to him. Jacob Vanderheyden, with whom Talleyrand was in communication, may, as an Indian trader, have been concerned in the transaction. But here we can only conjecture until further developments take place. (Appendix I.)

Arrived at Long Meadow, Eleazar was under an entirely new

* Letter from W. E. Smith, Milwaukee, Sept. 18, 1853.

series of influences and associations. I have made such inquiries concerning his condition, appearance, and estimation at this period as time permitted. The following extract, from the letter of a lady, now residing in New York, gives so lively a picture of the nature of the interest he excited, that I will let her tell her own story :—

"In early childhood my deepest sympathies were excited on his behalf, from listening to the rehearsal of anecdotes of him by my beloved mother, who knew him personally. When he, with his reputed brother, John, was placed under the care of Mr. Ely, my mother was spending some time with her brother, a resident of Long Meadows. She soon became interested in the lads, especially Eleazar, or Lazau. She found him possessed of fine traits of character, amiable, kind, sensitive, frank, generous, and gratefully susceptible to every overture of kindness. She often invited him to her brother's house, and found great pleasure in showing him kind attentions, and supplying many of his little wants. In the garden was a profusion of melons and cucumbers, of which he was very fond, and as his daily route to and from school led him directly by the house, she invited him always to call as he passed, and partake of them freely, and while enjoying the repast he would look up to her, with gratitude beaming on his countenance, and say, in broken English, 'Good Missy Gomee (Grosvenor), give poor Lesau cucummer, Missy Gomee very kind poor Lesau.' At one time he came to her, and said, 'Missy Gomee, poor Lesau very sick.' She found him pale and very chilly, although it was in midsummer. She tried various means to relieve him, and at length, took him into the yard, and with a blanket wrapt around him, seated him by the sunny side of the house, where he would feel the full influence of the sun, and she had soon the happiness of seeing him relieved. But it was the strangeness of his appearance and circumstances, and the deep mystery which hung around him, which excited her deepest pity. His total unlikeness, in his personal appearance, as well as character and habits, to his reputed brother, forbade, at once, the supposition of one and the same origin. While the latter was truly an Indian, with long black hair, his complexion and every feature, corresponding with his race. Eleazar had brown hair, hazle eyes, light complexion, and European features. The strangeness of these facts gave rise to various conjectures and speculations concerning him.

Although he was naturally cheerful, still, a tinge of thoughtful sadness would steal over him when interrogated with regard to his early history; and he would say, he couldn't remember much about it, and it gave him pain, apparently, that he could not. The prevalent opinion, in that vicinity, seemed to be that, he was a French boy, who was stolen from his family, and brought away at so early an age, as to render his recollections of other than Indian life, vague and unsatisfactory. So great was the interest felt in his case by my mother, and so great her desire and belief that the mystery which enshrouded him would be cleared away, that during her life, so long as was in her power, she kept herself advised of his situation and circumstances, and I well remember with what delight she heard the announcement, that he had been located at Oneida, twelve miles distant from her residence, and would remain with the Indians some time. She was then in feeble health, but she remarked, 'as soon as I am able to go so far from home, I must go and see Mr. Williams,' which intention, however, though she constantly cherished the hope of it, she was never able to realize.

"Very respectfully yours,

"JULIA M. JENKINS.

"New York, February 17th, 1853."

There must have been something very remarkable in one who could attract such attention, and awaken so much curiosity. This was not an isolated instance, but the same thing has attended him through life. People have been unable to reconcile his look, bearing, and intelligence with what they were told about him. He carried a mystery with him. It enshrouded him. It was felt, but could not be explained. In the letter of Mrs. Jenkins, allusion is made to his ignorance concerning the events of his childhood, which people, it seems, were, even then, anxious to pry into. I receive the same information, varied in details, from Mrs. Clarissa Dickenson, of New York, who was a schoolfellow of Mr. Williams, and who has no acquaintance whatever with Mrs. Jenkins, so that their testimony stands entirely separate, and affords the highest confirmation to the truth of the facts which they assert in common.

"He was a fine handsome boy," says Mrs. Dickenson, "sprightly and fair in complexion, and my father frequently told him that, he looked more like a Frenchman than an Indian. The scars were always upon his face, from the earliest period of my recollection, and one day, he came in heated with exercise, and the perspiration standing on his forehead; as he passed the mirror, his eyes fell upon the scars, and he turned quickly round and asked me, if I had ever noticed them, and if I had any idea when he got them? I replied, 'I suppose in childhood,' upon which he added, there were painful thoughts connected with them in his mind, which he could not bear to dwell on. At this period of his life, though usually happy, and frank in his disposition, he was, as the whole family remarked, frequently subject to fits of musing and abstraction, as if endeavoring to remember something, and when questioned as to the reason of it, he said that, there were painful images before his mind of things in childhood, which he could not get rid of nor exactly understand. I saw an asserted brother of Mr. Williams, who was sent to Long Meadows for education. He was entirely unlike Mr. Williams in appearance, being quite thin, dark, and like an Indian, whereas Mr. Williams was always full and portly in person.

"CLARISSA W. DICKENSON.

"February 18th, 1853."

There is another important letter which I will here introduce, and which will tell its own tale:—

"46, BANK STREET, NEW YORK,
"*September* 7, 1853.

"DEAR SIR:

"In reply to your inquiries respecting my acquaintance with the Rev. Eleazar Williams in early life, I beg to say that I was a schoolmate of his at Long Meadow. I am a descendant of the redeemed captive, the Rev. John Williams, who was my great-great-grandfather. According to the best of my recollection, Eleazar was about fourteen years of age, when he came to the care of Mr. Ely. There was no similarity whatever in appearance between him and any of his family, either his brother John, or his reputed father and mother, who I saw on their visit to Long Meadow. Thomas Williams I have seen frequently. Eleazar was a very studious boy—indeed, he seemed to do little but study; and I can well remember his remarkable proficiency in writing, and that the second winter after his coming to Long Meadow, he would say to me, 'Come, Cousin Mary, and hear my sermon,' when he would produce and read some MS. on religious subjects. There was something so remarkable in his character, attainments, and amiable and religious disposition, that the highest attention was shown him by the most distinguished persons, as he was not like other children, and was always in the company of gentlemen of literature and sobriety.

"Very truly yours,

(Appendix J.) "MARY W. JEWETT."

To these documents I must add another from Mrs. Temple, daughter of Nathaniel Ely:—

"DEAR SIR

"The efforts made by my dear departed father, deacon Nathaniel Ely, to educate and qualify you for usefulness among your countrymen, as well as to prepare you for glory, honor, and immortality, have given me so deep an interest in you, that I should feel pleasure in complying with any reasonable request of yours. I, therefore, state in writing, as you desired, that there was an entire and striking dissimilarity between yourself and your brother John, in the features of your face, your general appearance, and also in your predilections and character.

"Your early and sincere friend,

"Rev. Eleazar Williams. "MARTHA E. TEMPLE.

"January 24, 1851."

I have already alluded to the practice of Mr. Ely, of keeping a regular diurnal record of the principal events of his life; and as this has exercised a very important influence on the character and habits of Mr. Williams, I will, before I proceed further, give the reader a specimen of it, from the page which records the first coming of Eleazar Williams to Long Meadow:—

"1800. January 21. Monday, Stripping Tobacco, &c.

" 22. Tuesday, at do., &c., &c.

" 23. Wednesday, at do., &c., &c., our cousins from

Connawaga came, viz.: Thomas Williams and his sons, Lezau and John Sir Wattis Williams.

1800. January 24. Thursday, at home, &c.

" 25. Friday, about home.

" 26. Saturday, Rode to Springfield, &c.

" 27. Lord's Day. Attended Divine Service. Mr. Storrs Preached, and Baptized Patty, Daughter to Martha Suh, &c.

" 28. Monday, Rode to Somers with Cousin Thomas, and Returned.

" 29. Tuesday, about home.

" 30. Wednesday, Rode to Wolcott Brussels, &c.

" 31. Thursday, attended Samuel Keep's Wedding.

February 1. Friday, Cousin Thomas Set of for Albany.

" 2. Saturday, about home, it Snowed, &c.

" 3. Lord's Day, attended Divine Service, Mr. Storrs Preacht and Baptized Chancey, son to Luther Cotton."

And so the good old conscientious man went on, to the day of his death; recording every ride, every storm, telling how at such a time he "did chores," and got his "slay shod," and how "the scholls in the streeat met," and how he "visited the scholls in the middle deastrict," and how Lord's Day, after Lord's Day "Mr. Storrs Preacht." On May 1, 1808, he wrote, "Sacrament day—my mind is very tender with the thought that this is the last time I shall ever commune with the Church Militant!!!" Had it been possible, he would, doubtless, have recorded how he died, June 13, 1808, aged fifty-seven years, and that Mr. Storrs preacht the funeral sermon, and said that "both in the male and female line his ancestors were distinguished for piety and good sense, for usefulness and respectability;" and that "for more than twenty years he had sustained the office of a deacon in the church, and so discharged the appropriate functions of that office, as to purchase to himself a good report, and promote the spiritual welfare of his

Christian brethren." By the convictions of my mind, and the feelings of my heart, I am a churchman; but there is something in the character of the old-fashioned Congregationalist of New England, of which Deacon Ely seems to have been so good a sample, that makes me bow my head in reverence and love; and, though we worship in different sanctuaries below, may we meet in the temple that is above. Under this good man it was that young Williams acquired the habit of journalizing which has been continued, with occasional breaks, throughout life. But, with the intuitive good sense of a highly superior mind, he improved upon his model. The earliest journal of Mr. Williams in my possession was written, as handwriting and internal evidence show, as early as the year 1803, but it dates back to January, 1800; and the portion which relates to that and the following year were then composed from recollection and previous memoranda. Like Mr. Ely's, it is written on sheets of paper sewn together, but instead of giving the events of every day it only records the most important circumstances, such as visits from his supposed father, journeys, changes of residence, &c. It begins thus:—

"MEMORANDUM FOR THE YEAR 1800.

"*On Journey of Life*, 1800.

"I have written from time to time, and now collected in part by recollection: First, my coming to England in the year 1800. I, Eleazer Williams, aged 13 years, and John Williams, my brother, both of us came to Long Meadow, it being Wednesday, 23d of January, 1800, this being the day we began with Nathaniel Ely. After a long tedious journey we arrived at this place safely, through the kindness of Providence—praised be God for our preservation. We was receive wilcome to our friends here and treated kindly by them. My brother and I was not able to converse with them, and went to school next day after our arrival. Mr. Ely, Mr. Cotton, and my father went with us to school house. Mrs. Hale kept the school, and we was treated kindly by her. I hope I shall remember her amiable disposition. Mr. Ely and my father went to [illegible] and from thence, Mr. R. and my father went to Hartford, and returned with him to

Long Meadow, and brought us little books, a present from Rev. Dr. Strong, of Hartford. We receive them very thankfully.

" *Long Meadow*, *Feb.* 11, 1800.—FRIDAY.—My father set out for home with Mr. Fitch and his wife, by way of Albany. The occasion, his going that way that the counsel [i. e. Indian Council] was then sitting in that city, and he was the member. Mrs. Fitch is cousin to my father, Mr. Williams' daughter, of this town. We heard from them in course few days. The first da they went from here, they went as far as Chester, to Rev. Mr. Bascom, and kept Sabbath with him, 30 miles from here, and Mrs. Bascom is cousin to my father.

" We heard no more from our father until he came down again to see us next October. It was great trial to me when he left us, more so on account that we could not speak the language. However, we soon learn the languag—so as to be able to converse, and the family were very agreeable and kind to us. The blessing of the Lord rest upon them.

" *October* 3, 1800. Thanks be to God for his loving kindness towards us. We have been very well since our father left us, and came to see us this month, and we have reason to bless God that all our friends at north, were well. Went down to Hartford with him, and Mr. Ely went with us. We went to Mr. Pitkin, and dined there, from thence went over the river to Rev. Dr. Strong, and lodge there one night. And give us many little books, story books. Friday, my father and I set out for Tolland. Mr. Ely and John return to Long Meadow. We arrived, toward night, at Rev. Dr. Williams, we was received kindly by the Gov. and the family, and this being the first time I am in this place, we set out next morning and dine at Rev. Dr. Backer's—Sommers—from thence we start for Long Meadow, and arrived about sundown, this being Saturday, and my father set out for home this week, and my brother was very anxious to go home with him—but it was soon over—his home sickness—hoping the Lord will be with my father on his journey, and return him safely to his friends. If I only consider the blessings I have received from my common father which is in Heaven, oh, how ought I to give him praise which is due to him. I could exclaim in the language of the good Jacob, " I am not worthy the least of all thy mercies." Oh, my soul, forget not all the benefits which thou hast received from thy father of all mercies. Praise him. Praise him, oh my soul. This being written by the recollection. The end 1800.

The only entry which is made for the year 1801, is the following:—

"*Memorandum, year* 1801.

"*Jany.* 1, 1801.—The God of all mercies preserved us and brought us to see another of New Year's day. Let every created being give him thanks and praise. Oh that men would praise the Lord for his goodness and his wonderful works towards the children of men!

"*Meditation on the Anniversary of the New Year's Day.*

"O Lord, thou art the great preserver of men. I give my humble hearty thanks for my preservation and protection the year past. Thou hast been so kind and merciful as to bring me to see another New Year's Day. Oh, may I serve thee this year more faithful than I have done hitherto. Assist me, most gracious God, to devote myself wholly to thy service and glory—preserve me from sinning against thee, and I pray thee forgive me all the sins which I am guilt of, and prepare me for thy whole providential dealings with me, whether life or death—and I beseech thee to bless my friends wherever they may be; may thy name be known on earth—may all flesh see thy salvation. I ask thee in the name of Jesus Christ, thy beloved Son. Be all honor and praise be given to the Father, the Son, and the Holy Spirit, now and ever more. Amen."

Now, these entries in his journal seem to have been written somewhere about 1802 or '3, but they are copies in part of previous MSS., and partly composed from recollection. At first, he scribbled his thoughts on little scraps of paper, some specimens of which, in the year 1805, remain; and then, afterwards transferred them to larger sheets, and wrote with greater care. The journal itself bears every mark of great age, and there is a providential test of its accuracy and authenticity in the journal of Mr. Ely. There is an invariable correspondence in the entries in the two documents, a specimen of which it may be well in this place to exhibit. Whenever young Eleazer writes down, in full, with all attendant circumstances, any event, to him remarkable, such as the arrival or departure of his father, you find it briefly noted, in a line, in the diary of the deacon.

This agreement is best shown in parallel columns.

E. Williams.

"*Long Meadow, Dec.* 9, 1802.—God is once more pleased to send our father. He came to-day about sun down, and brought us news that my sister is sick. God be praised.

"*Long Meadow, April* 2, 1803.—God is merciful towards his children—he does everything that is right and for their good. Let the whole earth give him praise for his loving-kindness towards them. This day I receive a letter from my father, as follows:—

"'Dear son, I take this opportunity to let you know of our welfare. I arrived here in ten days after I left you, and found two of my children very sick, and now I am to inform you that they are taken from me by immortality, &c.

"'Since that time we have lost one of your brothers, six years old,' &c.

"*Long Meadow, April*, 1803.—I am going to live with Mr. Brockway, Ellington."

N. Ely.

"1802.

"*Dec.* 9, *Thursday at home, &c., &c.*—Thomas Williams, of Connawaga, came to our house.

"1803,

"*April* 2, *Saturday*.—Met at Lieut. Hezekiah Hale's on select mens business, heard of the death of three of Thomas Williams's children, of Connawaga, viz. 2 daughters and one son.

*N.B. This was written by an interpreter, Thos. Williams being unacquainted with English*

"*April* 30, *Saturday*.—Rode in chaise with Lazau to Elington, left him with Mr. Brockway, &c., &c., &c., and returned."

There can thus be no doubt, and if there were, personal inspection of the documents would at once remove it, of the entire authenticity of the remarkable and most interesting record of Mr. Wiliams's early life contained in his journal. But what a strange problem it presents by itself. A child, taken from the midst of savage life, is within a year or two master of the English language so as to write it with a fluency, ease, and precision of expression—notwithstanding marks of simplicity which create a smile—usually attained only after long and painful study, by those born to the use of it. His observations and reflections are all just, he exhibits a mind previously disciplined in the ways and feelings of civilization, his conscience is cultivated, his religious sentiments are those of a mature intellect, and, in a word, in a very short space he has made a progress in learning and morals almost miraculous. If I had stated all this without having the documentary evidence to produce to the world, and the ability to annihilate scepticism by fact, with what incredulity should I have been met. A distinguished gentleman has expressed doubts as to Mr. Williams having ever kept a journal—because he could see no use for it. Why, the school-boy, fresh from the wilderness, found the utility of preserving a record of his thoughts, feelings, religious convictions, domestic sorrows and joys; and, as if with an instinct, unaccountable except as the inspiration of Providence, that all these random effusions might some day be of interest, has treasured them, amid all the vicissitudes of an adventurous and checquered life, and now produces, when forced by circumstances and in self-defence to do so, to the gaze of the world, the words penned with no idea that any eye but his own and God's would read them.

Now these papers show that from the very outset, civilized life was natural to him. There is every token that education came to him as a recovery. There is none of the impatience of the half-savage Indian accustomed only to the wigwam and the hunting ground, and unable to endure the thraldom of civilization, but every token that he felt himself at home among books, and in the use of the pen, and in religious meditation, so as actually to outstrip, within a short period of his residence in New England, the good Deacon who had been the Providential instrument of withdrawing him from the barbarism in which he had been engulfed, and would soon have been everlastingly and indistinguishably buried. The moment that he is placed in civilized society, his mind expands upon it, and grasps the whole. Though murky clouds of oblivion roll between him and a past life, emitting, through their gloom, but faint, intangible, and mystic rays, which only bewilder and perplex him, the discipline of that life, both to the mind and conscience, remains in its effects. It is in its psychological aspect that Mr. Williams's case has, from the first, next to sympathy with his misfortunes, interested me, and the perusal of his early journals deepens the interest excited by his most singular mental condition. I feel certain that the best intellects will have their attention riveted to this point, as to a problem worthy of profound study, and exhibiting a new phase in the laws of mental action, only capable of development under circumstances the most exceptional and extraordinary.

In the beginning of the year 1802, there was a great revival, as it is called, among Congregationalists and others, of religion, in Long Meadow. The principal trace of it in Mr. Ely's diary is the record that other ministers were then preaching in Mr. Storr's faithfully occupied pulpit, and the texts, "Sirs, what must we do to be saved?" and "If any man have not the Spirit of Christ he is none of his," show the nature of the exhortations then employed. In addition to which, under date of 5th and 6th March, the following entries occur:—

"1802. *5th March, Friday.*—At home. Conference Preparations at our house; Mr. Harris present, Lazeau Williams much affected, &c., &c.

"*6th March, Saturday.*—About home. The minds of the children affected, &c., &c., the Spirit of the Lord is at work," &c.

But, all which the good deacon, who was the very soul of brevity, indicated by &c., may be found at large in Eleazar Williams's journal. "Wonderful works in the month of February. God was pleased to pour out his Holy Spirit in the hearts of the people in this place, many are inquiring the way that leads to eternal life or the holy city of God. It is wonderful the great revival of religion in this place; O Lord, be pleased to show us our unhappy state, and make us inquire *what we should do to be saved* from thy wrath." It was, according to Mr. Ely's journal, on the 21st of this month, that Mr. Enos Bliss preached from this text, and the incidental coincidence is curious and important. "Say to our heart," continues the journal, "tremble ye not—believe in and look to thy Creator, and Jesus Christ thy Saviour, and the Holy Spirit thy Sanctifier, and keep my commandments, and thou shalt be saved.

"*Long Meadow, Feb.* 28, 1802.—Many of the young people now begin to speak with freedom to one another, concerning the interest of Christ's kingdom. In the evening conference, meeting was attended by a large number of people, both old and young." In Deacon Ely's journal this conference meeting is also spoken of.

But, I may here avail myself of his convenient, &c., and spare my eyes the pain of deciphering from the faded MS. whole pages, which follow, of Eleazar's revival enthusiasm. I do not believe it was in this school he first acquired his religious feelings; but that the devotional tendency of his mind was from a pre-existent life. His piety, however, was here fanned into a flame, and has, through all vicissitudes, burned steadily and uniformly. The death of his reputed relatives, in 1803, seems strongly to have affected his mind, and gave rise, in his journals, to long reflections on the uncertainty of life, and prayers to God that he might be prepared for his own departure. He went in April, 1803, to reside at Ellington, and remained there until July 20, when Mr. Ely brought him back to Long Meadow.

This gentleman, as was generally understood, had undertaken the education of the two boys at his own expense; but his means being very moderate, he soon found the necessity of applying to others for assistance. His first application was made to the Massachusetts Missionary Society, who granted him fifty dollars; and in

November, 1802, he applied also to the Hampshire Missionary Society, who made him a similar donation, upon a report from a committee consisting of Joseph Lathrop, D.D., Rev. Richard Storrs, and Justin Ely, Esq. In their report, these gentlemen state the ages of the children to be, at that time, fifteen and ten years of age; although in an account of expenditures by Mr. Ely, to which their signatures are attached, it is said that Eleazar was nineteen, and John twelve years of age in January, 1800. They are represented as having made "remarkably good proficiency in school learning, to exhibit strong proofs of virtuous and pious dispositions, and seem likely to make useful missionaries among the heathen." This praise, though thus bestowed indiscriminately on the two lads, was only, in its full extent, deserved by the eldest; for, in the course of a few years, it was found impossible to cultivate the mind of John, whose passion for savage life was irrepressible, though in many respects a fine young man. He could not be broken into the trammels of civilization, and returned home to live and die a mere Indian. Dr. Jenkins, of New York, informs me that years ago, he heard an aged gentleman, now dead, speak of the singular impression made on his mind by the contrast in the conduct of the boys, as well as their appearance, when he took them out one day for a walk in the fields. John would not come near him, but played about in a shy, wild, manner; while Eleazar kept close by his side, and asked him questions on all subjects, politics, religion, history, and geography.

Whatever solitary distress the school-boy experienced, in the dim and shadowy reminiscences of horrors whose intangible features escaped him whenever he attempted to grasp them and give them form, time, name and locality, he was now in the midst of scenes and influences which left their own impress on his character and mind, and claimed the prominent share of his attention. He was in Massachusetts, among enthusiastic religionists, as the embodiment of the Deerfield tragedy, and all the treasured traditions of a century of prayer meetings, mournful and stern recollections of invasion, fire, and blood, hostility to Romanism, veneration for the memory of John Williams, and piqued affection for the poor Eunice, whose perversion was looked upon rather as a misfortune than a crime, all centred in him, so that he found himself a hero from the alphabet, a predestined crusader and missionary of Protestantism, and became tinctured with all the feelings in the social atmosphere around him. Naturally of an ambitious turn of mind, he had an idea, as I am informed by a schoolmate, that he was superior to every one, and when questioned as to the reason for this feeling, which he took no care to conceal, would impute it to his Indian blood. His friends, on the other hand, were captivated by his frankness, grace, and intelligence, and felt proud of a kinsman, who issued from the bosom of barbarism, with such susceptibilities for refinement and culture. All this has been remembered and treasured up, apart from the interest recently excited, as something most remarkable. He exhibited a grace and polish of manner, unusual in a New England village, at that period, and seemed rather to give than to receive the polished manners of social life. He was called familiarly "the plausible boy."

The Williams family felt justly proud of him, and clung pertinaciously then, as some of them do now, against all external evidence, to the idea that he was a descendant of Eunice, and were in the habit of carrying him round the country to exhibit to different branches of the wide extended stock, as one by whom an honor was conferred upon them.

The strength of this feeling is shown, in a somewhat eccentric and ludicrous manner, in the following extract from a letter written by the Rev. Thomas Williams, of Providence, R. I. and published in the papers at the beginning of the year :—

"We thought ourselves to be highly honored by such a kinsman as Eleazar Williams, on account of his conversion from Popery, his native genius, his firm health, his manly form, his pleasant countenance, his cheerful and peculiar conversation, and the happy union of Indian shrewdness with our Welch ardor. I took him with me from Hartford to my father's in Pomfret; from Pomfret to Dr. Emmons in Franklin, whose wife was Martha Williams, whose father and my father were first cousins. From Franklin I went with cousin Eleazar to Boston. Since those days I have frequently had information respecting the Rev. Mr. Williams. But if I had ever had the least reason to believe that he was not our beloved and honored cousin, as descended legitimately from Eunice Williams, and only a son of Louis XVI. of France, I never should have rejoiced and gloried in him as one of our family."

Eleazar, on his part, repayed the affection of the Williams family with gratitude and love; and although there was ever an obscurity in his mind, concerning his origin, yet being unable to lift the veil of mystery from the past, he fell passively into the state of things in which he found himself, and took as much pride and pleasure in considering himself the descendant of Eunice, as her relatives took in calling him so. Adopted, to apparent identification, by the family, he identified his feelings and interests with theirs, adopted their traditions, their sentiments, their principles, and has continued, up to the present time, to entertain for them all the love which springs from the most cherished and honored ties of relationship. His situation was most peculiar. Against the tangible and evident claims made on him by his reputed kinsmen, the every day realities of life, and all the endearing associations which spring from the reception of a thousand marks of kindness, social and pecuniary, he had nothing to oppose but thick clouds and darkness brooding over his early childhood, faintly lighted up by mysterious dreams of unknown things, to which he could assign neither date nor place.

If, in long after years, when the events of his life had become inextricably confused and complicated, we find him the sport of contending feelings, and the prey of a corroding anxiety which did not permit him to rest, and showed no avenue of escape, leading to apparent inconsistencies of conduct in perfect harmony with the incongruities and anomalies of his lot, we should rather pity him for the soul crucifixion, entailed by his position, than harshly and superficially judge him to be a deceiver, because he still continued, nominally, to identify himself with his adopted kinsmen, at a time when grave and well-founded doubts as to the truth of his personality were torturing his spirit. An unjust and unjustifiable attempt has recently been made to injure him in public estimation, simply because, within a few years, he has, within the circle of his nominal kindred, spoken of himself as a member of the Williams family. This is not the place to enter into the question, which belongs historically to a later period, and I only allude to it, in passing, because suggested by the circumstances of his boyish days, and the associations in the midst of which he was reared.

On the 15th January, 1804, Thomas and Mary Ann Williams visited Long Meadow. Their coming, at that time, recorded in the journals, is well remembered by Mrs. Jewet, a descendant of the Redeemed Captive, who was at school with Eleazar, and who, though a child, was struck with the incongruity in appearance between him and all his reputed relations. After staying a few days, and visiting with the boys in various places, all of which is duly recorded, Mr. and Mrs. Williams returned. "Oh, it was grevious to my heart," says Eleazar, "I hope God will be with them."

In May, being quite unwell, and suffering from pain in the head, he was taken to Boston for change of scene and recreation. He now attended various missionary meetings, and says, concerning one, "Here I saw the largest assembly that ever I have seen before." Alas, poor boy, thou hadst probably witnessed vaster and wilder gatherings. Previous to their return home, Mr. Ely made application to the House of Representatives of Massachusetts, for aid in supporting and educating the lads, acknowledging the assistance he had received from the missionary societies, and saying that a reverse in his circumstances had put it out of his power to fulfil his original design of educating them at his own charge. Together with his petition he presented a specimen of Eleazar's writing, in large and small hand, which Mr. Williams has preserved among his papers, and which is now before me. A resolution passed by the Senate, 13th June, 1804, that three hundred and fifty dollars should be paid for this purpose, was concurred in by the House of Representatives, June 15th. Shortly after, Mr. Ely set forth an account of his expenditures with the quaint heading "The Humane, the Noble, and the Charitable of every name to Nathaniel Ely, of Long Meadow, Massachusetts, Dr. To expenditures for the education of Lazau Williams and John Surwattes Williams," but with what success this appeal was attended there is no means of ascertaining. From a letter written by a Mr. David Avery, it appears that in some minds there was a violent prejudice against them, because they had been "soaked with the blood of their relatives slain by the Indians from Canada." But this feeling must have been quite exceptional.

From October, 1804, to May, 1805, the journals are missing. By the latter date, he had obtained great precision and considerable elegance of style:—

"1805. *15th May.*—To-day I am to set out with Mr. Ely on a journey for my health.

"*15th, Coventry.*—Came from Long Meadow this morning; I am much better.

"*26th, Coventry.*—Lord's Day, evening. I am more unwell to-day. Dr. Hunt is very kind to me. I went to meeting part of the day; Mr. Brockway preached from Genesis iv, 16, and Proverbs iii, 20.

"*27th, Thompson.*—Monday, from Coventry to-day. We called upon Mr. Welch, of Mansfield, and found him not at home; and from thence went to Ashford, and dined there.

"*28th, Roxbury, Evening.*—From Thompson to-day; I am more unwell. Exceeding pain in my breast. Mr. Ely is very attentive and kind to me.

"*29th, Boston.*—We rode six miles this morning, and took breakfast here. After breakfast, rode out in a coach with several gentlemen—went to the court-house, and from thence to the meeting-house. I was introduced to several clergymen, and also to young gentlemen. I was invited to dine at Mr. T's., Boston. I went out to Roxbury last evening, and returned this morning. I dined at Mr. D's.; and this afternoon I went over to Charlestown, agreeably to the request of the Rev. Dr. Morse, and took tea with him. I was agreeably entertained while I stayed, looking over his books. I am somewhat better to-day. How thankful I ought to feel to the Divine Providence that I am no worse than I am. Praise ye the Lord, O, my soul. Since I have been in town, I have been invited into company of some of the most respectable families. I ought to be very humble, that so much notice is taken of me. I have visited all the ministers as I was invited, and they treated me with utmost respect, and gave me good advice.

"31*st*, *Boston*.—Rode out to-day to Cambridge to see the college, and took tea at Mr. Ps'. I am better, I trust the journey will do me good. Let me always remember that I am in the hands of God, and trust him at all times."

After visiting Roxbury and Providence they went to Newport, and here attended the Protestant Episcopal Church, and the Baptist meeting. The sermon preached at the latter is thus recorded :

"Mr. Emerson preached from Eccle. xi. 9. The preacher pointed out in the latter part of his discourse, that the thoughts of men, their actions and conduct, God will bring to light in the day of judgment. He admonished all to live in such a manner as that they may give a good account of their conduct in that day, when God shall bring every secret thing to light."

A few days after, occurs the following entry :—

"I had a bad turn to-day, bleeding at my breast, which I feel at this very moment. I am in the hands of a wise and holy God. Oh, must I die in my younger days? O, my God, cut me not off in the days of my youth, but spare me a little longer that I may do a little to thy honor and glory. It is a solemn thing to die."

But, travelling about in various places, his spirits soon revived; and in a day or two he writes :—

"I am much pleased with Mr. Smith; and my friend Storrs is very attentive to his lovely daughter. This place (Montauk) is most delightful, and I am entertained very agreeably, indeed."

Again:—

"There are several ladies going with us to-morrow to New London. *The ladies requested me to sing French tunes.*"

The italics are my own. They went out on a sailing excursion, and had a pleasant time; but the ladies were sea-sick, and called on him for help though he was very feeble. "The ladies were very thankful for my attention to them."

The journey was concluded on the 22d June, when he writes:—

"I have seen a great many things since we have been gone. How thankful I ought to be to Mr. Ely for his kind attention to me. Surely this is a very substantial evidence of his friendship."

But although he had derived much pleasure and temporary benefit from this ramble, his health still continued in a very feeble state, and the light of life seemed flickering in its socket. The physician advised him to try a journey to the bracing air of the north, and though this was much opposed by his friends, it was finally determined he should go. Before setting out, he "thought much about his eternal state," and prayed that God would make him wise in the things which belonged to his everlasting peace." Passing through Cambridge, Greenwich, Salem, and Albany, he came to Lake Champlain, with the scenery of which he expresses great delight:—"Lake Champlain is rolling under me. Here it is fifteen or twenty miles wide, lined with mountains on both sides of the shores, whose summits seem to touch the clouds. I thought much upon the works of creation. I said to myself, Great and marvellous are thy works, Lord God Almighty." Arriving at Montreal, he thus describes that city. "Montreal is pleasantly situated on the north side of the river St. Lawrence, the streets are wide and well paved, the houses generally built of stone, from two to three stories high. I went to the market this morning about sunrise. I found it quite full. The market itself is a curiosity."

There must have been something about him at this period of life remarkably attractive and captivating, for, it is easy to perceive, from the following brief and modest entries in his journal, that his presence in Montreal occasioned a general sensation in the highest circles, and called forth attentions not usually paid except to the most distinguished persons, and which in the case of one by reputation an Indian youth, could not possibly have been drawn out had there not been a personal fascination and superiority which cast in the shade all other considerations.

Thomas Williams, alias Tehorakwaneken, his reputed father, was a wandering Indian hunter, and Mary Ann Konwatewenteta, his reputed mother, a squaw in a blanket, not very distinguished personages in the eyes of the dignitaries and literati of Canada—but all this in his presence was forgotten as absolutely inexistant.

"*1st October*, *St. Louis.*—The Hon. Sir. J. Jarvis, secretary of state, came to see me this afternoon, and I had a very agreeable interview with him.

"*3d October.*—I rode out to-day to Chautagay, I spent my time very agreeably with several young French gentlemen and ladies—they were very polite indeed.

"*4th October.*—To-day, I visited Mr. Lorimier, the British agent of the Indian department.

"*5th October.*—To-day, I visited and dined with the Rev. Mr. Van Felson, Roman Catholic clergyman in this town. He treated me politely.

"*12th October.*—*To-day, I had the honor to be admitted as a member of the Historical Society.*

"*1st Nov.*—I have been to the Roman Catholic church to-day, the annual festival of the dead.

"*2d November.*—I have been to La Prairie to-day, and I attended the Mass. Rev. Mr. Boucher preached, a Roman Catholic clergyman. I think he is the most eloquent orator I ever heard in my life, and has the most graceful gestures. After meeting I went to Mr. Perault's, and dined there—and there I saw Mr. Thomas—to be remembered, &c., &c., &c. Yesterday several men came to see me, &c., &c.

"If I am honest I will speak the truth.

"*25th December*, *St. Louis.*—The commemoration of the birth of our blessed Lord.—I have just returned from church. The altar was dressed very fine. There were about 20 levites attended upon the High Priest."

ELEAZAR WILLIAMS.

*Fac-simile of Pencil Sketch by Fagnani, from Original Portrait, by J. Stewart of Hartford in 1806.*

G. P. PUTNAM & Co. N.Y.

No evidence, which it is possible to collect, at this distance of time, from others, can equal in life-like and vivid portraiture, the artless representation of himself which the poor youth here gives. I do not wish to anticipate, but in the strange commixture of argument and history I am writing, I wish to remind the reader that he has before him the Indian boy, who, according to a certain forged affidavit, was nine years of age in 1800, and who, on his return to Canada, was laid up at Caughnawaga with ulcers on his knees. Notwithstanding all this, he was certainly sufficiently active, had attained a surprising maturity of mind, and exhibited an acute perception of men and things, which would have done credit even to the best instructed lads.

No wonder he was looked upon in New England as a prodigy, and his cousin, Thomas, felt proud of his kinsman. He writes in the style of a young gentleman of finished education, on his travels —demeans himself with well-bred courtesy and affability—attracts the attention of distinguished foreigners, mingles with easy grace in the society of ladies, and is the hero of their girlish festivity—but, stranger than all, has the honors of a savan conferred upon him, and is elected member of a historical society. A happy compound, indeed, of "Indian shrewdness and Welch ardor." Providentially, a painting of him, at this period of life, has been preserved. It is the rude daubing of some New England genius, left to invent for himself an art, in which he had no models to guide him. The hair is a blotch, but the countenance is fair, with an expression of great sweetness and innocence, combined with thoughtful and almost Quaker gravity. It is one of those faces which indicate a nature to which integrity, honor, gentleness, and love, are almost a necessity, and where the seeds of divine grace fall upon a soil naturally prepared to receive them. Of all words in the world, shrewdness, is the most inapplicable to such a being. There is not the remotest sign of cunning on that countenance, but a bland sincerity which thinks and wishes nothing but good for all that breathes It strongly resembles, allowing for the necessary advance of age, the pictures of the Dauphin, and exhibits in the most marked manner the lineaments of the Bourbons. It is scarcely possible, but that the Romish priests and dignitaries with whom he was, at this period of life, so frequently in company, if they had the remotest intimation that the young Prince was among the Indians, must have detected the truth; and his journal exhibits traces of a mysterious character impressed upon his first intercourse with them.

The beginning of 1806 found him still in Canada, and the journal of that year opens, as usual, with religious meditation.

> "Oh, I wish I may live this year to the honor and glory of God. As I live may I live in the flesh by the faith of the Son of God; a faith which purifieth the heart, worketh by love, and produceth obedience. May I be humbled under a sense of my past vileness, and labor after that purity of heart and holiness of life without which no man can see and enjoy God. May I ever realize that here I have no continuing city and the vast importance of religion to render me useful and comfortable while I live and happy when I die."

He left Canada on the 23d January; but to the last was in the society of the British consul, surrounded by French ladies, and receiving calls from gentlemen of Montreal. He took under his charge in going to New England a boy named Rice, in order to put him to school. All this was five years from the time when he emerged from barbaric life.

There is nothing deserving notice in his journal for some time, though crowded with the details of daily life, attendance on missionary meetings, associations, and so forth. He was at this period studying under Dr. Welch, at Mansfield. In May, 1806, he accompanied a reputed relative, the Rev. Mr. Williams, to Boston, and was examined respecting his studies by several ministers. Mr. Ely, who was at that period in the legislature, joined them. It was at this time that the interview occurred between him and the Rev. Mr.—afterwards bishop—Chevreux. The only trace to be found of it upon the journal, which is here very brief and fragmentary, is the following entry :—

" *Boston, Saturday, June* 3.—This week I have been to several lectures.

"*Lord's Day*, 4. Blessed be God for another of his holy days. To-day, went in forenoon to Roman Church, and this afternoon over to Charlestown, with Dr. Morse. June 5. I have been to the Roman Church to-day with Mr. Ely.

" *Boston, 15th, Lord's Day.*—I have been here some time, but I have not kept particular account since I have been, and I have seen a great deal of wickedness."

It is unfortunate that he did not record the conversation with Chevreux, as he did so many things of less importance; but we cannot foresee what is to have a bearing on the future. The interview was brought about by an Irish Roman Catholic gentleman; and the ostensible cause of the somewhat mysterious visit of Ely, a rigid Puritan, to a Romish place of worship, was his passion for music. He was introduced, to Chevreux, as an Indian youth, studying for the ministry—and the priest immediately questioned him as to the practice of the Indians in adopting French children, and also whether he had ever heard of a boy being brought from France, and left among them. Chevreux could not fail to perceive that he was of French extraction, and, probably, from his marked lineaments, at once divined the secret, or may have known it before; and asked the question to ascertain whether he had himself any knowledge or suspicion on the subject.

I pass over pages crowded with religious reflections, prayers, confessions of sin, reports of sermons, ordinations, conferences, visits, journeys, and similar things incident to his character and position, till on the 14th May, 1807, we find him at Hartford, Massachusetts :—

" Here I was introduced to President Dwight. The good president took me on one side, and said that, he had been wanting to see me this long time, and had pleasure to see me now. He gave me very affecting advice. 'If you are to have happiness in this world,' he said, 'you must have religion. The happiness of the world consists in religion only; and from no other source can we hope to attain felicity, in another world.' He thus conversed with me an hour; at last, he took my hand and left me, saying, 'It is my most earnest prayer to Almighty God, that he will raise you up to be useful in the world, in the day of your generation. The blessing of the Lord be with you always.' I had the pleasure to see many other ministers, and their advice to me was too much. It overcame my mind, so that I was obliged to retire to my lodgings until meeting time, when my friend S. came to me and said, 'The president gave you good advice. I would give anything to be regarded and noticed by so many venerable men in New England.' I answered, 'This is my grief; I don't deserve any notice to be taken of me.'"

President Dwight, in his travels in New England and New York, alludes to this interview in a manner which claims attention in this place, as an additional confirmation of the difficulty which all observant persons had in reconciling the personal appearance of the youth with his imputed Indian parentage. After recounting the history of Eunice Williams, he continues:—

"One of her grandchildren"—[he should have placed the relationship a remove farther]—"has been educated at Long Meadow, in a respectable manner. I have seen this young man—he has a very good countenance, pleasing manners, a good understanding, and apparently an excellent disposition, with scarcely a trace of the Indian character. He is destined to the employ of a missionary."*

Until historical research and scientific examination proved the contrary, there was necessarily an acquiescence, not, however, without protest, in his extraction, as represented by his New England relatives, but accompanied with curiosity, affectionate interest, and a feeling that there was something behind which required explanation.

On 27th May, 1807, an entry occurs which shows the soundness of his mind, rising, by the force of its own constitution, above the

* Dwight's Travels, vol. ii. p. 69.

narrowness of the theological system, in the midst of which circumstances placed him:—

"Dr. Williams and I had an agreeable conversation upon different subjects, and we disagree in some particular points of Christian doctrine—such as total moral depravity, election, redemption through Christ, effectual calling, adoption, justification through the righteousness of Christ, and the saints' perseverance. The Protestant divines, in my opinion, go too far in some particular points. I wish the doctrine of the great Captain of salvation could be preached in its purity."

As all the mental phenomena exhibited by Mr. Wliliams, in early life, are deserving of close and attentive study, since they must either confirm or militate with the theory of his origin here maintained, I would call the attention of the reader to the action of his mind upon religious subjects. Taken at the age of fourteen or fifteen from the bosom of Indian barbarism, and a religious atmosphere, impregnated with the most ignorant superstitions and slavish subserviency to Rome, in which, had he lived all his life in the enjoyment of his senses, he must by that time have become, like Eunice Williams, who did not go among the Indians and Jesuits until she was seven years of age, a bigoted devotee to the system. But he comes to New England in the strange condition of a youth with his mental faculties in the fullest and most vigorous activity, as if they had previously been matured, by almost excessive culture, and yet absolutely without any prepossession whatever, either for Indian life or Romish superstition, and cleaving to the past by no links but those of the social affections. He falls at once, into the kindly moral spirit of New Englandism, and twines his heart-strings around its altars; but his intellect acts independently, and refuses to adopt the peculiar theological tenets of those whom he loves and honors. The phenomenon here exhibited, is that of a mind with its powers cultivated, and yet destitute of prepossession in favor of any particular system. Whence could he obtain his early maturity of judgment? and how are we to account for the absence of any leaning towards Romanism?

The journals afford so many indications of the nature of the man, that the reader will not blame me for presenting him as I proceed, with more copious extracts, than I have yet done. In Nov., 1807, Eleazar set out on another journey for the benefit of his health. He arrived at Hanover, and formed an acquaintance with the President of the College, and other gentlemen. "Hanover," he says, "is a fine place. The College and other public buildings are elegant. The village contains many handsome houses, surrounding a spacious plain which, in summer, is always covered with verdure, the whole appearance is charming, and the inhabitants are noted for their hospitality and polite attention to strangers. I was introduced to Rev. Dr. Smith, Professor of the learned languages. I was agreeably entertained with several of the students. I have experienced that there are many temptations to which a young man is exposed, but if he is inclined to sustain a good character, he must associate only with those who are virtuous. The young gentlemen appear to be scholars, but I perceive that there is something wanting in them to make them complete gentlemen. Modesty is the ornament of a person."

In May, 1808, a friend named Dr. Lyman urged Eleazar to go as a missionary to the heathen. He writes, "It is certainly an encouragement to me to go as a missionary when I hear that young nobles and others in England are promoting the cause of the Blessed Redeemer. I feel perfectly willing to go and suffer for the sake of advancing the glorious Gospel of Christ. God is doing wonders in the world. I pray God to make me an instrument for promoting His own cause."

In the month of June he became indisposed, with severe pain in the head, and a renewal of his old disorder, which appears to have been excruciating, and called forth earnest prayers for patience and fortitude.

In the midst of these bodily sufferings he received the sad intelligence from Mrs. Ely, of the death of her husband. "The intelligence," he writes, "was overwhelming to me. Yes, my soul was troubled, and with a throbbing heart, I exclaimed, 'O let me die the death of the righteous, and let my last end be like his.' Although my lamentations were in secret, yet the Lord, my heavenly Father, heard my cry. The spirit of resignation was given me, and I was enabled to say amen to what God had done."

The loss of Mr. Ely, his first friend and benefactor, who had been the Providential instrument of withdrawing him from the sepulchre of barbarism, in which he would otherwise have been entombed, brought to a close the first scene of his life in civivilized society in America. But he had now made friends for himself on all sides, and was known far and near as a young man of mark and promise, and yet around whom hung a mystery which no one was competent to solve. Who was he, this Indian youth, who yet was not an Indian?

Of the current views of the most distinguished New England Society on the subject of his race, Mr. Theodore Dwight has furnished me with a conclusive proof in the fact, that about this time he became attached to a connection of his family, and although the match was not effected, it was neither for want of esteem and admiration of his character, nor any objections on the score of Indian blood, because neither the lady herself, nor any other persons of discernment regarded him in reality as the descendant of Eunice Williams, though, by the necessity of the case, he nominally passed as such.

Eleazar remained at Mansfield and Long Meadows, making occasional visits to other places, until Dec. 22, 1809, when he was put under the tuition of Rev. Enoch Hale, of West Hampton, Massachusetts, with whom he continued till the month of August, 1812, though during a great portion of the time he was absent on journeys to various places, which are minutely recorded in his journal, and was also engaged, under the patronage of the American Board of Missions in a missionary visit to the St. Louis or Caughnawaga Indians, to ascertain what prospect there was of introducing Protestantism among them. It is impossible to peruse the earnest and simple outpouring of his feelings in his journals, without perceiving the entire devotion and dedication of his soul, mind, and powers to the work of converting his Indian brethren. His residence among Europeans, his instinctive delight in the refinements of social intercourse, the attentions shown him by all classes of persons, had not, for one moment, diverted his mind from the great purpose for which he conceived himself created—that of carrying the Gospel to the heathen. But his health continued very feeble, and severe pains in the head and chest rendered it difficult for him to continue his studies uninterruptedly. At times he seems almost to have despaired of life, but the activity of his mind and body, rising superior to indisposition, soon dissipated the gloom. His friends and physician advised him in April, 1810, to give up study, for a time, and travel southward, which, after some delay, he did. It was on this occasion that he first became acquainted with his future friend and Bishop, Dr. Hobart, who even at that early day was attracted by him and showed him much attention.

On his return to Massachusetts, his pains returned, and every few pages some record of his sufferings occurs. In the beginning of 1811, it was again thought expedient for him to travel, and he went to Canada, to see his family, taking every occasion of conversing with the Indians upon religious subjects. The Romish priests warned their people against listening to him, but the attention paid to him encouraged him to enter on what he designed should be the work of his life.

## CHAPTER XI.

### THE SECRET CORPS.

THERE are few who do not find actual life unlike as possible their youthful imaginings. Some happy beings, though the number is daily lessening, become what they purposed, and resemble forest trees, whose roots cleave in age to the soil which nourished their first fibres. But most of us seem the sport of circumstances, and, in the struggle of life, are bruised, battered, and misshapen, till we emerge something, we can only recognise by faith in continuity of remembrance.

> "There's a destiny that shapes our ends,
> Rough-hew them how we will."

In the beginning of 1812, Mr. Williams set out on another journey to Canada, but this time as agent of the American Board of Missions. His health did not permit prolonged application to study, and, as it was deemed necessary he should survey his proposed field of missionary labor, and, by mixing with the Indians, perfect himself in the use of their language, he interrupted his literary preparation for the Congregational ministry, in order both to recruit his strength, and probe the sentiments of his reputed countrymen. He arrived at the Sault St. Louis, near Montreal, on Saturday, January 18th, and set to work zealously to accomplish his design, visiting the Indians all along the northern frontier, and discoursing wherever he went of "death, judgment, and eternity." But, for the most part, those he addressed, "acted as if they were possessed by the evil one." Addicted to intemperance, lax in their morals, devotees to heathenism, or equally blind adherents to Rome, he found it, to the last degree, difficult to produce any effect on them. His feeble condition and shortness of breath were also very discouraging. He continued, however, his missionary tour until March, 1812, when he received a token that, although his religious exhortations might produce little result, he had personally acquired the esteem and confidence of the Indians. A message was sent him from the chiefs and counsellors of the Iroquois, requesting his attendance, and on presenting himself at the council house, he was declared a chief of the nation. The name given him was, Onwarenhiiaki, or Tree Cutter, the same which had been applied to Sir William Johnson. A complimentary speech was addressed to him on the occasion, to which he replied in nearly the following terms:—

"Most honorable chiefs and counsellors of the Iroquois nation, I rise to speak a few words to your ears. I give you, with peculiar pleasure, many thanks. Your choice is very honorable to me. I am unfit for so high station in the nation. But as I desire to render important circumstances, I accept with diffidence the seat, which the chiefs and counsellors have pointed out to me, and shall ever endeavor to promote the best interests of the nation. May unity and harmony ever prevail between me and the senior counsellors, and may the chiefs and counsellors of the Iroquois nation, be ever interested in its welfare, and the people ever respect and be guided by them."

When he ceased speaking, they thronged round and congratulated him, and he took advantage of the occasion, "to press upon them with tenderness the things which belonged to their eternal peace." They listened with courtesy and parted with expressions of regret.

But, though there was much to encourage him, he found it impossible to accomplish anything at that time. "When you talk on political matters," said a chief, "you talk like a wise Indian counsellor—but, when you converse about religion, then you talk like a Frenchman." "How deplorable," he writes, "is the situation of the Indians. When I consider that they are ignorant of the character and perfections of that Being who made them, and the way of salvation by Jesus Christ, then I am almost overwhelmed with grief and sorrow. O Lord, I beseech thee to send thy light and thy truth among the Ancients of America, and make them know thee, the only true God, and Jesus Christ whom thou has sent."

Such were his occupations, feelings, and aspirations, when the war broke out between England and the United States. He had returned to West Hampton, when, in July, his reputation for ability, and for influence among the Indians, known in the highest quarters, caused his immediate selection by government, as the best person, to prevent his reputed countrymen from taking up arms against the United States. The peaceful and devotional tenor of his thoughts and hopes was, therefore, broken in upon by the request that, he would repair immediately to the head-quarters of General Dearborn, and receive instructions concerning the views and objects of the General Government. Thomas Williams was at the same time invited to enter into the service of the United States—which invitation he finally accepted. The St. Regis Indians, who occupied so critical a position between the two belligerent powers, and were undecided what course it was best for their interest and safety to pursue, also applied to Eleazar for advice in the emergency, and, thus, a variety of influences forced him, at a moment's warning, to abandon the peaceful seclusion of the parsonage, at West Hampton, for the hot haste of military life.

"I am sent for," he writes, under the date of July 27, "to prevent the Indians from taking the hatchet against the Americans. I tremble, my situation is very critical. Indeed, I hope God will direct me what to do." It was with great unwillingness that he entered on his new avocations. The prudential committee of the American Board of Foreign Missions, shortly after, spoke thus concerning him, and his late missionary tour.

"Mr. Eleazar Williams, the Indian youth proposed for an Indian mission, and who is in a course of education for that purpose, made a visit during last winter to his tribe, a journal of which has been seen by the committee. It is an excellent journal, affords great evidence of the piety and good sense of Mr. Williams, details some facts highly favorable to his reception among his red brethren, when the time shall come for him to be sent to them. When that time will come, is known only to Him who has all events under his sovereign direction. At present, the prospects regarding the contemplated mission to the Caughnawaga Indians are darkened by the war, but this darkness may be dissipated, and brighter scenes open than man can foresee."

All immediate prospect of prosecuting his mission, being thus cut off, and duty calling him to the scene of war, he set out for Greenbush, where General Dearborn was then encamped, and arrived there on the 8th August. But, before plunging into the exciting scenes that followed, the reader will, I am sure, read with pleasure the following reflections of Mr. Williams on war, which I found among his papers, and which exhibit an amplitude of mind which has not been attributed to him, and show how little we can judge of the character and powers of men, when we see them only in obscurity and depression:—

"Many of the citizens in this state were opposed to the war. When in their company, the expediency or propriety of the war was often brought into view. It has been contended that, the more any people are civilized and Christianized, the greater is their aversion to war; and the more powerful exertions are necessary to excite what is called the war-spirit. Were it not for the influence of a few ambitious or revengeful men, an offensive war could not be undertaken with any prospect of success—except where the mass of the people are either uncivilized or slaves. If, then, as great exertions should be made to excite a just abhorrence of war, as have often been made to excite a war-spirit, we may be very certain that rulers would find little encouragement to engage in a war, which is not strictly defensive. And, as soon as offensive wars shall cease, defensive wars will be, of course, unknown. It is an affront to common sense to pretend that, military officers and soldiers have no right to inquire whether war be just or unjust; and that all they have to do is to obey the orders of the government. Such doctrine is fit only to be taught to slaves without souls. If a man is called to fight, he should be faithfully informed and fully satisfied that he is not to act the part of a murderer, that the blood of man may not be required at his hands. Every soldier ought to be impressed with the idea that offensive war is murderous; and that no government on earth has any right to compel him to shed blood in a wanton and aggressive war. Yet, in the present state of general delusion, the soldiers and most of the citizens are treated as having no more right to judge of the justice or injustice of a war, than the horses employed in military service. On one side, a war is certainly unjust and murderous. Yet, on both sides, it is considered the duty of soldiers to submit to the orders of government, and fight, whether it be murder or not murder. With the same propriety it might be considered as the duty of a citizen, to obey an order of government for murdering an individual of his own nation."

Let the mind that conceived such sentiments have been on a throne, and he would have been accounted a model of political liberality. And yet this man has been the mark of obloquy and scorn, maligned, abused, ridiculed, defamed, driven from one place to another, cheated, reduced to poverty, and, because poor, scarcely deemed worthy, by his own brethren in the church, who had not discernment to understand his character, of common civility.

On his arrival at the camp, Mr. Williams was treated courteously by General Dearborn, and remained two days closeted in his cabinet, with him and Gov. Tompkins, to learn what was required, and express his views as to the best method of carrying the objects into effect. Notwithstanding the religious tone of his mind, and his devotion to the ministry, there was something in his nature which was stirred by the pomp and circumstance of war, and he was made captive, as he expresses it, by "plumes, epaulettes, red sashes, and glittering arms." In an instant he was in the vortex, and, with a facility which belongs to some natures, of adapting themselves to all circumstances, hasted to the north, to accomplish a mission very different from that which had so recently carried him there. With the excitement of his new employment, his health revived, and we hear little more of indisposition, except a great weakness in the eyes, and occasional headaches after fatigue. At first, he had no idea of permanently entering the service of the government; but, being entrusted with military powers, and brought under military law, he was forced by circumstances to continue in the path which had thus, fortuitously opened before him, and was appointed Superintendent-General of the Northern Indian Department, with the most ample powers, having under his command the whole secret corps of Rangers and scouts of the army, who spread themselves everywhere, and freely entered in and out of the enemy's camp. There was an understanding that all communications between him and the government should be entirely secret, lest the lives or interests of individuals should be compromised. But, as there was no prohibition against keeping a journal, a thing which, probably, did not enter into the ideas of General Dearborn, or the War Department, he faithfully chronicled all his movements, though often without mentioning the special object he had in view. The body of men who were placed at his command, were the most reckless, daring, and unscrupulous in the army, and he frequently speaks of it as "the terrible corps," and trembles at the accountability he assumed in placing himself at their head. Spread out in every direction, they reported to him every movement of the British forces, and the manœuvres of the American army were, in a great measure, governed by the information received from him, as to the necessity of despatching troops to particular positions. He was thus the instrument of defeating the English, both by land and water, in the north and west.

Parting from General Dearborn, who gave him letters to Colonel Clarke, of Burlington, and Major-General Mooers, of Plattsburg, he crossed the river about four o'clock, on Thursday, August 6, and, the next morning, set out for Vermont. At Poultney he met a British officer, General Baynes, with a flag of truce, accompanied by Major Clark, of the militia. On Sunday evening, August 9, he reached Burlington, and had an interview with Colonel Clarke, who kept him concealed, and, the following morning, crossed the lake with him. On Monday evening they arrived at Plattsburg. The necessities of war not permitting the strict observance of the Lord's Day, almost every week brings its confession of sin, and prayers that God would pardon the enforced violation of his law. He delivered his letter to Major-General Mooers; and, in the afternoon of the 11th, a council of war was held, consisting of the General, Colonel Clarke, Lieut.-Colonel Bedell, and Major Warford, at which, according to his discretional powers, he made a partial disclosure of the objects of his mission. General Mooers despatched him on his journey, with the following letter to Captain Tilden, o Constable:—

"PLATTSBURG, *August* 12, 1812.

"SIR:

"You are hereby requested to render any assistance in your power to the bearer hereof—Mr. E. W., by giving him information relative to the situation of the enemy, Indian tribes, &c., &c., and keep the same to yourself relative to Mr. W., &c. What passes between you and him, let it be kept in perfect secresy. Mr. W. will keep this if he thinks proper. He will show it you.

"BENJAMIN MOOERS, Major-General.

"Captain Rufus Tilden."

He was also provided with the following passport:—

"PLATTSBURG, *August* 12, 1812.

"The bearer hereof, Mr. E. Williams, is on business, and is going into Franklin County. Being a stranger he might be interrupted, and I have, therefore, handed this for his protection.

"BENJAMIN MOOERS."

It was raining hard, and the roads were horrible, but he continued on his journey, when, at an inn in the Chautegay Wood, he met Colonel Lewis, who was in the secret of his mission; and, after consultation with him, found it necessary to return to Plattsburg, to meet some Indian chiefs who were expected there to receive money. He found them friendly to the United States, and obtained much information as to the condition of things at the north. The officers paid great attention, from policy, to the Indians. He then returned to Albany, which he reached on the 24th, and sat up with General Dearborn all night, communicating intelligence and arranging plans for the future. The excitement over, he fell sick, and all the conscientious scruples, natural to one with his feelings and position, began to torment him. "Oh, that God," he writes, "would make all men peaceful, and live together in unity. I am in distress for my sins—they are great. Oh, most gracious God, for Christ's sake, pardon them, and assist me to manage the affairs I am upon with integrity."

After forming acquaintance with General Bloomfield, he again set out for the north, on the 1st September, from Whitehall, in a little sloop, and a storm coming on, was in great danger on the lake. He reached Plattsburg on the 8th—the next day, General Bloomfield arrived, and was saluted by the gun-boats; and, in the evening, Mr. Williams laid before him the reports of the Rangers, and had a long conference with him, "in relation to the Indians, the force of the enemy, the state of his defences, the movements of his troops, the strength of his navy, and the condition of the roads from Champlain to the La Acadia plains."

The next day he set out from Plattsburg, with protection from General Mooers, addressed to Major Young, in the following terms:—

"PLATTSBURG, *September* 9, 1812.

"SIR:

"The bearer, Mr. Williams, proceeds to your post and to the westward, on business of an important nature, which entirely meets the approbation of General Mooers; you will, therefore, afford him the protection necessary and proper to facilitate his purpose.

"By order of the general,

"JOHN WARFORD, Aide-de-camp.

"Major Young."

Having delivered this letter to the Major at Chautegay, he proceeded with a corresponding passport from him to Turner's Inn, where he met Captain Tilden, the commander of the station. He was carefully concealed from the sight of the Indians, but at French Mills, had a secret conference with the chiefs, whom he harangued, distributed to them money, and obtained the promise of adherence to the American cause.

Returning through the woods, to Plattsburg, on the 16th, he dispatched a confidential messenger to the Sault St. Louis, and though now irretrievably engaged in the business of the war, was troubled with conscientious scruples as to the morality of attempting to withdraw the British Indians from allegiance to their government. He had a conference with Gen. Bloomfield on this question, and says with great simplicity, "we agreed that if we can bring them over to the American side, it was proper and justifiable." Every day and hour brought its occupation, and he was hurried hither and thither. On the 21st September, he received a communication from the Commander-in-chief, to which he sent a reply express, by way of Lake George, and immediately set out to the lines, to meet his Rangers and receive their report. Hearing of the capture of seven Indians by the British, he was fearful lest his messenger, William, whom he had dispatched to St. Louis, was among them, and set out on Sunday, 27th, to Chazy, to ascertain the fact, but had the happiness to find him returned in safety, and spent the remainder of the day in conversing with him and some Indians on religious subjects. Several chiefs now arrived from the Sault St. Louis, and on Monday were presented to Gen. Bloomfield, to whom the General and Col. Clarke presented their swords. Col. Clarke also gave his rifle to William the messenger, who Mr. Williams despatched to St. Regis, and to the Indians of the Lake of the two mountains, to inform them that powder was ready for them. He now returned to Albany, carrying two chiefs with him to present to General Dearborn, who was highly delighted with the success of the enterprise. A brilliant entertainment was given, but in the midst of officers and ladies, and music and general merriment, young Williams—the excitement of enterprise being now over—was moody and melancholy, between the effects of sickness and conscientious difficulties. But not much time could be given to reflections of this kind. The next day after the entertainment, Oct. 8th, the following entry occurs:—

"As the enemy have had in contemplation for some time past to send troops to St. Regis, to attack the Indians, and Captain Montigny, the resident agent has made great efforts to rouse the war spirit of the friendly part of the tribe against the Americans, from self-preservation—which is the first law of human nature—that post must be attacked. I have received orders to this effect from the Commander-in-chief, but am left in a great measure to my discretion, and the necessity for such an attack. The order is issued upon Major Youngs, at Chautegay, to march with his corps, attack and carry the place, but have a care not to injure the friendly part of the tribe. The Rangers are required to give a faithful account to the Major, of the strength and position of the enemy. If the Major is true, he will succeed. Bravery is not wanting to him."

The attack proved successful. St. Regis was carried—a number of prisoners captured, and the first flag taken from the British during the war. Mr. Williams again set out from Albany, on the 14th October. From Plattsburg, which he reached after a variety of adventures, on 3d November, he went to Cumberland's Head, to issue orders to the Rangers, and on the 5th, by the invitation of Gen. Bloomfield, attended a secret council of war, at which he presented his report, which he had written while lying in bed. The result of the council was an order to prepare for the winter campaign, and repair the boats and wagons for transportation. On 7th November, he received an order from the Commander-in-chief, to return to Albany, but, before starting, was able to communicate to Gen. Bloomfield intelligence that the enemy were preparing for an attack. The first artillery train arrived. In the evening, Gens. Bloomfield and Mooers discussed with him the plans of the ensuing campaign; he sent out orders in different directions to the Rangers, and information to the Indians, and the next morning was on his way to Albany, express, issuing orders as he went, to some of the posts. In the afternoon he heard a heavy cannonading in the direction of the lines. Arriving at Albany on the 10th, he dined with the Commander-in-chief, received from the war department a complimentary communication, concerning the efficient services of his corps, and further instructions in relation to his department. He left for the north the next day, but snatched a few moments to have a conversation with the Rev. Mr. Clowes, an Episcopal clergyman, at Albany, and obtain some religious advice. The troops were now moving in all directions for the lines—for which he himself set out post, issuing orders to the whole corps of observation. He returned from the lines to Plattsburg, on the evening of the 18th November, having performed all the duties assigned him, and sent his report to the Commander-in-chief.

Under date of November 20, he writes:—

"A council of war was held to-day, in which I appeared somewhat conspicuous, as I was the only person who could give the information desired. In this council disclosures were made, to a certain extent in relation to the campaign, which were entirely contrary to my expectations, and far from being honorable to the public service. Still there is hope for a revision of the decision of this council, and this must be upon certain circumstances in regard to the enemy, but in the meantime, every demonstration must be made by the American army of its intended invasion of the British Province. By the reports of the Rangers, the enemy is not so formidable in our front as to give any fears of the unfavorable result if our advance was made upon them. The Canadians are still unwilling to bear arms against the Americans, since they had a skirmish with the royal troops at La Chine, in August last. They are forced into the service, and no dependence can be placed upon them."

The season was too far advanced for much to be accomplished. The corps of observation, under command of Mr. Williams, was, however, incessantly active, and the slightest movement on either side faithfully reported to him, and provision made for every emergency as it arose. At the latter end of November the artillery train moved towards Plattsburg for winter-quarters, and the campaign being over, he returned to Charlotte in Vermont. The troops were dying in great numbers. "I had an interview," thus the journal for 1812 concludes, "this afternoon (Dec. 12) with Gen. Mooers, and made arrangements with him in regard to the movements of the Rangers. I have apprised them of my removal, with orders to direct their reports accordingly. One is with me now and takes my orders, and will issue them to others. God bless them."

## CHAPTER XII.

### THE WAR JOURNAL.

WITH the intuition pertaining only to the highest order of minds, the divinity student had displayed the abilities of a military officer, been admitted to the secret councils of those highest in command, and honorably and successfully performed some of the most arduous duties which could be assigned to man—duties which a Christian nation at war could only, with a just regard for its own honor, consign to one who united rare ability with strict fidelity and unassailable conscientiousness. But though he had thus proved himself, intellectually, equal to any position in which Providence might place him, and been engaged in occupations the hardest to reconcile with devotional feeling, his humble and unfeigned spirit of piety was unaltered.

The Journal for 1813 opens thus :—

"*Jan'y* 1.—A pleasant morning. I am permitted to see the beginning of another year. What shall I render unto the Lord for all his benefits? May I live more to His glory. How ungrateful I have been for the many and undeserved mercies I have received from his benificent hand. I will endeavor, by the help of God, to live more like a Christian. O my God, give me grace to love thee above all things, to live and walk in the ways of thy commandments, and preserve me from all the temptations with which I am surrounded. This has been a solemn day with me. My meditations have been upon death, judgment, and eternity."

My intention was to have epitomized the following journal. But it is sacred as an historical document, and though very long, I transcribe it entire, since nothing can more thoroughly exhibit the man, and show the claims he has on the esteem of all men, and especially of the citizens of the United States, than the simple pages in which he has jotted down, with careless hand, his actions and feelings during these trying times.

"I am ordered by Col. Larned to repair to St. Regis. I am preparing for the jaunt.

"*In Chautegay Woods*, *Jan'y* 2.—Left Plattsburg this morning early, in a sleigh. My waiter with me. Now, at Robert's Inn. It has been a cold day. Here I learned the movements of the enemy, at St. Johns and Chamblee. I have sent an express to Plattsburg.

"*French Mills*, *Jany*. 3, 1813.—Arrived about 10 o'clock, this evening—suffered much from the cold. I have sent out two faithful Indians who I found here. Yesterday, a heavy detachment of the enemy passed through Cornwall, for the Upper Country. I met here one of our secret Rangers. His report will be useful for the commanders of Sacketts Harbour and Plattsburg.

"*French Mills*, *Jany*. 4, 1813.—I met in council, four of the American chiefs. They are still firm to remain neutral in the present contest. Capt. Peters delivered a lengthy speech, on the occasion, the substance of which is intended to be communicated to Major-General Dearborn, Gov. Tompkins, and Gen. Mooers. I exhorted them to remain firm to their resolution, and continue to be faithful to the Americans. We parted with many friendly expressions. May God bless them, is the sincere desire of my heart. I made some arrangements with the Commissary Hastings, to continue to issue rations to them.

"*Evening*.—I am informed that the enemy are making a great preparation at Kingston, to attack Sacketts Harbour. I shall hear more of this.

"*Chautegay*, 4 *Corners*, *Jany*. 5, 1813.—From the French Mills, this morning. I am greatly concerned for the St. Regis Indians. The British governor threatens to annihilate them, but the American part are determined to resist him. Sir John Johnson is active in persuading them to join the English forces. Col. Scott, the commandant at Couteau du Lac, has issued an order for my arrest, if possible. I have, this evening, issued an order to the whole secret corps of our Rangers—and that in positive terms, in case of my arrest by the enemy, to take and make prisoners of as many as it may be in their power, of the high officers of the British army, and even Sir Geo. Provost. The faithful and brave H., captain of the corps, accepted the order with joy, and promised it shall be performed to the full extent. 'Now,' said he, 'life and death are with us.' This is the first desperate order I have issued to the corps, but there is no alternative in the case.

"*Plattsburg*, *Jany.* 6, 1813.—Left Chautegay early this morning, but not without fears that I may be waylaid and caught in some extensive woods I had to pass. I apprised my waiter of this, who, like a brave soldier, prepared his rifle for resistance, but reached safe, and suffered no inconvenience but the cold. The sun was bright, the sky clear, but the air piercing. I have a heavy cough upon me, and am somewhat feverish this evening. At Robinson's Inn, I was informed by a person who came, yesterday, from the lines, that the enemy were reinforcing the garrison at *Isle Aux Noix*, and a party of Indians were stationed at La Cole.

"*Plattsburg*, *Jany.* 7, 1813.—I sent my report to Col. Larned, this morning, at Burlington, as I am not able to go myself thither, being much indisposed. The garrison physician is in attendance.

"*Evening.*—Gen. Mooers called upon me, and I communicated to him the substance of my report to Col. Larned. Rev. Mr. Weeks also called, with whom I had an interesting conversation upon the subject of religion. He is a pious and godly man. My religious meditations have been greatly interrupted from the many duties which are just now pressing upon me. Oh, let me not forget my duty to God, but may I walk more closly with him, and that daily, as one who loves him with all the heart. Let me not forget thee, O my God, in whom I live, move, and have my being. O Heavenly Father, have mercy on thy unworthy servant, forgive all his sins for Christ's sake. Give him grace to love thee more—make him by faith to be united to thee, and enable him by grace to walk in the ways of thy commandments.

"*January* 10, *Plattsburg*, 1813.—It is to be regretted that the northern army is in a sick condition—ten or twelve men are daily buried. Dysentery and diarrhœa are the principal diseases, which are often combined with typhus fever. Colonel Pike, who commands this post, is doing all in his power to assuage the sufferings of his troops, by making the medical department do its duty—the noted Dr. Mann being at its head.

"*Plattsburg*, *January* 29.—The order issued on the 4th instant by me, at Chautegay, upon the whole corps of Rangers, I am happy to say has been responded to with the greatest cheerfulness; and they will exert themselves to the utmost, to fulfil the import of the order. B. H. and L. have engaged to take the Governor-General a prisoner, and bring him safely into the United States.

"*February* 3, 1813.—Information has been received that the enemy has been concentrating his disposable force at Kingston, Upper Canada, distant thirty miles from Sacketts Harbor, with a view to attack that place, upon which I ordered the Rangers to be on the alert. For further information, one was despatched for that place. Three days after, another was despatched to Ganonnaque.

"*Burlington (Vt.)*, *February* 10, 1813.—I came here to have an interview with Brigadier-General Chandler, and communicated to him a certain intelligence, which caused him to delay his former intentions in regard to his military operations in this quarter. Here I received further information from the Rangers, that the enemy were sending troops to Kingston, and that some troops have been sent from Quebec to Montreal, and more are expected.

"*Plattsburg*, *February* 17.—I am fully persuaded, by the information of the Rangers, near Montreal, that the enemy is contemplating to attack Sacketts Harbor. I shall, at all events, apprise General Dearborn this day.

"*Plattsburg*, *February*, 1813.—We are informed that Major Forsythe, from Ogdensburg, crossed the St. Lawrence, and surprised the guard at Elizabethtown; took fifty-two prisoners, one major, three captains, and two lieutenants.

"*Plattsburg*, *February* 20.—The preparation of the enemy, at Kingston, is very certain. The Rangers have returned. Their reports are corroborated from other respectable sources. My duty requires me to make a formal communication to Major-General Dearborn, at Albany, who will, I trust, duly appreciate the alarming intelligence. I have also ventured to apprize the commanding officer at Sacketts Harbor, of the intentions of the enemy upon that post.

"*Plattsburg*, *March* 6, 1813.—We are informed that, on the 21st ultimo, the enemy attacked Major Forsythe, at Ogdensburg, and succeeded in expelling him from the town, after a short conflict.

"*Plattsburg*, *March* 9, 1813.—General Dearborn has duly appreciated the intelligence conveyed to him, in relation to the enemy's movements and intentions on the port of Sacketts Harbor. He will make, or has already made, a quick movement for that post.

Both sides appear to be preparing for some heavy stroke upon each other, in the ensuing campaign.

"*Plattsburg*, 14*th March.*—I am informed it is in contemplation for Colonel Pike's regiment to repair to Sacketts Harbor, without delay.

"*Evening.*—The colonel has called on me for information of the route he intends to take on his way to the Harbor. I am ordered, immediately, to repair to Malone, and French Mills. So I will proceed to-morrow morning; my waiter will accompany me.

"*Chautegay, Four Corners, March* 15.—French news from Canada by one of the Rangers. Sent on an express to Colonel Pike, at eleven o'clock, with intelligence I have received.

"*French Mills, March* 17.—Heard much of the movements of the enemy. Saw the Indian chiefs. Their future conduct was explained to them.

"*Plattsburg, March* 19.—I made my report to Colonel Pike. He appeared to be satisfied. He has himself received his instructions to proceed with his regiment to Sacketts Harbor. I am informed that General Dearborn has gone thither.

"I had a long conversation this evening with one of the officers of artillery upon religion, who is to all appearance an infidel.

"*Plattsburg, March* 27.—Colonel Pike has gone with his regiment, by way of Malone. I regret much that this amiable and accomplished officer is taken from this post. His whole regiment were conveyed in sleighs. The inhabitants were pressed for their teams. It was a strange sight to see so many of them together.

"*Plattsburg, March* 30, 1813.—By the Rangers I have heard that since the arrival of General Dearborn, at the Harbor, and the movement of Colonel Pike, the enemy themselves are alarmed lest they be invaded by the American force.

"*Burlington (Vt.), April* 4, 1813.—I came here to confer with Colonel Clarke, who commands this post, about some money concerns. The Deputy-Paymaster, Mr. Hatch and Mr. Sheldon, are concerned in the matter. The expenditures in my department are rendered and settled. The secret service-money of the government is wholly expended. Orders are made out, to the quarter-master-general, for more.

"I had a pleasant interview with the Rev. Mr. Haskell, of this place, who, with President Sanders, has directed my theological studies. I have read Stackhouse's Body of Divinity—Hopkin's

System—Edward's on Redemption, and other theological works which they have placed before me. I have read much for this two years past. The Rev. Mr. Weeks, of Plattsburg, has assisted me in obtaining books, &c. Indeed, all the Congregationalist clergy in this quarter seemed to be interested in my welfare.

"*Charlotte* (*Vt.*), *April* 12.—At the hotel of Colonel Williams, I have made my head-quarters. It is my home. I have a retired room, where I have spent many pleasant hours in reading the Scriptures, and meditations upon that sacred volume. Prayer and praise have been offered to my Creator and bountiful benefactor. O, thanks be to God for those happy hours I have enjoyed in communion with him. At the same time, many unhappy hours have I passed, because my sins were set before me. I saw that I was a sinner. I was made to see and feel that unless my heart was sanctified by the Spirit of God, I was none of his. But, by prayer and supplication, I was made joyful in the Lord.

"*Charlotte*, *April* 13, 1813.—My mind has been in a very comfortable state since my return to my solitary room—here I would wish to be in communion with my God.

"The two great contending parties appear to be, for the present, in a tranquil state; preparing, however, for a severe and bloody conflict. O, that God would be pleased to put an end to all wars, and advance the spiritual kingdom of Christ upon earth.

"I am again called on by the war department to perform certain duties which are delicate and dangerous in the extreme. I have issued my orders to the whole corps of Rangers, to be in readiness to perform the duties assigned to each of them. This is a terrible and efficient corps in the service of the government. No movement is made by the enemy but it is known to them. They are constantly, as it were, within the enemy's camp, or on every side of them. This corps was embodied by Col. Isaac Clark, of 11th Regt., in connection with the secretary of war. As to my position with them, my order is final. No appeal can be made from it. They are constantly exposed to martial-law and to death. Their courage, bravery, and fidelity save them, the war department often applauds their daring conduct, and rewards their services with high wages. They are faithful to the government. My orders they are always ready to obey, at which I have often been surprised. When I am absent from the department, Major-Gen.

Mooers takes my place. He was an officer during the Revolution, under his uncle, Col. Hazen.

"*Plattsburg*, *April* 16.—By the request of the deputy quarter-master, I am, to-morrow, to proceed to Albany.

"*Albany*, *April* 19.—I had an interview with Governor Tompkins, who laid a certain communication before me from the war department, to which I answered, with the assistance of Mr. Vanderhayden. It is secret and confidential in its nature.

"*Albany*, *April* 20.—To-day, again, I had a long conference with the governor, who committed to writing much of my communication, and was highly pleased with my management of certain manœuvres of the enemy. The quarter-master-general has once more replenished the secret service money. I am to return to-morrow. I called upon the Rev. Mr. Clowes, and had an agreeable interview with him. He presented me some books.

"*Poultney*, *April* 21.—I came to Troy yesterday afternoon, and called upon the Rev. Mr. Butler, an Episcopal clergyman, who labored with me to study the claims of the Episcopal church. It was wholesome advice. I shall attend to his directions.

"*Middleburg*, *April* 22.—I was visited by several officers, and spent the evening pleasantly with them. Paymaster Sheldon joined our company. He is an amiable young gentleman.

"*Burlington*, *Vt.*, *April* 25.—The conference with the Rev. Mr. Haskel and President Sanders was serious and affecting. O may I improve them.

"*Plattsburg*, *May* 15.—We have a melancholy intelligence to-day, that on the attack upon Toronto, Upper Canada, Col. Pike was slain, but that the place was carried and taken on the 27th April. I lament the loss of the amiable and brave Col. Pike.

"*Plattsburg*, *May* 18.—I was called upon this afternoon by Lieut. Montieth, of the navy, with a note from Commodore McDonough, to meet him and other officers of his station, to-morrow, at 3 o'clock, in a council of war. Gen. Mooers is unwell. I have had no reports from the Rangers, and I am somewhat concerned. I have sent on an express to Champlain, to-day. There are various reports in circulation of the movements of the enemy. The duties assigned to me by the government are arduous and difficult—to the actors, dangerous in the extreme. May they escape detection. If detected they are lost. One of the enemy's secret agents is now confined and strongly guarded. He must, I fear, suffer death in accordance with martial-law.

"*Plattsburg, May* 19.—My communications in the council, yesterday, were received with attention. Gen. Smith was highly gratified, and ordered something extra to the Rangers, to encourage them in their fidelity to the government. The extensive power invested in me, I have endeavored, constantly, to exercise with the greatest moderation. The great and glorious principles of religion have governed all my acts, as I trust. Thus far the war department have approved my acts, and also the officers, with whom I have been immediately connected in these frontiers. Major-Gen. Mooers and Mr. Sailly, of the custom department, have been very useful to me in my movements.

"*Plattsburg, May* 21.—Received communication from the west to-day, which has the appearance that the enemy is meditating an attack upon some posts on Lake Ontario—Oswego or Sacketts Harbour perhaps.

"*Plattsburg, May* 23.—I learn, by the Rangers, that Sir George Provost has passed Prescott for Kingston. I have, by express, communicated this to proper officers at Ogdensburg and Sacketts Harbour, and requested the latter to alarm the officer at Oswego.

"*Plattsburg, June* 1.—As I expected, information has just reached me, by the Rangers, that the enemy made an attack upon Sacketts Harbour, on the 29th ulto., and were defeated by Gen. Brown, with a considerable loss on our side. Cols. Backus and Mills are among the slain. I believe the timely information from this department, has saved Sacketts Harbour. Would to God that our officers were more vigilant, and the government active in its operations on these frontiers.

"*Plattsburg, July* 3.—A heavy cannonading is heard from the north, about 10 o'clock this morning. Lieut. Sidney Smith, with two armed schooners (the Growler and Eagle), went yesterday to the lines—he is undoubtedly attacked.

"*Plattsburg, July* 4.—By the Rangers I am informed that at the extreme end of this Lake, Smith met some of the enemy's gunboats, by whom he was attacked, and pursued so far into the Narrows that he could not return with his vessels against the south wind, other heavy gun-boats from the *Isle aux Noix* attacked him. After a severe resistance, of three hours, against a superior force, he was compelled to surrender. By this unfortunate catastrophe Commodore McDonough is reduced to a single schooner and a few gunboats. Lieut. Smith was imprudent to venture into the Narrows—he was undoubtedly decoyed by the enemy. He is a brave and daring officer. The British are now masters of the Lake. They will, no doubt, soon show this. I was requested by General Mooers to call out the regular troops at Pike's encampment to make their appearance on the Lake shore. They did so.

"*Plattsburg*, *July* 10.—I have information from the Deputy Quarter Master, at Albany, that Gen. Wade Hampson is to assume the command of the Northern Army. Strange that the government should appoint southern men to such responsible stations at the north. Gen. Mooers ought to have this appointment, Montreal would be in his possession in a month. He is a brave, judicious, and prudent officer, and, withal, extremely popular with his fellow-citizens. They would follow him with the greatest cheerfulness.

"*Plattsburg*, *July* 16.—Some of the St. Regis Indians came in today. From them we received some interesting information of the movements of the enemy. Col. Lewis, an influential chief of this tribe is here. He was a confidential friend of Gens. Washington and Schuyler during the Revolution. His friendship is firm to the Americans. He says that the English will be beaten in this war.

"*Plattsburg*, *July* 18.—I have received from the war department, through Gov. Tompkins, a communication which, to me, is somewhat curious, and shows how little those great men are acquainted with northern affairs. In my communication to the department I have respectfully represented to the government that the reduction of Montreal, if this is in their contemplation, is to be effected by concentrating its whole force on the Northern Frontiers, at Lake Champlain, and force its way by removing the abbatis at the river La Cole to the plains of La Arcadia, where, undoubtedly, in such a case, the first battle would be fought, between the regular armies, on the issue of which will depend the fate of that city, the fortress of Isle Aux Noix, St. Johns, and Chambly, and when Montreal is once occupied, by an American army, the communication between the Upper and Lower Canadas is cut off, the British army, in the upper province, must inevitably die. If it exist it must fight through the American army at Montreal, to reach Quebec. All this, and much more was respectfully submitted to the war department, as I was requested to give my opinion and sentiments on this delicate subject. I was happy to find that Gen. Mooers and the Hon. Judge

More, of Champlain, concurred fully with my opinion, and sentiments.

"*Plattsburg, July* 21.—I have heard several able discourses from the Rev. Mr. Weeks, on the Decrees of God, concerning which I cannot agree with him in every respect. Gen. Mooers seems to submit to them as in accordance with the Scriptures. Gen. Skinner, my particular friend, dissents from them. He pleads the agency of man. He is well versed in the Scriptures, *i.e.*, he retains much in memory. Mr. Nichols, a lawyer, is greatly opposed, he is willing to hear the subject discussed.

"*Plattsburg, July* 24.—I am informed by the Rangers that the enemy at St. Johns and Isle aux Noix appeared to be preparing for an immediate expedition, but to what point, of course, it is not known.

"*Plattsburg, July* 25.—I received a note from General Hampton's aide-de-camp, last evening, in which I am requested to repair to his camp, and report myself. I am to start to-day by way of Essex. Captain Stevenson had informed me, who had an interview with the General, that he was in a bad humor with my department. This hastens me to have an interview with him. I understand that he is by no means popular with the troops. This is most unfortunate for him and the public service.

"*Plattsburg, July* 26.—I was unable to start yesterday on my intended jaunt to Burlington, in consequence of my receiving despatches from the War Department which required my immediate reply. General Mooers has called on me, to inform me that he had an interview to-day with several American merchants, who, by permission, left the Canadian provinces; and learned from them that the enemy were preparing for an expedition. This is only a corroboration of what I knew before. I have apprized the General of my intended jaunt to Burlington.

"*Burlington, July* 30.—I arrived here, this morning, from Charlotte; and, at eleven o'clock, I had an interview with General Hampton, who, at first, seemed very polite and flattering in his language; but, in the discussion in regard to his military operations against Canada, he was out of tune. He said, he knew the course he intended to take to be successful in his campaign, that he had fine troops under his command, and that they would do all that he would ask them. But, he was reminded that they were raw troops. Upon this he uttered tremendous oaths, and intimated that any man who would hint anything of the kind was not true to the American cause. This brought on an altercation between the General and myself. I was aware he knew my position with the General Government; and I, knowing at the same time that I was beyond his reach, dared to confront him. I frankly stated to him that I knew my duty, and should faithfully perform it, as required by the War Department; and if he did not wish to avail himself of the benefits which my department was capable of rendering to the government, its armies, and generals, I should continue to do my duty. When the General found I was firm, and stood in no fear of him, he lowered his tone, and said, 'Well, I suppose I must look to you for information.' 'That,' said I, 'you may do as you please. But, you may expect to be attacked by the enemy in a few days.' 'In a few days,' he said, and appeared to be surprised. 'Yes, the enemy are certainly preparing for some expedition. I cannot say to what point.' 'If so,' said he, 'you will prove to be a true prophet.' With this, I took my leave of the most unpleasant commander of the American army I have met with.

"*Charlotte, July* 31.—This morning I started to return to Plattsburg, and went as far as Grand Isle, at the Bar; there I met, about twelve o'clock, Mr. Myers, who informed me it would be dangerous to proceed, as the enemy were in force, advancing by water to Plattsburg, and he presumed they were already in possession of the place. I, therefore, returned to Burlington and Charlotte.

"*Plattsburg, August* 2.—I returned last evening to my post, and found that the enemy had been here, and no resistance was made to their landing. Their force was twelve hundred men, under the command of Colonels Murray and Williams, who destroyed all public property, and then wantonly burnt store-houses and the residences of several of the inhabitants. The same day the British flotilla passed Burlington, and threw some shots into the town; and General Hampton had his five thousand men in battle array, on the bank of the lake, as if he was to be attacked by land. He ought to have had at least a part of his force at Plattsburg; but this is one of the many blunders he has already made in the command of the northern army.

"My report of this affair to the Department of War, and that of Governor Tompkins, were drawn up in cautious language; but yet I spoke, somewhat plainly, of my fears in regard to General Hampton. I am informed that the Secretary of War will soon be at Sacketts Harbor, to see, himself, the preparations of the grand army, before its descent to the St. Lawrence.

"*Plattsburg, August* 10.—There is another important communication; I say this, although I do not know precisely its language, yet I know its import. I forwarded it to-day, by one of the confidential Rangers, to its destination. I am politely requested to pay no regard to General Hampton's rough language—but to aid him to the full extent which my department is capable, which may be of great benefit to the public service.

"*Plattsburg, August* 16.—An officer from General Hampton has been with me to-day, and I have received a certain requisition at his hand. It is somewhat curious, but shall be performed as far as this Department is able to execute it.

"*Plattsburg, August* 22.—I have made out a communication for General Hampton, which I have forwarded to him to-day. The chiefs from St. Regis have been here, and received their annuity from the people of the State of New York. We received from them some important intelligence, in corroboration of that received from the Rangers. They have had a communication from the Caughnawaga chiefs, which is friendly in its import. The chiefs expressed to General Mooers their sincere attachment to the American cause.

"*Plattsburg, September* 6.—By communication from the Adjutant General, I perceive General Hampton is soon to make a move from Burlington, for the lines. I am requested by him to reconnoitre the position at La Cole river, and examine the possibility of his penetrating, with the army, from Chautegay Four Corners into Canada. I shall consult with those who are best acquainted with that section of the country, and send some of the Rangers thither. Governor Tompkins has no confidence in General Hampton as a general to command an army.

"*Plattsburg, September* 8.—General Mooers has had an interview with General Hampton. Commodore McDonough's flotilla is on the lake. *Evening.*—I understand that General Hampton is about to move with his army from Burlington. I am ordered by him to meet him on his arrival at Cumberland Head.

"*November* 9, 1813.—In consequence of a fall from my horse, I have been unable to write until now. *Recapitulation.*—As requested, I had an interview with General Hampton, at Cumberland Head.

Through him, I was requested by General Wilkinson, from Sacketts Harbor, to advance within six miles of Ogdensburg, and there remain until further orders—that is, till his arrival, with his army, at that place. To this General Hampton made no objection, but refused that, when there, I should be subjected to the orders of General Wilkinson, and, finally, opposed my going at all. When he saw that the public service required it, he gave me orders to proceed, with positive instructions not to remain there two hours after accomplishing the duty assigned me. In this interview I learned from him the route he intended to take to enter into the British Province—the difficulties of which, as well as the many obstacles he would encounter, were he to attempt to reach Montreal by that route, were pointed out to him. He was also, in vain, told that the enemy were weak in his front, and that the great road from the river La Cole to the La Acadia plains, and St. Johns, was the only practicable route, at this time, for his army to pass, and the abbatis might be removed by one hundred and fifty axemen, protected by a sufficient corps. If he met any opposition in these woods, it would only be by the Canadian militia and Indians. After reaching the plains, he would contest only with the regulars, which were few, while, by his cannons, he could keep the militia and Indians at a respectful distance from him. By taking this route, he would distract the enemy, and divide their forces so as to favor the descent of the grand army down the St. Lawrence, from Sacketts Harbor. I informed him that, according to the reports of the Rangers, there were, at this time, at Montreal, about two hundred sailors, and three hundred and fifty marines. The numbers of the militia were not known, and some regulars were expected from Quebec. As for the Isle Aux Noix, it might be left untouched, and kept in awe by a strong militia force. It is contrary, indeed, to military rule, to leave an enemy in the rear, yet its position, and the necessity of the case, may justify its infraction. The garrison would be cooped up in the fortress, offer us no hinderance, and, if the attack on Montreal be successful, must ultimately surrender. I also told him that great efforts were made to distract the Indians, and that they had been informed by some of the Rangers, that Montreal is about to experience the fate which happened to it in 1760, when it surrendered to two armies, under Generals Amherst and Haviland, one of which advanced by way of the St. Lawrence, and the other by that of

Lake Champlain—that the Americans have no desire to shed their blood, nor do they even ask them to espouse their cause; but their object is to save them, if they continue neutral, from the horrors of war, educate their children, and make them, like themselves, happy, through the influence of Christianity and civilization, while the British Government occupy their land, but give them no payment for the same. They were staggered by this intelligence, and great dissension was produced, in the midst of which the Rangers made a narrow escape.

"Having communicated all this to the General, I left him and his army near Champlain, I proceeded to the place of my destination. I called upon the Hon. Pliney Moore, and consulted with him upon certain points. The information he gave was very useful. He is one of the most honorable gentlemen in these parts, although his political sentiments may be different from those of the present administration, yet he is a true friend to his country, and will do all in his power to maintain its honor. At Chautegay 4 Corners, I was, for the first time, since my coming on these frontiers, alarmed for my safety. By a confidential friend I received information, that the enemy's scouts were frequently seen on the lines in that quarter, and had occasionally approached the great road from Plattsburg to Malone—the commander had also inadvertently hinted the object of his being in that neighborhood, and actually employed one of the inhabitants to inform him, should I again appear there—but the person being faithful to his country, to prevent any mischief happening to me, communicated the intelligence to one of the Rangers, and sent also the news to Plattsburg, which I had not received. It was supposed, at the time, that the scouts were then in my front, and to avoid coming in contact with them, I lost no time in procuring a hunter or woodsman, as he styled himself, for a guide. With him and my waiter I took a pathless route through a dreary wilderness, and at night, like a true son of the forest, made my lodging beside a log, with my cloak for my covering, and my valise for a pillow. Next day, by ten o'clock, I was beyond reach of those who sought my life. From the French Mills I sent a confidential agent to Prescott, to obtain information of the movements of the enemy. I then discovered, as I supposed, one of the enemy's emissaries, but on examination I found he was, more or less, connected with one of our Rangers. I exhorted him to be faithful or his life would be forfeited. I went to Malone and back to the French Mills. The British agents were temporizing with our Indians. Capt. David Irwin, who commands the post at the French Mills, does what he can to keep the Indians faithful to the United States. They are fed, and draw rations from the post, an arrangement which I had much difficulty to effect in 1812, with the government, but finally accomplished it, with the assistance of Gens. Dearborn, Mooers, and Tompkins.

"On my return from the west, I found Gen. Hampton and his army at Chautegay. As the duty assigned me rendered it necessary that I should be at Plattsburg, at a certain time, I left him, having received orders to join him in four days.

"At Robinson's Inn, within twelve miles from Plattsburg, one of the Rangers reported to me that, Gen. Hampton had already made demonstration of entering Canada, at Champlain, but that his movements were yet a subject of mystery to the enemy, who watched him, and that in anticipation of his entering somewhere at the west into the province, Sir George Provost was throwing his forces into St. Louis, on the south side of the St. Lawrence, and that the Canadian militia were called out in mass, to oppose the American army—that the Indians were not to be relied on by the British, though Sir John Johnson had lately held a council with them, and exhorted them to be faithful to His Majesty's cause, and co-operate with their forces against the common enemy. I have information as to the strength of the regular troops at Montreal and La Prairie. I communicated the news to Gen. Hampton. On account of duty I was not able to join him till 10th October. The St. Regis Indians were in his army on 20th August, had been ordered to be in readiness to serve the government. On 25th, it was reported to him that they were under arms, and ready to march to meet the enemy.

Capt. Irwin, of the F. Mills, opposed the requisition of the General, on the ground that the government did not wish them to interfere in the contest, but was strong enough to handle the enemy herself. She wished them to stay at home in peace, and protect their wives and children, and she would feed them. But it was overruled. The plea was retaliation. The British had employed the Indians in the west, and their cruelties called for vengeance; besides, the friendly part of the St. Regis Indians were anxious to co-operate with the American army. When this subject was brought before me, my situation was delicate in the extreme, as I knew the sentiments of the government in 1812, and had no intimation of any change. Gen. Hampton had given me no information of his intentions to arm the Indians. I immediately made inquiry of Gov. Tompkins and the war department. The answers put an end to my anxiety. The Indians were permitted to coöperate with the American army, and did so as scouts. On the same day, 19 Oct., as before stated, I found the General. It was reported there was a detachment of the enemy at Cornwall, ready to fall upon his rear, which the enemy could do within thirty-six hours. To ascertain the truth I was despatched, on the 20th, towards St. Regis, and an officer to another part. The General intends to enter into Canada once more. I perceive he regrets that he did not enter Canada by way of La Cole and La Arcadia, as he was recommended by this department. He little understands the many difficulties he will encounter. He sees now the obstacles which were formerly represented to him, by the route he is now taking. He appears to have little reliance on the discipline and perseverance of his troops. On my return to the Four Corners, on the 26th, a note was handed me from the General, requesting me to join him without delay; so, after having obtained fresh horses, I proceeded with all speed in search of him. On my arrival at headquarters, I found there had been a sharp skirmish between his advanced corps and the enemy. About this time a council of war was held, where several communications were presented to the council for their consideration, which eventuated in the falling back of the army to its former position. The disclosures were somewhat extraordinary, from the tone and temper of the commanders towards each other. There was great discord in their views with regard to their military operations, which was highly detrimental to the public service. In the close of the day succeeding that on which I joined the army, I was informed that an express had just come in from the west, and it was not long before I was requested to appear before the General. After an hour's conference, I left him, to meet Gen. Wilkinson, according to his orders, at Morristown and Ogdensburg. For this purpose, at 11 o'clock at night I left the camp with a dragoon and my waiter. On the 6th Nov. I met Gen. Wilkinson and his army above Ogdensburg, by whose orders I returned the same day down the river as far as St. Regis. Some of those Indians who had put themselves under the protection of the

United States, were employed by him to act as pilots to his numerous boats, on their passage down the Long Sault Rapids, and by whose guidance not a single boat miscarried. Mr. W. Gray, the interpreter, aided me in this matter and came up with them. On the 10th instant, at night, I returned to the Long Sault, and so on, and, early the next morning, had an interview with the General, who was at this time confined to his barge, by indisposition. Just at the close of the conference the cannonading commenced between the British and American gun-boats, upon which, after receiving his instruction, I retired. The battle of Chrystlers Farm, as it is called, soon after commenced on the opposite shore. The sight was grand as well as terrific. The cannonading on the water, and the musketry on land was kept up for a time with great spirit and resolution on both sides.

" Agreeably to my instruction I hastened to Plattsburg, and took the French Mills on my way, where I remained time enough to complete certain arrangements which were necessary to be made for the benefit of the St. Regis Indians.

" On my arrival at Plattsburg I found the place was already occupied by a portion of the Northern army.

" *Plattsburg*, *Nov.* 29.—I have made an arrangement with Gen. Mooers, in relation to my department, and I am preparing once more to cross the Lake, for my old quarters at Charlotte. The enemy is rejoicing to see that our armies are going into winter-quarters. Peace be with him.

" *Charlotte*, *Dec.* 2.—I am informed by several officers to-day, from Wilkinson's army, that Col. N. Pinkney was sent to arrest Gen. Hampton, but timely information was given him by a confidential friend, at the French Mills, which enabled him to elude the above officer. The moment, as it were, he received the intelligence, he resolved to decamp, and, fortunately for him, a steamer had just come into the port, which, without delay, he pressed into the public service, and was soon on his way for Whitehall. Thus, he escaped from being arrested, his sword taken from him, and the northern climate which, it is said (as a southern man), he dreads more than the enemy.

" The General is a gentleman of warm temperament, on account of which, he may have sometimes given unnecessary offence to those who have a jaundiced eye upon his private acts and military operations. He has, undoubtedly, erred in the latter, and this, not from the heart, but in judgment, and for adhering too much to ignorant and evil advisers, but he is a brave and good officer, who sincerely wishes to sustain the honor of his country. May his noble son (who is acting as his aide-de-camp), imitate his honored father, in his patriotism.

" *Charlotte*, *Dec.* 4.—The cold weather has commenced with all its severity, in this northern climate. My health is extremely feeble —this, I trust, is for my good—it reminds me of the uncertainty of my existence here—and, oh, that I may improve my time in preparation for the world to come. O merciful God, fit and prepare me for death and judgment. My father and brother are with me here —Col. Williams has just returned from his command, at the Lines, several officers are with him.

" *Charlotte*, *Dec.* 8.—I have been at Burlington, and met with one of our Rangers, and I have his report, which is so important that I have communicated it to the war department, and partially to the commanding officer at Burlington, who will communicate the same to the officer at Plattsburg. I have received a letter from Judge Ford of Ogdensburgh, who makes certain inquiries of me, about which I am unable, at present, to give him information. I have received also a letter from Mr. Hastings at the French Mills, in relation to the rations issued by him. I shall write to the Commissary-General.

" *Charlotte*, *Dec.* 11.—I have written to Mr. Hastings to delay his determination until I can hear from the commissariat department.

" *Charlotte*, *Dec.* 14.—I am requested by Gov. Tompkins to repair to Albany, and shall go thither as soon as my present engagements permit. Captain McNeil, of the 11th Regt., and Col. Fassett called upon me, and had a pleasant interview.

" *Charlotte*, *Dec.* 15.—I am requested by the commanding officer at Plattsburg, and Gen. Mooers, to visit that post without delay. I start to-day, although I am somewhat feeble, yet the urgency of the request impels me to go.

" *Plattsburg*, *Dec.* 17.—Had an interview with the commanding officer, in presence of Gen. Mooers and Mr. Sailly. The object of my call was arranged, and I hope it will be beneficial to the public service.

" *Charlotte*, *Dec.* 18.—Just returned from Plattsburg. I am greatly fatigued, and have suffered much from the cold, being on horseback. My waiter is sick. My father, Col Williams, and Major

Stone, are in high spirits—they have been out on a chase, and killed two foxes. There is to be a ball this evening, I am invited to attend —but no! My Bible shall be my company this evening, and may God give me a heart to understand His holy word.

"*Charlotte*, *Dec.* 11—I intend to start for Albany to-morrow morning in a stage. How many things at present come in my way, which disturb my feelings, in my religious meditations. Much of it is, perhaps, my own fault, that my communion with my Heavenly Father is not so close as it might be. O, how sweet it is when I am with Him by prayer and in reading His holy word. Come, thou Holy Spirit, take possession of my soul, kindle there Thy sacred fire —warm my cold heart—stir me up to devote my whole self, and all my time and talents to the glory of my God and Saviour. Sanctify my heart by Thy divine influence, and make me a true child of God. O my God I once more give up myself to Thee, and wilt thou accept of me, unworthy as I am, but for Christ's sake have mercy upon me and mine in the Saviour.

"I had a long conversation with my father upon religion, this evening—it was pleasant to me.

"*Albany*, *December* 23, 1813.—I arrived here greatly fatigued. I had a pleasant interview with the Rev. Mr. Clowes. Our conversation was much upon the church, its discipline, and government. Lieutenant-Governor Taylor came in the course of the evening, and was somewhat urgent upon me to attach myself to the Episcopal Church.

"*Albany*, *December* 24.—I had an interview with Governor Tompkins, who had received communications from the War Department, in relation to my corps, which were flattering to my department, and urging its continuance. But this is uncertain, as the corps complain for want of more pay, and I have not been able to give them a satisfactory answer. It is a wonder thus far that they have not been caught by the enemy—their life is in their own hands. They know their fate, if taken.

"*Albany*, *December* 25.—I heard a Christmas discourse from the Rev. Mr. Clowes—it was an excellent sermon—took a Christmas dinner with Lieutenant-Governor Taylor. In the evening went to Mr. Walsh's, and spent the evening pleasantly with a small party.

"*December* 30.—I had an interview with the Commander-in-chief, and several officers.

"*December* 31.—Made my report as I received it from the Rangers. In the evening, Governor Tompkins revealed to me the intentions of the government, either to attack Prescot or Montreal. There was a long discussion on this delicate point. By the reports of the Rangers, Prescot was a strong fortress, and to succeed in taking it there must be a regular siege, perhaps, it will take ten or fifteen days; whereas, Montreal was much weaker, and it being the second city in the lower province, if conquered, would redound more to the honor of the American arms, than the conquest of Prescot. It was left to the Commander-in-chief of the New York forces to make his choice in regard to an attack.

"*December* 31.—I am to start for Plattsburg this afternoon.

"*Burlington, January* 3, 1814.—Reached here this evening, greatly fatigued from the roughness of the roads and the cold I experienced on the way. I have great reason to bless God that I am still in the land of the living, and see the commencement of another year. May I live a new year unto righteousness.

"*January* 4.—Had an interview with the commandant of the post, who appeared to be alarmed at the movements of the enemy, on the lines. But, by the reports of the Ranger, who met me here, I learn that the detachment hovering on the lines is a corps of observation.

"*Plattsburg, January* 6.—Several of the Rangers have come in, whose reports are not worth observation. The enemy is strengthening his fortress at the Isle Aux Noix; forty-five Indians are encamped in the neighborhood.

"*Plattsburg, January* 8.—The troops here are at their ease. They have now good quarters. Colonel Smith commands the post.

"*Plattsburg, January* 13.—I had an interview with General Mooers. I have received an important communication from the Department of War, which impells me to repair to the French Mills.

"*French Mills, January* 15.—General Wilkinson's army have occupied this post, a portion of which have already moved to Malone, and others will soon follow them. This was an unfortunate campaign. For a southern man to be put at the head of the northern army, is considered by the public prints to be one among the many errors that the present administration have committed. To put this army, on the 1st November, in motion for a campaign, was preposterous beyond calculation. The Secretary of War, on his visit to Sacketts Harbor, was duly apprized of this—but no attention was paid to the representations of my department. The hints I have received, that the remarks made upon them were, that government was determined to commence the campaign—as its army was organized, and its transportation was ready—and more, it must. In vain, the lateness of the season was represented, and the difficulty of conveying such an army down the St. Lawrence, on account of the many and dangerous rapids it had to pass. It was apprehended that by these and the climate, more men would be destroyed than by the sword of the enemy—as was the case in Bonaparte's campaign to Russia. As was expected by this department, the campaign ended without accomplishing its object.

"*Plattsburg*, *Jany*. 20.—By the request of Gen. Wilkinson, the fortress at Isle Aux Noix, is more closely to be examined, and its strength ascertained. In accordance with this, I have issued my orders to the Rangers—also the Stone Mill, on the river La Cole, which the enemy occupied as a guard-house, is to be examined.

"*Plattsburg*, *Jany*. 24.—Although I am in the midst of the din of war, yet I do not forget my duty to my God. This day has been consecrated by me as a day of humiliation, fasting, and prayer, for my sins of omission and commission. It has been a blessed day with me—what can be more happy to a sinful creature than a close communion with God? I have found one officer only who can and does pray—he spent the evening with me in prayer and praise to Almighty God, for his merciful care of us, and the religious privileges that we enjoyed. All sorts and conditions of men were remembered.

"*Plattsburg*, *Jany*. 26.—Received a letter from Col. Brady, at Sacketts Harbor, who distrusts the fidelity of the St. Regis Indians to this government—I have referred him for his satisfaction to the commandant of the post at French Mills. I am not aware of the cause of his mistrust, but it shall be attended to, and I have hinted it to the Commissary Hastings, at the place.

"*February* 4.—By the orders of the General, I am to repair to Burlington—thence to Swanton Falls, and approach Missisiquoi Bay, as far as it may be practicable and safe to my person.

"*February* 8, *Grand Isle*.—I have thus far returned from a jaunt of observation—passed last midnight at Aburgh, where we were fired upon, but received no injury from it. Our horses suffered much, as they were pushed at a great rate on the ice, to avoid our being overhauled by the enemy's dragoons. We were too fleet for them, as we had the start.

"*Plattsburg*, *February* 9.—Made my report to the General, who was satisfied. I perceived, in this interview, he intends to invade Canada this winter.

"*Plattsburg*, *February* 13.—There was a council of war. Gen. Mooers was requested to attend. I was called upon to make certain statements, which I did. The council were divided. Invasion of Canada was the subject of this discussion. Three routes were pointed out to the council. It was finally concluded, to attack the Stone Mill on river La Cole.

"*Plattsburg*, *February* 27.—I was called by the secretary of war to state the strength of the fortress at Isle Aux Noix, and the practicability of its being forced if an attack was made immediately, and when the information is obtained to communicate the same to General Wilkinson. The information desired was soon obtained—although the strength of that fortress was well known before—yet in compliance with the requisition of the war department, re-examination was made, and further information gained as to the force of the enemy at that place—St. Johns, Chambly, La Prairie, and Montreal. On the occasion, one of the Rangers was taken upon suspicion of the object of his visit, but, fortunately for him, escaped.

"*Plattsburg*, *March* 5.—A partial report was made to the General. By this he was sure of his game. Many detachments had been preparing for some days for an expedition.

"*March the* 6*th*.—The final report was made of the information received of the Rangers. There was a discussion between the General and myself, as to the expediency of the immediate attack of the aforementioned fortress. The General was referred to the reports, and, at the same time, reminded of the difficulties and obstacles he and his army might encounter should he attempt it. He contemplated an attack upon the Stone Mill, whose walls were strong, and would resist the six pounders he intended to take—so, to succeed, it would be necessary for him to take several pieces of heavier calibre, say, eighteen and twenty-four pounders to batter down the walls of the Mill, and those pieces of ordnance ought to be mounted upon sleds, to make it easy for their transportation, and to have their carriages accompanying them, and used when necessary. To this the General remarked, that he had ordered one eighteen pounder on a carriage, and several field pieces to accompany the detachment. He was again reminded, that if successful in his intended attack upon the Stone Mill, as he would be then in the neighborhood of Isle Aux Noix, it was presumed, his next attack would be upon that fortress—and if so, it was of the greatest importance to his success there, that his fire of artillery should be superior to the enemy. The fort must be destroyed by his artillery, as it would be preposterous to attempt to take it by storming, since it was doubly fortified at present—as the fort stands on the island, and care is taken every day that the ice is broken, and moved for thirty feet all round the island, and this must be surmounted before the ramparts of the fort can be reached and attacked. Its ramparts are well protected by heavy guns and three small batteries. The General appeared to be somewhat disconcerted with the first obstacle, viz. the water all round the fort.

"It was again represented, if a regular siege was intended upon that fort, he would meet many difficulties—and that if the place was not taken by the point of the bayonet, it must be by a heavy cannonading—to raise redoubts, at present, for his heavy pieces, would be a great labor, as the ground was then in a frozen state. But the General could not see there were any hinderances to his intended invasion. The honor of the army must be retrieved.

"*Plattsburg, March* 7.—To-day I communicated to the War Department the hints which were given to General Wilkinson, and one, in short, to Governor Tompkins. I am happy to find that General Mooers' sentiments coincide entirely with mine, in every point which was suggested to General Wilkinson. If I am not mistaken, the General will find there were some truths in the friendly suggestions made to him.

"*Plattsburg, March* 8.—I am indisposed to-day, and as this indisposition has been increasing for more than two months, I have concluded to visit Dr. Pomeroy, at Burlington.

"*Burlington*, 28.—I am now convalescent, my nerves have been deeply affected by a cold I took at Plattsburg. My nervous system is in a feeble state, and my eyes are so weak that I am unable to read. Grant, merciful God, that this sickness may have the effect of weaning me from the world, and bringing me in deep humility and repentance to thee. Restore, O Lord, my health to me, and may my future life be devoted to thy glory. My friends from

Charlotte have been kind and attentive. The Rev. Mr. Haskell, of that place, has been attentive as a good pastor. I bless God for his goodness and loving-kindness to me, his unworthy creature.

"*Burlington, April* 3.—I have watched, with intense anxiety, all the movements of General Wilkinson. He failed in his adventure of the Stone Mill, at the river La Cole. Without a military eye, and due preparation in the artillery, &c., it could not be otherwise than a defeat. They had a sufficient force in the field to have taken the Mill, at least, but were discomfitted and compelled to retreat before an inferior number of the enemy. Much praise is due to Major Hancock, of the British, for his noble defence of the post assigned him. This is the second disgrace General Wilkinson has brought on the American arms. If court-marshalled, he would not escape from being cashiered. The government may assist to screen him from a public censure.

"*Plattsburg, April* 12.—General Izard, I understand, is to assume the command of the northern army; a goodly number of troops are here. Saw General Mooers but a few minutes. I am to call upon him to-morrow.

"*Plattsburg*, 29.—I have been on the lines, by the request of the commandant of the post. I have been absent six days. I moved much with the movements of the enemy. Sent despatches to ——, confidential in their nature.

"*Plattsburg, May* 4.—I have been indisposed for a considerable time, yet I am able to perform my duties.

"*May* 13.—Had an interview with General Izard, and was pleased to learn from him that he would rely on any information that may be communicated to him from my department. The Ranger was introduced to him, whom he exhorted to be faithful to his duty.

"*Plattsburg, May* 16.—Dined with General Mooers, Judge More, General Woolsey, and Mr. Sailly. There was a long discussion among the gentlemen, of the past military operations on these frontiers.

"These gentlemen are my confidential friends, and much praise is due to them for their patriotism to their country. They were of great service to me, on various occasions, and in some instances their advice was of the greatest importance to my department.

"*Plattsburg, May* 20.—The same gentlemen mentioned on the 16th, met me at the house of General Woolsey, and half the day was spent in discussion upon the future military operations on these frontiers. With my approbation, a long document was produced and read, showing the present commander of the northern army his course, and the only one which was considered to be feasible for him to pursue, in order to his success over the enemy. I must confess the document was an admirable one, and well calculated to call the attention of the General to many important points which were suggested therein. I readily concluded it was the united opinion of the gentlemen present, as they highly recommended the sentiments and suggestions expressed in the document; I myself joined with them in the propriety of adhering to it. It was finally hinted, whether I did not think it would be for the good of the public service, and the honor of the American arms, to present the same to Gen. Izard, for his inspection and consideration. I replied, 'Gentlemen, you are northern men. You have critically observed the movements of the former disastrous campaigns. You have seen with pain the great faults that were committed by those to whom the American armies were intrusted. Your patriotism to your country and anxiety to sustain her honor, has led you to suggest many important points which may prove to be of great service to the General. The document not only reveals the errors that were committed by the former commanders, but most judiciously points out the course that may be pursued by the present commander, in order to his success. I shall with pleasure present the paper to General Izard, if I am permitted to do so. I presume, gentlemen, he will duly appreciate its contents, and he may be benefited by them.'

"The document was presented at a proper time.

"*May* 26.—I was called upon by the General, in relation to the paper which I had presented him, with which he was pleased.

"*Plattsburg*, *June* 3.—There is a report that General Izard will move a portion of his army to Chazy or Champlain. I have no intimation of the kind, as yet, from him.

"*June* 8.—I have forwarded a certain communication to the war department, which is confidential in its import.

"*June* 12.—I have received a communication from Governor Tompkins, asking for an information in relation to the St. Regis Indians. I perceive an attempt is made to stop the rations which have been issued to them by the General Government. The Governor is friendly to them. I called upon Gen. Mooers and Mr.

Sailly, to sustain me in this matter, and they have done it to my satisfaction.

"*June* 14.—Commissary Hastings, from the post at the French Mills, called upon me this afternoon, who is somewhat alarmed lest his issuing the rations to the Indians should be discontinued by the government. He was informed, that an exertion was making for its continuance. I advised him to repair to Albany, and have an interview with the general of the commissariat department, whom I addressed once more upon the subject. Mr. Hastings has gone to Albany.

"*June* 21.—Some of the St. Regis Indians came in yesterday. The intelligence they have communicated is somewhat exaggerated. The enemy is, no doubt, active in his preparation, either for the invasion or self-defence.

"The gun-boat, on the Lake of St. Francis, is somewhat troublesome to the American inhabitants on the shores of the St. Lawrence. This department has recommended its being taken or destroyed. It is now, as I understand, in preparation of being effected. The volunteers from the post at the French Mills, may be drafted for this expedition. One of the lieutenants from the navy of Lake Champlain, will be put at the head of the detachment. I have had several interviews with the Commodore McDonough upon the subject, who approves the plan. May the expedition be as successful as Major Young was upon St. Regis, in 1812.

"*Plattsburg, July* 4.—This has been a festival day with the citizens here. I dined with them; Capt. Sperry, appeared conspicuous on the occasion. Mr. Sailly, of the revenue department, delivered a handsome and eloquent speech at the table, which was highly applauded. He is a French gentleman of great respectability.

"*July* 10.—I am preparing to visit the lines. Three Indians are to accompany me.

"*Evening.*—I visited the American camp at Chazy, and was treated politely by the officers—passed to Mooerstown, and am now lodging in the woods or wilderness. Here I met a certain messenger, and received from him despatches, and obtained from him many particulars of the movements of the enemy, &c., among others, that they are daily expecting to receive reinforcement from Europe, as Bonaparte has ceased to be a terror to the European powers, so that the troops can now be spared from the continental service. Thus we may now expect to contend with the Duke of Wellington's heroes—but the American army is now, in a measure, organized, and they will meet them, as they did in the Revolutionary War. There will be hard battles fought this season on these frontiers. The army is now in fine order, and eager to meet the enemy.

"*July* 20.—A communication has been presented to me from Gen. Izard, which has greatly disturbed my feelings. I immediately sent to the General, requesting him, to have the goodness to give me the name of the author, or he might be seized under the martial-law, and have him sent to me for investigation of his reports. I asked this favor of the General, as I considered the subject came within my department.

"*July* 23.—Gen. Izard was pleased to send the person, under the guard of two dragoons. The paper was placed before him which he had presented to the General. He was mute, and his eyes fixed upon the paper. He was questioned, but no reply. He was told that his life and death was in his own hands, as there was a strong suspicion of what he was, and who employed him—that although by the military law of this government, he was exposed to death, if convicted of what is charged upon him, or what he is supposed to be; but if he would candidly confess and declare his object in making such representations as he does in the paper before him, he may hope for mercy.

"He saw his escape was hopeless, and to save himself, there were disclosures made of the intrigues of the enemy with the American citizens on the lines, which astonished this department. Certain officers, in the Indian department, are seeking to seize my person, &c. The disclosures made, just stated, are seasonable and important at this period of the war. The plan of the enemy, had it been effected, would have been most mischievous to the military operations of the northern army, but the discovery was so important, it compelled me to have an interview with the General, which lasted about two hours. It was a delicate and difficult subject—although his case was remediless in the view of martial law—yet mercy prevailed, for several important reasons it was concluded it would be most politic and conducive to the American cause, to dismiss, as easily and as silently as possible, the person in question. He was, therefore, permitted to depart, after receiving from him a pledge to be at peace—with a strong caution, from this department, to be quiet and withhold his hands from the concerns of the war. Names were obtained of the American citizens (some of these were smugglers from Massachusetts), who were actually in league with the enemy —conveying to them secret intelligence of our position and strength. In consequence of the foregoing, I immediately issued an order to the whole corps of the *Rangers* to have a watchful eye upon the persons named in the order. Names also were obtained of the enemy's secret agents in Canada—they were to be looked after, and taken if they were found within the American lines.

"*July* 25.—I am much indisposed in consequence of the warm weather we now experience. Commodore Macdonough called upon me for information (if in my power), of the naval force of the enemy at *Isle aux Noix*, which I was not able to give him.

"I have been just informed that some troops have arrived at Quebec, from Europe, but the report, however, is somewhat vague.

"*July* 30—Dr. Moore has been with me for this three days past, being so much indisposed. I am, however, somewhat better to-day. The General and some of his officers have called upon me, and very kindly tendered their services, for which they have my sincere thanks.

"*Plattsburg, August* 3.—By the Rangers, the enemy's largest ship is in a fair way to be soon completed. I have reported this to Commodore Macdonough. Mr. Macdonough is the only navy officer, I have found who appears to be pious, and attends upon the divine institutions.

"*August* 9.—There is a report that General Izard is soon to move with a portion of the northern army to the Niagara frontier; if so, this will be another blunder of the present administration. I have sent one of the Rangers to Gen. Izard according to his request.

"*August* 10.—I have ascertained to-day that a portion of the northern army is to move to the Niagara frontier, to fill up the loss which Gen. Brown had sustained at Chippeway and Lundy's Lane.

"*August* 13.—I have received communication from the war department through Governor Tompkins, in which I find that the determination of the government in the removal of the northern army from this quarter, is a most extraordinary step in the military policy. It is well known that the enemy is receiving reinforcements from Europe. Already it is believed there is a considerable force in the vicinity of Montreal. If our army is withdrawn from this post, the enemy may invade this section of the country and attack Plattsburg.

"*August* 14.—The General has communicated to me, that it is the final order of the government for his taking a line of march for Sacketts Harbor—thence on board of the fleet for Niagara.

"Now, this is most impolitic, as well as contrary to the military tactics, to leave such an important post as Plattsburg, just at this time, where the government has everything here to sustain the campaign. Artillery of various calibre, abundance of munition of war, provisions and arms for ten thousand men, 700 batteaux complete for use, and a navy ready for action. I am somewhat disheartened with the manœuvres, and errors of the government. Commodore Macdonough is greatly chagrined at the intentions of the government in regard to this matter.

"*August* 15.—In the warmth of my feelings to sustain the American flag, I have addressed the war department, through Governor Tompkins, in which I respectfully remonstrated against the policy of the government, in withdrawing the troops from this quarter, and forewarned them that the enemy may besiege Plattsburg.

"*August* 16.—As I have anticipated, so I am informed that the British are now assembling their troops at La Prairie and La Acadia plains, and that their object is for the invasion of the State of New York.

"*August* 18.—The northern army is now in motion to the place of its destination. I remarked to the General, that I feared, that by this move of the government, they were taking from him all the glory of beating the enemy—with this he appeared to be greatly moved—and remarked, he was a soldier, and must obey his superiors; but he observed, with a placid smile on his countenance, 'Friend Williams, you ought to be at the head of the war department, instead of those who now control the army.'

"*August* 19.—General Macombe will be left with one thousand five hundred men to protect and defend this important post. I had a long interview with him. I did not wish to alarm him, but hinted that his post may be in danger of an attack from the enemy. He thought there was but little danger of this, especially when the enemy shall be informed of General Izard's march for the west, and if they had any troops to spare from Montreal, they will send them up to oppose him on the Niagara frontier.

"Thus ended my first interview with him as a Commander-in-chief of the post at Plattsburg.

"*August* 21.—General Macombe called upon me this morning to ascertain the truth of what he had learned from some of the American merchants, who were retiring from Canada, under the proclamation of the Governor-general, Sir George Provost. 'I wish to know, sir,' said he, 'from your department, as to the truth of the information which I, last evening, received from several Americans from Canada—that the enemy is in force at La Prairie and La Acadia plains.' I stated to the General that I was in possession of the same information—as to their numbers, I was unable to say—but that from the Rangers I was daily and hourly expecting to hear and learn on this point, and when I did he would be informed; with this he retired.'

"*August* 22.—At 3 o'clock, P.M., a Ranger arrived, and the intelligence he brought was immediately communicated to the General, which was somewhat alarming in its import.

"*August* 23.—At 2 o'clock, P.M., General Macombe called upon me, and appeared to be somewhat in agitation. 'I wish, sir,' said he, 'to be informed more correctly as to the truth, which was communicated to me, yesterday, of the enemy's force at *La Prairie* and *La Acadia* plains,' and with strong emphasis, added, 'if your department needs any money to obtain correct information required, please to make your requisition for the sum upon the deputy-quarter-master-general.' I took the hint of the General's expression. I retorted upon him, 'General, the department does not require an extra sum to obtain the information desired. The reports made by this department have always been correct, so it shall be now. Especial order shall be issued, to-day, to the Rangers for more activity and vigilance, and for a further information.'

"*August* 24.—This morning I had an interview with General Macombe and Commodore Macdonough. I am to start for the lines, this afternoon, to be accompanied by one of the officers of the navy, in a citizen's dress. The General, as I understand, has ordered the whole garrison to labor upon the forts for their completion.

"*August* 25.—I have just returned from Champlain (now, two o'clock at night), where I arrived last night at twelve o'clock, and there met some of the Rangers, and the information received from them, is in corroboration of that which had been received from other sources, of the force of the enemy and their destination, viz. Plattsburg. On my arrival I had an interview with the General, who, I perceive, has decided to make an effort to defend the post. To-morrow a council of war is to be holden, and General Mooers is invited to attend.

"*August* 26.—A council of war was held to-day. My department was called upon for information of the strength of the enemy and its intentions, as far as it was known. The information being given, the council was satisfied on this point, for it could not be otherwise, that the enemy was gradually advancing towards the lines, that his intentions were to invade the State of New York, and that Plattsburg was his object. General Mooers was requested to call out the militia en masse, and to invite the Vermonters to assist in the defence of Plattsburg, and the patriotic citizens to aid in completing the forts. There is, at present, a general alarm among the citizens of the place, and the inhabitants in this vicinity, of the expected invasion of the enemy. Some have already began to leave the village, taking their effects with them. It is not only melancholy, but distressing, to see the poor taking their *all* upon their backs, and flying from their peaceful abodes, and seeking an asylum in places where they are unknown.

"*August* 27.—The anxiety of the General is now so great at the movements of the enemy, as to require me for a report once in ten hours. I sent one of the Rangers to the lines, who has just returned. He took a view, as he said, of the enemy's fleet, and ascertained, as near as it was possible, the calibre of his guns. This requisition was made by Commodore McDonough's request. He took one of the government horses, with permission to sell it to the enemy, to cover his visit.

"*At* 4 *o'clock*, *P. M.*—A Ranger has just arrived with an important information, with which I immediately repaired to the General's quarters—who, I found was marching with his men, with a heavy pine stick on his shoulders, which had painted him with its black coat, so that I could scarcely know him. Every department is now all in activity. Several redoubts are raised as batteries. The inhabitants are flying from their homes.

"*August* 28.—A great anxiety now prevails among us all. Gen. Mooers and his staff are in the field. A Ranger has come in, who has been in the enemy's camp for four days—he made a close observation of his forces—viz. fourteen thousand regulars, most of whom were lately from Europe; two thousand Canadians and two hundred Indians; thirty-six guns, and about one thousand carts. Three thousand of the above troops were thirty-six miles above Montreal, on their way into the Upper province. When the news reached Montreal that General Izard had left Plattsburg with his army (excepting a heavy guard), on his way to the west, they were recalled.

"*Evening, at Chazy*, 8 *o'clock, P. M.*—After an interview with Generals Macomb, Mooers, and Commodore McDonough, I placed myself upon my horse, with my waiter, and in great haste came hither. I saw Judge Treadwell on my way, from whom I received a certain intelligence—and met here Judge More, from Champlain, and Mr. Ransom, of this place, with whom I consulted in regard to our present peculiar and dangerous situation. From these intelligent gentlemen I am relieved from the object of my present jaunt toward the lines. It would appear that the enemy are so confident of their strength and our weakness, they do not hesitate to declare openly that Plattsburg was their object.

"The reports of the Rangers are now more frequent, as they are now close to me, and they have nothing else to do but to observe the movements of the enemy; daily, useful information is now received from this brave, daring, and active corps.

"*August* 29.—The enemy are advancing gradually towards the line. Our forts, redoubts, and batteries are almost completed—should the enemy attempt to appear before them, no doubt, but that they will receive hard blows.

"As to the naval force of the enemy, we have ascertained it, and the calibre of his guns, with which intelligence Commodore McDonough is pleased, as he has been somewhat troubled in not knowing the metal of the enemy's naval guns.

"*Plattsburg, Sept.* 2—A portion of the enemy have crossed the great territorial line, and are encamped at Champlain.

"*Sept.* 3.—The enemy have crossed the Champlain river, and are somewhat in advance of the village. The militia, under Gen. Mooers, are assembling, and forming an encampment in the rear of the forts and at Salmon river.

"*Sept.* 4.—The enemy's advance guard is within eighteen miles from us. Some of the bold and brave militia-men have exchanged shots with them.

"*Sept.* 5.—A council of war was held last evening. My department was again called upon to state the force of the enemy. Every arrangement was made and settled how to receive him. All are in activity—every kind of instrument of death is in preparation, and our fleet in the Bay are manœuvering—the gun-boats are exercising near the shores, in preparation to annoy the enemy whenever he may approach and attack the village. All are solemn—it cannot be otherwise, knowing as we do our weakness, and the strength of the enemy—but resistance will be made, whether to effect or not. Gen. Hull's surrender at Detroit, is in their minds, and spoken of by the soldiers—they are determined that Plattsburg shall not be attacked or surrendered, without the expense of British and American blood. The word *Saratoga* is in the mouth of many.

"Major Aplying, with his Rifle corps, will occupy the bridge, at Dead Creek, near Gen. Mooers' house. This corps has already seen hard service.

"*At night*, 12 *o'clock.*—I have just returned from Gen. Mooers' encampment, at Calwell's Hill. His position is well chosen to receive the enemy, who are now at Douglas Place, at the separation of the Lake and the Back Road, as it is called. It is presumed they will advance on both. A small detachment, headed by my brother John, have gone to spy out the enemy's encampment.

"*At Night*, 5 *o'clock.*—A Ranger has just come in, who left the enemy's camp at two o'clock; and, at that early hour, they were in columns, ready to march. I presume they will be upon us to-day. Although I am not strictly bound, according to my office, to take the carnal weapon into my hand; yet, connected as I am with the army, and all the secret intelligence of the formidable preparations of the enemy, for the invasion of the State of New York, passing through my hands—the feeble state of the American force—half a million of property of the government at the place—the extensive and unfinished works to defend—the distress of the inhabitants, who are now deserting their houses—the general excitement and alarm on the northern frontiers—and the anxiety manifested by the commanding officer, are such as to raise my war-spirit. I have been even called upon several times during the day and night, for information of the progress and movements of the enemy. I had put the whole corps of *observers* in motion to watch him, who were so faithful and daring as to give intelligence from the very centre of the enemy's army, in less than thirty hours; the import was frightful, that the enemy was fourteen thousand strong, with a formidable train of artillery—fearful odds against the American army of fifteen hundred men. Under these exciting and distressing circumstances, and at the same time, with strong but respectful request from General McComb and Mooers for my co-operation, I am thus at length under the necessity of putting on my armor and buckler, to sustain the honor of the American Government.

"To repel the invaders, who are now about twelve miles from Plattsburg, General Mooers advanced this afternoon with seven hundred men to Beckmantown, and, in the evening, Major Wool followed, with two hundred and fifty of the regulars.

"*Evening, September* 6, *at* 10 *o'clock.*—The enemy had been making gradual approaches upon Plattsburg, until this morning, he made a rapid advance in two columns upon two distinct points, and an engagement immediately followed, between Major-General Powers' brigade, supported by a demi-brigade of General Robinson and General Mooers, of the New York militia, supported by a detachment, under Major Wool, who set the militia an example of firmness, for the regulars disputed the road with great obstinacy; but the militia could not be prevailed on to stand for any length of time, notwithstanding the exertions of their general and staff-officers. The State Dragoons, of New York, wore red coats; and they, being on the heights to watch the enemy, gave considerable alarm to the militia, who mistook them for the British, and feared lest they would be getting in their rear. The field-pieces, however, did considerable execution among the enemy's column; and so undaunted were they, that they never deployed in their whole march, but continued pressing in close column, with the exception of a cloud of skirmishers on their right and left. The field-pieces were, finally, ordered to retire across the bridge, and form a battery for its protection, and to cover the retreat of the infantry, which was accordingly done. It was here, for the first time, I was initiated how to manage heavier guns than rifles. The cannonade was kept up upon the enemy with great spirit until sunset. This had been a day of anxiety and gloominess in the little American army. There was no prospect of retaining their position against such overwhelming force as that of the enemy. They had been compelled to recede about six miles before such a cloud of skirmishers and a heavy column of the enemy, as to impress them with an idea of their own weakness, and their inability to withstand the invaders. This was not only extremely disheartening, but humiliating to the American soldiery. General Macomb was silent and thoughtful—he saw too much, no doubt, of his dangerous position —but the garrisons were committed to him for safe keeping, and he would defend them to the last extremity, or be buried under them. In the council of war, which was held on the night of the 7th, at their recommendation, I concluded to place myself at the head of the artillery, with such volunteers as might be collected. The Ranger I had sent to ascertain the strength of the enemy's fleet, returned at two o'clock; and I went with him immediately to our fleet. I had an interview with Commodore Macdonough. He was pleased with the communication, and, no doubt, he will make good use of it. At intervals during the day, we have cannonaded at the enemy's works, and had skirmishing at the bridge.

" General Mooers' division are bivouacked at Salmon river. His advance-guard extends to Pike's encampment on the Saranac. His scouts are vigilant and active; and there is no corps more useful and watchful than the one under the command of Captain Aikens and Lieutenant Flagg. All the Rangers are in, excepting two, for whose safety I am somewhat anxious.

" *September* 8.—The Vermont militia have began to come. Captain Farsworth, of St. Albans, with his rifle company, ninety-six strong, have just arrived. This is a fine and noble corps.

" *Evening.*—Generals Macomb and Mooers, and Commodore Macdonough were together this evening, in consultation, the result of which is, that I am once more compelled to put the whole corps of Rangers in motion.

" *September* 9, *Friday.*—We again cannonaded at the enemy's works. I am quite deaf this evening. A detachment of the enemy attempted to cross at the upper-bridge, but were repulsed by Captain Vaughan's corps. This corps is one of the finest in General Mooers' division. On the 6th, although compelled to retreat, yet they did so in good order, and disputed the ground with the enemy for five miles.

" The volunteers from Vermont are now arriving by companies and regiments. Col. Williams, of Charlotte, eight hundred strong, landed, this afternoon, at Peru. Several of our men were killed and wounded in a skirmish at the lower bridge. By the request of Generals Macomb and Mooers, this Department was compelled to issue an order to the Rangers, on the 8th inst., to take an officer of the enemy. Accordingly, an officer of the artillery was taken, and brought in this evening, and presented to the Generals.

"I have just received a note, in reply to mine, from Colonel Fasset, commanding at Burlington, in which it is proposed to play a *coup de main* upon the British General. Preparations will be made to carry this matter into effect. The same have been submitted to Generals Macomb and Mooers, which was approved. The most active and bravest of the Rangers is selected to perform this difficult and dangerous duty. He accepts, with cheerfulness, the hazardous task.

"*September* 10.—Last night, a corps of the regular troops, under Captain MacGlassin, about 11 o'clock, crossed the Saranac, and stormed, at the point of the bayonet, a bomb-battery of the enemy, near Weight's printing office. My brother John was the leader of this detachment, and was the cause of the death of the engineer of the battery. Having accomplished the duty assigned them, they returned to the forts whence they had issued, with honor and victory.

"A rifle company, under Captain Aikens and Lieutenant Flagg (composed of the young gentlemen of Plattsburg), are not only useful in watching our front line, but they are brave and daring in skirmishing with the enemy. Yesterday, three of this noble corps came nigh being taken or destroyed by the enemy, viz. Allen, Traverse, and Williams. The daring spirits of these young warriors carried them beyond prudence. They crossed the river Saranac to spy out the enemy, as well as to supply themselves with certain articles which they knew were deposited in a barn, and the house was not far from it which was occupied by the guard of the enemy. Just at the moment they were supplying themselves with such articles as they would take, volley after volley of musketry was poured upon them, but they fortunately escaped uninjured. But it is said that the enemy paid dear for this. The youthful band had anticipated this opposition, and were prepared to defend their comrades. The whole corps answered the enemy's fire with such firmness and precision, as to compel the enemy soon to retire. By the report of a Ranger from Grand Isle, we may now daily expect to see the enemy's fleet in our bay. Both parties are preparing for a conflict. The militia from Vermont are still coming in. General Strong and Major Lyman have arrived. Their division is encamped at Pike's cantonment.

"*Plattsburg*, *Sept.* 14.—The British General having made a disposition of his fleet and land forces for a simultaneous attack upon the American position, the first gun on the 11th was the signal for a general action. Sir George Provost instantly opened his heavy batteries upon the works on the opposite bank of the Saranac. A tremendous cannonade ensued—terrific was the noise of more than two hundred pieces of cannon; bomb-shells, shaapnells, balls, and congreve rockets, were thrown into the American lines during the whole day.

"Our position was in the range with one of the enemy's batteries, and was placed there to answer it, and to oppose them by cannonading should they attempt to ford the river. As it was expected, they made the attempt more than once, and at first, by two heavy columns, and when they arrived at the brink of the river they were saluted with such a storm of shot and grape from our battery, as to compel them to fall back, and make their way into the houses, shops, barns, and ditches. Thence they kept up a heavy fire and contended with our riflemen, who were in two mills near the bridge. While the cannonading went on, we either answered the enemy's fire, or poured shot into every body of their troops, that presented a tolerable mark. Never, perhaps, were skirmishes, if such they deserved to be called, conducted with more bravery on both sides. If our troops, in this quarter, lacked skill, they more than made up by their daring. The result of the engagement between the two naval armaments, which continued upwards of two hours, ultimately determined the action upon land. The plans of the British General were completely frustrated by its issue; the whole of his larger vessels having struck to the United States flag; three of the row gallies being destroyed, and the remainder escaping from the bay in a shattered condition. The annihilation of his fleet being announced to Sir George, he immediately withdrew his forces from the assault of the American works. From his batteries, however, he kept up a constant fire until the dusk of evening, when, being silenced by the guns of the fort and the batteries, he retired from the contest, and at nine o'clock at night, sent off his artillery, and all the baggage, for which he could obtain a transport. At midnight, he made a precipitate and disgraceful retreat, leaving behind him all his sick and wounded. Towards the close of the day, when the enemy appeared to make his last efforts to silence our batteries, I was wounded, though not to that degree as to compel me to leave the corps. As soon as it was known, in the morning, that the enemy had retreated, a general order was issued to several divisions and detachments, to pursue the enemy. Our corps was ordered to follow them, and at seven o'clock, we commenced our route for the north, under the equinoctial storm. The rain had been pouring down with such torrents during the night, as to put the road into such a state as to become almost impassable. It had been passed over, during the night, by more than four hundred carts of the enemy, besides his battering train of artillery, so that by twelve o'clock, our progress had been but eight miles. The cavalry, riflemen, and light infantry were several hours in advance, while we were thus drudging in a road, with mud sometimes almost up to our knees, gun after gun stuck and upset in the quagmires, and the horses were staggering and reeling under their burdens.

"Happily for us, in the midst of these difficulties, orders came for us to retrace our steps; and it was not until after dark that we reached the place whence we took our departure in the morning. On reaching my marquee, not a thread on me was dry—shivering under the north-westerly wind, fatigued, and hungry. My wound had now become quite painful, which no care had been taken of, more than what had been done by my waiter, who occasionally washed it with brandy. The wound was not dangerous in its nature, and no inconvenience would have resulted from it, had I not taken cold from the heavy showers of rain that fell upon us during the night and the following day, to which I was exposed.

* * * * * * *

"The cause for great anxiety had now passed—the enemy had retreated—and, although victory was on our side, yet in sober and serious reflections, there were grounds and reasons not only for painful sensations, but sorrow. Many promising young men had met an untimely death. Among them were our friends and acquaintances, whom we loved and esteemed, whose exit we greatly lamented, and whose dead bodies were still in an exposed state. Is this the fate of war? Were they prepared to die thus? And had I been one of them, what would have been my destiny in the future world? In the midst of these inward interrogations, I was interrupted by the appearance of General M'Comb and Major M'Neil, who congratulated me on my safe return, and sympathised with me on account of the painful sensations which I was now suffering from my wound. After many jovial words, and hearty laughs at certain transactions, by some of his officers, during the siege, the General left me, with promise that I should be immediately attended to by the medical gentlemen; but this was objected to by my father, who would act on the occasion as my physician, under whose fostering hand I was carefully attended, and in five weeks I was so far restored as to go abroad once more.

"It was in the hours of my confinement, that I have resolved again and again, if God be willing, to carry to the Indians the faithful saying, and worthy of all acceptation, that 'Christ Jesus came into the world, to save sinners.' How far I am actuated in these from holy principles, may I say that as far as I know my own heart, my aim is for the glory of God, and the advancement of the Redeemer's kingdom."

The military life of Mr. Williams closed with its most brilliant, if not its most arduous and trying hour. Entering the service of the United States, in the first instance, merely from a sense of duty, and without any desire for personal distinction, which allures so many into the army, he had fulfilled the part of a noble-minded commander and gallant soldier. The nature of his office, though responsible in the extreme, and demanding the highest qnalifications, mental and moral, kept him necessarily in the back ground. Though he had the full confidence and esteem of the government and high military officers, who rightly estimated his worth, because they reaped the fruits of it in almost every important event of the war, the public at large knew little of the wisdom, integrity, fortitude, courage, and moderation, which he had displayed. His services were too deep and vital to be blazoned in newspapers or recorded in despatches, and would never have come to light but for his practice of keeping a journal, from the dawn of boyish intelligence, in which, I think, so clearly the hand of Providence may be traced. If the war had continued, it is probable, he would have been offered the command of a brigade, had he chosen to remain in the service of his country, as an intimation to this effect was given him by Governor Tompkins.

This discussion has had one benefit—that of introducing Americans to one of the most noble, though humble-minded of their fellow citizens, and who, if I rightly understand their character, they will see has *all which truth and honor can claim—fair play.* No one, not deeply prejudiced, or lost to discernment, can read the simple war journal of Mr. Williams, unostentatiously truthful as a dying confession, without feeling that here, in all the elements which make man, he is a man. There are few tests of character like that of military life. Whatever a man has of good or evil in him it calls out, and no preux chevalier of olden time, could more modestly or stainlessly—I say nothing of courage, for that, apart from other qualities, is animal—with more of the spirit of Christian moderation and self-sacrifice, have played his part, than Eleazar Williams. During the whole of the war he never relinquished the idea of becoming an Indian missionary—but retired at every opportunity to his quiet room for prayer, meditation, and study—having kindly thoughts even for his national enemies, and in the spirit of one of the noblest hearts that bled during the civil wars of England, supplicating God for peace, even on the field of blood.

War was not his element, though his mind was for a time stirred by its excitement, and carried away by its brilliancy. "As soon as it was practicable," he says, in his memoranda for 1814, "I closed my military concerns with the General Government, and like a monk, entered into my cell for meditation and reflection." He was confined several weeks by his wound, during which time he was sedulously attended by his reputed father, Thomas Williams, who restored him to health and strength by Indian herbs. While feebly reposing on his sick bed, his thoughts and aspirations rushed back to their original channel, and he determined to consecrate the remainder of his days to preaching the Gospel.

## CHAPTER XIII.

### THE LAY MISSIONARY.

MR. WILLIAMS had peculiar qualifications for a missionary to the Indians. He possessed that key to their understandings and affections—without which no great success can attend any efforts to convert the heathen—a perfect knowledge of their language, customs, and modes of feeling and reasoning. His acquaintance with the Mohawk tongue, deficient in childhood, and impaired by long residence in New England, had been revived and increased during the war, and thus, his military life was a partial education for the ministry. Regarding himself, also, as an Indian, he entered on his task with a zest and fervor which can rarely attend the missionary to the heathen, who generally sacrifices to a sense of duty, the love of country and the associations of home. Heart-rending were the feelings of Martyn, when, from the jungles of India, he thought what might have been his earthly lot, had he not violently divorced himself from all he loved. In the case of Mr. Williams, there was no such surrender. He was as much at home in the hut of the Indian, as in the abodes of civilization, while he carried to his work European amplitude of mind and warmth of heart, accompanied with native grace and dignity of manners, sometimes mistaken for pride, but, nevertheless, imposing and attractive to the savage.

An interview with some Oneidas, at Albany, in August, 1814, led to a visit to Oneida Castle in the following November, when he carried with him a wampum from Governor Taylor, of Albany. He was affectionately received by the chiefs, and addressed in a formal speech by one of the orators of the nation, who "arose," he says, "like a Roman senator, and, perhaps, not less in dignity, holding the wampum on high." He replied in the same strain.

There were, at that time, about twelve hundred Indians at Oneida, one half of whom were Christians of the Presbyterian persuasion, and the remainder pagans and adherents of the Prophet Kanyatariyo. This distinction had existed since 1766, when the Gospel was first introduced among them by the Rev. Samuel Kirkland.

A minister of the Scotch Kirk, the Rev. Mr. Jenkins, was, at the time of this visit, instructing the Christian party—but he was ignorant of their language, and the Indians complained of his fragmentary and disjointed mode of preaching through an interpreter. The morals of the nation were at a very low ebb, and the Christians distinguishable from the pagans in little but in name. Before leaving them, Mr. Williams addressed the whole nation, in council, on the duty of believing and obeying Christ; and, after his departure, both translated and composed simple works for their religious instruction.

Shortly after his return to the north, he writes:—

> "The joyful intelligence reached us of the treaty of peace having been concluded between the British and American Commissioners. This event was celebrated by illuminations and demonstrations of joy on these northern frontiers. Thus terminated an eventful and memorable war of two years and six months—a war pregnant with important admonition to Great Britain and to America. Both countries had to experience the mortifying reflection that, all the blood and treasure expended in the contest had been lavished in vain, scarcely any of the objects which were the ostensible cause of the war having been obtained."

He now applied himself, more closely than ever, to his preparation for the ministry. During the war we have seen he had frequent interviews with the clergy of the Protestant Episcopal Church, the solemnity of whose ritual, in the first place, attracted his attention, and so devotionally impressed his heart that, in spite of all the associations of his early years in New England, and the cherished and never to be forgotten kindness of his Congregational friends, to whom the honor is due of having first rescued him from barbarism, and supplied all his wants with a lavish affection, he attended the worship of the church, on all convenient occasions.

A little incident which occurred during the war, when visiting the Rev. Mr. Clowes, of Albany, and which has, I believe, been published in a newspaper by the surviving brother of that gentleman, who informed me of the fact, is deserving of record. A brilliantly illuminated missal, of the character in use in cathedral churches on the continent, lay on the study table of Mr. Clowes, at the sight of which young Williams, who was remarkable for his usually quiet and self-possessed demeanor, became suddenly agitated, to an astonishing degree, so as almost to give the impression of temporary insanity, and in the most earnest manner, as if some mysterious chord of feeling was touched, besought that it might be given to him. The request was refused, not so much on account of the value of the book, as, because, it was looked on as an act of unaccountable eccentricity.

To his predilection for the Protestant Episcopal Church, was added the belief that her ritual and discipline would be more serviceable to the Indians than the extemporaneous worship of other denominations, and, accordingly, in the month of May, 1815, he made a journey to New York, to lay his plans and feelings before Bishop Hobart, and receive his advice.

"I wish to make known to the Bishop," he writes, "my feelings in regard to the Episcopal Church. Her ministry, doctrines, government, discipline, and mode of worship, I am fully persuaded, are in accordance with the word of God. I have read much upon the claims of this church, and I now firmly believe she is the true and sound part of the Church Militant, or the Church of Christ. I pray God to enlighten me more on this most important and interesting subject. Church history has been my companion for more than one year. Five different authors I have read on this subject.

"*Troy, May* 11.—I have had several friendly interviews with the Rev. Mr. Butler, who has labored most earnestly to make me see that the Episcopal Church of the United States is the sound part of Christ's Church His arguments are more powerful with me than those offered in my former interviews. He was very affectionate to me, and how could I do otherwise than love him, who takes such an interest in my spiritual welfare. By me, he will write to Bishop Hobart, to the Rev. Mr. Clowes, and Lieut.-Governor Taylor, of Albany. Mr. Butler has warmed my heart on the subject of religion.

"*New York*, *May* 14. *Lord's Day Evening.*—I arrived here in safety, to-day, about noon, went this afternoon to St. Paul's Church, and heard Mr. Creighton, and, this evening, heard Dr. Roymaine.

"*Thursday* 18—I called upon the Rt. Rev. Bishop Hobart, and presented the introductory letters I had received from my friends in the north. The bishop received me with great cordiality, and appeared to be much gratified.

"*New York*, *Monday*, 22.—I took breakfast at Dr. Hosack's, with Mr. Eddy, and the Rev. Mr. Steward. I was introduced to young Dr. Francis, pupil of Dr. H., with whom I was highly pleased for his polite attention to me. He is a young man of promise. I cannot be too grateful to Dr. H. and lady for his polite invitation.

"*New York*, *May* 29.—Bishop Hobart has requested me to take my board with the Rev. Mr. Onderdonk, to-morrow I shall go there, with which Mr. Ogden appears to be much gratified."

The bishop acknowledged the duty of the church to the Indians, and promised his hearty co-operation in the designs of Mr. Williams. In the record of their interviews the following scene occurs, equally honorable to both. We have seen, on various occasions, that the extreme doctrines of Calvinism did not harmonize with Mr. Williams's sentiments, but it was impossible to have mingled so much as he had with those who entertained them, without being tinctured. "When I touched," he says, "upon some controverted points of theology, the bishop abruptly observed that I was straining too much on those points which were considered, by some, to be in close alliance with the Calvinists. "Rt. Rev. Father," said I, "it is not my wish to know, on the present occasion, Calvin, Luther, Arminius, or Wesley, but Christ and him crucified. I have no desire to embrace the opinions of men, further than they follow Christ. It is my wish always to appeal to the law, and to the testimony, and if their religious opinions are not in accordance with the Holy Scriptures, I, of course, reject them." To this the bishop, with a placid countenance, replied, "Right, my son." I continued, "you see, father, I am somewhat free and independent in my views, in regard to the high doctrines of the Gospel. If I am to be a teacher in the Episcopal Church, I trust I shall not be compelled to receive anything as an article of faith, which I may view as repugnant to the word of God. I acknowledge the Thirty-nine Articles are such as to command the approbation of orthodox Christians, and contain a vast amount of important truth, yet they were composed by fallible men. I will cheerfully adhere to them as far as they agree with the word of God." "This is all," said the bishop, "we can ask of you," and then continued with a solemn voice, "My son, holding the mystery of faith in a pure conscience, let no man despise thy youth, but be thou an example to the believers in word, in conversation, in charity, in spirit, in faith, in purity."

For the first time in his life, he received the communion in St. John's church, on the 21st May, from the hands of the bishop and the Rev. B. T. Onderdonk. Of the kindness of the latter he speaks in terms of gratitude and affection.

It was determined by the Bishop to send him among the Indians as a catechist, lay reader, and schoolmaster; and in this humble capacity he continued for many years, performing all the duties of the ministry, except the administration of the sacraments. So unobtrusive was he, in this respect, that although his labors were crowned with the most ample success, and he enjoyed the full confidence of Bishop Hobart, he was not ordained until the year 1826. He had as little desire of self-aggrandisement in the church, as in the army. Provided he did the work assigned, he was satisfied. Other persons, with his endowments, would have despised the wigwam of the Indian, and sought for popularity and station in cities, and in the applause of the wealthy and intellectual. But personal display was not in his nature. Almost instinctively he seems to have attached himself everywhere to the highest and most gifted minds, and there are few men who have adorned the annals of this country, from John Randolph to Gen. Taylor, who have not enjoyed his society and esteem. But through all vicissitudes, his affections reverted to the Indian huts, on which his eyes had first opened in boyhood; and to preach the glad-tidings of salvation, in sounds, to others barbarous, but to him, most meaning and most musical, was the one absorbing desire of his heart.

He mentions, at this period, several interviews with the Rev. E. C. Steward, of St. Armand, Lower Canada, who was a son of Lord Galway, and expresses delight that one of noble blood would rather "be an humble messenger of the Lord of Hosts, than enjoy the ease and luxuries which are to be found in palaces." "O how powerful," he exclaims, "is that grace which gives divine life here, and eternal glory in the coming world!"

Through the influence of Bishop Hobart, who, on the 23d May, 1815, addressed an appeal to churchmen, for contributions for the purpose, he undertook the revision of former translations of the Prayer Book into the Mohawk language, and also attempted to establish a school for the Indians, at St. Regis. In the latter project he was disappointed, owing to the political feuds in the tribe, and the opposition of many against him, in consequence of the part he had taken in the war of 1812. He wrote, under date of August 3, 1815, a full account of the difficulties under which he labored, to the Rev. Mr. Onderdonk. The purest intentions, and the most self-denying conduct, are not sufficient to ensure success, and those who have no criterion for worth, but success, will often be unjust to those most deserving commendation. The Romish priest, at St. Regis, backed by all the influence of the British government, used every effort, justifiable and unjustifiable, to injure Mr. Williams in the estimation of the Indians, and we shall see, in the sequel, the lengths to which his successor has dared to proceed. But truth and innocence have only to be patient, and bide their time, and the moment of retribution will come.

Baffled, for the time, by Romish influence and political prejudices, in his efforts at St. Regis, he turned his thoughts to Oneida, the chiefs, warriors, and counsellors of the nation, having applied to Bishop Hobart, that he might be sent to them as a religious teacher. He arrived there, with a letter from the bishop, on 23d March, 1816. The minister of the Presbyterian Kirk was recalled at the request of the chief, by the Missionary Society who had sent him, and Mr. Williams accepted by the whole nation.

It is not my purpose to enter into the endless details of his labors among the Indians, which are ample enough to form a work of absorbing interest, to those who can sympathize with the struggles of the humble missionary, but simply to state results and leading events. On his arrival among them, he found the Christian part of the nation, in the most deplorable moral condition, and the heathen given up to idolatry, witchcraft, and drunkenness, while all of them, though attached personally to him, as one who could address them in their language, were indisposed to receive the ritual of the Protestant Episcopal Church—but by preaching and oral conferences, in which he explained their difficulties, and met the various objections, infidel or sectarian, they brought, with a quiet practical wisdom and simplicity which might serve as a model for a missionary among the heathen in any part of the world, he not only converted, in a brief space of time, the whole of the heathen party, but united the whole nation, in adherence to the doctrine, discipline, and worship of the Protestant Episcopal Church, achieving a victory over prejudice and unbelief, absolutely unparalleled in our ecclesiastical annals, in this country.

The following document, exhibits the result of his labors:—

"*To His Excellency the Governor of the State of New York.*

"May it please your Excellency:

"We, the chiefs and principal men of that part of the Oneida nation of Indians, heretofore known and distinguished as the "Pagan Party," in the name of the said party, beg leave to address your Excellency on a subject which, we hope, will be as pleasing to your Excellency as it is to us.

"We no longer own the name of pagans. We have abandoned our idols and our sacrifices, and have fixed our hopes on our blessed Redeemer. In evidence of this assertion, we here tender to your excellency, solemnly and unequivocally, our abjuration of paganism and its rites, and have taken the Christians' God to be our God, and our only hope of salvation. We believe in God the Father, the Creator and Preserver of all things, as omniscient and omnipresent, most gracious and most merciful We believe in Jesus Christ, that He is the Son of God, the Saviour of the world, the Mediator between God and man, and that all must believe in Him, and embrace Him, in order to obtain salvation. We believe in God the Sanctifier and Comforter of all the children of men. We believe in a general Resurrection, and a future judgment in which all men shall be judged, according to their works. We believe the Scriptures to be the Word of God, and that in them are contained all things necessary to man's salvation. We present to your Excellency this abstract of our faith, in order to demonstrate the impropriety of our retaining any longer the name of pagans. We trust that, through the mercy of God, we have abandoned the character of pagans. Let us also abandon the name. We, therefore, request your Excellency, that in all future transactions with this state, we may be known and distinguished as the 'Second Christian party of the Oneida nation of Indians;' and we pray that your Excellency will take such means as may be necessary and proper to cause us to be known and recognised in future by that name. And in the name of the Most Holy Trinity, we do here sign ourselves your Excellency's most sincere friends.

"Done in General Council, at Oneida, this 25th day of January, 1817."

The following Indians subscribed to the above, each one making his mark:—

| | |
|---|---|
| CORN. OTHEASHEAT, | PETER SANTHECALCHOS, |
| ARIRIUS TEHORANIOGO, | NICHS. GARONGONTIE, |
| JOHN. CANNELIUS, | MOSES SCHUYLER, |
| JACOB ATONI, | WM. TEGARENTOTASHON, |
| WM. TONIATESHEN, | WM. TEHOIATATSHE, |

PETER TWASERASHE.*

* Christian Journal, p. 62, vol. i.

"It was an affecting sight," writes Mr. Williams, speaking of the council in which this document was drawn up, "to see the aged and venerable chiefs, counsellors, matrons, and warriors, with uplifted hands, and with countenances indicating that their minds were deeply affected, unitedly, with a loud voice, renouncing the principles of paganism, and making their profession of the Christian faith."

As a substantial token of their sincerity in the adoption of the Christian religion, the chiefs gave Mr. Williams one hundred acres of land, which, however, were used and expended for the benefit of the nation—and they also contributed four thousand dollars towards the erection of a chapel.

During all this time, with the exception of his salary from the Missionary Society, of one hundred and twenty-five dollars per annum, Mr. Williams received nothing from the church, and as, from motives of delicacy he declined aid proffered him by his New England friends, whose communion he had conscientiously left, though, to their lasting honor be it said, this made no difference in their affection for him, or their willingness to contribute to his support, he continued, until he had expended all, in the service of the church, to subsist on his hard-earned remuneration from the United States Government.

The intimacy formed in 1816 by Mr. Williams with the Rev. M. Stewart, of St. Armand, Canada, soon ripened into friendship. Letters frequently passed between them respecting the spiritual interests of the Indians and translations into Mohawk; and after the elevation of Mr. Stewart to the Episcopate of Quebec, his affection for Mr. Williams continued unabated. Before he left America, in later years, for ever, he wrote to Mr. Williams to come and see him. "I went," says Mr. Williams, "to the place appointed for the meeting, and there, after many prayers by ourselves, I, with many tears and a bleeding heart, took the hand of my most beloved and sincere friend, for the last time. I left him, with heavy and sorrowful heart, to return to my distant abode in the west, and he to the eastward to lay his body—yea, mingle his ashes, with his ancestors. O, my God! what a meeting and what a journey was this, mingled with joy and sorrow."

Hitherto, with the single check he had received in his efforts to establish a school among the Indians at St. Regis, the course of Mr. Williams had been a constant series of successes. A storm, which, at first, was only like a little cloud in the horizon, began now to brew at a distance.

The Menominie and Winnebago Indians, having ample territories on the borders of Lake Michigan, which they were unable to occupy, were desirous to share them with their eastern brethren of the Six Nations, and made a generous proposition to surrender to the New York Indians many thousand acres of land in the neighborhood of Green Bay. A general council of the Six Nations was held in 1817, at Fort Meigs, on the Maumee river, to which the young Missionary Chief of the Oneidas was invited. De Witt Clinton, then Governor of New York, knowing his influence among the Indians, was anxious that he should attend, and wrote to Bishop Hobart asking his permission, as Mr. Williams, with military fidelity, refused to leave his post without the consent of his superior. The Bishop gave his consent, but Mr. Williams did not go to the council. Indeed he was at that time opposed to the project of removal, though afterwards he got entangled in this political measure of the General and State Government, which created a dislike to him in the minds of a portion of the Indians, which, fostered by other causes, in which he was entirely innocent, has continued till the present day.

Though merely a lay reader, from the necessities of the case, he performed all the duties of an ordained minister, except the administration of the sacraments, and it is curious, considering the ardent nature of his Protestantism, and the influences under which he had been educated, to read the following entry in his journal for 1817, at a time the Episcopal Church in this country was quaker-like in the unadorned simplicity of its worship. "The joyful festival of the Nativity was celebrated by the natives with peculiar solemnity. On Christmas evening our chapel was dressed up with evergreens in beautiful order. In celebrating the Divine Service and the august ceremonies of the Holy Church this night, *I chanted at the altar, Gloria in Excelsis, and Te Deum Laudamus, and other parts of the service*, with which the congregation were highly gratified." This event reminds one of the anecdote of the missal related by Mr. Clowes. There must, indeed, have been a somewhat strange state of things at Oneida, although it was with the full knowledge and approbation of Bishop Hobart. Though merely a layman, Mr. Williams wore a surplice in performing divine service, and, according to a practice of the times, had his hair powdered; and, worse yet,—I cannot forbear a smile at the dismay the sight would have occasioned some of my friends—was attended with a bevy of little Indian boys, similarly clad. But this was only in accordance with the policy afterwards pursued by the Congregational missionaries among the eastern churches; and Bishop Hobart, who knew the Indians required ceremony and outward display, like a man of common sense, who could distinguish a doctrine from a vestment, did not suspect the lay missionary of Romish tendencies, because he donned a white garment in the sanctuary, and arrayed in snow a few copper-colored cherubs. Controversy makes things odious and, I grant, pernicious, very harmless in themselves. At the Bishop's visitation, the little surpliced Oneidas, like choristers in English cathedrals, walked in front of him. *Honi soit qui mal y pense.*

The bishop also permitted the zealous layman to preach his own sermons. Indeed, he could not have done otherwise, as there were no hot-pressed Iroquois homilies to which he could resort. The church, if she would be useful, must adapt herself to circumstances, and eschew Procrusteanism in accidents. Cut and stretch according to the creed, but allow latitude in the canon, arm-like action from a fixed centre of principle—here is power.

Notwithstanding the ability Mr. Williams manifested in everything calling for the display of the highest endowments of mind, in that peculiar region where the moral faculties are required to aid the intellectual, there was an absolute want in him, of that which, in a mercantile community, is regarded as constituting the man—viz. the power of keeping money when he had got it. He had received $10,000 from the United States, for his services during the war, but allowed it to get beyond his control, and would have lost it, but for the friendly exertions of Chancellor Kent, Gov. Taylor, the Hon. Nathan Williams, and Morris S. Miller, of Utica. He was left, for a time, in almost entire destitution, with nothing to support him but his $125. In a long communication to Bishop Hobart, which, with the bishop's affecting answer, may be found in the "Christian Journal," vol. ii. p. 268, the Oneida Indians say, "agreeably to your request, we have treated our brother with that attention and kindness which you required of us: we have assisted him all that was in our power, but we cannot do a great deal. Though our brother has lived very poor since he came among us, he is patient and makes no complaint: we pity him, because we love him as we do ourselves. We wish to do something for his support, but this is impossible, as we have lately raised between 3 and 4,000 dollars to enable us to build a little chapel."

Burning with zeal for the advancement of Christ's cause, he hoped that his unparalleled success among the Indians would stimulate the church, into whose ranks he had entered, from conscientious motives, to extend the mission among the rest of the New York Indians, who were desirous, if he could be supported, to receive the Gospel at his hands, but he could wring nothing from the treasury but the munificent sum of $125. Thus reduced to despair, with a generous self-sacrifice, which few can even understand, he solemnly consecrated to God's service his $10,000 as soon as it was assured him by the exertions of his friends. "All this," he writes, "I trust was spent with the greatest economy, as a faithful steward—as one who must render an account of his stewardship."

In the summer of 1818, his health being very feeble, on account of his many trials and arduous labors, Mr. Williams undertook a journey to the north, accompanied by La Fort, a young Onondaga chief of fine abilities, who embraced Christianity, and had for several months been studying with him the English language. La Fort afterwards received an excellent education, under the patronage of the Protestant Episcopal Church, but finally relapsed into Heathenism, in a great measure in consequence of depression of spirits, owing to his neglect by the church, and the unpopularity of Christianity among his Heathen brethren. At Morristown, on the St. Lawrence, they were entertained by Judge Ford; and at Waddington, by Hon. D. A. Ogden, at whose house they met the British and American Commissioners, who were deciding the boundaries between the British and American provinces.

On their arrival at St. Regis, the Rev. Mr. Marcoux, the Romish priest, put into his hand a letter of introduction to the Rev. Mr. Dufresne, at Caughnawaga, who gave him another to the Rev. Mr. Richards, formerly a Methodist minister, but then residing at the Seminary, at Montreal. He went to see this gentleman on 4th August. Richards was, at first, constrained in his manner, but at last assumed a more cheerful appearance, and said, "I believe, sir, you must be the gentleman, noticed in the public prints, as a missionary, who is doing much good among the Oneidas. I once passed through their settlement. You are connected, I believe, with the Episcopal Church, and Dr. Hobart is your Bishop. I am surprised that you have connected yourself with that false church, a church that has no lawful ministry. The Church of Rome is the most ancient church. The Church of England is of yesterday." Mr. Williams hereupon reminded him of the reply of Queen Elizabeth to the Jesuits, when they petitioned her to restore the "ancient Catholic faith," to the effect, that their own records made them liars, and proved that Christianity existed in England independent of Rome, long prior to the time of Austin. Richards dropped the subject, showed him the library of the Seminary and the parish church, and invited him back to his room, when the following conversation occurred.

"I believe, sir," said Richards, "that you are the gentleman of whom the Abbé de Calonne, of Three Rivers, has often spoken, as a person whose history was hidden in the womb of mystery, in regard to your descent, and the cause of your adoption among the Indians of this province." "This excited my curiosity," writes Mr. Williams, "to ask him what mystery it might be which the Abbé supposes to be about my birth and family?" "He supposes," said he, "you are a foreigner by birth, and of high family." "If this be the opinion of the Abbé," said I, "he must have some evidence of it." "He has, of course," he replied, "but as to the extent of it, I cannot say." "I am, however, inclined to believe that it is a mere conjecture with him, for when I have pressed upon him to be more explicit, he would evade the question by saying—'It is in a great measure conjectural with me.'"

"I then observed to him, it would be highly gratifying to me, were I to know my family, and the cause of their putting me among the Indians." "This, I presume," he said, "the Abbé would not say, so long as he himself is not fully satisfied on the point. I am satisfied he has more information upon this subject than he is willing to communicate. There are known circumstances, which are strong in their nature, and which would prove, it seems, that you are not the son of an Iroquois chief. I would be happy, if in my power to unveil this mystery to you. I will see the Abbé again." He then gave me a pat on the shoulder, and said, "You are, I suspect, of higher grade by blood than the son of an Iroquois chief."

"These extraordinary declarations produced some sensations in my feelings," he writes, "although it was not the first time such hints were thrown in my way. On reflection, however, my conviction was that I had been taken for one of those youths and children who had been given to the Indians by the poor French Canadians."

On his return to the Sault St. Louis, by the permission of the missionary priest, he examined the parochial register, and found that all the names of the children of Thomas Williams were registered excepting Eleazar, "at which," says Mr. Williams, "the priest appeared greatly surprised and vexed, as in my former interview he would make me appear as if I was the child of the Romish Church by baptism."

This was the first time that serious doubts were awakened in his mind as to his belonging to the family of Thomas Williams, but having nothing tangible to support them, they died away gradually. While absorbingly occupied with present interests, duties, and trials, he referred the whole subject to Providence and futurity— and having nothing before him but vague suspicion, for which there seemed little foundation, continued in everything to act and feel towards his reputed kinsmen, far and near, as he had always done.

On the 3d September, 1818, Bishop Hobart visited Oneida Castle, and confirmed eighty-nine persons, who had been prepared for that holy rite by Mr. Williams. The bishop produced a great effect on their minds, and months after, they told Mr. Williams that, when they thought upon the scene, they imagined they felt his hands upon their heads, and heard his voice, saying, "Defend, O Lord, this thy servant."

In the ensuing Convention the bishop spoke in the highest terms of applause of the zealous labors of the missionary. Indeed, it was impossible to speak in terms of laudation too strong of the exertions of Mr. Williams, at this time, in the cause of Christ. He was not only laboring hard as a missionary, catechist, and lay reader, and performing the practical duties of a pastor, but was supporting and educating, in a great measure, at his own expense, several young Indians for the ministry. Besides which, extending his exertions from the Oneidas to the Onondagas, he created such a sensation in favor of Christianity, as to lead to the convening of a general council of the Seneca, Cayuga, Tuscarora, Mohawk, Stockbridge, and St. Regis Indians, to take into consideration the duty of embracing the Christian faith. The services of the Church were solemnly performed with chants and hymns, and a debate ensued which lasted several days, but led to no results, owing to the fierce opposition of the Pagan party. The subject was referred to a future council, to meet at Buffalo Creek, on the 8th October, 1819.

Between the session of the two councils, the chapel at Oneida was consecrated by Bishop Hobart, and the most devout feeling prevailed among the Indians.

The discussion was resumed at the appointed time, and the substance of many of the speeches on both sides, presenting choice specimens of eloquence, not unworthy the halls of a civilized legislature, have been preserved by Mr. Williams, who, as an Oneida chief, being a delegate to the council, on this occasion, and the main pillar of the Christian cause, was opposed to the famous Red Jacket, and maintained with him, for three days, a fierce debate, in which everthing that the malice and ingenuity of a strong minded and eloquent idolator, sharpened by the necessities of forensic strife, and winged with sarcasm, could urge against the Gospel, or the lives of its adherents, was brought forward on one hand, and on the other the truth, the beauty, the divinity of the Christian religion, and the folly, absurdity, superstition, and degrading tendency of Heathenism. Wearied at last, and overpowered, though not convinced by an eloquence, perseverance, wisdom, and resolution, superior to his own, Red Jacket abandoned the contest. "His language," says Mr. Williams, "was certainly beautiful. His arguments, as far as they went, were powerful, yet he was placed in an unfortunate position, he was opposed to a subject with which he was little acquainted. His position was studied and examined, his arguments well weighed, but by his antagonist promptly met. For he understood his language—it was, therefore, a fair combat. Hitherto had he boasted, and his adherents with him, that he had beaten all the missionaries who had attempted to meet him. When he was excited, as he was at times in his declamations, then his eloquence was at its height. It was then, indeed, that the flow of words and arguments, the music of his voice, the graceful gestures of his arms, and the ease and majestic motions of his body, were exciting and animating in the extreme. He appeared to the best advantage on the first day of his declamations, in which he occupied the floor the greater part of the time. There was only time for me to make a few preliminary remarks upon the points which would form the subject of my discussion on the following day, before the council adjourned. One of the Pagan chiefs observed to another that, 'Red Jacket, the King of the Orators of the Six Nations, has just commenced his oratory, and before he finishes he will make the young missionary feel the weight of his power.'"

A vote was obtained from the council more favorable than could have been expected at so early a period, in the death conflict between the hereditary superstition and the newly introduced Gospel, permitting the establishment of schools, though as yet they would not consent to the introduction of missionaries. It was regarded as a victory by the Christians, for in the conflict of parties, both on a small and great scale, that which wavers and declines must ultimately fall, and every foothold of advance is a step towards ultimate triumph.

It is sad to think that zeal so unbounded, self-sacrifices so noble, and successes so great, should have passed out of the mind of the church as if they had never been; and sadder still, to think that there was not sufficient missionary zeal in the ranks of the Episcopal Church to listen to the exhortations of Bishop Hobart, or appreciate and sustain the efforts of Mr. Williams.

The reader will have noticed throughout Mr. Williams's history, that while his mental powers were most vigorous, and his exertions intense, every season of exertion was followed by a prostration of health. It was so in the present instance. He continued, however, laboring unweariedly—for his duties were such as scarcely to admit cessation—when at length, in the midst of his favorite Christmas solemnities, his voice failed while chaunting, and bleeding of the lungs ensued. He was, therefore, compelled to leave, and travel for his health, the only remedy he had from boyhood found available.

He was also summoned to Washington, at this time, on public business of the highest importance to the Oneidas, and, as it eventually proved, of most disastrous consequences to himself. The government of the United States had now determined to attempt the removal of the New York Indians to the west, and, relying on the ability of Mr. Williams, and his influence with the nation, summoned him to its councils.

The subject of removal had engaged his attention for many years, and he was at first much opposed to it, but observation, reflection, and consultation with others, had all contributed to change his views.

The Indians had no longer the ample territories and hunting-grounds they once possessed. Encroached upon, on all sides, by the rapid strides of civilization, and dwindling, as barbarism ever must, in power and numbers, when in contiguity with a great civilized people, they had lost, piecemeal, a large portion of their lands, and the prospect was, they would be entirely swallowed by the swelling tide which hemmed them in on all sides. Besides which, there were many claimants to the Indian lands in the State of New York, foremost among whom were Messrs. Ogden & Co., who, as far back as 1796 or '7, had actually purchased large portions of these lands from the colony of Massachusetts, which, in the adjustment of boundary difficulties between it and New York, had obtained a pre-emption interest in the Indian country, with right of extinguishing the Indian title, which passed over to the purchasers, who had thus a joint interest with the General and State Governments in causing the removal of the Indians.

In December, 1819, the Rev. Dr. Morse, on behalf of the United States Government, visited Oneida, and Mr. Williams convened the nation, in general council, to hear his address, in which he urged them, by such considerations as those above, and by showing the impossibility of their continuing to lead a hunting life in the State of New York, to consent to retire to the lands formerly occupied by the Menominies and Winnebagoes, in the neighborhood of Green

Bay—negociations concerning which with the Six Nations, began even before the war of 1812, but, interrupted by that event, had been renewed. He also read the memorial of the Sachems and chiefs of the Six Nations to the President of the United States, in November, 1815, on the subject, with the answer of the President. It was a subject too weighty to admit of immediate decision, as the Oneidas were greatly divided in opinion; but the visit of Dr. Morse led to a correspondence between the government and Mr. Williams, which ended by his being invited to Washington. On his way, he called on Bishop Hobart, in New York, who gave him a letter of introduction to President Monroe, and expressed the greatest sympathy, both with his infirm condition of health and the business on which he was engaged. The Bishop, who took an enlightened and statesman-like view of the subject, had for several years regarded emigration westward, as the only means of saving the Indians, and had persuaded Mr. Williams to use his influence in furtherance of the design. It is necessary to understand all this to perceive how he was first withdrawn from strict missionary duty, and placed in political opposition to a portion of the Oneidas.

President Monroe and Mr. Calhoun, Secretary of War, received him kindly at Washington; but though much attention was shown him on all sides, his favorite appears to have been John Randolph, in whose society and conversation he took great delight. On the arrival of Dr. Morse, an expedition to the west was determined, and the War Department agreed to furnish means for prosecuting it, according to plans furnished, at request of the Government, by Mr. Williams. The party was to consist of Dr. Morse, Mr. Williams, and eight Indians, delegates from the Six Nations.

The Secretary of War, under date of February 9, 1820, wrote to Governor Cass and General McComb, stating that the expedition was undertaken with the approbation of the President, and recommending Mr. Williams to their care, besides sending fuller communications to them, and the commandants of the different posts in the west.

Governor Clinton, also, charged Mr. Williams to obtain for him extensive statistical information respecting the traditions, language, customs, numbers, and government of the western Indians; which he subsequently embodied in his discourses before the New York Historical Society. And Bishop Hobart, likewise, wrote to him, before his departure, giving him permission to leave his missionary station for the purpose contemplated; "satisfied," he says, "as I am, that it is your supreme desire to promote the temporal and spiritual welfare of your countrymen, and, further, the benevolent views of the government."

On the arrival of Mr. Williams and the deputies at Detroit, July 11, 1820, they found General Cass absent at Maumee river, making a treaty with the Potowatomies, and could obtain no aid from Lieut.-Gov. Woodbridge, with whom they conferred, as he said he had no authority to assist them. To their surprise, also, on the return of Dr. Morse, who had preceded them westward to Green Bay, they learned that the agent of the United States, Colonel Boyer, at that place, had purchased by treaty, from the Indians, the very lands they had gone out to survey—a transaction they imputed to General Cass, who, as Governor of the territory, was at the head of the Indian department—it being in no way probable, that a subordinate would act in such a manner, at such a moment, without the knowledge and approbation of his superior. Baffled and disappointed in their undertaking, the deputies memorialized the government on the subject, and expressed their chagrin at the transaction. They then returned eastward from Detroit; and Mr. Williams was compelled to proceed to, and spend the winter at, Washington, to oppose the ratification of the treaty, which he did successfully, with the approbation and assistance of the President and the Secretary of War. Permission was then given to the Six Nations to make arrangements with the Menominies and Winnebagoes for the purchase of the lands, and it became necessary for Mr. Williams to set out again to the west. As the mission at Oneida had suffered greatly in consequence of his absence in 1820, he procured immediately on his return from the west, in the fall of that year, the services of a young gentleman of the name of Ellis, to act as lay reader. The health of Mr. Ellis was weak, and, in the spring of 1821, Mr. Williams determined to take him with him to the west for the benefit of his health. With the sanction of Bishop Hobart, he entrusted the care of his mission, during the second absence, to a poor young man, of pleasing manners and seeming piety, named Solomon Davis, whom he furnished with clothes and other necessaries, and left in care of his house and library.

Before the departure of Mr. Williams, the bishop, who was now deeply interested in the project for the removal of the Indians to the west, addressed the Oneidas in a long letter, from which I will insert the following passages :—

"My Children.—I am fully satisfied that it is the benevolent wish of the Government of the United States, in all their plans, to promote your good.

"My Children.—Your friend and brother and instructor, Eleazar Williams, I am fully persuaded, has you constantly in his heart; and it is the object of his thoughts, and cares, and plans, and labors, to make you good, and respectable, and happy.

"My Children.—It is expedient that he should go on a journey to the west, to see if he can find some territory, where the Stockbridge Indians and others, who are disposed to go, may reside; and particularly to ascertain whether your western brethren are inclined to embrace the Gospel of our Lord and Saviour, Jesus Christ, which is the great and only means of making us good and happy, here and hereafter.

"My Children.—Let Mr. Williams go, and aid him all you can in the important objects of his journey.

"John H. Hobart."

To show the deep interest taken in this expedition, so unfortunate to Mr. Williams, I need only further insert the following testimonial with which he was furnished, by the Governor of New York :—

"*De Witt Clinton, Governor of the State of New York, to all to whom these presents shall come, greeting:*

"Mr. Eleazar Williams, and several of the chiefs of the Six Nations resident in this state, being on an exploring tour to the west, on business of importance, I do hereby recommend them to the protection and hospitality of all persons to whom they may apply for the same.

"In witness whereof, I have hereunto affixed my hand and the privy seal of the state, at the city of Albany, this 17th day of May, A.D., 1821.

"DE WITT CLINTON."

The deputation from the Six Nations, with Mr. Williams at their head, arrived at Detroit, July 12, 1821. Governor Cass, being absent, deputed Mr. Trowbridge to act as agent for the government, and he accompanied the party to Green Bay. "We are very fortunate," writes Mr. Williams, "that such a gentleman as Mr. Trowbridge was appointed to superintend, on the present occasion, the concerns of the New York Indians."

On July 31, they left Detroit in the steamer, "Walk in Water." The Rev. Dr. Yates, of the Reformed Dutch Church, and Rev. Dr. Richard, of the Romish Church, were of the company. On 3d August, they touched at the island of Michilimackinac and admired "its beauty and majestic appearance," and passing through the Straits of Lake Huron and Michigan, arrived August 5, at ten o'clock, in the Fox River, opposite Fort Howard.

Communication was immediately opened with the Menominies and the Winnebagoes. At first, the latter were desirous of making a *present* of the land to the New York Indians; but this was declined, on account of the insecurity which would attend the title, in future times. It was finally agreed the land should be purchased, by treaty, which was accordingly done on August 17, in a grand council—the terms being two thousand dollars, five hundred of which were to be paid immediately and fifteen hundred within one year. Having accomplished his mission for the government and the Indians, Mr. Williams returned home, and arrived at

Oneida Castle, September 28, 1821. He received the thanks and congratulations both of the General and State Governments, and also of Bishop Hobart, for the ability with which he had conducted the affair.

"I congratulate you," wrote De Witt Clinton, in transmitting him a check for two hundred and fifty dollars, "on the success of your mission." This, I may remark, being a mere payment of expenses, was all which Mr. Williams has ever received for services by which the State of New York has so largely benefitted in consequence of the sales of land by emigrating tribes to her.

But now, in earnest, began the troubles of his latter years. The reader will remember that the Oneida Indians were divided into two parties, formerly Christian and Pagan; but, since the successful missionary efforts of Mr. Williams, known as the First and Second Christian parties. Of these, the First was favorable, and the Second, opposed to emigration. Political prejudices, fostered by certain religious teachers, for their own ends, alienated the Second Christian party from the man to whom they were indebted for the faith of Christ, and who had been laboring to the best of his ability, and the neglect of his own interests, to promote their welfare and that of the whole body of the Indians.

It was, at this time, that system of calumny began, so well continued and imitated by others up to the present time, and the effects of which can only be counteracted by such an exposure to the public eye as I am now making of the life, character, and actions of the man. Happy for every one if their past lives would bear scrutiny as well as that of Eleazar Williams. The Second Christian party of Indians, or rather a few individuals among them, repudiated, in the name of the whole nation, any connection with the recent delegation to the west, which they represented as a fraudulent attempt, on the part of Mr. Williams, to draw them from the homes of their forefathers, and repeatedly wrote to Bishop Hobart on the subject, requesting that he would withdraw him from being their teacher, and appoint Mr. Solomon Davis in his place. The bishop paid no attention to them, and did not even deign to reply. They sent a delegation to Washington, who were at once informed that the affair had the sanction of the President, and that Mr. Williams had in everything acted honorably and uprightly. And the First Christian party, meeting in council, declared that they had appointed the delegation which accompanied Mr. Wiiliams to represent them, exposed the influences by which the opposition to him had been fomented, and expressed the fullest affection for, and confidence in him.

Unable to injure Mr. Williams in the estimation of Bishop Hobart, the party of opposition wrote to the Rev. Wm. B. Lacy, of Albany, requesting him to use his influence for the removal of Mr. Williams, and the appointment of Mr. Solomon Davis. "Our affections for him," they say, "are changed. We cannot reverence and respect him as we once did. He has tried by every means in his power to draw us from our lands. While he continued faithful to our spiritual interests, and remained with us as a teacher of good things, we loved him and endeavored to assist him, but when he became discontented with his situation, neglected us, and often left us, we became jealous of our rights. Ambition appears to be the ruling passion in his breast. *The humble cottages of the natives* ill suit the dignity of his mind. We, however, forbear personal reflections and solicit relief. Our wishes centre in Mr. Solomon Davis."

As this gentleman was said to be the instigator of this communication, Mr. Williams kindly wrote to inform him of the fact, at the same time giving him some friendly advice respecting the prosecution of his studies. Mr. Lacy enclosed the letter of the Indians to Bishop Hobart, with the following remarks:—"Although I have a high opinion of Mr. Williams's zeal and fidelity to the cause, I am afraid he has lost his influence among the Oneidas. Prejudice, founded on invincible ignorance, is often unconquerable, and the best way to avoid its consequence, is generally, in the case of clergymen, to flee from it. Under this impression I am inclined to think that the sooner Mr. Williams enters on his mission to Green Bay the better it will be for him and the church."

While difficulties, not of his own creation, were thus thickening around him at Oneida, his missionary exertions for many years past were justly appreciated by the more intelligent portion of the community, and he records in his journal an interesting correspondence, in January, 1822, with Mrs. L. H. Sigourney, who wrote for information respecting his mission, and the condition and habits of the Indians, in which both she and her husband took a lively interest.

Mr. Williams had now, though unordained, been laboring as a missionary under the auspices of the Protestant Episcopal Church for seven years, and during that time he had received, according to the account of Genit H. Van Wagenen, Esq., the treasurer of the Missionary Society, of New York, now before me, $1,119 3, being on an average, about $160 per annum. During this space of time he had expended in behalf of the church, with the exception of $4 or $500, all his little fortune received from the government. It is not necessary to recapitulate the services he had rendered to the church, or ask the reader, with this simple statement of facts before him, whether, as a missionary, he seems to have been actuated by worldly motives, or by a sincere love to God, and a desire to promote the temporal and spiritual welfare of the Indian race. If a cloud rested on the latter part of his career at Oneida, it certainly was not of his own creation. Poor as was his compensation, he would not have deserted his post, unnecessarily, even for an hour, had he not been called from it by a sense of duty to the people to whom he ministered, and who were too ignorant to appreciate his principles or feelings.

It seemed now necessary that he should seek another field of labor, and precede his people into the promised land of the west. After conference with Bishop Hobart, he resigned the station at Oneida, and set out for Green Bay, in July, 1822, with the design of being on the spot, when the portion of the Indians who were in favor of emigration should arrive there. In doing this he depended solely upon Providence. He went out without missionary station or stipend, *a Christian layman, who had devoted his life to God*, and patiently awaited the time, when he might be deemed worthy of serving his Divine master in the lowest ministry of his church.

---

## CHAPTER XIV.

### MARRIAGE AND ORDINATION.

THE reader has now traced, step by step, and, almost, day by day, the career of Mr. Williams, since his first arrival in Massachusetts. He has seen the wonderful development of his intellect, accompanied by every manifestation which man can afford, to his fellow-men, of the purest piety; he has been admitted, by his journals, into the inmost feelings of his heart; he has followed him through the exciting scenes of his military life, and marked the success which attended his missionary efforts—together with the influences which broke in upon the simple and retired devotion of his life at Oneida.

In the midst of a rich and cultivated country, surrounded by those he had civilized and Christianized, he had hoped to spend his days, ministering to his rustic flock, and worshipping in the beautiful little church, whose spire he had taught to rise amid the wigwams and hunting-grounds of the Indian, a centre of good influences, both to his own nation, and to the church, who, by his example, might be quickened in missionary zeal.

The advice of his venerated bishop, the urgent request of the President of the United States, the Secretary of War, and the Govenor of the State of New York, Hobart, Monroe, Calhoun, De Witt Clinton—compassion for the condition of the Indians, reliance on the faith of treaties, and the most ample minded and philanthropic views for the social regeneration of the aborigines, throughout the continent, had induced, or rather compelled him to lead the way, as at once a religious and a political pioneer, to the west, in order to induce the New York Indians to follow him, to what was designed as the perpetual seat and guarded haven of a down-trodden race.

To vindicate the character, and detail the history of Mr. Williams, as a man, and as a Christian, it is necessary to put the reader briefly in possession of the transactions relative to Indian affairs, in which he was engaged.

In the early part of the century, the Winnebagoes and the Menominies were the possessors of several millions of acres of most valuable land, on the borders of Lake Michigan. A general idea may be formed of its nature and extent, by drawing a line on a map from the mouth of the Milwaukee river westward to Fort Winnebago—from thence northward to the high lands bordering on Lake Superior—and then south-eastward to Noquet Bay, opposite the entrance to Green Bay. It was well watered, and richly wooded—abounding in game, and fish, adapted alike for agricultural and hunting purposes—but ample beyond the wants or desires of its uncivilized inhabitants. With the generosity of the savage, they proposed to share this noble territory with their eastern brethren. We have seen how the General and State Governments approved of and fostered this proposition; and how, at length, in 1821, in a treaty between the Winnebagoes and the Menominies, on the one hand, and the delegates of the Six Nations on the other, with the United States, in the person of its agent, standing by as a paternal witness, to afford its solemn sanction, and throw over the contracting parties the mantle of its protection, the New York Indians had purchased a certain portion of this territory. Beginning several miles from the mouth of the Fox river, it ran back in breadth seven or eight miles to a longitudinal extent of about seventy. This tract of country, was not, however considered by the Six Nations sufficiently large—and, with the sanction of government—application was made for an extension of the cession, in the year 1822, and Mr. Williams went to Green Bay, not only as a settler, but as a member of a delegation commissioned for this purpose.

He was requested by General Cass to act as United States agent, on the occasion; but, deeming the duties of this office incompatible with being a party to the transaction, he honorably declined it. A treaty was entered into between the New York Indians and the Menominies only, on the 23d September, by which, for certain considerations—the latter admitted their eastern brethren to a full joint ownership of the half of the whole territory, possessed, previously, in common by them and the Winnebagoes—with certain reservations, however, to guarantee individual rights, of which I shall speak more fully hereafter.

Now, it is true, that, according to civilized valuation, the amount paid by the New York Indians was entirely inadequate for the just purchase of land, which, at a small estimate, exceeded a million and a half of acres. But, to view the negotiation in this light, is most absurd. It was an arrangement, between Indian tribes, for their mutual convenience and benefit, not only sanctioned, but encouraged by government, for its own ends.

The New York Indians, in purchasing this western territory, and consenting to removal, sacrificed to the State of New York, and to the pre-emption companies, their own valuable possessions in the east, and exchanged an ample, cultivated domain, for a wilderness, in the hope of obtaining an asylum for the red man, where, geographically protected by the lakes, and defended by the arm of government, he might remain for ever safe from Anglo Saxon cupidity, and grow up in wealth, civilization, morality, and religion.

The dream of Mr. Williams, which he indulged in common with the excellent bishop, and the great statesmen who had encouraged the project of removal, was, that all the remains of the Indian race in the territories of the United States, should be there gathered into one vast community, where the savage tribes might be won over to civilization and Christianity, by intercourse with their already civilized brethren.

He hoped, at some future day, to establish a great Indian college, in which the red man from Canada, as well as the inhabitant of the States, might be instructed and trained in all things conducive to happiness here and hereafter. With this unselfish hope, he braved the hardships of the wilderness, poverty, and isolation, and patiently awaited the hour when he should be repaid by the sight of the prosperity of his people.

But, while negotiations were still in progress, difficulties began, in consequence of the interference and chicanery of the whites, in the neighborhood of Green Bay, who strove to sow dissensions between the contracting parties, and neutralize the benevolent designs of President Monroe. They represented to the Menominies, that the New York Indians, in consequence of their superior knowledge, had already overreached them, and were endeavoring to do so again; and that, if they had sold the land to the government, they would have obtained far better conditions. But, notwithstanding their efforts, the treaty was concluded to the full satisfaction of the Menominies, who were most urgent with their eastern brethren to take immediate possession, that, by occupying the country, they might keep off of it the "long nails" of the white man.

At a subsequent period, the Menominies were induced, by interested persons, to deny their bargain with the New York Indians, on the plea that they had been overreached, and Mr. Williams was compelled to spend his time and substance to maintain their rights, against the efforts of knavish traders and intriguing statesmen. But, for the present, the evil hour was postponed; and, as soon as he was settled at Green Bay, he began to look round him and examine the mixed elements of which society in the Indian territory was composed, and take measures for the establishment of religious worship.

His old friend and comrade in the war of 1812, Col. Pinkney, was in command of the garrison at Green Bay, and, together with his officers, received him with kindness. He had carried with him Mr. Ellis, for the purpose of instituting a school for the religious education of the Indians. Still a layman, unmarried, with the world before him, he was under no obligation but that of a conscientious devotion to Christ, and affectionate regard for the Indians, to apply himself to missionary work, or remain at Green Bay. He might easily have gained wealth, had money been his object. He might have acquired political importance, had ambition been his ruling passion. But he was simply an enthusiast for the welfare of others. Immediately on his arrival at Green Bay, he held public service in the garrison, and, finding a respectable and increasing attendance on divine worship, made an appeal in February, 1823, to the officers of the post and the citizens, to provide a place of worship, which was promptly and cheerfully responded to. In a short time a neat chapel was fitted up in the garrison. Mr. Williams had the honor of being the first person who performed the service of the Protestant Episcopal Church west of Lake Michigan. But the religious instruction of the Indians was still uppermost in his mind. Only a few families had yet arrived from the State of New York, but a great many were expected, and he desired to be in readiness for their arrival. He accordingly opened a correspondence with the Missionary Society of the Protestant Episcopal Church at Philadelphia. His plan was to erect a mission house, in which he would place, as superintendants, one of the most respectable Indian families, with accommodation for the boarding, lodging, and schooling of 100 children, who were to be provided with gardens and fields for their amusement. He was, meanwhile, educating Mr. Ellis for the ministry, and while prosecuting his studies, proposed that he should act as school-master to the mission, which was to embrace children of all the Indian tribes. At the same time exertions were made by the officers and residents of Green Bay to effect the same object; and, with the sanction of Bishop Hobart, and the recommendation of Gov. Cass, application was made at the east, by Mr. Ellis, for funds to carry the design of Mr. Williams into effect, but owing to the illness of that gentleman, very little money was collected.

Soon after his arrival at Green Bay, Mr. Williams had become acquainted at the garrison with a young lady of French and Indian extraction, named Magdeline Jourdan, of great personal attractions, considerable accomplishments, and prepossessing sweetness of disposition. They were united in marriage at Green Bay, on 3d March, 1823. By his marriage with this lady, Mr. Williams came into possession of between 4 and 5,000 acres of land on the borders of the Fox River, a few miles distant from Green Bay. In explanation of the manner in which Miss Jourdan became entitled to this fine property, I may remark that, among the Menominies, while in general the lands were common, certain tracts were held immemorially, as hunting-grounds in particular families; and at the time of the cession, by purchase, of a portion of their country to the New York Indians, reservation was made of these, by express treaty stipulation, for the benefit of the parties interested. The land in question was one of these tracts, and had long been the hunting-ground of the Jourdan family. To avoid all future doubt concerning the title to this property, it was, on the 22d August, 1825, made over to Mrs. Williams, by a deed from the chiefs, warriors, and head men of the Menominie nation, in which they say that, "for, and in consideration of their love and friendship for Magdeline Williams, and her heirs of the Menominie nation, and in consideration of the sum of fifty dollars, they gave, granted, bargained, sold, and quit-claimed" the said property, to her and her heirs for ever. In Article 9, of the treaty of 1838, between Ransom H. Gillet, Commissioner on the part of the United States and the chiefs of the New York Indians, this property was guaranteed to Mr. Williams, in fee simple, by patent from the President. Hereafter I shall have occasion to speak more on this subject; but here, I shall only beg the reader to remember that this property had no connection with any remuneration of Mr. Williams for services rendered to the Indians, but was his wife's estate, owned by her at the time of their marriage.

In May, 1823, Mr. Williams wrote to Bishop Hobart a report of his proceedings and prospects of success, as a missionary at Green

Bay, and applied for deacon's orders, which, at Oneida, he had out of modesty declined, though strongly urged to enter the ministry by the Bishop.

In the fall of 1823, considerable alarm existed in the minds of the New York Indians, respecting the validity of their claims on the lands ceded them, in consequence of the efforts of some government agents, at Green Bay, to create dissension between the two Indian tribes; and it became necessary for Mr. Williams to visit Washington, and confer with the President and the Secretary of War, in relation to the affair. He left Green Bay for this purpose, on November 1, and was entirely successful in his mission to the seat of government. The parties were still in power under whom the treaties had been made between the Indians, and prompt measures were taken to redress the ills of which the New York Indians complained.

Bishop Hobart was then absent in England, whither he had repaired for the benefit of his health, not long after the application of Mr. Williams for deacon's orders. During the bishop's absence, Mr. Williams was subject to severe annoyance in consequence of false, frivolous, and vexatious reports circulated to his discredit, the purport or the author of which he could not, for a long time, ascertain, but which, at length, were shown to emanate from a young person whom he had formerly befriended. The whole details of this affair have been preserved by Mr. Williams, and will form a curious chapter, if ever published, in the natural history of slander. He spent "the whole winter of 1823, and the winter, spring, and summer of 1824, in trying to ascertain the substance of false reports," during which time he had to travel about three thousand miles, and be at an expense of one thousand dollars, merely to find out that he was charged with a leaning to Romanism, and other things equally absurd and unfounded. Among other means of defamation resorted to, was the circulation of a hand-bill, which drew forth a reply from the chiefs of the First Christian party, at Oneida, in which, after denying the truth of everything alleged, they say, "Mr. Williams has been among us ever since the year 1816, and his acts of kindness have been constant, and he has gratuitously ever since been doing us many and various services. We have looked to him as a friend and adviser, and he has conducted himself towards us, with the utmost fidelity and disinterestedness, and yet these his acts, and this his conduct, is now to be misconstrued."

Mr. Williams, during his residence at Green Bay, had officiated regularly to the garrison and the inhabitants, and raised a numerous and respectable congregation, who were strongly attached to him. The attendance on divine service not unfrequently amounted to three hundred persons; but his labors, with the exception of occasional gratuities from the officers, were without remuneration. He had no stipend, either from the congreation or any missionary society. His health again became infirm, and the weakness of his lungs increased, and as he had never designed to continue in a ministerial capacity at Green Bay, itself, and the Oneidas were now rapidly arriving at the neighboring settlement of Duck Creek, where he intended to plant a church, he applied to the society, at Philadelphia, to send some clergyman to the station, who might take his place, and raise a school and mission for the instruction of the Menominies. The Rev. Mr. Nash was accordingly appointed. The failure of this gentleman at Green Bay is well known to those acquainted with the history of the mission; but everything was done by Mr. Williams, previous to his departure, for the east, where he purposed to spend the winter of 1825–6, to render him comfortable, and make his services efficient. In consequence of sickness, Mr. Williams remained at Oneida until the spring of 1826, in the midst of his friends, but at the same time exposed to the ungenerous assaults of his enemies. To bring the attacks against him to immediate issue, he now applied for deacon's orders. The signatures to the canonical recommendations were of the most respectable kind, and the bishop appointed Oneida as the scene of his labors, and the residence of his enemies, for his ordination.

At Vernon, on the evening preceding the ordination, Mr. Solomon Davis called, with several chiefs, on Bishop Hobart, and withdrew the charges he had made against Mr. Williams; though I am sorry to add, that this gentleman has not ceased to blacken the reputation of a man every way his superior, and whose literary labors even he has not hesitated to pass for his own. A translation of the Prayer Book, published some years since, as the compilation of Mr. Solomon Davis, is the work of Mr. Williams. The bishop, with the clergy who accompanied him, the Rev. Mr. Anthon, of Utica, the Rev. Mr. Bulkley, of Manlius, the Rev. Mr. Perry, of Rome, the Rev. Mr. Holister, of Paris, the Rev. Mr. Young, of Perriville, the Rev. Mr. Treadway, of New Hartford, the Rev. Mr. Griffin, of New York, and the Rev. Mr. Burgess, of Connecticut, were met at Vernon by a party of Oneida chiefs and others, and escorted to the church. Mr. Solomon Davis, catechist and lay reader, said the morning prayer. The bishop then made an address to the Indians, which was interpreted to them. It has been preserved, and is an admirable specimen of apostolic simplicity. At its conclusion, several of the chiefs advanced, each one placing his hand in token of assent on the right shoulder of the one who stood before him, and the foremost placing his hand upon the shoulder of Mr. Williams, who thus, as the representative of all, addressed the bishop on behalf of that portion of the Oneida nation who adhered to and designed to follow him to the west, praying him still to extend his paternal care over them, in spiritual things, after their departure to their distant and new home at Green Bay, to which the bishop affectionately responded. The address to the candidate for ordination was marked by all that fervor which was characteristic of the zealous bishop. "You are now," he said, "to make very solemn vows. You are to make them in the presence of Him who cannot be deceived, and who will not be mocked. You are to seal the sincerity with which you make, and the fidelity with which you mean to fulfil them, by partaking of the symbols of the body and blood of the Lord. Need I say to you—and what I say to you I say to my brethren and myself—how tremendous the guilt, how horrible the punishment, if those vows be not made in sincerity, if those vows be not faithfully fulfilled. In an extensive region to the west, the greater portion of your countrymen will be gathered, advancing in all the arts of civilization and social life, under the guidance of that religion which best perfects and secures every human blessing; the time may come, when the descendants of those who once roamed, scattered bands, wild as the wilderness around them, which they now behold bright with the fruitful fields, the populous villages, and the busy cities, of the more powerful, because civilized race, who possess the soil of which they once were lords, may take their stand, a compact, honored, independent body of enlightened freemen, in the highest ranks of their white brethren, and participate in all the inestimable blessings of those civil and religious institutions, which are the just pride of our happy country. You go forth to aid in this great, this glorious, this most benevolent design. You go forth, the first Indian vested by our church with that commission, without which no man can minister in holy things. God grant I may have cause to thank Him for making me the instrument of commissioning you to His service. Duties and difficulties you will have of no ordinary kind. To discharge those duties, and overcome those difficulties, exert all your powers, and call forth that grace of God's Spirit, which you must constantly implore. Great your labors, great your difficulties, but great also may be your reward. How great the reward in the view of your scattered, and in too many respects, degraded countrymen, rising to that rank in civil and in social life, for which God has designed them—what a transcendant reward in the prospect of the fulfilment to you of that gracious promise, 'they who turn many to righteousness shall shine as the stars for ever and ever.' "

With these words ringing in his ears, the Sachem knelt at the feet of his friend and bishop, and received, in ordination, the apostolic laying on of hands. The prospect seemed, once more, bright before him, and, surrounded with the fruits and evidences of past labor, and with a heart beating high with hope of converting into a smiling garden the western wilderness, which was to be the scene of his future toils, he rose to carry thither the cross and Gospel.

---

## CHAPTER XV.

### REVERSES.

Armed with the ministerial commission, Mr. Williams returned to Green Bay, to spend his life in missionary labor, among the people he loved, who were now crowding to their new homes in the west. His position was peculiar. He was not merely the spiritual pastor of the Indians, but their secular champion. While a layman, he performed the duties of a clergyman; and, when in the ministry, it was impossible for him, as the most intelligent person in the Six Nations, who had, also, been engaged in all late transactions between them and government, to cease defending the title to their newly acquired possessions. He was bound, in honor and duty, to fight for them, as he had been the chief instrument of government in withdrawing them from their old habitations; and they might well have accused him of treachery, had he tamely permitted them to be despoiled, by unprincipled politicians, of what was designed to be the magnificent heritage of their children.

While the right of the Oneidas to the land purchased near Lake Michigan was still unquestioned, Mr. Williams induced them to erect a chapel at Duck Creek; but, in the midst of their labors to establish themselves as a civil and religious community, the intelligence came that government was about to enter into a treaty with the Menominies. They were at no loss to foresee the bearing of such a treaty on themselves. On its face, it bore an attempt to defraud them of their possessions, and deny the validity of the treaties between them and the Menominies, entered into with the sanction, and at the instigation of the United States Government. The then existing administration was bound by the acts of its predecessors;

and General Cass, who had superintended the negotiations between the Indians of the east and west, was still governor of the north-western territory, and fully cognizant of all the details of those transactions, and of the integrity and good faith in which the New York Indians had obtained their lands at Green Bay. From its most incipient stage, General Cass had been, we may say, a party to the cession. On the 10th July, 1817, he wrote to E. Granger, Esq., Indian agent at Buffalo, "The government is friendly to the proposed cession. Were it otherwise, I should not consider myself at liberty to *co-operate* in the projected negotiation." In 1818, in a long letter to the Hon. D. A. Ogden, he represented the removal of the New York Indians to the west, as a change fraught with benefit to the government, on account of their civilization and proved fidelity, which would render them a barrier against the incursions of the savage tribes, and be the means of reclaiming them from barbarism. Mr. Trowbridge, who, by his appointment, had been present on behalf of the United States, at the treaty of 1821, had reported to him the whole proceedings, making mention, among other things, "of the correct moral deportment, and statesmanlike conduct of the deputies from the Six Nations, under the direction of Mr. Williams, whose personal exertions," he added, "have been very great." Mr. John Sergeant, jun., in making his report, of October 16, 1822, to General Cass, concerning the second treaty, in which an extension of the cession was obtained, says:—"Some of the French people in this place have taken much pains to create a party among the Menominies, *to frustrate the designs of government, and the New York Indians*, in the aforesaid purchase, and have been entirely unsuccessful in their attempts; and I have the pleasure, further to state, that the Menominies appear to be much pleased with the bargain and their new neighbors." So that, if ever there was a purchase made in good faith, it was that of the New York Indians, and General Cass knew it.

"My fears in regard to the contemplated treaty with the Menominies," writes Mr. Williams, in his journal, "were at length fully realized. By a communication from government, I was informed that an appropriation had been made by Congress to carry the above into effect, and that General Cass and Colonel McKinney were appointed as commissioners; the main object being to curtail the land conveyed to the New York Indians, as all the tract of country lying on the west side of Lake Michigan must now soon be erected into a territory."

Of all transactions in the history of the United States, the treaty of Butte des Morts is the most dishonorable. The commissioners, without asking the consent of the New York Indians, purchased from the Menominies the most valuable portion, including improved lands, of the tract, ceded by previous treaties to them, shutting them out entirely from access to the Fox river, from its mouth to the rapids of the Grand Kakalin. The Menominies and the Winnebagoes were summoned to the council, and the New York Indians had to stand by and see their possessions wrested from them by the strong hand of power. After the treaty was opened, Governor Cass said, "We have observed for some time the Menominies to be in a bad situation as to their chiefs. There is no one we can talk to as head of the nation. If anything should happen, we want some man who has authority in the nation that we can look to. You appear like a flock of geese, without a leader, some fly one way and some another. To-morrow, at the opening of the council, we shall appoint a principal chief of the Menominies. We shall make inquiry this afternoon, and try to select the proper man. We shall give him the medal, and shall expect the Menominies to respect him."

On August 7, two young men were called in front of the commissioners (one was named Oiscoss, alias Claw, the other was called Carron). Col. McKinney then addressed them, and put medals round their necks. Oiscoss or Oskashe, as the name is spelled in the printed treaty, was made head chief, and the future organ of communication with the commissioners—and thus, by his instrumentality, the property of the New York Indians was given over to the United States.

A short story which Mr. Williams once told me in conversation, will show who Oiscoss was, and what "a proper person" was found in him.

One morning, at dawn of day, about a year previous to the treaty of Butte des Morts, a young half-breed Indian, who was a distant relative of Mrs. Jourdan, the mother-in-law of Mr. Williams, was paddling in his canoe down Hell Creek, a branch of the Fox River. It was still dark, so that objects could not be distinctly discerned. As he glided by the tall rushes growing near the bank, he observed them move, as if some animal was among them. Supposing it to be a deer, he fired at the spot where he saw the motion, and then paddled through an opening in the reeds to see the effect of his shot. To his inexpressible horror, he found an Indian, in his canoe, which was half-drawn on shore, drooping lifelessly over the side of his bark, with a shot through his head. As the deed was accidental, he had no wish to conceal it, and putting the body in his own canoe, paddled down to Green Bay, to the encampment of Oiscoss, as the Indian killed belonged to his party. On landing, he went strait to Oiscoss, and informed him of what had happened, when Oiscoss, who was drunk at the time, drew his knife, and plunging it repeatedly into his body, continued stabbing him till he was dead. He was arrested for murder, but as he was a man of great influence among the Indians, was acquitted. But though he had escaped the law, there was another tribunal of a different kind to which he was still exposed. There is a traditional institution among the Indians, very similar to the avenger of blood. Mrs. Jourdan, as the relative of the slain, and *a medicine woman*, had only, according to the custom of the nation, to take a pipe and a war-club, and lay them down at the feet of any of the chiefs of Menominies, and pronounce the name, "*Oiscoss*," in order to insure a just and immediate retribution. When the day appointed for the council at Butte des Morts drew near, fearing, that unless he was reconciled with her, his life might be taken, he proceeded to her house, acknowledged the murder, threw himself on her mercy, and implored pardon. It was granted, and the only punishment he received was the fierce invective which the eloquent tongue of an indignant woman could bestow. When he appeared at Butte des Morts, he was taken by a half-breed (L. G.) to the judge before whom he had been tried, and told, " There sits the man who saved your life—now do whatever he tells you." Such was the head chief, the medal man, " the proper person," of Butte des Morts, by whose influence, in a great measure, the lands of the New York Indians were consigned by the Menominies to the commissioners.

Many of the speeches delivered by the Indians, at Butte des Morts, and that by Mr. Dean, who spoke on behalf of the Six Nations, were taken down, at the time, by Mr. Polk, of Washington, and Mr. Williams, and are yet preserved by the latter gentleman. The indignation and distress of the Oneida, Stockbridge, and Brothertown Indians, was extreme. "Before we left the treaty ground," writes Mr. Williams, "it was proposed to me, by the whole delegation, to proceed to Washington and meet the treaty just concluded with the Menominies." An eloquent appeal and petition, from the Six Nations, was drawn up, and Mr. Williams set out for Washington, in the fall of 1827, to oppose the ratification of the treaty. He had the good fortune to interest Mr. Van Buren, Mr. Benton, Mr. Calhoun, and other distinguished gentlemen, in the senate, in behalf of the New York Indians, and, by their kind exertions, the consummation of the proposed iniquity was prevented. Nothing, however, was done that session. As the hopes of the Six Nations depended on the efforts of Mr. Williams, it was of the utmost importance to those who desired the ratification of the treaty, to withdraw him from their cause, and a politic but fruitless appeal appears to have been made to his cupidity. He received the following letter from Gen. Cass :—

"*Detroit, Jany.* 29, 1828.

"DEAR SIR:—By the present mail I have written to the War Department, recommending your appointment as sub-agent, at Green Bay. I hope you will be appointed,

"I am, dear sir, sincerely yours,

"LEW. CASS.

"REV. E. WILLIAMS."

So much anxiety was shown that he should get this, that two copies were sent, one to Washington, the other to the care of Col. McKinney, by whom it was forwarded to Bishop Hobart, that it might reach him in New York. He was confined in that city, after the termination of the session, with a severe fit of sickness, and was not able to leave until June, 1828. He then returned to Washington, to inform the President, agreeably to a communication he had received, that the Six Nations would consent to the ratification of the treaty, provided the claims of the New York Indians were allowed.

In August, 1828, Mr. Williams was appointed, by the Missionary Society at Philadelphia, missionary to Duck Creek. His salary was $62,50 per quarter; and for this munificent sum, he was not only to perform all the ordinary duties of a clergyman, but "to keep, or cause to be kept, without additional charge to the Society, a permanent school for the instruction of the children of the Oneida Indians, and *such others as may desire it.*" He hired a teacher at a salary of $150 or $200 per annum, and the surplus constituted his own remuneration. All this time, and for years after, he had to defend the rights of the New York Indians at his own expense. It is necessary all this should be exposed, that the discouragements of every kind under which he labored may be seen. How many are there who would have labored on such conditions? Since his leaving Oneida, except occasional presents, at the option of the officers of the garrison at Green Bay, he had not received a farthing in the shape of salary from the Church.

On the occasion of the appointment of Mr. Williams as missionary, the Indians at Duck Creek made an address to the Society, in which they say:

"FATHERS AND BROTHERS.—We have hitherto hanged our heads down, and our hearts were sorrowful, because we were weak in our religious affairs. Our brother, who was disposed to instruct us in the ways of God, was weak also. No society encouraged him in his labor of love. We were grieved to see him thus situated. We were not able to aid him; we were poor ourselves. We now raise our heads, and rejoice at the news that you have taken pity on us and our brother, by giving him such assistance as to enable him, *in some measure*, to preach the Gospel to us *without laboring at the same time to maintain himself*."

Mr. Williams, too, in reporting his labors to the Society, returns them thanks, and offers the prayer that "the name of Jesus may be glorified, and all men may be blessed in Him, and all nations call him blessed." His health, however, continued infirm, and with difficulty he performed his ministerial duties, until the spring of 1830, when he began to amend.

With the return of health he was once more called into the exciting and thankless scenes of political life.

A new commission was appointed to negotiate with the Indians, and just prior to its meeting he received a visit from an old friend and school-mate, at Long Meadow, the Rev. Mr. Colton, who records it in the first volume of his able work on the American Lakes. The account of Mr. Colton is interesting, as it presents a lively picture of the man in the scene of his labors and disappointments; gives a just idea of the simple grandeur which attaches to his person and character, and which no depression can efface; and exhibits his lofty views and extensive plans for the amelioration of the condition of his supposed countrymen, which were all blighted by political dishonesty. It is also curious on other accounts. To do justice to it, the account of Prof. Colton should be read as a whole. I can only furnish some brief extracts. Mr. Williams took his friend in a canoe up the Fox River, from his residence, and "as may be imagined," says Mr. Colton, "we talked over and lived again the scenes of childhood. 'And here we are, Mr. Williams. How strange! What a scene is this!'

"'Indeed, sir; and did we dream of it when we ran around the brick school-house in the street of Long Meadow, and played our boyish pranks in that never-to-be-forgotten and delightful retreat?'

"'And do you remember the dress you wore when first your father brought you from Canada, and what infinite sport you and your brother John made for the children of the school, by the strangeness of your manners, and your Indian whims, before you had learned to accommodate yourselves to such a state of discipline?'

"'My memory,' said Mr. Williams, tapping his forehead with his finger, *as much like a Frenchman as an Indian*, and winking a smile of great significance, 'records those scenes as if they were the occurrence of yesterday.'"

This shows how, apart from any theory to suggest the idea, Mr. Williams bears the polite Frenchman in his very aspect and manner. The friends landed. "After being made acquainted," continues Mr. Colton, "with Mrs. Williams, who set before us refreshments, a walk was proposed and taken along the elevated brow of a sort of amphitheatre, overlooking the river, and enclosing a spacious and rich plain a little above the highest floods. It was indeed a beautiful and commanding eminence, itself the margin of another plain, stretching back under the sombre and apparently boundless orchard of oaks. 'Here,' said Mr. Williams, 'on this spot, and along this line, I had fondly indulged the dream, would one day, not far distant, be founded and erected a literary and scientific seminary for the education of Indian youth. Next to the removal and establishment of our eastern tribes, in these delightful abodes of the northwest and along Fox River, and such a confirmation of our privileges as to afford a security for future exemption from the incursions of the white man, I had conceived and fondly cherished the project of this institution. This wide and beautiful country was to be our inheritance, in common with the tribes of whom we purchased, and with whom we entered into friendly alliance, under the guidance and auspices of the President and Government of the United States. For the first time in the history of our public injuries, and of the successive ejectments of our tribes, from the east to the west, in the progress of two centuries, and of the gradual wasting away, of whole nations, as well as the constant diminution of these small remnants which still retain a name and existence—a fixed and permanent position was here pledged to us, and seemed to be gained without fear of disturbance. Here opened to our imagination and to our hope, and, I might add, to our sober judgment, a theatre for the regeneration of our race. And is there any hope, think you? The lamp of hope has long since expired. We can never move again. We have no courage. Our tribes have no courage. For where is the faith on which we can rely? You shall see the state of things in the developments of the sittings of this commission.' "

Well does Mr. Colton say, "These once hopeful instruments, and this individual man will have labored in vain, except as the disclosure and ascertainment of their injuries shall awaken a repentance and a sympathy in the bosom of that community, which ought long ago to have thrown in the shield of its protection, and saved the Indians from these disasters, and even then, such a man as Mr. Williams cannot be raised from the grave; or if he should be among the living (which is not very probable), a state of health worn out, and a constitution broken down by these cares; *a mind originally vigorous and heroic*, but the courage of which has been well nigh subdued by this irresistible accumulation of calamity, over the heads of his race —would require little less than a miracle to fit him to cherish again the hopes, and again to wield the burden of such an enterprise, as he must have the credit of having once conceived. '*May a Phœnix yet arise from the ashes of his hopes consumed, and wing its way to a brighter destiny.*' To this I say amen."

To dispossess the Indians, and erect a new state upon the ashes of their council-fires, was now the firm resolution of interested politicians. All things seem to be considered fair in politics—concience is a jest, and expediency the rule of action. Dissensions, which never would have existed among the Indians, but for foreign interference, had been created, and since, if the poor people were left to themselves, their differences would soon have died out, they were diligently fomented. The treaty of Butte des Morts had been the entering wedge. Something had been accomplished. A claim had been set up to the effect that, even after the sanction of treaties between the Indians, by the President, they were capable of being set aside by him; and now, in August, 1830, a commission, consisting of Erastus Root, John G. Mason, and James McCall, was sent to Green Bay, on the plea of arbitrating between the Menominies, and the Six Nations, which terminated in an invitation being extended to the pretended disputants, to send representatives to Washington, that the President, out of his paternal love and wisdom, might compose their differences. Mr. Williams was then dragged off again, by political chicanery, from the scene of his ministerial labors. On their way the representatives had an interview with Gov. Cass, at Detroit, in which speeches were made by the Menominie chiefs, complimentary to their father the Governor, and their father Colonel Stambough, the United States agent, and their great father the President. The New York Indians, with a better understanding of their position, were as guarded in their compliments as courtesy would permit. Mr. Williams merely acted as interpreter. On this occasion Gen. Cass gave him the following letter, which I insert, as an honorable testimony to the worth of Mr. Williams, by a person who has recently made an anonymous attempt to injure his reputation, in the "New York Herald," and hold him up as an impostor to the scorn and ridicule of Christendom.

"*Detroit, December* 5, 1830.

"SIR:—The Green Bay agency is the most important upon this frontier, both with respect to the number and character of the Indians. It embraces three distinct tribes, the Winnebagoes, the Menominies, and the New York Indians, all speaking languages radically different. Besides these, there are scattered bands of the Chippewas, Ottawas, and Pottawatomies, who reside within the limits of the agency, and resort to the agent for aid and advice. Col. Stambough is determined to revive the affairs of the agency, and leave no means untried to place them in a situation commensurate with their importance. He should have a Winnebago, a Menominie, and an Oneida interpreter, together with one sub-agent at the Bay, and one up the Fox River. The latter is already filled, but should any event render the appointment vacant I beg leave to recommend the Rev. Eleazar Williams, as a proper person to fill the vacancy. This gentleman is an Episcopal clergyman of very respectable standing, and partly descended from the Iroquois Indians. He rendered essential services to the United States during the late war, in which he was actively engaged, and badly wounded; the effects of which will probably continue during life. I understand he enjoyed the confidence of some of our highest and most distinguished officers, and bravely led a heavy column at the battle of Plattsburg. He is a gentleman of education and talents, and, from his position and association, can render important services to the government and the Indians.

"LEWIS CASS.

"HON. JOHN H. EATON, *Secretary of War.*"

The delegates from the Indian tribes arrived at Washington, and were quartered at one of the principal hotels. And now began a scene of fresh political profligacy. While the New York Indians were amused with the idea of submitting their differences with the Menominies to the arbitration of the President, a treaty, without their knowledge or consent, was actually entered into by John H. Eaton, Secretary of War, and R. C. Stambough, Indian agent, on the part of the United States, and the ignorant and savage Menominie chiefs, in which the rights of the Six Nations from New York, were entirely denied, and the Menominies, on the ground *that they had not yet disposed of any of their lands*, sold to the United States two million five hundred thousand acres of land, consenting, *as a favor*, that five hundred thousand acres should be appropriated to the New York Indians, whose delegates, with every token of humiliation, as intruders and robbers, were called in to witness this very cool disposition of their property, besides which, in token, that even the small tract allotted to them was held in sufferance from the United States, the government were to pay the Menominies twenty-five thousand dollars for it, becoming thus proprietors of the lands of the New York Indians, by purchase, and having the power, on this plea, at any time, to dispossess them.

The contest of parties on this question ran high, for the New York Indians were not without powerful and able friends, who rightly appreciated the injustice done to them. Mr. Williams and Mr. Quiney, delegate from the Stockbridge Indians, exerted themselves to the utmost, to cause the defeat of the treaty in the senate, which they had the satisfaction of seeing accomplished. The senate also refused to confirm the appointment of Col. Stambough, and the session of 1830–31 closed without anything having been effected towards the settlement of the difficulties.

All this time, Mr. Williams was suffering from severe indisposition, which, after his leaving Washington, increased with such violence as to detain him at Oneida during the summer, and here his scanty means gave out, and he was under the humiliating necessity of appealing to the clergy of the church for assistance to enable him to return home. Bishop Onderdonk furnished him with the following testimonial, which I insert as proof both of his misfortunes and his sacrifices.

"*Hudson, June* 13, 1831.

"The bearer, the Rev. Eleazar Williams, having by various expenditures, while in the spiritual service of his brethren, the aborigines of our country, and in consequence of long and severe indisposition, become seriously embarrassed in his circumstances, is hereby respectfully and affectionately commended to the Christian beneficence of the members of our communion. I also introduce him to my clerical brethren generally, as a clergyman of respectable standing and attainments, and good, moral, and religious character.

"BENJ. T. ONDERDONK.
"Bishop of the Diocese of New York."

The pecuniary benefit of this application was about sixty dollars.

Unable to fulfil his engagements with the Missionary Society of Philadelphia, in consequence of ill health, and enforced absence, he resigned his station of missionary at Duck Creek. His old friend, Mr. Solomon Davis, now contrived to prejudice the mind of Bishop Onderdonk against him, by accusing him of officiating at Oneida, without his permission, *although he had expressly granted that permission*, and the bishop supposing, of course, that the representation was correct, rebuked Mr. Williams for violation of the canons.

The pen almost grows weary with recording, even in the briefest manner, the troubles, disappointments, injuries, and insults heaped on this suffering man. From first to last, it is impossible to discover any instance in which he departed from the strict course of duty and honor. All who have aided to increase the burdens of his life, have, at some period, borne witness to his worth. But the complicated web of wrong, goes on steadily increasing to the end, and some of the last developments of injustice are among the strangest.

When the session of 1831–2 opened, it was necessary for him again to repair to Washington, to advocate the cause of his countrymen, in company with the other delegates of the Six Nations. An able memorial was drawn up to the Senate of the United States, setting forth the rights and grievances of the New York Indians; but, though the hardships of their situation were felt, the necessities of a tortuous policy were too compelling to permit full justice to be done; and the treaty of 1831, with the Menominies, was finally ratified, on June 25, with the addition of a saving clause in favor of the New York Indians, which, though it did not alter the amount of land assigned them by the treaty, gave them somewhat more favorable terms in respect to location of lands, payment for improvements, and acknowledgment of individual rights. During this session, worn down in health and spirits, and reduced to poverty, Mr. Williams, having achieved all he could, was compelled to abandon the long contest and retire from the delegation. Efforts were, however, made by his friends to create sympathy in the church, in his behalf, and Bishop Onderdonk, with prompt kindness, summoned a missionary meeting, at Christ Church, New York, on 7th April, 1832, in which energetic appeals were made to the benevolence of the church, to sustain the mission, at Duck Creek—but, like most affairs of the kind, there was more sound about it than substance, and the small collection made on the occasion, and the few dollars Mr. Williams obtained in Connecticut and Western New York, were of little permanent benefit to the mission. Feeling his physical inability for exertion, he was anxious to retire from the station, but agreed to continue in it for one year, at the request of the bishop. At this time, he was to have been admitted to priest's orders, from which, out of diffidence, he had hitherto abstained, but the approach of the cholera hastened his return to the west, that he might be at his post provided the pestilence attacked his people.

On his return to Green Bay, Mr. Williams found that, during his absence, many evils had crept into the little flock he had been compelled to leave untended, in spiritual things, while struggling to preserve their temporal rights. Drunkenness, dissension, and immorality prevailed; parties had been raised, and everything was in a state of disorder. It became, in his estimation, his indispensable duty, with the consent of the religious portion of the congregation, to subject the refractory and immoral members to discipline, and among them, it was his painful task to include one who had been united with him in the delegations to Washington, and in the efforts of years to obtain justice for the Indians. I do not understand the principle on which a deacon or a congregation could excommunicate—but this, at the worst, was a failure in judgment, although Bishop Hobart, in former years, knowing the necessity of preserving order among such a lawless class of people, had permitted Mr. Williams to act in such matters at his discretion. Bishop Onderdonk was informed of what had been done, and of the crime by which the peace of two families had been broken up—which had caused the excommunication of the individual especially referred to. Much happened at this time, which I refrain from chronicling, because it is not necessary for the vindication of Mr. Williams, and the bare statement of facts might seem to imply censure in quarters to which there is no antagonism, as, doubtless, there was no design of committing injustice.

On the 8th September, 1833, Mr. Williams, finding the dissensions among the congregation, growing out of the act of discipline, could not be allayed, and having neither heart nor strength to contend with those to whose service he had devoted his life, resigned his charge, and preached his farewell discourse, which he concluded thus:—"Brethren of the communicants of St. Thomas Church, I now bid you farewell. Live in peace, and the God of peace be with you. Remember that the eyes of Heaven and earth are upon you. How holy is your calling—how solemn your profession—how delightful your service—how rich your reward. Relax not in any duty. We must now separate, and you hear my last words. If you have discerned anything of the Saviour in me, imitate it. What you have seen in me contrary to the spirit of the Gospel reject it. I was set for your spiritual guide, but now my work is done. Though the cause of our separation be unpleasant, I shall rejoice to see you walking in the truth. Discipline is the life of a church. We have endeavored to reclaim offenders. It is to be hoped that the delinquents will come to sober reflections and repentance. What I have done, in this respect, I have done from the purest motives. Let us pray for one another, and give all diligence that we may arrive at our Father's home. All is not lost, though your friend and pastor is gone. God and His promises remain to comfort you; and beyond the grave is a state of peace where Christian friends will part no more."

If ever there was a man who had proved he had at heart the temporal and spiritual welfare of his people, and his desire to spend and be spent for them, it was Mr. Williams. During his whole career, as a religious teacher, both before and after his ordination, it is not too much to say, that he had labored without remuneration—for the paltry sums he had received cannot be set in the balance against his immense pecuniary sacrifices. It was his misfortune to be the pastor of a semi-barbaric race, who, as a general thing, are not noted for gratitude, nor truthfulness, and who were surrounded by those whose interest it was to foment discontent, at a time when political contentions, social disasters, and change of residence, rendered them refractory, immoral, and restless. But, it is to his honor that, notwithstanding all the ingratitude he has met with at the hands of the Indians, he has never ceased to love, and desire to serve them, feelings which continue unabated to the present hour, when in advanced life he is still laboring for them as a missionary.

He had now nothing left but to retire to his farm on the Fox River, and in peace and solitude recruit his health, worn down by fatigue, anxiety, and sorrow. He celebrated Christmas, 1833, with a few Indians, at his farm, and his journal for that year closes with an ascription of praise to God: "Blessed be the God and Father of our Lord Jesus Christ, who hath blessed us with all spiritual blessings in Him, and granted us to enjoy the day which the patriarchs foresaw, the prophets foretold, and the righteous men of the earth desired. Hosanna to the Son of David, who comes in the name of the Lord."

The winter, spring, and summer, passed rapidly away, when his thoughts once more turned toward his brethren at St. Regis, and, as he had not seen his reputed parents for a long time, he bent his steps thither. As his family and all his means of subsistence were at Green Bay, he did not purpose a permanent residence in the State of New York, but thought he might be instrumental in founding an Indian Protestant school which others might conduct.

In October, 1834, he left Green Bay, but being taken sick on his journey, did not reach St. Regis until December. The winter and spring were spent at Albany, under the care of a physician; and in June, 1835, feeling himself stronger, he returned to St. Regis, with the design of establishing his proposed school. He stated his views to some English and American gentlemen at St. Regis, Hogansburg, and Cornwall, and, with their co-operation and encouragement, undertook the task. He was, soon after, appointed, by Lord Aylmer, Governor-General of Canada, one of the government schoolmasters; and, notwithstanding the opposition of the Romish clergy, the school increased in numbers and prosperity.

But, his labors soon received an unexpected check, in consequence of receiving information from James Hughes, Esq., the Indian agent, that as a government schoolmaster, it was his duty "to tell the children that they were brought up in the Roman Catholic faith, that they had a missionary to instruct them in their religious duties, and should listen to his advice in regard to religion." Mr. Williams, in consequence, at once resigned his situation under the British government. "Christian sincerity and plainness of speech," he wrote to the Indian agent, "require me to say that, I cannot exhort the pupils who may be committed to my charge to attend the ministrations of a Popish priest. As a Protestant clergyman, and that, too, under a Protestant government, to be compelled to do this, I should regard as infringing upon the liberty of conscience which I have hitherto enjoyed." Under these circumstances, he wrote to inform Bishop Onderdonk, of his condition, praying for assistance that he might go on with the school, and preach the Gospel to the Indians. "My circumstances," he said, "have been this year exceedingly straightened, as I have been putting all my resources in requisition to maintain the school. Be assured, right reverend sir, that this request is made as a last resort, after having done what I could." The bishop, however, was unable to afford him any assistance. It is deplorable to reflect that the American church was too poor to uphold a man so conscientious and so desirous to perform his duty.

The Governor-General, in accepting the resignation of Mr. Williams, testified his sense "of the goodness and purity of the motives which induced him to offer it." The Rev. Mr. Archibald, of Cornwall, who throughout had been his firm friend, wrote to him on the occasion of his resignation. "I confess to you, my Rev. Brother, that I am glad to be rid of the patronage of the Government here. Whilst it continued you were in trammels. Now you are independent, and have only to look to the Lord Jesus as the Supreme Head, and if we seek His glory success must inevitably attend our exertions. God bless you." By the aid of Mr. Archibald, Mr. Chesley, and other friends, the school was kept in operation, and soon attained a flourishing condition, when in June, 1836, his health broke down, in consequence of confinement and want of exercise, and his domestic concerns required his presence at Green Bay. These causes, but above all, the approach of another government treaty with the Indians for the sale of their lands, compelled him to abandon his new field of labor and return to the west. His presence was required both by the Government and the Indians; for, however a portion of the latter might assail him in periods of quiet, they were sure to call for his assistance in the hour of danger, and that assistance was never withheld.

As much of the affliction of Mr. Williams in late years has grown out of this treaty, I will briefly recount the whole series of involved transactions up to the present time, referring the reader to the Appendix for the documentary evidence. Mr. Williams wishes no concealment, but desires to have all obscurity cleared away from his dealings with the Indians, and his treatment by Government and individuals. He has not obtruded himself nor his concerns on the public, but as events have taken the course they have, and even his misfortunes and wrongs have been tortured into evidence against him, in some instances by those he deemed friends, there is no remedy but to lay bare the whole. If there be inaccuracy as to facts, it is an easy matter for the parties concerned to point it out.

The final treaty between the Government of the United States and the New York Indians, was begun on 16th Sept., 1836, at Duck Creek, J. F. Schermerhorn acting as Commissioner on behalf of the Government, and was continued, at Buffalo, on 15th Jan., 1838, the name of Ransom H. Gillet being added to the Commission, which, in the treaty there made and concluded, adopted, as its basis, the provisions of the previous treaty at Duck Creek, which related solely to the Oneidas and the St. Regis Indians, while the additional articles then entered into, referred to the Senecas and other branches of the Six Nations.

When the treaty was brought up for ratification in the Senate, in 1840, the name of J. F. Schermerhorn, who had been the principal and almost sole agent of the Government in the transaction, was omitted or erased from the treaty, it is supposed, in consequence of fears that his unpopularity with the Senate would defeat its passage, and the name of Ransom H. Gillet left, as if he had been the sole commissioner.

The first eight articles of the treaty consist of "general provisions," respecting the cession, by the New York Indians, on certain specified conditions, of the whole land possessed by them in the neighborhood of Green Bay, with the exception of reserved tracts. The remaining six articles of the treaty contain "special provisions" for the different branches of the Six Nations and the St. Regis Indians.

The ninth article consists of special provisions for the St. Regis Indians, and contains two clauses; the first, relative to the payment and mode of distribution of certain moneys to the tribe, as, 1, a remuneration for moneys laid out, and, 2, for services rendered by their chiefs and agents in securing the title to the Green Bay lands, the sole chief and agent who rendered such services being the Rev. Eleazar Williams, who signed the treaty; and the second clause, securing to Mr. Williams a reservation of land on the bank of the Fox River, consisting of 4,800 acres, being his wife's estate previous to marriage, and of which the chiefs of the Menominie nation gave her a quit-claim deed in 1825, under which Mr. Williams claimed it in the territorial adjustment between the United States and the Indians. Before an acre of land had been sold by the Winnebagoes or Menominies to the Six Nations, this estate was the peculium of the Jourdan family, and had been held sacred by all parties as private property. Its introduction into the treaty of 1838, was only for the purpose of solemnly confirming an individual right previously existing; and in no shape or manner can it be considered as a donation from Government to Mr. Williams, except that the Government having, through its commissioner, the disposition of technicalities, threw it into the form of a patent grant, thus, in appearance, giving away what did not belong to it. Appendix K.

At the time, however, when the treaty was made, there was an express understanding that four out of five thousand dollars, covenanted to be paid by Government to the St. Regis Indians, " on their removal west, or at such other time as the President should appoint," was to remunerate Mr. Williams for his long and arduous services, as agent for the St. Regis Indians; and to avoid all dubiety on the subject, either as to the fact or as to the amount, the commissioner, J. F. Schermerhorn, certified the same to the President, under date of July 10, 1838, and the paper is among the Indian office files at Washington, marked W. 572. Green Bay, 1838. Appendix L.

In this paper it is candidly acknowledged, by Mr. Schermerhorn, that to the persevering efforts of Mr. Williams, the preservation of the lands of the New York Indians was attributable. All the Six Nations were thus indebted to him. But he had acted especially as the agent of the two parties with whom he was most closely connected, viz. the St. Regis and the Oneida Indians. For his services and expenditures, in behalf of the former, provision was made to remunerate him, in the treaties of Duck Creek and Buffalo. But while the latter treaty was in progress, a certain portion of the Oneidas became discontented with the course things were taking, and went to Washington to make a separate agreement for themselves. Mr. Van Buren appointed Carey A. Harris, as commissioner, to treat with them. By him, a treaty was made with the first Christian and Orchard parties of the Oneida Indians, residing at Green Bay, by which all their improvements, and 100 acres for each individual, amounting in all, to 75,000 acres, were secured to them out of the wreck. In this treaty, provision was made to remunerate the chiefs and agents of the Oneidas, and five thousand dollars was apportioned to Mr. Williams, although his claim, admitted to be just, by the commissioner, amounted to eight thousand dollars more. What is observable in this case is, that the wording of this treaty, under which Mr. Williams was allowed, and paid five thousand dollars for his services to the Oneidas, is precisely the same as that of Buffalo Creek, by which he was to receive four thousand dollars for services to the St. Regis Indians, with the additional security, in the latter case, of a certificate of his right, according to agreement, from the commissioner to the President.

One thousand dollars out of the five thousand dollars mentioned in the ninth article of the Buffalo treaty, was, according to stipulation, in a supplementary article of said treaty, paid over to the St. Regis Indians; the remaining four thousand dollars, being, according to their desire, at the time, reserved for Mr. Williams. Of this fact W. L. Gray, the interpreter, has given two affidavits. "They refused," he says, "to receive the whole of the five thousand dollars, because they knew that four thousand dollars of that money had been promised to Mr. Eleazar Williams, but they accepted and received one thousand dollars of the five thousand dollars, as may be seen in the supplemental article of the treaty."

The money thus due to Mr. Williams, remained unpaid for a number of years, no appropriation for the purpose having been made by Congress, when on June 17, 1850, the chiefs and warriors of the American party of the St. Regis Indians, addressed a petition to the President, in his behalf, stating that they had no claim whatever to this money, which was due to him as their agent, that he had expended a large sum in their behalf, and that the commissioner, Mr. Schermerhorn had certified his right. "Mr. Williams," they say, "is entitled to receive the four thousand dollars, as he has honorably fulfilled the stipulations of the treaty." "We have been remunerated for the moneys expended by the tribe—but not so with our agent, and we hope the four thousand dollars, as before stated, will be no longer withheld from him. He is the only person of our tribe who has rendered any service in procuring the Green Bay lands."

One would think if ever there was a clear case of right and justice it was this. But we shall see here how the most stainless characters may be assailed at the very moment the foulest injury is done to them. I shall not permit myself to utter a word of comment on the following facts. That I leave to the public.

In the month of January, 1851, the Hon. R. H. Gillet, wrote from Washington the following letter to John L. Eldridge, Esq., of Hogansburg. To avoid any charge of misrepresentation, or any temptation to remark, I give it entire in the text

"WASHINGTON, *January* 5, 1851.

"DEAR SIR:—I have just ascertained that Messrs. Bryon and Cochrane, Indian Claim Agents of this city, have succeeded in obtaining from the government of the United States certain moneys stipulated, by the treaty of 1838, to be paid to the Oneidas in New York. They are willing to make an effort to obtain payment of the $4,000 due the St. Regis Indians, the payment of which depends upon the action of the President. An appropriation has been made for the Oneidas, but none has been made for the St. Regis.

"The commission they propose, in this case, is the same that they received in that of the Oneidas, where it has been made, and the services much less. Presuming that it would be for their interest to employ agents here, as skilful and as responsible as I know these men to be, I have sketched the draught of a memorial and power of attorney for the St. Regis, which I forward to you, as their agent and ally, under the laws of the State of New York, presuming that you would, as such, or individually, obtain their signatures, and forward them to these gentlemen, to represent them. Seals should be attached to the power of attorney, and both should be signed by all the chiefs of the American party, in the presence of a magistrate, who should take an acknowledgment as of a deed of law, and his official capacity be certified by the county clerk. Then there should be an affidavit of yourself, as local agent, that you know that those who sign are the only chiefs living at the time. It would be well for the trustees, as such, to approve the memorial and power, and recommend the commissioner of Indian affairs to con firm the prayer of the chiefs, and to confirm their doings. If the chiefs have all died out, so that there are none to sign, then you should make affidavit of that fact, and let the papers be modified so as to read *trustees*, instead of chiefs. Great pains should be taken to make them understand the matter, so as to leave no chance of complaint, by them or any one else. It is important that this be all attended to immediately, so that proper steps may be taken to get an appropriation, which may be attended with some difficulty. Priest Williams is said to have a power of some sort, but informal and insufficient. But, without prompt and decisive movements, he will either get, and perhaps keep the money; but, if he cannot do so, he will be likely to try to defeat an appropriation, until he thinks his chances better. Personally, I have no interest in this matter, but, owing to my relation to the treaty, and the friendly terms I am on with the tribe, I will do what I can, freely, for them. If the papers are properly and correctly made, and forwarded to Messrs. Bryon and Cochrane, of this city, and they collect the money, they will retain, say twenty dollars, to reward you for your trouble and expenses, and remit it in any form you may direct. You had better engross the papers I send you, in a better handwriting than mine. If the papers are promptly sent to Messrs. B. and C., I have no doubt that, before spring, the St. Regis will get their money, which will greatly help them, and *add to the circulating medium in your vicinity*. I am here attending court, but return to New York soon. Whenever I am here, I shall cheerfully lend a hand, without reward, to aid my St. Regis friends. Should you be unable to attend to this matter, you had better employ some one on the proposed terms, and thus have it speedily disposed of. Yours truly,

"R. H. GILLET.

"JOHN S. ELDRIDGE.

"P. S. The money for the Indians, beyond the attorney's fees, will, probably be remitted by the U. S. sub-agent. It does not usually go into the hands of the attorney who prosecutes the claim. But if it does, B. and C. are responsible and safe men. R. H. G."

The facts in the case, then, and I shall confine myself to evident facts, are these, that after the St. Regis Indians had solemnly renounced all right and title to the $4,000 in favor of Mr. Williams, the Hon. R. H. Gillet, being aware of Mr. Williams's claim, made efforts to induce those Indians to apply for the money, promised Mr. Eldridge $20 on behalf of Messrs. Bryon and Cochrane, if he would undertake the business, held out to him the further inducement that the $4,000 would increase the circulating medium in his vicinity, and made out with his own hands the necessary documents for the Indians to sign. I do not say a word to impugn his perfect honor and disinterestedness. That is a question I will not touch. My only aim is to vindicate the character of Mr. Williams; but I cannot help questioning whether Mr. Gillet will ever write Mr. Eldridge a similar letter. Appropriation was made by Congress in the session of 1851–2 for the payment of the $4,000 in question; and, on the 27th January, 1853, Stephen Osborn, of Buffalo, was appointed commissioner to appropriate the money to the several claimants, according to the provisions of the treaty; and, on the 3d April, he reported to the office of Indian affairs, that he could "not come to any conclusion with the chiefs, they insisting that the entire amount should be paid to the American party of the Indians, while it is very evident," he writes, "to me, that the Rev. Eleazar Williams is entitled to the greater part, if not the whole of this money, under the facts and upon a just construction of article nine of the treaty." In this condition of affairs, the Indian bureau very naturally referred to the Hon. R. H. Gillet, for information "relative to the nature of the Rev. E. Williams's claim," and "for such facts connected with the subject within his remembrance, as would enable the department to pay over the money as was intended when the treaty was made." This honorable gentleman, therefore, the writer of the letter to Mr. Eldridge, communicated to the office of Indian affairs the information, that a "liberal if not extravagant provision" of land, worth, at the time, $10,000, by government valuation, was intended, at the time of making the treaty, "to indemnify him for the past, if he had claims, and to secure such action by him and the St. Regis tribe, as would vest in the government their interest in the half million acres of very valuable land;"

and concludes by saying, "I cannot see that Mr. Williams has special claims upon the fund, after receiving his valuable reservation, which certainly was equal to the value of any services rendered by him. A commissioner may well assent to its being divided per capita among those who constituted the American party of the tribe." The hesitancy with which Mr. Gillet speaks ought to have induced further inquiry. It was a question of aye or no. What was the intention at the time of making the treaty? Either Mr. Williams had claims or he had not claims. Mr. Gillet dare not deny that he had *claims*, but *he* could not see that he had "*special claims*," and *thinks* that a "commissioner may *well assent*," &c. The private property of Mrs. Williams, previous to her marriage, and which, according to the wording of the treaty of 1838, Mr. Williams *claimed in his own right and in that of his wife*, is represented by Mr. Gillet as an extravagant remuneration for his services. No wonder that the Government of the United States should enjoy a reputation for economy, if it can always purchase services like those of Mr. Williams, at the expense of the parties who render them. The result of the affair was, that Mr. Osborn was dismissed, another commissioner appointed, and the $4,000 belonging to Mr. Williams paid over by government to the very Indians, who, previous to the interference of Mr. Gillet, had renounced all right and title to it. The reader has, doubtless, heard of pecuniary difficulties between Mr. Williams and the Indians at St. Regis, and the great prejudices in their honest minds against him. He is now in a position to judge whether anything discreditable can be laid to his charge. If there be, he challenges investigation.

There is another transaction, of a pecuniary nature to which I should have made no allusion, had it not been officiously, offensively, and incorrectly brought before the public by a soi-disant friend of Mr. Williams, and for no reason, that I can see, except to display his personal acquaintance with one who was then a topic of general conversation, and whose character he took occasion in a public lecture, *for which he received payment*, to traduce, while compelled to confess that he knew nothing of him but what was favorable. I allude to Dr. Lothrop, an Unitarian minister of Boston. I copy the following passage from the appendix and notes to a recent edition of the Redeemed Captive, by Dr. Stephen Williams, whose remarks on the life of Mr. Williams I shall have occasion, hereafter, to criticise. It has been circulated extensively through the country by the daily press. "The Christian Register," of Feb. 26, 1853, published at Boston, says: "The Rev. Dr. Lothrop, of this city, delivered a lecture on Monday evening, before the Mercantile Library Association, on the lost Dauphin, in which he examined the claims of the Rev. Eleazar Williams. The speaker had known Mr. Williams for twelve years, visisted him in 1845 at his residence in Wisconsin, and received two visits from him in Boston. In his opinion there is not a particle of evidence in Mr. W.'s favor, except what depends upon his 'say so.'" The Transcript, from which we take the statement, gives the following interesting report on one portion of it. "It appears that Mr. Williams came to Boston with his whole property, consisting of a considerable tract of land in Wisconsin, encumbered by a bond and mortgage to the amount of $1,800, which bond, in the course of trade, had fallen into the hands of parties in this city who could not grant a renewal of extension. In twenty-four hours from the time these facts became known to Dr. Lothrop he was enabled, through the kindness of the late Amos Lawrence, to hand Mr. Williams a check for the whole amount, and to send him home with his bond in his possession redeemed and cancelled." If this report represents fairly Dr. Lothrop's statement, I am sorry to say that it is incorrect from beginning to end. The truth of the affair is not calculated to diminish the sympathy which the reverses and misfortunes of Mr. Williams must occasion, and it is necessary it should be understood, as many have been unable to reconcile the asserted poverty of Mr. Williams at the present time, with the statements of Dr. Lothrop, which represent him as owner of a fine estate. Let me apprise the reader at the outset, that the property of Mr. Williams has been for years in the hands of Mr. Amos A. Lawrence, of Boston, who claims the whole. The history of the affair is as follows.

During the whole period of his struggles for the recovery of the Indian lands, Mr. Williams had to make great outlays, considering his limited means, and often to borrow money, so that by the time of the final treaty settlement, he found himself burdened with debt. His remuneration for defending the rights of the Oneidas fell greatly short of what, in equity, it should have been, and the reader has seen the fate of the $4,000 due him on behalf of the St. Regis Indians. Had the latter sum been promptly paid him, as it should have been, he would have immediately recovered himself. Before he obtained the patent for his wife's estate from government, one of his creditors, Daniel Whitney, of Green Bay, recovered judgment against him in 1839, which judgment was assigned by Mr. Whitney in June, 1840, to T. Eustis, of Boston. In April, 1842, his lands at Green Bay were sold to satisfy the judgment, leaving him, how ever, until the 25th April, 1844, the right of redemption. At the earnest request of Mr. Williams, the time was extended from April to the 2d of September, 1844. Just as the last period of grace was expiring, Mr. Lothrop introduced him to the late Amos Lawrence, who advanced the necessary sum, amounting to about $1600, and *secured himself* by receiving from Mr. Eustis the judgment, &c., on land worth, by government valuation, $10,000, it being understood between Mr. Lawrence and Mr. Williams, that one half of the tract, or about 2400 acres, was a bona-fide purchase by the former, in order to save the remaining half for Mr. Williams and his family. On the part of Mr. Lawrence the act was, doubtless, one of pure benevolence, but still he received his equivalent, and purchased 2400 acres of land for $1600. Mr. Williams, instead of going home with "his bond and mortgage in his possession, redeemed and cancelled," left his whole property in the hands of Mr. Lawrence, in the shape of the papers transferred to him, and without any written voucher to show the nature of the agreement between them.

Mr. Eastman, of Green Bay, was, at that time, agent for Mr. Lawrence. He found there were other liens upon the land, which it was necessary to discharge in order to obtain a perfect title. Further advances to a small amount were made, which were to remain as a debt upon the portion of the land still belonging to Mr. Williams. In December, 1844, Mr. Williams and his wife conveyed to Mr. Amos A. Lawrence, at the suggestion of his agent, the whole tract of four thousand eight hundred acres, with the understanding that they did no more than constitute him conservator of the two thousand four hundred acres pertaining to themselves, until such time as Mr. Williams could recover from his pecuniary embarrassments, and pay off his creditors, and among them, Mr. Lawrence himself, for what had been advanced over and above the first purchase money. That such was the nature of the transaction, there are three decisive proofs. 1. If by the deed of December, 1844, Mr. Lawrence obtained the bona-fide title to the whole four thousand eight hundred acres, it must have been in consequence of the gift to him, without consideration, of two thousand four hundred acres from Mr. Williams, which is not supposable. 2. On January 2, 1845, subsequent to the conveyance, Mr. Amos A. Lawrence, wrote to Mr. Williams, making an offer to purchase more of the land at the same price that had been paid for the first portion, which he would not have done had the whole belonged to him. 3. On the 2d August, 1845, Mr. Eastman, agent of Mr. Lawrence, wrote to Mr. Williams in the following terms:—"This thing can be done if it meets your approbation. A friend of ours will advance you $1,642\frac{11}{100}$ on the tract of 2,190 acres (or half the value, at $1 50 per acre), at 10 per cent. interest, per annum, for five years—interest to be paid annually—the tract of 2,190 acres, the title of which is now in Mr. Amos A. Lawrence, of Boston, to be held by him as security for the money to be advanced, the taxes and assessments to be paid by you, or if paid by him, to be charged over to you, at 10 per cent. advance, &c." All this shows clearly that Mr. Amos A. Lawrence was not the owner as late as August, 1845, of any more than one-half the land, though he held the nominal title to the whole. Subsequently, the sum mentioned by Mr. Eastman, was advanced to Mr. Williams upon the terms specified. This, as far as I understand it, is the whole of the matter. But there seems to have been a misconception on the part of both Mr. Amos Lawrence and his son, the cause of which, with the data before me, I cannot comprehend. When, at the expiration of the five years, Mr. Williams, in accordance with the agreement, offered to repay the sum borrowed, which he was able to do by the kindness of a friend, and redeem his land, Mr. Amos A. Lawrence refused to accept.

Occupied with the oversight of a princely commerce, Mr. Amos Lawrence, seems to have bestowed scarcely a thought on the transaction so important to the humble missionary. Even the amount of land was a thing quite hazy in his mind. In writing to Mrs. Williams on the subject, he speaks of the property, which in all was only four thousand eight hundred acres, as consisting of ten thousand, probably confounding the worth of the land with its extent. "The purchase," he says, "was made in the first instance to save the whole ten thousand acres passing out of Mr. Williams's hand, as an act of proper liberality to secure for him a home, and of so small importance to me that I did not decide for a few days, to whom the conveyance should be made, and then decided that it should be made to my son. Since then he has purchased other lands there, and paid for these ten thousand acres more than could have been obtained in money for them from others, intending always to secure a home for you both, and the money thus paid by us *has not been for investment*, but for *relief* of yourselves." Mrs. Williams, on her part, expressed to Mr. Lawrence her gratitude, with a touching simplicity. "Respected sir," she writes, "a stranger who is not accustomed to writing, and one who was brought up among the Indians, on the borders of one of the great western lakes, would take the liberty to address you. I have been induced to this in consequence of seeing your polite and friendly note to my husband, on his departure from Boston, and a letter lately from your son. Not only these, but on account of your saving a portion of his landed property, has moved me at this time, from a deep sense of gratitude, to present you my sincere and hearty thanks for this benevolent act of yours towards us." The *design* of the transaction was, therefore, most benevolent on the part of Mr. Lawrence, though the practical effect has been to throw into the hands of his son, by the agency of Mr. Eastman, the whole property of Mr. Williams.

The value of land in the neighborhood of Green Bay, is greatly enhanced, and, perhaps, the two thousand four hundred acres of Mr. Williams, might now sell for five dollars an acre; but, in consequence of the transaction with Mr. Lawrence, so pompously set forth by Dr. Lothrop as an act of pure charity and munificence, he has lost his all. Mrs. Williams continues to live, by sufferance, on their farm, but the title of it is vested in another. The result, then, of all the exertions, from boyhood, of Mr. Williams, for the temporal and spiritual welfare of the Indians, has been the loss of everything—every event in life has gone against him—health, property, home, have been sacrificed, and reputation endangered, simply because he was unfortunate—and in mankind, as well as in some races of animals, there seems, often, an instinctive desire to destroy, utterly, those whom affliction has wounded. I have endeavored clearly to express, in few words, affairs sufficiently intricate; and I feel convinced that the most laborious examination of details, which might be brought in to cloud these transactions, would not make any alteration in the substantial result. In fact, in both cases, events speak for themselves.

As I am not now writing a complete biography of Mr. Williams, but merely presenting such facts, in his history, as may enable the public to form some opinion of the character and trials of the man, I shall pass, briefly, over the most uneventful period of his life, reserving my remarks on the occurrences of the years 1841 and 1848, until they are brought up in the narrative of my personal acquaintance with him. After his resignation of the mission at Duck Creek, and the Indian school at St. Regis, he continued to perform the duties of his ministerial office whenever opportunity offered; although, being dispirited and afflicted, he remained a great portion of the time, at his farm, on the Fox River, where he frequently gathered his neighbors for Divine service at his own house.

Human nature can only endure a certain amount of hardship, disappointment, and trouble, and then the energies of the strongest will relax. His health was bad, his prospects clouded, his difficulties, of all kinds, daily increasing, every hope he had entertained for the regeneration of the Indian race, blighted by political chicanery and their own ingratitude; and, if he succumbed, in severe depression, under the accumulated burden, it is only what other persons would have done. Among churchmen he has been accused of neglecting public worship. To this, his reply is, that, he was weak, oppressed, lonely; that, all his efforts had been despised and rejected; that, he had no one to sustain and advise him; that, he was at a distance, in the wilderness, from any place of worship; and worn down with sorrow and disappointment, could do little more than sustain his own personal communion with God. He had consecrated his life to the service of Christ, among the Indians. He was not fitted by feeling or habit for pastoral duty, in a different sphere. Unable, by the very constitution of his mind, to manage, with success, his pecuniary affairs, a martyr to his efforts for others, and enduring the same kind of trials which have weighed heaviest on some of the noblest spirits in the ministry, in this country, he saw his property melt beneath his hands, without the power or the tact to save himself from ruin. And, then, in the very midst of afflictions calculated to depress the most energetic, came the bewildering and stunning intelligence that he was not of the name, nor race, nor country, to which he had supposed himself to belong; but that, severe as were his trials in late years, he had borne worse ills in childhood, and was the exiled survivor of a family who had endured mightier griefs and more terrible reverses.

How the tidings affected his spirits and harrowed his mind, the reader will hereafter perceive; and, instead of feeling suprised at his depression, every candid mind will rather be astonished that he rallied his powers sufficiently to become the cheerful, vigorous, and intellectual man he still is. Within late years he has resumed his missionary labors at St. Regis, and, having accomplished, by the kind aid of the provisional bishop of New York, a work he has long had at heart, the publication of a re-translation of the principal portions of the Book of Common Prayer, adapted alike to the use of the Indians both of the English and American church, he has now every prospect of being actively and successfully occupied during the remainder of his chequered life. Since the year 1848, the subject of his foreign birth has frequently been mentioned and discussed in the public prints. It was this which, in the first instance, led to my acquaintance with him, which, with its results, will occupy the following pages.

## CHAPTER XVI.

### OUR FIRST INTERVIEW.

My first acquaintance with the Rev. Eleazar Williams, was in the autumn of 1851. His name had been, for years, familiar to my eye, from seeing it in the record of missionary proceedings, but beyond this I had no knowledge of his history; when, one day, my attention was arrested by a paragraph in a New York paper, I believe it was the "Courier and Enquirer," containing the strange, and, at first sight, most improbable announcement, that there were strong reasons for supposing him to be the son of Louis XVI., and that he was said to bear a very strong resemblance to the Bourbon family. It struck me, at first, as being one of those idle stories we see so frequently in print, but it excited my curiosity, as I was at a loss to imagine what could have given rise to a report so wild and marvellous. I was then residing at Waddington, on the banks of the St. Lawrence, and did not even know there was any connection between Mr. Williams and the Indians at St. Regis, in my immediate neighborhood. It, however, occasioned me pleasure to learn, from a friend, that Mr. Williams had removed from Green Bay to St. Regis, and nothing but constant engagements prevented my going to see him, and ascertain what he had to say on the subject, though I had no idea but that he would contradict the story, and explain the circumstances out of which it had arisen. This, I find was the common feeling among his brethren of the clergy, who, not unfrequently, alluded to it, for the first time, in a laughing way, and were surprised to find he treated the matter seriously, and was sometimes immediately affected to tears.

As I was about to leave St. Lawrence county, I regretted not being able to see him, before my departure, when accident threw him in my way. I have already, in another form, given an account of our interview, and repeat here the substance of what I then said, because it explains the interest I have since taken in him, gives a correct picture of his manners, and apparent character, and is an introduction to the history of the last few months of his life. It also exhibits the casual manner in which the present agitation of the question has arisen, and exonerates him from the charge of having thrust himself before the public. I found him busily engaged in the sacred duties of his ministry, which he has ever since uninterruptedly pursued, without allowing himself to be diverted from them, by the excitement and investigation of which he was the centre. Verbal repetition, however unpleasant, is unavoidable, because, as a matter of evidence, the subject has assumed a certain definite form, from which it is impossible now to separate it.

Upon entering the cars, on the Ogdensburg railroad, on my way to New York, in the autumn of 1851, I observed a somewhat stout old gentleman, talking to two Indians in their own language, in a very animated manner, and was much interested in watching the varied play of their countenances while listening to him. He appeared to be very eloquent, used much gesticulation, and worked his hearers into a state of excitement more remarkable, when compared with the usual stolid expression of the Indian face. A gentleman on the seat before me, who was also watching the singular group, said, "He must be a half-breed," for we were all surprised at the freedom with which one of evidently European figure and face, spoke the Indian tongue. It then occurred to me that it was Williams, and on my saying so, and mentioning the mystery connected with his name, the gentleman who had first spoken rose, and asked the conductor, who confirmed my supposition. On hearing this, I introduced myself to Mr. Williams as a brother clergyman, apologizing for not having paid him a visit. I found him friendly and easy of access. He said he had been trying to convince his Indian friends, who were members of the Romish communion, of their errors, and that the poor fellows were much interested in what he had advanced. He was going to Burlington, Vermont, and from thence to Boston, and as our route lay down Champlain, we took the steamer together at Rouse's Point. While waiting on the dock for the arrival of the vessel, I was prepossessed in his favor, from noticing the unaffected kindness he showed the Indians, in directing them what to do, and aiding them with their luggage. I was perfectly familiar with the Indian lineaments and charcteristics, but was not sorry, that at my interview with him, I had so good an opportunity of attentively comparing his appearance with that of his reputed countrymen, and, the closer my examination, the more my curiosity was raised, for though his dress was not such as to show him to advantage, he presented, in every respect, the marks of different race and station from theirs, and my wonder was, that any attentive observer should ever have imagined him to be an Indian.

When we were seated on the dock, I told him, I had seen a statement in the newspapers, which had excited my curiosity, and should feel obliged, if it was not intrusive, by being informed if he believed the story of his royal origin, and upon what evidence the extraordinary claim was based. He replied, the subject was painful to him, nor could he speak of it unmoved, but would, with pleasure, give me the required information. "There seems to me," I then said, "one simple and decisive test of the truth of your claim, I mean, your memory of your childhood. If you have always lived among the Indians, you cannot forget it, and if you are the lost Dauphin, it seems scarcely credible that, being at the time of your mother's death more than eight years of age, you could have passed through the fearful scenes of the revolution, without a strong impression of the horrors attendant on your early years. Have you any memory of what happened in Paris, or of your voyage to this country?"

"Therein," he replied, "lies the mystery of my life. I know nothing about my infancy. Everything that occurred to me is blotted out, entirely erased, irrecoverably gone. My mind is a blank until thirteen or fourteen years of age. You must imagine a child who, as far as he knows anything, was an idiot, destitute even of consciousness that can be remembered until that period. He was bathing on Lake George, among a group of Indian boys. He clambered with the fearlessness of idiocy to the top of a high rock. He plunged down head foremost into the water. He was taken up insensible, and laid in an Indian hut. He was brought to life. There was the blue sky, there were the mountains, there were the waters. That was the first I knew of life."

"When, then, and how," I continued, "did you come to entertain the idea, you now do, concerning your birth? What is there to confirm it?"

"I was under the impression," he replied, "that I was at least partly of Indian extraction, until the time that the Prince de Joinville came to this country. One of the first questions he asked on his arrival in New York was, whether there was such a person known as Eleazar Williams, among the Indians of the northern part of the State; and after some inquiries in different quarters, he was told there was such a person, who was at that time a Missionary of the Protestant Episcopal Church, at Green Bay, Wisconsin, and was advised to apply for further information to some prominent members of the church in this city. He accordingly applied to Mr. Thomas Ludlow Ogden, who, at the Prince's request, wrote to me, stating that the Prince was then in the country, and before his return to France, would be happy to have an interview with me. I replied to Mr. Ogden, that I should be exceedingly happy to see the Prince at any time. I was much surprised with his communication; but supposed, however, that as I had resided a long time in the west, and had been chaplain to Gen. Taylor, he might desire some local information, which I could give him as readily as most men. Some time elapsed, and I heard nothing more on the subject, which was beginning to fade from my mind,* when one day, while on board a steamer on Lake Michigan, I had an interview with the Prince, who shortly after, at Green Bay, revealed the secret of my birth."

Mr. Williams then proceeded to give me many of the incidents connected with this memorable interview; but as I have, at a later period, drawn from him an account, in every way more circumstantial, of all that occurred, I will postpone further particulars until the subject recurs in the order of events.

To return again to our conversation. "Is your reputed mother," I inquired, "living—the Indian woman who brought you up? Is it not easy to ascertain from her, whether or not you are her child? What does she say upon the subject?"

"My reputed mother," he said, "is still living, at a very advanced age. She is now at Caughnawaga. I ought, as soon as the Prince told me the secret of my birth, to have returned to the east and seen her. But I unfortunately neglected to do so for some time, and when I did come, I found that the Romish Priests had been tampering with her, and that her mouth was hermetically sealed. Since I have been at St. Regis, I have learned from the Indians, that the

* The above account of our conversation was written months after it occured, and I must, in the last sentence, have partially misrepresented what Mr. Williams said, as there is documentary evidence that he went expressly to the west to meet the Prince de Joinville.

priests said to her, 'Suppose that this man should prove to be heir to a throne on the other side of the Great Salt Lake, what injury may he not do to the Church? He has been brought up a Protestant, and if he obtained sovereign power it would be the ruin of many souls. You must, therefore, say nothing one way or the other, but keep entirely silent.' And so all my efforts to extract anything from her were unavailing. Her immovable Indian obstinacy has hitherto been proof against every effort I could make. But I have not given up hope yet, and will try her again. When asked the direct question, Is Eleazar Williams your son? she will neither answer yes nor no—but keeps her mouth shut, and seems indifferent to what is said. When hard pressed indeed on one occasion, she has been known to say, 'Do you think that Eleazar is a bastard?' but that was all. If, however, the question is put to her in an indirect form, she will begin, in the monotonous manner in which ignorant people repeat a story, in which they have been drilled by others, and have told for years in one way, to give a list of her children, and the dates of their birth, bringing in my name at a particular place. But we have had the baptismal register at Caughnawaga examined, and the priest was made to certify to it, and though the names of all the rest of her children are recorded there, together with the dates of their birth and baptism, mine does not occur there; and the births of the children follow so closely upon each other, at regular intervals of two years between each, that it does not seem naturally possible I could have been her child, unless I was twin to some other child whose birth and baptism are recorded while mine are not—a thing which, when we take into consideration the exactness and fidelity with which such affairs are transacted in the Church of Rome, does not seem probable, and scarcely possible. The silence of the baptismal register may, therefore, be deemed conclusive proof that this Indian woman is not my mother.

"And then comes in," continued Williams, "evidence of a different description. A French gentleman died at New Orleans, in

1848, named Belanger, who confessed on his death bed that he was the person who brought the Dauphin to this country, and placed him among the Indians in the northern part of the State of New York. It seems that Belanger had taken a solemn oath of secresy, alike for the preservation of the Dauphin and the safety of those who were instrumental in effecting his escape, but the near approach of death, and the altered circumstances of the times, induced him to break silence before his departure from the world. He died in January, 1848. Now, the person who had charge of the Dauphin after the death of Simon, stabbed a man in a political quarrel in France, and fled for safety.* He it was, I suppose, who, with the assistance and connivance of others, carried the youth with him to the Low Countries, and thence to England. He must have changed his own name for greater security, crossed the Atlantic, and after depositing him with the Indians, gone to Louisiana and there lived and died.

"The next link in the evidence is yet more singular. A French gentleman hearing my story, brought a printed account of the captivity of the Dauphin, and read me a note in which it was stated that Simon the jailer, having become incensed with the Prince for some childish offence, took a towel which was hanging on a nail, and in snatching it hastily drew out the nail with it, and inflicted two blows upon his face, one over the left eye and the other on the right side of the nose. 'And now,' said he, 'let me look at your face.' When he did so, and saw the scars on the spots indicated in the memoirs, he exclaimed, 'Mon Dieu! what proof do I want more?'

"But that is not all," he continued. "In the same memoirs it is said, that the Dauphin died of scrofula, and that the disease was on his knees. My knees are eaten up with scrofula, and there are no other scrofulous marks on my body. Such are the main points

* The historic misstatements of Mr. Williams, in conversation, respecting events in France, only show he had at this time paid little attention to the subject, and picked up his information from others. He was utterly ignorant of the mass of historic evidence in support of his personal narrative.

of evidence on which my claim rests, and you may judge of their strength—and further I can only refer you to the alleged resemblance between me and Louis XVIII., and the Bourbon family in general. I remember a gentleman put his hand over the name attached to a picture of Louis XVIII., and asked a friend whose portrait it was, 'That of Mr. Williams,' was the reply. I have somewhat of a curiosity in my valise, and will show it you if you would like to see it. It is a dress of Marie Antoinette. It was given me by a person who bought it in France, and who hearing my story, and considering me the rightful owner, made me a present of it."

He then went forward, opened his valise, and returned with a small bundle under his arm, which he carried into the upper saloon for the sake of privacy. It is of course impossible to say whether the dress which he showed me is what it is asserted to be, but from its appearance it certainly may be so. It was a magnificent but somewhat faded brocade silk. It had been taken to pieces, and consisted of a skirt, back piece, stomacher, and train ten or twelve feet in length. The waist was very slender. There is pleasure in believing in the truth of memorials of the past, and I cannot envy the critical coldness of one who would ridicule me for surrendering myself, under the influence of the scene, to the belief, that the strange old gentleman before me, whose very aspect is a problem, was son to the fair being whose queenly form that faded dress had once contained, as she moved noblest and loveliest in the Halls of Versailles; and that in childish beauty and innocence, the heir of crowns, and the hope of kingdoms, the observed of all observers, he had rested fondly against its silken folds when the living loveliness of Marie Antoinette was within it.* However, I am not

* As the fact of this dress having belonged to Marie Antoinette has been questioned, I give the note with which the gift was accompanied :—

"Presented to the Rev. Eleazar Williams, with the respectful regards of Mrs. Edward Clarke, of Northampton. Being in England some years since, I had an opportunity there to purchase this dress, once worn by the Queen Marie Antoinette, of France. It had writing romance, but a matter-of-fact account of an adventure on a steamboat.

I now proceeded to scrutinize more closely the form, features, and general appearance of Mr. Williams, and to re-examine the scars on his face. He is an intelligent, noble-looking old man, with *no trace, however slight,* of the Indian about him except what may be fairly accounted for by his long residence among Indians. He is far more familiar with their language than with English, which he speaks correctly, and even eloquently, as far as style is concerned, but pronounces imperfectly. His manner of talking reminds you of a Frenchman, and he shrugs his shoulders and gesticulates like one. But he has the port and presence of an European gentleman of high rank; a nameless something which I never saw but in persons accustomed to command; a countenance bronzed by exposure below the eyebrows; a fair, high, ample, intellectual, but receding forehead; a slightly aquiline, but rather small nose; a long Austrian lip, the expression of which is of exceeding sweetness when in repose; full fleshy cheeks, but *not* high cheek bones; dark, bright, merry eyes of hazel hue; graceful, well-formed neck; strong muscular limbs, indicating health and great activity; small hands and feet, and dark hair, sprinkled with gray, as fine in texture as silk. I should never have taken him for an Indian. Some persons who saw him several years ago, tell me, their impression is that he looked partially like one, but admit, their opinion may have been influenced by their having been previously told he was of Indian extraction. I will here insert a description of him by another hand, furnished me by Mr. Williams. "His complexion is

been bought at the court by a gentleman, attached, at that time, to our embassy. I was informed that the dresses once worn by the queen, were afterwards distributed among the ladies of the court, who would sometimes dispose of them in this manner at auction.

"*Round Hill, Northampton,*
" *Jany.* 3, 1851."

rather dark, like that of one who had become bronzed by living much in the open air, and he passes for a half-breed. But his features are decidedly European, rather heavily moulded, and strongly characterized by the full, protuberant Austrian lips This, the experienced observer is well aware, is never found in the aboriginal, and very rarely among the Americans themselves. His head is well formed, and sits proudly on his shoulders. His eyes are dark, but not black. His hair may be called black, is rich and glossy, and interspersed with gray. His eyebrows are full, and of the same color—upon the left is a scar. His beard is heavy, and nose aquiline. The nostril is large and finely cut. His temperament is genial, with a dash of vivacity in his manners, he is fond of good living, and inclines to embonpoint, which is the characteristic of the Bourbon family."

While refolding the dress of the poor queen, I asked him if he could account for the conduct of the Prince de Joinville in disclosing so important a secret as that of his royal birth, and requesting him to give up rights previously unknown to him, and which, without information derived from the Prince, he would have had no means of ascertaining. He replied, in substance, it might indeed seem strange, but the only satisfactory explanation he would suggest was, that although he was personally ignorant of his origin, yet there were those both in Europe and this country who were acquainted with it, and that Louis Phillippe being at that time anxious to fortify his family in power by every possible means, contracting alliances with other royal lines of Europe, yet knew that in him existed an obstacle which might possibly prevent the accomplishment of all his designs, and had therefore, perhaps, delegated his son to reveal the fact to him so as to escape the consequences of its coming to light some other way. However, I may add that, at this interview, Mr. Williams positively declined stating all that passed between him and the Prince de Joinville. "I do not trouble my mind, he continued, "much about the matter, otherwise I might easily render myself unhappy by repining at the will of God. But I submit myself entirely to His will. My story is on the winds of Heaven, and will work its way without me. They have got it in France. Copies of my daguerreotype have been sent to eminent men there. God in His providence must have some mysterious ends to answer, or He never would have brought me so low from such a height. He has cast my lot among this poor Indian people, and I have ministered and will minister to them, if it please Him until death. I don't want a crown. I am convinced of my royal descent; so are my family. The idea of royalty is in our minds, and we will never relinquish it. You have been talking," he concluded, smiling between jest and earnest, "with a king to-night. Come, let us go down stairs, and I will show you something else." He then went again to his valise and took out some miniatures and a daguerreotype. "There is the picture of Madame," he said, putting into my hands the miniature of a very beautiful young lady. "That was how my wife looked when I married her. And there," giving me another, "is my likeness at the same time. I suppose you know who that is," he continued, taking back the miniatures and giving me a daguerreotype. It was his likeness such as he now is, but having a broad band fastened by an ornamented cross passed over the shoulder as worn by European princes. In the daguerreotype the lights and shadows of his marked and expressive face are brought fully out, and the sun's pencil makes him look every inch a king. Strange, indeed, if a St. Regis Indian could be the original of such a portrait, drawn by so unfailing an artist. The steamboat by this time was drawing near to Burlington, and Williams employed the few moments that remained, in describing his situation at St. Regis. He said that having left his wife in the west, he was living alone in a little hut, almost destitute of the necessaries of life, without books, without companions, except the Indians, and that he occupied his time in teaching a few children.

The boat stopped—he hurried down, and I parted with him.

## CHAPTER XVII.

### PUTNAM'S MAGAZINE.

When our interview was over, I had little idea I should ever again see Mr. Williams; but the strange story I had heard made a great impression on my mind. It haunted me. I could not get rid of it, and when I tried to throw it off, it would recur again. I had seen something of men, and been a not inattentive observer. Mr. Williams was one of the most simple men I had ever met, and apart from simplicity there is little excellence and questionable truth. I saw clearly all the difficulties with which his story was surrounded, but I reposed confidence in him; and I am happy to say that, although my confidence has often been put, in the course of discussion, to the severest test, it remains unshaken. Though I saw him under circumstances least favorable to impress the mind with ideas of noble birth—among Indians, in plain, simple dress, in poverty, in depression, in social isolation, and unfriended destitution—yet, there was nothing in his appearance or manner, his bodily or mental characteristics, to jar with the idea excited by his words. Everything was in keeping. Had any other person I ever met told me such a story, I should have laughed him in the face. He was evidently a man who had a history which did not lie on the surface, because nature never placed such a man in such a position. He was clearly an exotic. With no sign of the Indian, he bore every mark of a mixture of French and German blood, and good blood, too. But what chiefly led me to believe his statements were true, was, that he, soberly and seriously, told improbabilities as facts, without knowing what there was to sustain them. A pretender would never have done this. He would have had all his proofs cut, dried, and labelled, and his story, consistent or inconsistent, fully made out. With Mr. Williams it was entirely different. He mentioned certain strange things which had happened to him, and a few isolated hints of confirmation, merely showing there might be evidence fuller and more explicit. With nothing to gain, he risked, as the event has proved, everything.

I was surprised that no one had taken the trouble to probe the mystery which hung about him, since, if it were a case of deception, it was one of the most extraordinary the world has seen, and deserved on that account to be chronicled; and, if his statements were, indeed, true, there could not be a richer pearl of historic fact rescued from oblivion.

I repeated what he had said, to many persons, and made all possible inquires concerning him. He had mentioned the Hon. J. C. Spencer, of Albany, as one to whom he had communicated the facts I have detailed; and, meeting that gentleman, in Convention, I stated the impression his story had made on my mind, when Mr. Spencer, with earnestness, exclaimed, "His story made a great impression on my mind, too, sir—a very, very great impression;" and, then, went on to mention several facts of which I was previously ignorant, and among them, the omission of the Dauphin's name from the funeral solemnities. I had seen too much of the ripe judgment and legal acumen of Mr. Spencer, not to feel certain that there was something to be discovered in a historic question which had riveted his attention; and, though he concluded by saying, that, he feared it was now too late to gain positive evidence, and that the whole subject would, probably, remain a mystery like the man in the iron mask; the result of our conversation was to stimulate my desire to clear away the obscurity.

Shortly after, I repeated Mr. Williams's story to the Rev. Dr. Hawks, who was as much interested in it as I had been, and requested me to put what I had said in writing, which I did in the shape of a lettter addressed to him. He read my letter to some friends, and this drew from Dr. J. W. Francis, who was present, an account of a conversation with M. Genet, respecting the Dauphin. He said that, in the year 1818, there was a social party at the house of Dr. Hosack, in New York, at which there were present, beside himself, Dr. Macneven, Counsellor Sampson, Thomas Cooper, of Carlisle, Count Jean D'Angley, and M. Genet, formerly ambassador from France. In the course of the conversation, the subject of the Dauphin was introduced, and the inquiry started as to his fate. At length, Genet distinctly said, "Gentlemen, the Dauphin of France *is not dead, but was brought to America.*" The conversation continued, for some time, and M. Genet informed the company, among other things, that he believed the Dauphin was in Western New York, and that Le Ray de Chaumont knew all about it.

The issue here raised is a mere collateral one, and has no necessary connection with the main argument; but as the names of many highly respectable gentlemen are introduced, it may be as well to consider it in this place. The facts are simply, that M. Genet did make the statements referred to at the time, as he did also at many other times, and to many other persons, and, therefore, had his own reasons for supposing the Dauphin to be then alive in America, and that Le Ray was in the secret. In the latter he may have been mistaken. For many years, as I learn from members of his family, he entertained hopes of discovering the Dauphin, but seems to have relinquished expectations of success in his latter years, and especially after conversing with Billaud Varennes, in Philadelphia, who expressed the opinion that the Prince was dead. Though an ambassador of the Republic, Genet was warmly and affectionately attached to Louis XVI. and his family, and had himself been on the point of bringing, at the martyred king's request, both his children to America, when he came out as ambassador. A carriage, with a false back, in which the children were to have been concealed, was provided for their escape; but on the eve of the execution of the project, the carriage was seized and destroyed by the mob. This fact, and other circumstances, which cannot now be ascertained, may have induced him to believe the Prince was brought to his original destination by the intrigues of Louis XVIII., whose character and designs he well knew, having himself seen a letter from the Count de Provence to the Arch-anarchist. Again, Count Real and Count Jean D'Angley were in conference with Le Ray de Chaumont, in 1817, as stated by Dr. Francis, at a time when the existence of Louis XVII. was being agitated in Paris.

Apart from these circumstances, there is nothing to indicate that Le Ray had any knowledge of the affair, except an allusion in his conversation with Mr. Williams, in 1819 or 1820. Mr. Williams was at that time residing at Oneida, in which place there also lived a Col. de Ferrière, who had fled from France during the Revolution, and married an Indian woman, who is still living. Le Ray inquired of Williams concerning the health and welfare of De Ferrière, adding that he had been a great sufferer in the royal cause: that the King's family had been widely scattered, but that, notwithstanding all the misfortunes of De Ferrière, he was no greater sufferer than a member of the royal family, whom both Colonel de Ferrière and he believed to be in this country.

Now, in 1816 or '17, De Ferrière went to France, and took several Indians with him. Before starting, he obtained from Mr. Williams three separate signatures to some legal document. One of the Indians afterwards related that he had been introduced into the presence of some person of distinction in Paris, and asked, among other questions, who was then the religious teacher in Oneida, when he replied Eleazar Williams; he was again asked if he was certain as to his being there, and on his replying in the affirmative, was dismissed. It is a well known fact that De Ferrière went to Europe a poor man, that he returned a rich one, and that he was afterwards in correspondence with the royal family of France.

In October, 1852, I wrote to Mr. Williams for additional information, if he could afford me any, respecting the subject of our conversation on the steamboat, and asked if he had any objection to the publication of the facts he had mentioned, not knowing, at the time, that any fuller accounts than I had seen had been printed. In his reply, dated Hogansburg, Nov. 4, 1852, he informed me of the reception of a letter from Paris, purporting to proceed from the secretary of the President, making inquiries, in a respectful manner, concerning the events of his life, and also of similar communications from several eminent French ecclesiastics, but said that he had not replied to them, as the subject was "very afflictive" to him. "It has been, and is," he continued, "a very great annoyance, from which I would gladly be delivered. You cannot be surprised, reverend sir, when I say that my feelings have been such, at times, as no pen can describe, nor tongue express. I am in a state of exile among the Indians, and compelled, at times to beg my bread, although connected with a Christian Church, who has means in abundance to sustain her humble and self-denying missionary honorably. It is true I am allowed a little pittance, which is scarcely enough to clothe me; yet I still continue to labor patiently in the cause of my Divine Master, who suffered and died, but is now my exalted Saviour. I seek not an earthly crown, but heavenly, where we shall be made kings and priests unto God —to him be glory and dominion for ever and ever. Nothing keeps me in my present position but that gracious promise of my blessed Saviour, 'Be thou faithful unto death and I will give thee a crown of life.'"

His letter only increased my sympathy in his behalf, and, though he seemed quite indifferent to the publication of the strange story, it seemed an evident duty to him, to the church of which he was a minister, and to history, of which, provided his origin could be ascertained, he would form a portion, to make some effort to clear up the mystery.

I knew he must be in great want and destitution; that, as far as I could ascertain, he was laboring zealously among the Indians, and deserved more consideration at the hands of the church than he had received; and, therefore, after consultation with Dr. Hawks, who was deeply interested in his case, and strongly urged me to make some effort to ascertain the truth in the matter, I determined to visit the north and see him.

I accordingly left New York for this purpose, on 17th November, and arrived at Morra, in the neighborhood of his residence, on the following day; meeting an old resident who had known Mr. Williams for many years, named Harrington, I asked him which he thought the oldest, without intimating for what purpose I made the inquiry. Without any hesitation he replied, that he was himself sixty-eight years of age, but had always considered himself younger than Mr. Williams. He added, that Williams was, without doubt, an European. His son, an intelligent and respectable man, who has had every opportunity of knowing the truth in the matter, wrote, at my request, the following certificate:—"I was brought up at Hogansburg, and have served in the army as a private, under General Worth. I have known Indians of various tribes, especially the Seminoles and the Iroquois. I have known Indians as long as I have known white men. I am personally acquainted with the Rev. Eleazar Williams, and have known him since my childhood. I do not believe him to be an Indian. He is entirely unlike the rest of his family. I knew some of his supposed brothers, especially Jarvis Williams. They bore no resemblance to Eleazar. He looks like a German or Frenchman; they were undoubtedly Indians. The general impression among intelligent people, in this neighborhood, who know Mr. Williams, is, that he is not an Indian. His reputed mother does not acknowledge him to be her son. Mr. Williams bears an excellent character among us, and is highly respected. I know an Indian as well as I know a cow or a horse."

Every inquiry which I made in the neighborhood of Mr. Williams's residence, led to precisely the same conclusion. I found there were certain facts to which every one I conversed with, in Hogansburg and the neighborhood, was ready to testify, viz. that there was no personal resemblance between Williams and any of his nominal kindred, dead or living; that he had no marks whatever of being an Indian, in the estimation of persons who see Indians every moment of their lives; that old Mary Ann Williams preserved an unaccountable silence and mystery respecting him, and did not acknowledge him to be her son; that he was hated, opposed, and thwarted in every possible manner by the Romish priest and his people, but labored to do his duty faithfully under these discouraging circumstances.

His landlady at Hogansburg, said, "I don't know whether he is Indian or not. He does not look like one. If I had not heard that he was one, I should not suppose that he was, any more than you. He is not like any of his family. All the other children are dead." And I may add, they all died of consumption. I found the absence of his name from the baptismal register was undoubted; the Rev. Francis Marcoux, Romish priest, at St. Regis, having lately acknowledged the omission to the Hon. Phineas Atwater, formerly Indian agent, but endeavored to account for it by saying, that he was privately baptized on account of sickness, which certainly is no reason why his baptism should not have been registered.

His temporary absence on missionary service deprived me of the pleasure of seeing him, but I obtained full insight into his position, estimation in the neighborhood, and other things necessary to the formation of a correct judgment. He is missionary at St. Regis and Hogansburg, both miserable, lonely places, receiving no payment from the Indians among whom he labors, and but a small stipend from the Missionary Committee. The rigors of the climate are excessive; the thermometer in winter being frequently thirty degrees below zero, and one can scarcely conceive a situation for an intelligent mind more lonely, more unfriended, more destitute. His residence is on the Indian Reservation, a wild tract of woodland, partially cleared, here and there, at the edges. At the time of my visit, dead evergreen swamps, decayed vegetation, rude fences, half prostrate, surrounded the ricketty shed, admitting the cold at a thousand crevices, in which resided poor Williams and the old Indian woman, his reputed mother, whom he heroically treats as if she were his parent, though believing himself to be the son of the peerless Marie Antoinette. He had no church building, but was trying to build a school-house on the Indian

Reservation, which stood roofless in the piercing cold, the picture of desolation.

Having failed to meet Mr. Williams at Hogansburg, I went to Caughnawaga, in hopes of finding him, but was again disappointed. I, however, inquired among the Indians, as to their impressions of his race, and found the same opinion prevalent there, as in the vicinity of his residence.

On my way home I had another interview with the Hon J. C. Spencer, in Albany, from whom I derived many additional items of information. From him I learned, that Prof. Day, on his return from Europe, in an interview with Mr. Williams, threw some lithographs and engravings on the table; at the sight of one of which, and without seeing the name, Williams was greatly excited, and cried, "Good God, I know that face. It has haunted me through life," *or words to that effect.* On examination, it proved to be the portrait of Simon the jailer.

I afterwards received a letter from Prof. Day, in answer to inquiries made of him on the subject, in which he gave the combined recollections of himself and family. The incident occurred at Northampton, in the summer of 1850-51. Previous to seeing the engraving, Mr. Williams had spoken of a hideous countenance which had haunted him for years. At the time the portrait was shown to him, Prof. Day's hand was over the name. "He was silent," writes Prof. Day, "for a moment, and then said, 'that is the countenance,' *or words to that effect*—but added, that in one respect, it did not agree with his recollections, for the man whose features had haunted him all his life was bald. It was impossible to decide, from the lithograph, whether such was the case with Simon, or not, as he is represented, with his hat on, but on looking at the inscription, under the print, it was evident that he might have been bald, as he was fifty-eight years old when guillotined with Robespierre." Of course, in this, and all similar cases of recognition, the proof can only be conclusive to the individual who is the subject of it. Mr. Spencer likewise mentioned he had been informed by Mr. Williams, that he had ascertained from his reputed mother, that two boxes of clothing, and other articles had been left with him at the time of his adoption. One of these boxes has been carried off by a daughter of Thomas Williams, and cannot now be recovered. The other, there is every reason to suppose is still in Montreal, but efforts are made in certain quarters to conceal it. In this box were three coins or medals, one of gold, one of silver, and one of copper—fac-similes of each other—being the medals struck at the coronation of Louis XVI. and Marie Antoinette. The gold and silver medals being of value, were sold by the Indians in Montreal. The copper one was retained and is now in my possession. The gold medal has also been seen in the possession of a Romish bishop at Montreal or Quebec.

The probability that these traces of the Dauphin are to be found in Montreal is increased by the proximity of Caughnawaga to that city. Caughnawaga is a straggling Indian village on the St. Lawrence, opposite Lachine, and within sight of Montreal. It consists, besides a number of scattered huts, of two long narrow streets varying considerably in width. The houses are low and shabby, most of them of wood, but some of dark stone. The masonry is of the rudest kind. A Roman Catholic church, a solid stone building, of some slight pretensions to architecture, stands in the middle of one of the streets. In looking at the dingy houses, the narrow streets, the crowd of little Indian children; and considering the loneliness of the spot in former years before railroads and steamboats had brought it into connection with the busy world, one cannot help feeling how secure a hiding-place for the poor scion of royalty this village presented. And the same remarks apply more strongly still to St. Regis, which lies on the present boundary between Canada and the U. S. But from these secluded spots the Indians, who partake much of the character and roving habits of the gipsey, wander forth over the surrounding country, selling baskets, and bartering whatever of value comes into their possession. Those who placed the Dauphin among the Indians, might be sure that the tomb could scarcely be a more secret shelter; but at the same time if they desired to identify him, as their leaving these relics would intimate, they could have had little hope that the habits of the Indians would permit the retention of any traces of royalty.

Having obtained all the information I could without seeing Mr. Williams, I returned to New York. On Dec. the 7th, I received a note from him, stating he was in the city. Upon calling at his hotel, I found that, having heard of my journey to the north, he had come to New York to see me. He accompanied me to the study of Dr. Hawks, in whose presence he confirmed the statements he had previously made to me. In the course of the conversation which took place between us at my house, I drew from him a detailed account of the interview between him and the Prince de Joinville, alluded to in the early part of this narrative, to which I will now proceed, merely premising that, although given in an uninterrupted form, it was in a great measure elicited by dint of questioning and cross-questioning, so as to obtain all the particulars concerning the value of which Mr. Williams did not seem to be sufficiently aware; but there is no thought or fact he did not express, and the language, as near as a retentive memory can give it, is in his own words, though somewhat condensed. After describing the correspondence between him and Mr. Thomas L. Ogden, and re-affirming strongly the fact that the Prince had made inquiries concerning him, immediately on his arrival in the country, he said, in substance, as follows:—

"In Oct., 1841, I was on my way from Buffalo to Green Bay, and took a steamer from the former place bound to Chicago, which touched at Mackinac, and left me there, to await the arrival of the steamer from Buffalo to Green Bay. Vessels which had recently come in announced the speedy arrival of the Prince de Joinville; public expectation was on tiptoe, and crowds were on the wharves. The steamer at length came in sight, salutes were fired and answered, the colors run up, and she came into port in fine style. Immediately she touched, the Prince and his retinue came on shore and went out some little distance from the town, perhaps half a mile, to visit some natural curiosities in the neighborhood—the Sugar Loaf Rock and the Arch Rock. The steamer awaited their return. During their absence I was standing on the wharf among the crowd, when Captain John Shook, now at Huron, Ohio, who will confirm my statement, came up to me and asked whether I was going on to Green Bay, adding that the Prince de Joinville had made inquiries of him concerning a Rev. Mr. Williams, and that he had told the Prince he knew such a person, referring to me, whom he supposed was the man he meant, though he could not imagine what the Prince could want with or know of me. I replied to the Captain in a laughing way, without having any idea what a deep meaning was attached to my words, 'Oh, I am a great man, and great men will of course seek me out.' Soon after, the Prince and his suite arrived, and went on board. I did the same, and the steamer put to sea. It was, I think, about two o'clock when we left Mackinac. When we were fairly out on the water, the Captain came to me and said, 'The Prince, Mr. Williams, requests me to say to you that he desires to have an interview with you, and will be happy either to have you come to him, or allow me to introduce him to you.' 'Present my compliments to the Prince,' I said, 'and say, I put myself entirely at his disposal, and will be proud to accede to whatever may be his wishes in the matter.' The Captain again retired, and soon returned bringing the Prince de Joinville with him. I was sitting at the time on a barrel. The Prince not only started with evident and involuntary surprise when he saw me, but there was great agitation in his face and manner—a slight paleness and a quivering of the lip—which I could not help remarking at the time, but which struck me more forcibly afterwards, in connection with the whole train of circumstances, and by contrast with his usual self-possessed manner. He then shook me earnestly and respectfully by the hand, and drew me immediately into conversation. The attention he paid me seemed to astonish not only myself and the passengers, but also the Prince's retinue. At dinner time there was a separate table laid for the Prince and his companions, and he invited me to sit with them, and offered me the seat of honor by his side. But I was a little abashed by the attentions of the Prince, and there was an American officer who had attached himself to the party, and behaved in an obtrusive and unbecoming manner, which seemed to annoy them, and indeed one of the Prince's companions had expressed to me his disgust at his behavior. So I thought I would keep out of the circle, and begged the Prince to excuse me, and permit me to dine at the ordinary table with the passengers, which accordingly I did. After dinner the conversation turned, between us, on the first French settlements in America, the valor and enterprise of the early adventurers, and the loss of Canada to France, at which the Prince expressed deep regret. In the course of his remarks, though in what connection I cannot now say, he told me he left his suite at Albany, took a private conveyance, and went to the head of Lake George. He was very copious and fluent in speech, and I was surprised at the good English he spoke—a little broken indeed—like mine—but still very intelligible. We continued talking late into the night, reclining in the cabin, on the cushions, in the stern of the boat. When we retired to rest, the Prince lay on the locker and I in the first berth next to it. The next day the steamer did not arrive at Green Bay until about three o'clock, and during most of the time we were in conversation. Looking back thoughtfully upon what was said, I can now perceive, the Prince was gradually preparing my mind for what was to come at last, although then the different subjects seemed to arise naturally enough. At first, he spoke of the condition of affairs in the United States, and the American Revolution. He expressed admiration for our institutions, and spoke at large of the assistance rendered to the Colonies in the struggle with the mother country, by Louis the Sixteenth. He said he did not think sufficient gratitude was evinced by Americans to that monarch, and that, whenever his intervention was alluded to, it was attributed to selfish motives, and to a desire to humble the power of England on this continent, by depriving her of her fairest colonial possessions, but, in his opinion, Louis XVI. felt a true regard for America, and that on every return of the 4th of July, when, throughout the United States, the nation was celebrating its independence, there should be an especial salute fired to the memory of the king who had contributed so much to the result. Such was the substance of what was said by the Prince on that subject. He then turned to the French Revolution, and said, Louis XVI. was innocent of any tyrannical designs toward the people of France, and nothing he did personally could justify or excuse the excesses of the Revolution; that the last foundations of that event were laid in the preceding reign, and, the misconduct and misgovernment of Louis XV. were chargeable with the sad events which occurred, to a very great extent, although the storm had been slowly brewing for centuries. The people of France, though they had no just cause to complain of Louis XVI., yet had a right to do so of the oppressive institutions then existing, of the tyranny of the aristocracy, and the burdens laid on them by the church. He then referred to the changes which had since taken place in the form of government, and to the present amelioration of the condition of the French people under an elective monarchy. On our arrival at Green Bay, the Prince said, I would oblige him by accompanying him to his hotel, and taking up my quarters at the Astor House. I begged to be excused, as I wished to go to the house of my father-in-law. He replied, he had some matters of great importance to speak to me about, and as he could not stay long at Green Bay, but would take his departure the next day, or the day after, he wished I would comply with his request. As there was some excitement consequent on the Prince's arrival, and a great number of persons were at the Astor House waiting to see him, I thought I would take advantage of the confusion to go to my father-in-law's, and promised to return in the evening, when he would be more private. I did so, and on my return found the Prince alone, with the exception of one attendant, whom he dismissed. The gentlemen of his party were in an adjoining room laughing and carousing, and I could distinctly hear them during my interview with the Prince. He opened the conversation by saying, he had a communication to make to me of a very serious nature as concerned himself, and of the last importance to me,—that it was one in which no others were interested, and, therefore, before proceeding further, he wished to obtain some pledge of secresy, some promise that I would not reveal to any one what he was going to say. I demurred to any such conditions being imposed previous to my being made acquainted with the nature of the subject, as there might be something in it, after all, prejudicial and injurious to others, and it was at length, after some altercation, agreed that I should pledge my honor not to reveal what the Prince was going to say, provided there was nothing in it prejudicial to any one, and I signed a promise to this effect on a sheet of paper. It was vague and general, for I would not tie myself down to absolute secresy, but left the matter conditional. When this was done, the Prince spoke to this effect:—

"You have been accustomed, sir, to consider yourself a native of this country; but you are not. You are of foreign descent; you were born in Eurpoe, sir, and however incredible it may at first seem to you, I have to tell you that you are the son of a king. There ought to be much consolation to you to know this fact. You have suffered a great deal, and have been brought very low, but you have not suffered more, or been more degraded than my father, who was long in exile and poverty in this country; but there is this difference between him and you, that he was all along aware of his high birth, whereas you have been spared the knowledge of your origin."

When the Prince had said this, I was much overcome, and thrown into a state of mind which you can easily imagine. In fact I hardly knew what to do or say, and my feelings were so much excited that I was like one in a dream, and much was said between us of which I can give but an indistinct account. However, I remember, I told him, his communication was so startling and unexpected, that he must forgive me for being incredulous, and that really I was "between two."

"What do you mean," he said, "by being 'between two?'"

I replied that, on the one hand, it scarcely seemed to me, he could believe what he said, and on the other, I feared he might be under some mistake as to the person. He assured me, however, he would not trifle with my feelings on such a subject, but spoke the simple truth, and that in regard to the identity of the person, he had ample means in his possession to satisfy me there was no mistake whatever. I then requested him to proceed with the disclosure already partly made, and to inform me in full of the secret of my birth. He replied that in doing so, it was necessary that a certain process should be gone through in order to guard the interest of all parties concerned. I inquired what kind of process he meant. Upon this the Prince rose and went to his trunk, which was in the room, and took from it a parchment which he laid on the table, and set before me, that I might read and give him my determination in regard to it. There were also on the table pen and ink and wax, and he placed there a governmental seal of France, the one, if I mistake not, used under the old monarchy. It was of precious metal, but whether of gold or silver, or a compound of both, I cannot say. I think, on reflection, the latter; but I may be mistaken, for my mind was so bewildered, and agitated, and engrossed with one absorbing question, that things which at another time would have made a strong impression on me were scarcely noticed, although I must confess that when I knew the whole, the sight of the seal put before me by a member of the family of Orleans stirred my indignation. The document which the Prince placed before me was very handsomely written, in double parallel columns of French and English. I continued intently reading and considering it for a space of four or five hours. During this time the Prince left me undisturbed, remaining for the most part in the room, but he went out three or four times.

The purport of the document, which I read repeatedly word by word, comparing the French with the English, was this: it was a solemn abdication of the crown of France in favor of Louis Philippe, by Charles Louis, the son of Louis XVI., who was styled Louis XVII., King of France and Navarre, with all accompanying names and titles of honor, according to the custom of the old French monarchy, together with a minute specification in legal phraseology of the conditions, and considerations, and provisos, upon which the abdication was made. These conditions were, in brief, that a princely establishment should be secured to me either in this country or in France, at my option, and that Louis Philippe would pledge himself on his part to secure the restoration, or an equivalent for it, of all the private property of the royal family rightfully belonging to me, which had been confiscated in France during the Revolution, or in any way got into other hands. Now you may ask me why I did not retain, at all hazards, this document, or, at any rate, take a copy of it; but it is very easy for you, sitting quietly there, to prescribe the course which prudence and self-interest would dictate. A day or two afterwards all these points, and the different lights in which the thing might be viewed, came to my mind; but at the moment I thought of nothing except the question of acceptance or rejection. And then, remember, the sudden manner in which the whole affair came upon me, and the natural timidity and bashfulness of one who had always considered himself of such obscure rank, when called, without preparation, to discuss such topics with a man of high position like the Prince. Besides which, my word of honor had been so recently and solemnly pledged, and a sense of personal dignity excited by the disclosures of the Prince, that I never so much as thought of taking any advantage of the circumstances, but simply and solely whether or not I should sign my name, and set my seal to a deliberate surrender of my rights and those of my family. It was a deeply painful and harrowing time, and I cannot tell you, and you cannot imagine, how I felt when trying to decide this question. At length I made my decision, and rose, and told the Prince that I had considered the matter fully in all its aspects, and was prepared to give him my definite answer upon the subject; and then went on to say, that whatever might be the personal consequences to myself, I felt that I could not be the instrument of bartering away with my own hand, the rights pertaining to me by my birth, and sacrificing the interests of my family, and that I could only give to him the answer which De Provence gave to the ambassador of Napoleon at Warsaw, "Though I am in poverty and exile I will not sacrifice my honor."

The Prince upon this assumed a loud tone, and accused me of ingratitude in trampling on the overtures of the king, his father, who, he said, was actuated, in making the proposition, more by feelings of kindness and pity towards me than by any other consideration, since his claim to the French throne rested on an entirely different basis to mine, viz. not that of hereditary descent, but of popular election. When he spoke in this strain I spoke loud also, and said, that as he, by his disclosure, had put me in the position of a superior, I must assume that position, and frankly say that my indignation was stirred by the memory, that one of the family of Orleans had imbrued his hands in my father's blood, and that another now wished to obtain from me an abdication of the throne. When I spoke of superiority, the Prince immediately assumed a respectful attitude, and remained silent for several minutes. It had now grown very late, and we parted, with a request from him that I would reconsider the proposal of his father, and not be too hasty in my decision. I returned to my father-in-law's, and the next day saw the Prince again, and on his renewal of the subject gave him a similar answer. Before he went away he said, 'Though we part, I hope we part friends.' For years I said little on the subject, until I received a letter from Mr. Kimball, dated at Baton Rouge, informing me of the dying statements of Belanger, and then, when this report came from the south confirming what the Prince had said, the thing assumed a different aspect. This letter is, I think, among my papers at Green Bay, but for years I have kept a minute journal of everything which has occurred to me, and have, no doubt, an abstract of it at Hogansburg. Our conversation to-night will go down."

I was much struck with the little value, in point of evidence, which Mr. Williams seems to have attached to the Prince's asserted disclosures. After giving me the above account, however, he added—"I see more and more, that the matter rests between the Prince and myself, and I am quite willing that it should. I have been in hopes that some movement would be made in Europe in my favor; but, as you say, the affair must be begun here, and I will let the world know all. The Prince cannot deny what I say, and my impression is that he will keep entirely silent."

"But silence will be equivalent to confession."

"It will be so."

At this time, I learned that Mr. Williams had kept a journal during the greater portion of his life. He mentioned the circumstance casually, but seemed to have no idea that it could be of any service as evidence. I inquired if he had preserved any contemporary record of his interview and conversations with the Prince? He replied, he believed he had, but it was a long time since he had examined his old papers, and a great portion of them were at Green Bay—but, possibly, some of the journals might be at Hogansburg. The next time he went to the north, he brought me the portions of his journal relave to 1841 and 1848. The reader, who, by this time, has had sufficient evidence of a fact which General Cass considers apocryphal, is in a better condition than formerly to judge of the importance to be attached to these documents. I wish much that space would permit me to present the whole of the journal for the year 1841. I will give some copious extracts, because it is necessary to exhibit some picture of his mind and life at a time when not occupied with any parochial charge.

## JOURNAL FOR 1841.

"*Green Bay*, *Jan.* 1, 1841—Thanks be to God, I am permitted once more to see another year. How numerous have been the mercies of God towards me in the year past, and what thanks have I returned to the God of all mercies for the blessings he has conferred upon me? Bless the Lord, O my soul, and give him thanks for all his benefits. May I be humble for my ingratitude to that blessed God who has sustained my life to this time. O, Holy Father, enable me, by thy heavenly grace, to devote all my time and talents to thy honor and glory, and at last, by thy great mercy and the merits of my Saviour, may I be admitted to thy Heavenly Kingdom.

"*Little Kakalin, Jan.* 3.—It has been an unpleasant day. I read much all day in the Holy Scriptures. Somewhat indisposed.

* * * * * * * *

"*Jan.* 17, *Sunday Evening.*—I had a pleasant interview with several of the Oneidas, who are inquiring the way of salvation. I pointed out to them the proper and only object of their faith, the Lord Jesus Christ. I explained to them several passages of Scripture.

"*Jan.* 18—I went down to Green Bay, called upon the Rev. Mr. Potter, dined with him. There was a discussion between us upon the doctrine of the saints' perseverance.

"*Jan.* 22, *Friday.*—Went down to Green Bay to pay Judge A. $25, and had a long conversation about the Church. He is somewhat loose in his principles, yet he would be a churchman. Sanctification of the heart was strongly held up to him.

"*Jan.* 23, *Saturday.*—I am preparing to-day to officiate to-morrow. O, my Heavenly Father, prepare my heart for the services. May I be sincere and devout in my attendance upon thee, and give me grace and strength to proclaim thy Holy Gospel in a suitable manner.

* * * * * * * *

"*Green Bay, Feb.* 4, 1841.—I came down in haste this morning to visit a sick man—he is in a dangerous situation, both in soul and body. I have administered to him all the consolation which the Christian religion affords, and the prayers of the Church.

"*Green Bay, Feb* 5, *Friday.*—Called again upon the sick man; he is somewhat better. I again exhorted him to have a lively faith in the Lord Jesus Christ.

* * * * * * * *

"*Feb.* 15.—Our son is much better to-day, and I hope he will continue to amend. The weather is fine. I went to the sugar camp. The Indian boy knocks the snow from the roof, and I arrange the sap dishes. The Oneidas have been with us, and communicated to me many unpleasant news in relation to their missionary. I exhorted them to live in peace with him and adhere to his instructions.

"*Feb.* 16.—I have been at Duck Creek, and administered baptism to a sick child. I believe it is now sick to death. May God receive it to eternal glory. I saw many of my Oneida friends, and they wished me to come back to them.

"*Feb.* 19, *Friday.*—Very cold, but the sky clear. Went out to the sugar camp to see it was arranged and put in order. I saw several deer and wolves. My horse and myself were in the water some time, but we extricated ourselves after a hard struggle, by the aid of a Frenchman and an Indian, who had a hearty laugh at my misfortune.

* * * * * * * *

"*April* 10.—Mrs. Williams returned from the sugar camp, where she has been superintending, for three weeks past, the making of sugar. I have been back and forth to see the men did their duty. We have made at least 1000 lbs. of fine sugar. I have been left nearly for weeks alone. I cooked myself and took care of the cattle.

* * * * * * * *

"*May* 20.—Went down to Green Bay, and had an interview with Mr. Whitney in relation to our landed property; but no good resulted from it. It is hard upon us.

* * * * * * * *

"*May* 30.—I am still in a feeble state of health, but recovering in a gradual manner. The physician is doing what he can for me.

* * * * * * * *

"*June* 11.—How many painful tasks I have to perform. To-day I visited a sick man who professes to be a churchman, from Mass., and would have me visit him, as he understood I was a minister of the Protestant Episcopal Church. I did all the church required of me, as one of its ministers, towards the sick man. I exhorted him to have faith in Christ and repentance towards God."

* * * * * * * *

On June 22, 1841, Mr. Williams and his son set out on board the

De Witt Clinton, Capt. Squares, with the intention of going into the State of New York, and on Tuesday, June 29, reached Oneida. On his way to New York he was taken sick at Cahoes, and sent a Mr. Wilkinson to the city with letters to Mr. Thomas L. Ogden. His indisposition continued for several weeks.

On Tuesday, October 1, occurs the following entry:—

"We returned to-day from our journey to St. Regis; we went in a wagon all the way, and returned by the same route. We found our friends all well. We put up with Bowker, where I received all my Indian friends who wished to see me. I had an interview with the American chiefs, who were much troubled with the $500 which they received from the State of New York. The British part of the tribe are claiming for a portion of the same, but the American part are opposed to this claim. There has been a great altercation between the two parties, in relation to this affair. By the request of the two parties, the British and American commissioners are appointed to adjust this matter. I am strongly urged by the American party to remain and sustain their claim; but there are certain circumstances which have come to my knowledge, which hasten me to return as soon as possible to Green Bay. I am greatly disappointed in regard to my business with Mr. Ogden, which was the principal object of this journey. My time and expense are lost to me. We shall return to-morrow."

The reader will here observe, there was important business tending to detain Mr. Williams at St. Regis; but, simultaneously with the reception of information from Thomas L. Ogden, concerning his private affairs, he learnt something which obliged him to return immediately homeward. Let him now read the following certificate:—

"I hereby certify, that, in the year 1841, the Rev. Eleazar Williams was staying at my house, in Hogansburg, and left, abruptly, to go to the west, without concluding his business; and, in a letter received from him, shortly afterwards, from Green Bay, he informed me that the cause of his abrupt departure was an intimation which he had received of the visit of the Prince de Joinville, to Green Bay. I have read a copy of the letter then written me, contained in his letter-book, and recognise it as being correct. It is possible that I may have the letter itself among my papers, and I will search for it; but, at any rate, there can be no doubt as to the fact that he did write the passage in question, as I recollect it perfectly.

'ELIAS BOWKER.

"*Hogansburg, August* 24, 1853."

The letter referred to by Mr. Bowker bears date December 27, 1841; and the passage with which we are concerned, is as follows:

"I am anxious to learn what may be the decision of the American and British commissioners, who were about to meet and act as judges over the $500. At the time I left Hogansburg, Mr. Eldridge promised to write and inform me the result of the above meeting of the commissioners, but no communication have I received as yet from that gentleman. Will you be pleased to inform him that I should be happy to hear from him. It was my intention to remain in Hogansburg, till after the meeting of the commissioners, but I was hindered in consequence of the intimation of the Prince de Joinville of visiting Green Bay, and I was just in time to meet him on the route."

Thus, although, we have not, as yet, been so fortunate as to discover the letter of Mr. Thomas L. Ogden, circumstances come in to supply, almost entirely, the deficiency; and, if the reader could form a proper judgment of the immense mass of Mr. Williams's papers, of all kinds, and the condition that they are in, he would only wonder that anything could be found, and the measure of exactness attained, which, I hope, has been arrived at. There are, at the present moment, several large boxes of papers, &c., in Ogdensburg, and it is possible that further light may be derived from them. But, to continue the journal:—

"*Syracuse, October* 4, *Monday.*—Went out and visited my Onondag friends. I am still feeble.

"*Detroit, October* 11, *Monday.*—Arrived here this morning, and expect to go on this afternoon. My reflections to-day and yesterday upon death, judgment, and eternity, have been lively. O, that they may lead me to live more in preparation for those solemn events. O, merciful Father, grant me true contrition, and unfeigned sorrow, for all I have thought and done amiss; quicken me by Thy Holy Spirit, and enable me to live to Thee, and to glorify Thee in my body and my spirit, which are thine. I trust the sickness with which I have been afflicted has a tendency to drive me to think more upon God.

"*October* 14.—*On board of the steamer.*—I have written to Mr. Ogden, General Potter, and Mr. Le Fort, the Onondaga chief.

"*October* 15, *Friday Evening.*—On Lake Huron, the day has been very pleasant. By the request of the passengers, I officiated this evening—preached from Luke vi. 12. The audience were very attentive. I am again afflicted with a severe pain in my left side. May I feel that I am in the midst of death, and so number my days that I may apply my heart unto wisdom. My son is somewhat unwell."

* * * * * *

*Mackinac, Oct.* 16, *Saturday.*—The steamer arrived here at two o'clock, P. M. My son is somewhat indisposed, and on that account I am more willing to remain here, until the Green Bay boat comes.

I have had a pleasant interview with the Rev. Mr. Coit, of the Congregationalist Church. Mr. C. has spent his time much among the Chippeway Indians. In his labors of love he has been successful. I trust many souls have been converted under his ministry. *Evening.*—It is proposed to have the Divine Service to-morrow at the Presbyterian Meeting-house. In the morning I am to officiate.

*Mackinac, Oct.* 17, *Sunday Evening.*—I performed the service this morning—all the gentlemen of the garrison, the soldiers and the citizens of the place were in attendance. My subject was upon Apostasy, which gave great offence to Mr.——. I find he has been excommunicated for his apostasy. Truth will have its own weight upon the guilty conscience. Rev. Mr. Coit preached this afternoon to the same congregation; his discourse was well adapted to the occasion, and was heard with much attention. Several gentlemen of the place called upon me this evening, and I had a pleasant interview with them. I am invited to administer holy Baptism to-morrow morning.

Two soldiers called and asked for Prayer-books. I was only able to give them one, which was accompanied with some tracts.

My son is much better—still complains of pain in the head. May God give him grace to be submissive to his Divine will.

*On Lake Michigan, Oct.* 18, *Monday.*—The regular steamer for Green Bay (for which we have been waiting), arrived in the port of Mackinac to-day, at twelve o'clock. His royal highness, Prince de Joinville, and his suite, were among the passengers. On landing, the Prince and his party went immediately to visit the Arch Rock. In the meantime I had an interview, with Captain Shook, of the steamer, who stated that the Prince had made inquiries of him, two or three times since leaving Buffalo, about Mr. Williams, the missionary to the Indians at Green Bay, and that as he knew no other gentleman in that capacity excepting myself, I must be the person, the object of his inquiry. I replied, 'that cannot be, Captain. He must mean another person, as I have no acquaintance with the Prince.'*

I shall now inform the Prince, said the Captain, that there is a gentleman on board, of the same name as that of his inquiry, who is a mission-

* An obvious difficulty here presents itself, which was commented on upon the first publication of the affair, in February, and which the production of the fresh evidence, showing that he went out west expressly to meet the Prince de Joinville renders more startling. In reply to the captain's information that the Prince had inquired after him, he immediately says, "That cannot be, captain. He must mean another person, as I have no acquaintance with the Prince." Now, in explanation of the apparent discrepancy, I would remark—1. That it is true Mr. Williams went to the West to meet the Prince de Joinville, because the letter to Mr. Bowker, and the testimony of that gentleman, taken in conjunction with his journal, prove he did so, and that it is also true, the conversation recorded above occurred, because Captain Shook, as will hereafter be shown, confirms the statement of the journal. Both facts then stand, and there is nothing to prejudice the entire veracity of Mr. Williams's statements. The only question is, what was his meaning in his reply to the captain. I answer, simply to express the idea he afterwards advanced to the Prince, viz. that he imagined De Joinville himself mistook him for some other person. Though he had hastened his return to Green Bay, in consequence of the intimation from Mr. Ogden, he yet was unable to account for the anxiety of the Prince to see him, and, naturally enough, supposed it was founded on misconception, as he had no acquaintance with him. To this expression of doubt was added, as appears from his other account, a jocose remark, which shows how unsuspicious he was of what was coming—"Oh, I am a great man, and great men will seek me out."

ary to the Indians at Green Bay. Upon this, the Captain left me, and in about half an hour, he returned, and was followed by a gentleman, to whom I was introduced as the Prince de Joinville. I was struck at the manner of his salutation. He appeared to be surprised and amazed, as he grasped my hand in both of his, which was accompanied by strong and cheering gratulations of his having had an opportunity to meet me, and that upon the surface of one of the inland seas in the Western world, "Amazing sight!" he continued, "it is what I have wished to see for this long time. I trust I shall not be intruding too much on your feelings and patience, were I to ask some questions in relation to your past and present life among the Indians. We, the Europeans, to satisfy curiosity are sometimes too inquisitive. But I presume, Rev. sir, it will be a pleasure to you to satisfy the curiosity of the stranger now before you, who is travelling over the country and lakes which were first discovered by our forefathers." His eyes were intently fixed upon me—eyeing my person from the crown of my head to the sole of my feet.

The Prince in his cursory remarks upon the first adventures of the French in these western wilds was interesting. He spoke of La Salle, Fathers Hennepin, and Marquette (the latter, the first discoverer of the river Mississippi) in strains of commendation, as men of great courage, and possessing the spirit of enterprise in an unparalleled degree.

He spoke also with regret of the loss of Canada to France. He would attribute this to the want of energy and foresight in the ministry; that France could have easily, at that period, sent twenty thousand men into Canada, to maintain her possessions in that quarter, as her naval force was then nearly equal to that of England.

*October* 19, *Tuesday.*—This morning the Prince resumed his observations upon the French Revolution—its rise, its progress, and its effects upon France, and more particularly to the United States, which were affecting and touching in the extreme. The awful catastrophe that fell upon France, the dissolution of the royal family, and the destruction of the king, he strongly asserted originated from the American revolution, and that the people in the United States can never be too grateful to the unfortunate Louis XVI. for his powerful interposition in their behalf. "It is very evident," said he, "they do not duly appreciate the aid he afforded them in the day of distress. It is very evident also, that, from the very day when the Court of Versailles formed an alliance with America, the operations of the British against them were paralyzed; the naval force of France rendered more essential service to their cause than her land force. The Atlantic sea was soon covered with ships-of-war and privateers; these were a formidable barrier against England in sending her troops and munitions of war to America. In this war France lost thirty-five thousand men and twenty-five ships of the line. But, for these powerful aids, no monuments are raised to perpetuate their memory. Louis XVI. ought to be placed next to General Washington as a liberator of the American people. His interference in their behalf is attributed altogether to his political finesse and his hatred against England; hence he is not entitled to their praise or thanks. But, Rev. sir, were the American people duly to consider the important aid he gave them in their struggle with the mother country, its happy result, and the dreadful catastrophe that fell upon his government, his family, and himself; he would truly and justly be considered as a martyr to American independence. The king encountered an opposition from the Count de Vergennes and the Court, when he took the suffering cause of the Americans in hand. He was moved by the representations of the American commissioners, and the Queen was no less urgent to save the sinking cause of the American people. My grandfather and father were present when the last struggle took place between the King and the ministry upon the article of alliance with the United Colonies of America. That day—it was a happy day for Americans—but for the King, it was the day of his death! Yes, Rev. sir, on that day, when the King put his name to the instrument, he sealed his death-warrant. The ingratitude of the American people towards the King's memory is one of the darkest stains upon the stars and stripes of the American flag and independence."

This afternoon the Prince expressed his wish to take my son with him to France for an education. In connection with this he was informed that we had an infant who had not yet received baptism. He readily consented to stand as a godfather, and would give the name of his mother to the child. But, alas! on my first landing I received the melancholy intelligence that the lovely babe was in her grave—buried on the preceding Sunday, service performed by the Rev. Mr. Porter, of the Congregationalist

Church. When the news was communicated to the Prince, he appeared to sympathise with me, and remarked, taking me by the hand, "Descendant of a suffering race, may you be supported in this affliction."

About ten o'clock, the Prince was pleased to enter into his remarks more particularly, upon the family of the unfortunate king, which were, at first with me, somewhat curious and interesting; but as he proceeded in his narration. my feelings were greatly excited, as it filled my inward soul with poignant grief and sorrow, which were inexpressible. The intelligence was not only new but awful in its nature To learn, for the first time, that I am connected by consanguinity with those whose history I had read with so much interest; and for whose sufferings in prison, and the manner of their deaths, I had moistened my cheeks with sympathetic tears. Is it so? Is it true, that I am among the number, who are thus destined to such degradation—from a mighty power to a helpless prisoner of the state—from a palace to a prison and dungeon—to be exiled from one of the finest empires in Europe, and to be a wanderer in the wilds of America—from the society of the most polite and accomplished courtiers, to be associated with the ignorant and degraded Indians? Degraded as they are, as to civilization and polite arts, yet I am consoled at the idea, that I am among the lords of the soil of this western continent, who are are as precious in the sight of Heaven as the usurpers of their territories! O my God, am I thus destined! "Thy will be done." To be informed that I had rights in Europe, and one of these was to be the first over a mighty kingdom; and this right is demanded of me, to surrender, for an ample and splendid establishment. The intelligence was so unexpected, my mind was paralyzed for a moment; it was overwhelming to my feelings. There was a tremor in my whole system, accompanied with a cold perspiration. The Prince saw my agitation, and left the room, with an excuse, for ten or fifteen minutes.

A splendid parchment was spread before me for signature, to be affixed with the stamp and seal of Louis XVI. After consideration of several hours, weighing the subject with much and cool deliberation, it was respectfully refused. In those awful and momentous moments, it was happy that my mind was carried to the similar proposition and offers made to Louis XVIII., by Napoleon, in 1802. Being impelled from a sense of duty to sustain the honor of kings for centuries, the same answer was given

—"Though I am in poverty, sorrow, and exile, I shall not sacrifice my honor."

Gracious God! What scene am I passing through this night? Is it in reality, or a dream? My refusal to the demand made of me, I am sure can be no earthly good to me, but I save my honor, and it may be for the benefit of the generations yet unborn. It is the will of Heaven. I am in a state of obscurity. So shall I remain while in this pilgrimage state. I will endeavor, with all humility, to serve the King of Heaven, and to advance his holy cause among the ignorant and benighted people, which has been my delight.

Although the unexpected intelligence is a new source of trouble, which is already working in my inward soul with inexpressible sorrow, which will accompany me to my grave; yet I trust, that Almighty arm, which has hitherto " preserved me, will now sustain me. To the God of my salvation I fly for comfort and consolation, in this hour of distress. Let Christ be all, and in all. Saviour of the world, have mercy upon thy unworthy servant," and for the glory of thy name, turn from him all those evils that he most justly has deserved; and grant, that in all his troubles, he may put his whole trust and confidence in thy mercy, and ever more serve thee in holiness and pureness of living, to thy honor and glory. "For with God nothing is impossible." All that I have heard I will lay up in my heart, with the greatest secresy.

*October* 21, *Thursday.*—The Prince and suite left Green Bay yesterday, at twelve o'clock, and lodged last night at Capt. John McCarty's on the opposite side of the river to my residence. It rained all the afternoon.

The adieus between the Prince and myself were affectionate; he promised to write me, on his arrival at New York. The gentlemen officers presented me with their cards; were urgent to give them a call, should I ever visit France. May the best blessing of Heaven rest upon the whole party.

It is impossible to know how other persons are affected by this journal, but, under the proved circumstances of his having kept such a record, with more or less regularity, all his life, and the important entry, concerning his interview with the Prince de Joinville, occurring in the very midst of the yearly chronicle, and fortified, both as to character and authenticity, by all that precedes, and, as we shall see, by all that follows, it appears to me a testimony, which a reasonable person cannot lightly set aside. There is, it is true, much about the whole affair, passing strange, but, as regards the conduct of Mr. Williams, it is characteristically congruous, even in the midst of the eccentricity it exhibits. The conduct, throughout, is of a piece with the man. There is a singular mixture of simplicity, nobility, good feeling, absence of worldly tact and cunning, and a mode of viewing things, natural in one accustomed to the councils of the children of the forest; in which, when unpolluted by the intrusion of Anglo-Saxon chicanery, abstract right and justice are the fundamental considerations. He was, also, evidently bewildered by the strangeness of the event, and had no idea of turning it to his pecuniary advantage, which, in some minds, would have been the principal consideration. Even the manner in which he dismisses the whole party, with a blessing, is in keeping with the habit, which may be observed throughout the journals of Mr. Williams, of bestowing a benediction on every one, friend or foe, and as Mr. John Jay has well remarked, in a letter on the subject, is also in accordance with the forgiving disposition, history attributes to Louis XVII.

To regard this document as a forgery, you must suppose a noble and pious mind guilty of an amount of deception, absolutely unparalleled, and that, too, without any object; for it has evidently been written many years, and would never have been produced to the world but for me. Mr. Williams considered it a thing of no moment, and never dreamt of exhibiting it as evidence, and, in fact, ridiculed the idea, that anything which came from him, would be received by the public, in proof of his assertions. He looked upon his journal merely as repetition of his statement, whereas, under the circumstances, and especially the fortuitous manner in which the whole subject has been brought up, without any agency on his part, it has all the force of distinct, separate testimony. This will be exhibited more strongly as we proceed.

"*October* 23, *Saturday*.—I have commenced to collect materials for letter to be sent to the Prince de Joinville, in compliance with his request. My mind has been agitated since his departure, in consequence of the intelligence he communicated to me, which is startling in its nature. May God support me in these trying times, and keep my mind in a proper frame.

"*Little Kakalin, Oct.* 26.—Went down the bay; dined with Mr. Quindre. His lady (a Roman Catholic) informed me that the priest, Rev. Mr. Bondual, stated to her that the Prince was much pleased and highly gratified with his interview with me, and that the information I had communicated to him of the first visits of the French traders into this section of the country, was of great value to him, &c. I heard from the Prince this afternoon. I find he and his party had lodged at Cato's (a black man), in Stockbridge woods. This has created much laughter among some, as I understand. He was compelled to this as there was no other house near, it being already dark and in the midst of a heavy rain.

* * * * * * * *

"*Oct.* 31, *Sunday Evening.*—This has been a solemn day with me, on several accounts. My reflections have been upon my short-comings to the great duties enjoined upon me by that holy religion which I profess. Why is it I am so much troubled with my spiritual state? As to my foreign birth, it is not only new to me, but it is awful. This has changed my feelings materially. I am an unhappy man; and in my sorrow and mournful state I would often, with a sigh, cry out, O my father! O my mother! It is done—it is past; and, O my God, I would humbly submit to thy holy will in that which thou hast done towards us. Thou hast dealt towards us as thou didst towards Nebuchadnezzar in the days of old. We are afflicted, and in a situation of degradation and poverty. Shall we remain thus till we know that the Most High ruleth in the kingdom of men, and giveth it to whomsoever he wilt? Holy Father, remember not our offences, nor the offences of our forefathers, neither take thou vengeance of our sins. Spare us, Good Lord, whom thou hast redeemed with thy precious blood, and be not angry with us for ever. O grant me grace to consecrate myself entirely to thy service, and whatever painful trials I may be called on to sustain, wilt Thou support me under them and at length deliver me from them for Christ's sake.

* * * * * * * *

"*Nov.* 18—I have just returned from the Bay, and saw Mr. Ellis, who informed me Mr. Whitney has threatened to go against us in a suit. I have engaged Mr. F. to attend to this.

* * * * * * * *

"*Nov.* 30.—From some circumstances which have transpired within two days past connected with the intelligence I have received from the Prince de Joinville, my mind has been, and is now, greatly exercised. Why should I think on this subject, which is so unpleasant, or rather so afflictive? Yet it obtrudes itself, as it were into my mind in spite of my resistance. O, the fate of my dearest friends! My soul is troubled within me, at times, on account of them. I seek comfort and rest, but I find none. The awful intelligence has made me wretched, to which no language, no conception, can be true. Hours have I spent in the solitary wilderness, mourning over my fate and the fate of my family. Why was it permitted that I should know this? But to God, the Judge of all, I leave it.

* * * * * * * *

"*Dec.* 16.—Although I have had it in my head that I would read the history of the French Revolution, I have been afraid to read anything of the kind; but at length I have been induced to read a certain author, but my mind has been too much excited by the work, so that I have returned it to the owner.

* * * * * * * *

"*Dec.* 24.—I am preparing to go down to the Bay to attend the Christmass service at the Episcopal church. Pleasant day. Somewhat indisposed.

*Dec.* 25, *Saturday.*—This has been a good day to me for my religious exercises. O blessed Jesus, I praise thee that thou wert manifested in the flesh to be the Saviour of the world. Save me from my sins I humbly beseech thee."

Those who have objected to the truth of the statement of Mr. Williams, on account of the absence of pecuniary tact, in his dealings with the Prince, by which he failed to secure the tempting worldly advantages presented to him, may, when they read these extracts from his journal, acknowledge that, possibly, there may be moments and straits in existence, when the soul cannot turn its regards to dollars and cents, and when the weight of sorrow descends with a crushing and stupefying power, permitting only the appalling darkness of life's tragedy to be felt and seen. It may be lack of worldly wisdom, but, I own, I cannot sympathize with those who conceive, it would have been more natural for Mr. Williams, instead of acting in the high-spirited and unselfish manner, he describes, to have regarded the information of the Prince, merely in the light of a pecuniary God-send, and endeavored to see how much he could make of it. On the contrary, it was just the intelligence to drive the thought of money from the mind. It was like a thunderbolt, an avalanche, or anything that is most sudden and most terrible.

The necessities of space compel me now to pass on, without further comment, to the journal for 1848, when he received information of the dying disclosures of Bellanger, in New Orleans. The reader must remember that seven years have elapsed since first the tidings of his origin were communicated to him.

"*Green Bay*, *March* 10.—In the letter I have received from Mr. Thos. Kimball, from *Baton Rouge*, Louisiana, my curiosity is somewhat excited, and it may be a novel news.

"He states that the information he received from a respectable gentleman was such a startling news with him, as to induce him to communicate the intelligence to the person who was the subject of it, and with whom he was acquainted. He states by the death (in January last) of an aged and respectable French gentleman, either in New Orleans or Helena, that he made disclosures at the last hours of his life, that he was the person who aided in the escape of the Dauphin, or the son of Louis XVI., King of France, from the temple in 1795; his transportation to North America, and his adoption among the Indians; all this that he may live and be hidden, and live beyond the reach of his enemies, who had been murderers of his royal parents; and that the person alluded to as the Dauphin is no other than the Rev. Eleazar Williams, the Missionary to the Oneida Indians; and that the gentleman who had the principal agency in the escape of the Dauphin, was strictly and solemnly bound by the sacramental oath of the

Roman Catholic Church never to disclose, particularly in Europe, of the descent or family of the royal youth whom he was about to convey to North America; and that it was not until he saw himself drawing near to a close of his earthly career, that he would disclose the secret which had been locked up in his bosom for half a century; and that he would do this the more cheerfully now, without infringing his conscience, because he was in America, and that it may be a benefit to his most dear, beloved, but unfortunate friend, the Dauphin; in uttering the last his whole frame was agitated, and shed abundance of tears; and that near one of his last exclamations was, 'O! the Dauphin! may he be happy and restored!'

"The intelligence is so improbable, it had no weight nor consideration with me; and thinking at the same time there may be mistake as to the person, I shall wait patiently the meaning of all this, for a further information from Mr. Kimball upon this new and mysterious subject.

"*March* 13.—Went to Green Bay, and dined with the Rev. Mr. Porter, and had a long conference with Judge Aindt respecting the Oneidas, with whom he is at war in relation to some lumber which he had purchased.

"*March* 15.—Went to the Sugar Camp with Mr. Wartmen to make some inquiries. This is a beautiful day, and it was delightful to be among the lofty pines.

"*March* 16.—Received some letters from my friends in Oneida, in one of which I am informed that my father is in a feeble state of health.

"*March* 18.—I wrote to-day to the Rev. Joshua Leavitt, of Boston, in which I recapitulated the intelligence I had received from Mr. Kimball, in relation to the Dauphin of France. On mature reflection upon the subject, I must confess the news is becoming more startling with me. It is true that I have no recollection of my existence in the world until at the age of thirteen or fourteen: what passed with me previous I am unable to decipher. Since my recollection is perfect, there are some incidents connected with my life, I must confess, which are strange, and which I am unable to reconcile with each other. The suspicion in the minds of some that I am not the son of Thomas Williams may be mistaken, and the story of Van Derheyden of Albany, in 1814, has created in my mind an idea that I may be an adopted child, as I find the Iroquois have adopted more than sixteen persons of both sexes of the Canadian origin.

"*March* 24.—I have written to Mr. L. of Boston, and sent the letter containing the mysterious news in relation to my origin. Although this melancholy subject was communicated to me in 1841, and now again, it is renewed and brought before me from another quarter, I may truly say, that as often as the subject is brought to the mind the eyes of the afflicted man are filled with tears.

"Yes, in 1841, when the awful intelligence was communicated to me, my blood seemed to chill and my heart to rush into my throat, and I became affected in a manner which I now find it difficult to describe. May I humbly submit to the will of Heaven. O for more grace and Christian resignation!

"*March* 27.—Last evening there were several of the Oneidas lodged at my house, who made great inquiries after the history of the primitive church. They were referred to the day of Pentecost, and I dwelt largely upon it. They were very thankful for the instruction.

"*March* 28.—Went to Grand Kakalin, called upon Mr. Grignor, and dined with him, and soon Governor Doty joined with us.

"This evening I am invited to go to the Oneida settlement, to attend the funeral of one of the warrior chiefs. He was a communicant. *April* 3. Went to Green Bay, and was at the Fort, and had a long conversation with ——. He is an infidel. May the Lord show him the error of his ways.

"I have had many such people to deal with."

In the foregoing journal, Mr. Williams alludes to having written twice to the Rev. Joshua Leavitt, of Boston, in relation to the communication from the South. Learning that Mr. Leavitt is now a resident in New York, I called on him, and inquired what he remembered on the subject. He kindly gave me the required information, and wrote me two letters, from which I extract the following:—

"During my residence in Boston, from 1842 to 1848 inclusive, I was in correspondence with Mr. Eleazar Williams, and was visited by him several times, partly for relationship and partly on a matter of business, in which he wished my assistance. In the spring of the year 1848, I received from Mr. Williams one or two letters, in one of which was contained a statement concerning the decease of an old Frenchman, who declared that the

Dauphin of France was still living and in this country. This statement I procured to be printed in a small daily paper in Boston called the 'Chronotype,' where it appeared on the 12th April, 1848. In the autumn of the same year, Mr. Williams called on me, and greatly astonished me by saying that he himself was the supposed Dauphin. He seemed much disturbed and distressed about the matter, and even terrified at the possible consequences of the disclosure, and I thought wished not to have any further publication on the subject if it could be avoided. *He also expressed the regret he should feel in losing his cherished relationship to the Williams family, and declared that he should always feel towards them an unabated affection.*"

In the other letter, Mr. Leavitt, speaking of the disclosures made to him in the autumn of 1848, says that Mr. Williams "remarked, with sadness, on the disquiet the affair had caused him, interfering with his chosen work of the ministry, and even filling him with alarm for his personal safety." In his distress of mind, it was natural for him to apply to Mr. Leavitt, as this gentleman is connected by marriage with the Williams family, and had shown him much kindness in his troubles. A slip from the Chronotype, of April 12, 1848, is before me, containing the statement referred to, which is nearly literal in its agreement with the journal of Mr. Williams, except that the portion relating to himself is omitted, and the Island of Cuba is referred to in connection with Bellanger, which may probably have arisen from confounding the word Helena with Havana. This journal throws a curious light on the workings of Mr. Williams's mind. Deeply affected at first by the revelation of the Prince, he seems, in course of time, to have learned to treat the subject with indifference. It appeared to him entirely improbable. But the same tale comes from another quarter; and the first impression having faded away, it is looked upon as a novelty, and has no weight with him. Slowly his mind gathers itself up; awakens its recollections; renews its impressions; combines things widely separated, whose connection it did not at first perceive; and then anxiety begins, and he has recourse to a friend for advice;

timidly unfolds to him his griefs and his apprehensions, and wishes to hush the affair up lest it should injure him.

Having obtained from the Rev. Mr. Williams, and other available sources, most of the information and documents contained in this and the preceding chapter, I embodied the whole in an article which was published in "Putnam's Magazine," for February, 1853, the design of which was simply to awaken inquiry and investigation, and discover, if possible, what there was to substantiate the conclusion, to which the representations made to me seemed to lead, but which were, as yet, in too crude and unconnected a form to base upon them any other than a hypothetical inference. Fully conscious of all the difficulties with which the subject was environed, I carefully abstained from expressing any positive opinion, except my conviction, that Mr. Williams was mentally and morally incapable of inventing the story he had told me. Having recapitulated the main points of asserted testimony, which I left for the future to prove or disprove, I went on to say:—

Now there can be no question, that if all these points could be proved, the irresistible conclusion would be, that Louis XVII. and the Rev. Eleazar Williams are identical. Even in the imperfect degree in which I know and have stated them, they would carry conviction with them; much more, if brought out in detail, with all attendant circumstances.

Questions of identity are among the most difficult and interesting with which law is conversant. The settlement of them requires varied and peculiar evidence. The negative and the affirmative have both to be clearly shown. Two apparently different things must be demonstrated to be one. Resemblances must be proved to be not accidental, but inherent to the degree of sameness.

Where the utmost stretch of human ingenuity has been used for concealment; where more than half a century has passed since the supposed divergence of a life from its natural line; where evidence, scanty at the best, has been destroyed, both purposely and negligently, absolute demonstration, perhaps, cannot be attained; but we may reach, even under such circumstances, a degree of moral certainty, second only to demonstration, and amply sufficient to enable a sound mind to render a decisive verdict, satisfactory to the intellect and the conscience.

Now prove to me the truth of all that I have alleged as asserted and probable, and no course would be left but to pronounce such a judgment in favor of identity; for the evidence before us goes to show, I apprehend, exactly what it is requisite to have shown.

1st. That Louis XVII. did not die in 1795.

2d. That he was carried to the region in which Mr. Williams spent his youth.

3d. That Mr. Williams is not an Indian; and,

4th. That Mr. Williams is Louis XVII.

These are the four propositions which the case presents for proof —a negative and an affirmative one, with reference to each character, under which one and the same individual has at different times and places appeared.

The testimony is multiform, direct, indirect, documentary, circumstantial; but notwithstanding its exceedingly varied nature, it is wonderfully consistent. It would require extreme ability to fabricate it out of nothing—the utmost mendacity and hardihood, to build it up on a baseless foundation.

The history involves many most curious inquiries into human motive among persons in the most widely different positions in life. It would be impossible, without writing a volume, to do justice to these. I will just indicate one or two.

Mr. Williams asserts that the Prince de Joinville told him in the manner I have described, that he is the son of Louis XVI. Now here is the direct testimony of a responsible person to a simple fact. The assertion is either true or false. If false, it involves the degradation of Mr. Williams from the ministry. If true, it settles the whole question of identity, unless we can imagine it possible that the Prince de Joinville took the trouble of travelling from

Paris to Green Bay to speak at random, or to tell a falsehood on a subject of paramount importance to himself and to France. It is not supposable that such a person would say and do what he is asserted by Mr. Williams to have said and done, without having previously attained to the last degree of conviction pertaining to the possibility of human convictions, and, moreover, without being vested with authority from Louis Philippe himself to make the disclosure; and thus his words issued from the innermost arcana of France, proving that not a day elapsed from June, 1795, in which some watchful eye did not keep knowledge of the exiled Prince. On the other hand, what possible inducement can there be for Mr. Williams to say what is untrue on this subject? The clergy of the Protestant Episcopal Church value their commission too highly to throw it away by telling unmeaning falsehoods tending to nothing but disgrace and ruin. Mr. Williams is, I know, a sane, sober-minded, practical man, who has had all his life to deal with the sternest realities, and I believe he speaks words of truth and soberness. He has not the capacity to invent such a dramatic scene as that between him and the Prince, and if he has, he might long ago have turned it to account. What conceivable motive can such a man have to fabricate an airy and vain fiction, that he, the poor Indian missionary, is the descendant of long lines of European kings, and that a prince royal of France, now living, and who can be brought face to face with him, told him so. Again, if Mr. Williams's statement be correct, the motives of Louis Philippe in making the disclosure are a problem. I am inclined to believe that pity and commiseration entered largely into them. At the same time Bellanger was living, and De Ferrière, and Le Ray. The secret was known in Canada, and the citizen-king may, as Mr. Williams writes me, have "seen an object in that quarter, who might sooner or later be an obstacle to his ambitious views, and defeat the permanency of his throne, and the securing of the same to his family." As to the improbability that a poor man like Williams would reject, on a point of honor, offers so splendid and liberal, I own, it is great; but his own explanation of his feelings is before the reader, and nothing but the regally proud and romantic heroism it displays, so rare in this age, renders it incredible.

Not only the physical but the mental characteristics of Mr. Williams, curiously correspond with what the Dauphin would probably be if alive, and in such a position after such a complicated career. He possesses a great amount of native talent; an easy grace and dignity of manner when in polite society, which seems innate; a winning sweetness of disposition, and much simplicity; apparently warm religious feelings; but his judgment in matters of self-interest is not of the strongest; fluent and eloquent in diction, his ideas are not always well-assorted—a mystery to himself as well as to others, subject to perpetual questionings, he is sometimes abrupt—accustomed to Indian life, there is semi-barbarism mingled with courtly grace, and roving habits with warm affections—in a word, he seems like one jumbled out of place by destiny, a partial wreck, shattered, but not broken. And the peculiarity of his character must be taken into account, in forming an estimate of his conduct, the singularity of which will create in many minds a prejudice against his veracity, since they will be unable to understand how a poor man could reject offers so splendid, or a man of the world neglect the opportunity of establishing his regal birth, which the communication of De Joinville afforded. In his situation they would have acted differently. True, but he and they are very different persons. It is but justice to say that, whatever may prove the ultimate truth of his claims, the origination of them does not rest with him; unsought evidence has found him out, and new proofs are rising from unexpected quarters. He has never tried to make capital of his story. The present publication does not proceed in any way from his suggestion, though he has given his consent to it.

Nearly equal in importance with any point in the evidence, is the early idiocy of Mr. Williams corresponding with the condition in which the Dauphin is known to have been. It goes far to substantiate the truth of the story, for since Williams could not have been born an idiot, there must have been some fearful acts lying at the basis of his history to reduce him to such a condition. In all recorded cases in which the memory has been destroyed by sudden injury to the brain, the whole chain of lost knowledge has been brought back as by an electric shock. But, in this case, the destruction of memory was not sudden, but owing to the benumbing process of a long series of sufferings, mental and bodily, which took away the power of perception, and weakened that of retention. The soul fell into a merciful sleep, and when it again awakened, there was nothing to recall except a few vague ideas and one terrible image of the past, which was burnt into his soul. A draught of Lethe gave to one man two lives. Born the second time without birth, he who died a prince was regenerated a beggar, and the heir of kings surviving his own death, and the overthrow of his race, is metamorphosed into a red man, and having been baptized by a Romish bishop amid the pageantries of a European court, lives to preach the Gospel in America fifty-seven years after his exile. Republics, constitutions, kingdoms, and an empire, have, during that space, been overthrown. They who moved and ruled them have passed away, and the present occupant of Versailles and the Tuileries may follow them, while the veteran missionary is still in possession of his wigwam on the St. Lawrence.

Complicated and mysterious as this matter is, it has a fearful simplicity when brought to a direct issue between Mr. Williams and the Prince de Joinville. The latter has the reputation of being a high-minded and honorable gentleman, and I trust will act openly and candidly on a question of so much importance.

LOUIS XVII.

*From the picture in the Bryan Gallery, New York.*

G. P. PUTNAM & Co. N. Y.

## CHAPTER XVIII.

### TOKENS OF PERSONAL IDENTITY.

It seems necessary, briefly, to consider, in a separate chapter, the tokens of personal identity between Louis XVII. and the Rev. Eleazar Williams; and I will do this without interrupting the thread of my narrative. This is a portion of our subject of the highest importance—because, were there a failure here, all other arguments and evidence would be of no avail. If there were certain known, unchangeable peculiarities, in the person of the youthful king, all or *any* of which were absent from the person of Mr. Williams, it would be impossible to make out a case of identity: but, if it can be clearly shown, that *every* ascertainable peculiarity in the person of Louis XVII., both natural and accidental, exists in the person of Mr. Williams, I have established the *sine qua non*, and laid a firm foundation on which every other portion of the evidence can rest.

The publication of my article, in Putnam's Magazine, drew forth the almost universal criticism of the press, which was favorable, beyond the deserts, in a literary point of view, of a piece hastily written, and whose main object was to excite discussion and elicit truth. By many writers, it was regarded as a final argument, in a controversy it merely opened; and thus, by some, the strength of the evidence, as it then stood, was much overrated; and, by others, great injustice was done to me and to the historic question; and what was strictly tentative, was regarded as an exhibition of credulity.

The Rev. Mr. Williams was then staying in New York, to prepare, and simultaneously print, his translation of the prayer-book into Mohawk, and soon became the object of general curiosity and remark. Many gentlemen, and especially Frenchmen, and others familiar with the lineaments and peculiarities of the Bourbon family, called on him, to test, by personal examination, the truth of the asserted resemblance. It was a severe ordeal, and one I was curious to see how he would pass. A person playing a part must almost inevitably have failed, and exhibited some sign, by over or under-acting, of insincerity. But, Mr. Williams had no part to play, and his simplicity of character, quiet, dignified, good nature, and the freedom from all apprehension, attending an honest heart, with nothing to conceal and nothing to pretend to, carried him safely through.

I do not remember a single instance of a person leaving his presence with an unfavorable impression—not one who did not seem to feel—and, in many cases, this feeling was warmly expressed—that, whatever might be the ultimate issue of the investigation, the idea of deception, on his part, was out of the question.*

* A published account of one of these interviews is so graphic and honorable to all parties, that I perpetuate it in a note. It is from the pen of M. Arpin, then editor of the *Courrier des Etats Unis*. "In a modest chamber of an unpretending hotel, we found a man, possessed of a very simple exterior, his face quite good-looking and prepossessing. He received us with cordial courtesy. Mr. Williams is the type of the missionary whom religion sends out among the uncivilized. He has nothing of that dry austerity we too frequently find among those who have the cure of souls in large cities. His affable manner, impressing us at once with his good nature, and his eye so readily assuming a look of gentle cheerfulness, are in harmony with the work he is called to fulfil. It is obvious that persuasion rather than authority is his means of drawing the Indian listeners within the Christian church. He is an apostle of the primitive style. If we were less profoundly struck than his partizans with his resemblance to the Bourbons—if we do not discover in him *the most characteristic trait of the race*, the Bourbon nose, we must, nevertheless, confess, that the brow and lower portion of the face, offer striking analogies with certain physiognomies of the family. Thus Mr. Williams instantly reminded us of Louis XVIII., whose features are strongly impressed on our memory. The sight of the respectable missionary, certainly, does not carry entire conviction, but it is very far from forbidding it. It only remains to add, that Mr. Williams has an air of perfectly good faith, and that, while our conversation with him, and deliberate scrutiny of his person have not wholly converted us, we are compelled to pursue the inquiry of which he is the object further—for, underneath this outside, upon which candor and bonhommie are so strongly imprinted, we cannot realize that either a dupe or an impostor is concealed.

To show the impression made on M. Arpin's mind at the time, I may add to his narrative, that as he was bidding adieu, he said to Mr. Williams, in a tone of respectful

The result of the personal scrutiny, to which he was subjected, was no less favorable. The marked resemblance of person and physiognomy to the Bourbon family was universally admitted. He might differ from this or that individual of the race, in particular features, but the impress of blood and descent was on the man.

But, there is one point of family resemblance so strongly marked that, it cannot fail to strike every attentive observer, who is acquainted with the Bourbon lineaments. I allude to the formation of the lower jaw and ear. You may go back for centuries in the royal family, and in all their portraits, where the arrangement of the dress and hair permits, you will find the same marked conformation, which that of Mr. Williams exhibits. The ear, large and full at top, lessens almost to a point at the lower extremity, and, without any indentation at the bottom, joins the rounded sweep of the jaw. The same peculiar curve might be interchangeably used in the portraits of Louis XVI., Louis XVIII., Charles X., the Duchess D'Angoulême, the Duc de Bordeaux, and the Rev. Eleazar Williams; and a skilful artist might amuse himself by successively producing the six heads on the same base line. But, the likeness is not merely that of feature, but also of bodily form. There is before me a full length portrait of Louis XVIII., in the dress so well described by Lamartine. Making allowance for its immense obesity and fantastical attire, it is the image of my friend, from top to toe; the same lines in the face are there—the same shaped head, growing, as it were, without neck, out of the broad shoulders—the same length and squareness of body to the hips—the same short legs—and the hand and fingers in the same attitude most familiar in conversation with Mr. Williams.

The closer the investigation was pushed, the clearer it was seen that, peculiarities which, at first, excited doubt, tended more strongly to identification.

but manly candor, "Were you seated on the throne of France, sir, I should deem it my duty to oppose you, as a Republican; but, in your present position, and for the truth of history, I will gladly do anything I can to aid in the investigation."

Thus the Bourbon nose, as it is called, which all the pretenders possessed to a marvel, was found wanting in all the portraits of the young Prince, whose nose corresponded, as much as that of a child could with a grown person's, with the nose of Mr. Williams. Whoever will take the trouble of examining, will perceive, the Dauphin could, at no period of life, have had a strongly-marked acquiline nose; and, however, such a feature is connected in most minds with the Bourbons, the possession of it by Mr. Williams would have been fatal to his identity with the Prince. In all but profile, however, there is no discernible difference between his nose and that of Louis XVIII.; the general size, shape, and position of both being the same, and the central protuberance being alike, but more faintly indicated in one than in the other.

So also with the color of the eyes. Those who took their impressions from popular histories, found difficulty in the hazel hue of Mr. Williams's eyes, which they expected, as those of a Bourbon would be blue. A member of the New York press told me that, meeting Williams at the house of a friend, his impressions, otherwise favorable, were against him on this account; but added, he soon found he was, himself, in error, and called my attention to the portrait of the Dauphin, in the Bryan Gallery, in which the eyes are identical with those of Mr. Williams. I went to the Gallery, when Mr. Bryan said, he could pledge himself for the authenticity of the portrait, having purchased it at the sale of the collection of M. Prousteau de Mont Louis, in Paris, in 1851. This gentleman was a royalist, and enjoyed a high reputation as a connoiseur and collector; and his name is a sufficient guarantee that whatever came from his collection is genuine. In this portrait, not only the eyes, but the lower part of the face, jaw, and lips, might even now serve as a representation of Mr. Williams. It was evidently taken during his imprisonment in the Temple, as it bears tokens, in the emaciation of the form, and the pinched and painful expression of the features, of disease and suffering. The accompanying outline drawing gives a faithful representation of it, which the reader can compare with the portraits of Mr. Williams in 1806 and 1853.

While speaking of pictures I will introduce the testimony of the Chevalier Fagnani and M. B. H. Muller, both eminent portrait painters in this city.

M. Fagnani has had every means of forming a correct judgment on the subject, having lived, since childhood, in intimate acquaintance with the families of the Sicilian and Spanish Bourbons, of whom he has painted no less than ten portraits. The eyes of a skilful artist are not likely to be deceived by faint resemblances, nor to overlook indications of identity of blood, which escape an ordinary observer. He met Mr. Williams, for the first time, in a crowded room, and I was curious to observe his conduct on the occasion. Standing at some little distance at the outside of a group, he eyed him from head to foot with the calm, critical gaze with which he would have scrutinized a statue or a picture; dwelt on the contour of his face, the play of his features, and the manner of his address and conversation; and then, as if satisfied, turned quietly aside. A friend, who was much interested in ascertaining his opinion, inquired, "Well, Fagnani, what do you think as to his being a Bourbon?" "I don't think at all," was the reply, "*I know.*"

The following letter, which is of historic interest, was written after M. Fagnani had repeated interviews with Mr. Williams, and painted the portrait from which the engraving in the frontispiece is taken:

"NEW YORK, *February* 14, 1853.

"REV. JOHN H. HANSON:

"MY DEAR SIR.—In complying with your request to inform you of my impressions with regard to the identity of the Rev. Mr. Williams and Louis XVII., the Dauphin of France, and what acquaintance I have of the peculiar lineaments of the Bourbon race, I must premise by informing you that of the immediate family of Louis XVI. I know nothing, beyond having seen the original portraits of them at Versailles; but with the features of the Sicilian and Spanish Bourbons, who are closely allied by intermarriage as well as blood, with those of France, and strongly resemble them, I have been familiar from childhood. To enumerate those whose portraits I have painted, besides having seen and known many others, I may mention the Dowager Queen of Naples, mother of the present King Ferdinand II.; the Prince of Capua, and Count of Trapuna, brothers of the King, and grandsons of Caroline, sister of Marie Antoinette; Queen Christina of Spain, widow of Ferdinand VII.; Isabella II., the reigning Queen of Spain; and her sister, the Duchess of Montpensier; and two daughters of the Infant Don Francis de Paul, Uncle to Queen Isabella. Of the House of Hapsburg I have painted the portraits of the Arch-Duke Charles, brother of the Emperor Francis II.; and the Arch-Duchess Augusta, daughter of Leopold, the present Grand Duke of Tuscany. From the particular examination an artist must necessarily make of his sitters, many points strike him which would escape a more superficial observer. In painting the portrait of Mr. Williams, I noticed many of the peculiar characteristics which are developed in a greater or less degree in most of the princes of the House of Bourbon whose portraits I have taken. When I first saw Mr. Williams, I was more particularly impressed with his resemblance to the portraits of Louis XVI. and XVIII.; and the general Bourbonic outline of his face and head. As I conversed with him, I noticed several physiognomical details, which rendered the resemblance to the family more striking. The upper part of the face is decidedly of a Bourbon cast, while the mouth and lower part resemble the House of Hapsburg. I also observed, to my surprise, that many of his gestures were similar to those peculiar to the Bourbon race.

"Had I met Mr. Williams, unconscious that he was in any way other than his name would indicate, I should immediately have spoken of his likeness to the Bourbon family; and although a resemblance of the kind might possibly be an accidental freak of nature, still, taken in connection with the facts you have brought before the public, and the quantity of corroborative testimony adduced, it leaves no doubt in my mind of the very great probability that Mr. Williams and the Dauphin are the same person. Hoping that this interesting historical problem may be speedily and satisfactorily solved, I remain, my dear sir, very truly yours,

"GUISEPPE FAGNANI."

M. B. H. Muller, residing in Howard street, New York, was a pupil of the celebrated revolutionist David, and also of Gros. He was employed to take, after death, the picture of Louis XVIII., of whom he still preserves an admirable crayon sketch. The features, in their deep repose, are the very image of Mr. Williams, when asleep. I called on M. Muller, in company with Mr. Williams and Mr. A. Fleming. It was in the evening, and the room, at first, but dimly lighted; yet his recognition of the likeness to the Bourbon family was immediate, and his expression of it intense. As soon as he saw him, and almost without explanation of the cause of our visit, he declared the resemblance would have struck him anywhere, and, with characteristic nervous rapidity of action, proceeded to indicate the many points of marked and minute similarity. "The eyes, the eyes, too!" he exclaimed. "He has the eyes of the Dauphin." I asked him how he knew. He replied, from seeing portraits of him in France. By a strange coincidence Muller was well acquainted with the present Emperor while in New York, who, he said, had frequently sat on the old hair sofa on which Mr. Williams was then seated. I have elsewhere spoken of the testimony of M. Muller respecting the body exhibited as that of Louis XVII. in the Temple.

On another occasion, a French officer, who had been in the body guard of Louis XVIII., calling on Mr. Williams, said, the longer he looked at him, the more he recalled the image of the king, not only in feature, but in familiar indefinable gestures.

A gentleman of high rank, on the continent, who happened to see him in the pulpit, immediately touched a friend who was sitting beside him, and said, "There, that is the Bourbon they have found, if there be any truth in physiognomy," and expressed his full conviction, afterwards, from what he had heard in Legitimate circles, in Europe, that Louis XVII. was alive, and his belief, from the published statements, that Mr. Williams must be the man.

It was often a matter of amusement to me to watch the effect of introduction, on some ardent, impressible Frenchman, who, previous to seeing him, had ridiculed the affair with a "Bah, bah," but who, after looking on him, for a minute, and interchanging a few hurried words, would begin to speculate on the probable political consequences of the affair, and could hardly be made to understand that Mr. Williams was a clergyman, and made no political pretensions.

It has not unfrequently happened, that persons meeting him casually in the streets, for the first time, have, without any other clue, but the resemblance, at once addressed him by name.*

The Count de Balbi, an illegitimate son of Louis XVIII., who was in this country, is said to have been remarkably like Mr. Williams, and many persons have recognised the one, from having seeing the other. I have accumulated evidence on this point, because, I wish to place it historically above the reach of contradiction, and to show the remarkable character of the resemblance, bearing the test of rigid artistic scrutiny, as well as obvious to every one who has an eye for proportions and form. All this gives it an importance not due to the generality of resemblances, which are partly the work of forgetfulness, and part of fancy, and disappear when subjected to rigid comparison. Were France, and not the western wilderness the scene, the wonder would be less. It may be easy to find persons with Bourbon physiognomy in Paris, and as easy to account for it; but, by itself, it is a startling phenomenon to find, among the Mohawks, a man exhibiting the physiognomical traits of the House of Bourbon, and, notwithstanding such a life as that of Eleazar Williams, retaining, also, their familiar gestures, and not only so, but presenting precisely those modifications of the

* Several instances of this have fallen under my own observation. The following is deserving of preservation:—"As to the personal likeness of Mr. Williams to the Bourbon family, we are glad to put on record this fact, that the writer of these lines having heard that likeness spoken of, recognised Mr. Williams long after, when he saw him for the first time, simply from the Bourbon cast of his complexion and features, and, without introduction, saluted him by name. We venture the assertion, that Mr. Williams would not appear in any room filled with persons acquainted with the portraits of the Bourbon family, without that resemblance being at once generally recognised.—*Boston Daily Advertiser*, February 17, 1853.

Bourbon features, which characterized the unfortunate Louis XVII. But there was a still closer scrutiny through which it was necessary Mr. Williams should pass. If, of Indian descent, it was not probable that, however his European aspect might deceive the unscientific observer, the eyes of professional men would discover no trace of Indian blood, when his person was subjected to rigid, medical examination.

There are certain characteristics of the Indian race which are all but indellible, and appear, after the lapse of centuries, even on the cheek of beauty. When the fact of origin has died into a tradition, you can mark the red blood coursing with a duskier hue beneath the mantling blush brought from other climes, and imparting fixity and palor to its softness. Skin, hair, craniological formation in the closer degrees of affinity, present ready and infallible tests.

It was also requisite that the various marks on the body of Mr. Williams should be examined and certified. Observing scars on his knees, Mr. Williams had supposed them to be scrofulous, and I so stated them to be, on his authority.

On referring to the work of M. De Beauchesne, I found it necessary, for the identity, that there should be the scars of tumors, also, on the wrists and elbows; and, on examination, found them on the arms of Mr. Williams, in the spots indicated, though he had not observed them. I then obtained a formal examination of his person, by Drs. Francis, Kissam, and Gerondelo, who, after consultation, and without knowing Desault's opinion that Louis XVII. was not affected with scrofula, came to the conclusion of the non-scrofulous character of the scars on the person of Mr. Williams, which fact, while otherwise favorably impressed, they considered fatal, though, as it turned out, it is exactly confirmatory of the identity. I give their certificates below:

"New York, *February* 12, 1853.

'Rev. Mr. Hanson:

"Dear Sir.—We respectfully inclose to you the following statement, as the result of an examination made at your request. The physical development of Mr. Eleazar Williams, is that of a robust European, accustomed to exercise, exposure to the open air, and indicative of the benefit of generous diet, and a healthy state of the digestive organs. He might readily be pronounced of French blood. His general appearance and bearing are of a superior order: his countenance in repose is calm and benignant: his eyes hazel, expressive and brilliant, and his whole contour, when animated, indicates a sensitive and impressible organization. His cerebral development is nowise noticeable, and his mental manifestations are in harmony therewith. If any peculiarity is predominant, it is his apparent indifference to the pretensions or claims of his advocates. There are no traces of the aboriginal or Indian in him. Ethnology gives no countenance to such a conclusion. This fact is verified by anatomical examination, and no unsoundness of mind or monomania has been manifested, by any circumstance evinced in communion with him. His age might be estimated as approaching seventy years. After a careful examination of the several cicatrices which are to be seen in various parts of the surface of his body, more especially those discernible about the articulations of the knees, we are fully convinced that the joints themselves are in a perfectly normal condition, and that they have never been affected by scrofula or any deep-seated inflammation. The scars, which are more numerous on the right than the left leg, are colorless and superficial, indicating an ulcerative process of the integuments at an early period of life; these marks show no strumous diathesis, but might equally be the result of early bodily severities inflicted by, or consequent upon, a protracted confinement in impure or deteriorated air, restricted or bad diet, and other deprivations, or by the habits of a wandering and imbecile youth amidst the wilds of nature. The remnants of diseased action found on the arms, above the elbows, and about the wrists, though less conspicuous, are of a like character. The face, in the vicinity of the brows both of the right and left eye, exhibits proofs of wounds. These manifestations of injury cannot so easily be traced to a definite period of life, inasmuch as they are in some measure masked by the eyebrows themselves; but they partake of the character of incised or lacerated wounds. The cicatrix on the superior part of the right side of the forehead, being somewhat more than an inch in extent, would appear to have originated from a simple incised wound.

With all consideration, your most obedient friends,

"John W. Francis, M.D.

"Richard S. Kissam, M.D."

'New York, *February* 12, 1853.

"Rev J. H. Hanson :

"Rev. and Dear Sir.—You have requested me, as the medical adviser of the Rev. Eleazar Williams, to render an account of his personal characteristics, and the marks of former disease visible on his body. He has a lofty aspect, strongly marked outline of figure, obviously European complexion, and a slight tinge of scrofulous diathesis. His age seems to border on seventy—his share of native intellect is above mediocrity, and his mind, sound in its integrity and pertinent in judgment, is as unaspiring as his heart is cordial and affectionate. The limit of his ambition appears to be faithfully to fulfil his mission as a minister of Christ. The scars I have examined are located on both keees, particularly on the right—both elbows corresponding in character with those on the lower articulations—and both arms, near the wrists, more obscure than the former. They must all have occurred in childhood—and, particularly those about the knees and elbows, are such as would be left by ulcers, produced by a morbid condition of the system, brought on by unwholesome diet, exposure to damp foul air, and great depression of mind. They are in no sense scrofulous, but might have been accelerated, perhaps slightly *aggravated*, by a superficial taint of that particular diathesis. With a sincere hope you may succeed in settling the question which the most palpable facts have propounded,

"I remain, very respectfully, yours truly,

"B. Gerondelo, M.D."

After the publication of these letters in the April number of Putnam's Magazine, my attention was called, by Mr. A. Fleming, to the letter of Madame de Rambaud to the Duchesse D'Angoulême, in which she states that the Dauphin had on his arm inoculation marks, of which one was in the shape of a crescent. Upon this, we we went together to Mr. Williams, and requested permission to examine his arm, when we found precisely the scars indicated. To place the fact historically beyond reach of doubt, I requested Dr. J. W. Francis to re-examine him. He did so, and made the following addition to the certificate:

"It deserves to be stated that there are two distinct marks of inoculation on the upper part of the left arm, one of which is of a semi-circular or crescent shape on the outer margin.

"JOHN W. FRANCIS, M.D."

It is but very recently that inoculation or vaccination has been introduced among the Indians; it was unknown by them in the childhood of Mr. Williams; the scars have every appearance of age; and he has not been inoculated within his memory. That he should have the marks of inoculation is, therefore, remarkable—that they should coincide in shape with those on the arm of Louis XVII., is still more so. In addition, I would call attention to the further coincidence of the scar on the eyebrow corresponding with a blow given the Prince, by Simon, by which he nearly cut his eye out.*

To the foregoing medical certificates, I now add the following:

"REV. J. H. HANSON:

"DEAR SIR.—You have requested me, as a physician, living in the immediate vicinity of the St. Regis Indians, and in habits of close professional intercourse with them, to state my opinion as to the race of the Rev. Eleazar Williams. I beg, therefore, to state, briefly, that, in my opinion, he has no ethnological connection with the St. Regis Indians, nor with any other Indians I have ever known, and that my opinion is based on professional examination of the persons of the Rev. Eleazar Williams, and of several Indians, as well as a minute knowledge of the particular characteristics of the Indian race. If Mr. Williams be an Indian, it is in the absence of all those ethnological signs discernible in form, feature, texture of the skin, hair, and other similar tokens well-known to the profession, which, as far as my observation and information extend, are considered decisive.

"Very respectfully, your obedient servant,

"H. N. WALKER, M.D.

"*Hogansburg*, *New York*, *August* 25, 1853."

It is, then, I conceive, satisfactorily established, that, while the Rev. Eleazar Williams is, infallibly, not of Indian origin, every personal token, natural and accidental, necessary to establish identity

Hué.

between him and Louis XVII., exists; that he has not only the strongest indications of being a member of the Bourbon family, but also the known individual peculiarities of the Dauphin, and scars upon his body in character, location, and shape, such as would be on the body of the unfortunate Prince, if alive. But, for the sake of clearness, let me present the subject in a tabular form :—

| | |
|---|---|
| Louis XVII. resembled the rest of the Bourbon family in form and feature, with the exception of the absence, in him, of an aquiline nose. He had hazel eyes, tumors on both wrists, both elbows, and both knees, a scar on the eyebrow, and inoculation marks on the arm, one of which was of a crescent shape. | The Rev. E. Williams resembles the Bourbon family in form and feature, with the exception of the absence, in him, of an aquiline nose. He has hazel eyes, the scars of tumors or sores in early life on both wrists, both elbows, and both knees, a scar on the eyebrow, and inoculation marks on the arm, one of which is of a crescent shape. |

Remarkable as these coincidences are, I beg to inform that class of candid critics, who, when at loss for argument, can ridicule, without that which gives to ridicule all its force—adherence to truth—and, in the absence of which, it is like the cackle of the bird that saved the capitol, without its accidental utility, that I only attach to them, in my argument, the force of a *sine qua non.* I do not say Mr. Williams, on account of these things, is Louis XVII., but, simply, that he may be. May, however, is a word of very graduated significance, and I wish some arithmetician would calculate the probabilities of finding in the person of an Iroquois chief, everything physically necessary to identification with an European monarch, natural and accidental. And, if to this calculation he would add another, and decipher the further probabilities that, in the Indian chief, presenting all the above physical coincidences with the king, there should centre all the other tokens of identity, derived from circumstantial evidence which this volume contains, I should be glad to learn the number of figures composing his arithmetic.

## CHAPTER XIX.

### THE PRINCE DE JOINVILLE AND M. A. DE BEAUCHESNE.

IMMEDIATELY on the publication of the February number of "Putnam's Magazine," copies of it were sent to the Prince de Joinville, by various persons; and I awaited with some curiosity, but no apprehension, the response that gentleman would give to the appeal made to him. Desiring to ascertain the truth, I had so worded my article as to insure a reply of some sort, which I thought would materially aid the investigation. Sincerity has its own expression, which it is as difficult to feign, as it is easy to discern.

I felt convinced if the Prince had been wrongly accused, the fact would appear on the surface of his reply; and if rightly, he must either make a candid acknowledgment, and spare me the trouble of further investigation, or involve himself in some palpable contradiction, leading, by a more circuitous route, to an equally satisfactory result. It is true, I ran one risk. It was the policy of the Prince, if he desired to conceal the truth, to make a line of himself, and present the smallest amount of surface to the shot of an opponent. Prudence might thus ape the semblance of dignity, and hypocrisy adopt the language of sincerity. It was possible, therefore, he might reply:—"The Prince de Joinville denies having made the disclosures asserted by M. Williams."

This was all the public required, and had he said, merely, this, it would have been almost impossible to bring the charge home to him, however true—ridicule would have been cast, by his cool indifference on the affair—the investigation would, probably, have stopped, and if further evidence relative to the interview, came to light, room would have been open for explanation adapted to the requirements of circumstance. But I was playing a game of chess, in which, acting alike with candor, and boldness, I had to calculate the probabilities of oversight on the other side. The Bourbon family had never exhibited much practical acuteness, to say nothing of wisdom ; and indeed, I am afraid, certain critics, when at a loss for other arguments, will say, Mr. Williams has too much sense to come of the stock. I did not, therefore, anticipate the wisest management. Human nature is the same in prince and plebeian, and every one who has not the perverse genius of a Talleyrand, which I knew De Joinville had not—if conscience tells him he is in a dangerous position—will become nervous and throw in unnecessary explanations, defences, and palliatives, which will make against him if the case be of sufficient importance to demand critical scrutiny. I looked, in case an insincere course was adopted, for a reply extra-prudentially long, and I was not mistaken.

The acknowledgment of the interview, by the Prince, was all important, because even this fact was considered apocryphal by many. This was natural in England, where distance gives a shadowy character to events in America, and I was not astonished to read in the "London Morning Chronicle," the following passage:—"We are aware that the success of certain fantastic literary impostures by the gifted Edgar Poe, may have tempted other writers to try their hands at hoaxing the public, and that this article may be a specimen of vraisemblable inventions. But, at any rate, this would leave it the merit of much ingenuity and readableness, while it would be open to condemnation for the impertinent use of the names of living persons, amongst others of the Prince de Joinville."

In this country, where characters were capable of being easily ascertained, the case was different. But ridicule was thrown on the affair, *while in process of investigation*, and when brought forward by respectable and responsible names, simply as a historic problem, in a manner not creditable to the press of a free country. There were many and noble exceptions. But let this pass.

One article alone I am compelled to notice. A writer in the

Romish papers, the "Phare de New York," and the "Freeman's Journal," above the initials, "H. D. C.," which were understood to be those of Mr. H. De Courcey, represented me as being instigated in the publication, which he entitled, "Un Roman d'imagination," while he politely called me the Romancer of Putnam—by hostility to the Church of Rome. He further alleged, that three Protestant ministers had put their heads together to concoct a drama. I am not aware that Protestants, with all their faults, and they are legion, ever resorted, for quasi religious purposes, to falsification of history and forgery of pretended testimony to injure the Roman communion. This would be a work of supererogation. We need not resort to fiction when we have a storehouse of facts, endless as the meritorial treasury of the saints. Men are very apt to suspect others of practices which lie nearer home. We shall see hereafter.

The expected reply of the Prince came at length. It was in the shape of a letter, addressed, by M. Trognon, his secretary, to the London agent of Mr. Putnam, and showed the nature of the ground on which he had determined to take his stand. As this document is of the highest importance, I give it both in the original and in a translation.

*Claremont*, *Surrey*, 9, *Fevrier*, 1853.

Monsieur.—Le Prince de Joinville, a reçu le numéro du *Monthly Magazine* de New York, que vous avez bien voulu lui transmettre, et a lu l'article sur lequel vous avez appelé son attention. Sa première pensée était de traiter avec l'indifference qu'elle mérite, l'absurde invention qui fait le fond de cet article : mais en réfléchissant qu'un peu de vrai s'y trouve mêlé à beaucoup de faux, le Prince a cru qu'il était bon que je vous répondisse en son nom quelques lignes destinées à faire, au milieu de cet amas de fables, la part exacte de la vérité. Vous ferez, monsieur, de cette réponse l'usage qui vous paraitra le plus convenable.

Ii est très vrai que, dans un voyage qu'il fit aux Etats Unis vers la fin de l'année 1841, le Prince se trouvant à Mackinac, rencontra sur le bateau à vapeur un passager dont il croit reconnaître la figure dans le portrait donné par le *Monthly Magazine*, mais dont le nom avait entièrement fui de sa mémoire. Ce passager semblait fort au courant des événements qui se sont accomplis dans l'Amerique du Nord pendant le siècle dernier. Il racontait une foule d'anecdotes et de particularités intéressantes sur les Français qui prirent part à ces événements et s'y distinguerent. Sa mère était, disait il, une Indienne, appartenant à la grande peuplade des Iroquois, fidèle alliée de la France; il ajoutait que du côté paternel son origine était Francaise, et allait jusqu'à citer un nom que le Prince s'abstient de rapporter. C'était là ce qui l'avait mis en possession de tant de détails curieux à entendre. Un de ces récits les plus attachants était celui qu'il fasait des derniers moments du Marquis de Montcalm, mort entre les bras d'un Iroquois, son parent, à qui le vaillant capitaine avait laissé son épée. Ces details ne purent manquer d'intéresser vivement le Prince, dont le voyage à Mackinac, à Green Bay, et sur le Haut Mississippi, avait pour objet surtout de rechercher la trace glorieuse des Français, qui les premiers ouvrirent à la civilization ces belles contrées.

Le Prince pria M. Williams (puisque tel était le nom de son interlocuteur) de lui faire parvenir, sous forme de notes, tous les rensiegnments qu'il serait en mesure de se procurer, et qui pourraient jeter quelque jour sur l'histoire des établissements Français dans l'Amerique du Nord. De son côté M. Williams, qui ne paraissait moins curieux de connaitre á fond cette même histoire, demanda au Prince de lui transmettre tous les documents qui y etaient relatifs, et qui devaient se trouver dans les archives du gouvernement Français.

Arrivé à Green Bay, le Prince y fut retenu pendant une demi journée par le difficulté de se procurer le nombre de chevaux nécessaire au voyage qu'il allait entreprendre, M. Williams le presser vivement de l'accompagner dans un *settlement* d'Indiens Iroquois établis près de Green Bay, chez qui disait il se conservait encore le souvenir de leurs Pères d'Orient, et qui accueilleraient avec bonheur le fils du Grand Chef de la France. Le Prince declina cette offre, et poursuivit son voyage.

Depuis lors, quelques lettres ont été échangées entre M. Williams et les personnes attachées au Prince, au sujet des documents dont il vient d'être question. Ainsi la lettre de M. Touchard citée dans l'article du *Monthly Magazine* doit être authentique, M. Williams aurait pu egalement en produire une que je me souvienne de lui avoir écrite pour le même objet.

Mais là finit ce que l'article contient de vrai sur les relations du Prince avec M. Williams. Tout le reste, tout ce que a trait à la révélation que le Prince aurait faite à M. Williams, du mystère de sa naissance, tout ce qui concerne le prétendu personage de Louis XVII. est d'une bout à l'autre une œuvre d'imagination, une fable grossièrements tissue, une speculation sur la crédulité publique faite on ne sait à quel propos et dans quel bût. Si par hazard, quelques uns des lecteurs du *MonthlyMagazine* étaient disposés à y avouer creance il faudrait les engager à faire venir de Paris un livre qui vient d'y être tout récemment publié par M. de Beauchesne ils y trouveraient, sur la vie et la mort de l'infortuné Dauphin, du vrai Louis XVII. les détails les plus circonstanciés et les plus positifs. Il me reste à vous répéter, Monsieur, que vous pouvez faire que vous jujerez convenable, offrir en même temps, l'assurance de ma considération distingué.

AUG. TROGNON, ancien precepteur
et secretaire des commandements du Prince de Joinville.

"CLAREMONT, SURREY, *February* 9, 1853.

"SIR.—The Prince de Joinville, has received the number of the Monthly Magazine, of New York, which you have kindly thought fit to transmit to him, and has read the article to which you have called his attention. His first thought was, to treat with the indifference which it deserves, the absurd invention on which this article is founded—but on reflecting that a little truth is there mixed with much falsehood, the Prince has deemed it right that I should, in his name, give a few lines in reply, to show the exact portion of truth there is in this mass of fables.

"You can make, sir, of this reply, the use which you think proper.

"It is very true, that in a voyage which he made to the United States, towards the end of the year 1841, the Prince, finding himself at Mackinac, met on board the steamboat, a passenger whose face he thinks he recognises in the portrait given in the Monthly Magazine, but whose name had entirely escaped his memory.

"This passenger seemed well-informed concerning the history of North America during the last century. He related many anecdotes, and interesting particulars concerning the French who took part, and distinguished themselves in these events. His mother, he said, was an Indian woman, of the great tribe of the Iroquois, faithful allies of France. He added, that on his father's side, his origin was French, and went so far as to cite a name which the Prince abstains from repeating. It was by this means that he had come in possession of so many details curious to hear. One of the most interesting of these recitals was that which he gave of the last moments of the Marquis of Montcalm, who died in the arms of an Iroquois, who was his relative, and to whom the great captain had left his sword. These details could not fail vividly to interest the Prince, whose voyage to Mackinac, Green Bay, and the Upper Mississippi, had for its object to retrace the glorious path of the French, who had first opened to civilization these fine countries. The Prince asked Mr. Williams, since such was the name of his interlocutor, to send to him in the form of notes, all the information which he could procure, and which could throw light upon the history of the French establishments in North America. On his side Mr. Williams, who did not appear less curious to understand thoroughly this same history, asked the Prince to transmit to him all the documents which related to it, and which could be found in the archives of the French government.

"On his arrival at Green Bay, the Prince was detained during half a day, by the difficulty of procuring the number of horses necessary for the journey, which he was about to undertake. Mr. Williams pressed him earnestly to accompany him to a settlement of Iroquois Indians, established near Green Bay, among whom, he said, were still many who remembered their Eastern fathers, and who would receive with delight, the son of the Great Chief of France. The Prince declined this offer, and pursued his journey.

"Since then, some letters have been exchanged between Mr. Williams and the persons attached to the Prince, on the subject of the documents in question. Thus the letter of M. Touchard, cited in the article of the Monthly Magazine, must be authentic. Mr. Williams could also equally have produced one which I remember to have written to him upon the same subject.

"But, there ends all which the article contains of truth, concerning the relations of the Prince with Mr. Williams. All the rest, all which treats of the revelation which the Prince made to Mr. Williams, of the mystery of his birth, all which concerns the pretended personage of Louis XVII., is from one end to the other a work of the imagination, a fable woven wholesale, a speculation upon the public credulity. If, by chance, any of the readers of the Monthly Magazine should be disposed to avow belief in it, they should procure from Paris a book which has been very recently published by M. Beauchesne. They will there find, concerning the life and death of the unfortunate Dauphin, the most circumstantial and positive details. It remains for me to repeat to you, sir, that you can make of this letter such use as you may judge proper, and to offer to you, at the same time, the assurance of my distinguished consideration.

"Signed, AUG. TROGNON.
Former preceptor, and secretary for the commands of the Prince de Joinville."

After re-examining this document carefully, with the advantage of having before me a letter from the Prince himself, addressed to a gentleman in this country, in which he goes over, almost verbally, the course travelled by his secretary, showing that the words of the latter are the production of De Joinville's mind, I can arrive at no other conclusion than that expressed in Putnam's Magazine, in which I do not find a word to alter, and therefore insert it in a note;* while, in confirmation of the view then taken, I will again

* The Prince de Joinville represents himself, not only forgetful of the name of Mr. Williams, but *ascribes to chance his meeting with him* "Finding himself at Mackinac, he met on a steamer a passenger." The *suppressio veri* is the *suggestio falsi*. And from the ground which he has taken, I cannot permit him to move. *The Prince de Joinville, it can easily be proved, sought the interview with Mr. Williams. There was no accident in the meeting.* He was rather young at the time as a diplomatist, and permitted the world to know too much of his errand. The following testimony, from respectable American gentlemen, is decisive :—

The editors of the *Buffalo Courier* and of the *Northern Light* show that, long before the Prince got into the neighborhood of Mackinac, he was inquiring about Mr. Williams. Capt. Shook confirms entirely all the statements of Mr. Williams in which he is concerned. It is then a fact that not once, but several times, during the journey from New York to Green Bay, he had inquired of a variety of persons concerning Mr. Williams, and that, when he saw him, he showed surprise and agitation, and paid him such unusual attention, that it is remembered vividly by eye-witnesses, after a lapse of twelve years.

And yet the Prince, who knew his name so well before he ever saw him, and whose memory is so very faithful concerning everything which he thinks will make against him, now declares that the meeting was accidental, and that his name has escaped briefly consider the Prince's letter, in connection with the testimony of other gentlemen, in order to answer objections made to my position.

When the Prince read my article he was evidently at a loss what to do. "Say nothing," whispered prudence. "It is only a magazine article—stand on your dignity—call it, if questioned, an absurd

his memory. But, in many respects, his statements are important. The Prince says he acknowledged himself the son of an Indian woman. This shows how erroneous are the misrepresentations in many circles, which have charged him with having had a monomania of twenty years' standing, that he was the Dauphin, and confirms, by the authority of the Prince, the statement of Mr. Williams, that up to this time he considered himself of Indian parentage. As to his being of French extraction on the father's side, Mr. Williams never could have said that, unless he intended to accuse his supposed mother of infidelity, which it is not likely he would have done to a stranger. The Williams family are of English origin. There was a surmise that his mother had French blood in her veins, but it was some generations back. Again: The nature of a great part of the conversation between Mr. Williams and the Prince, on the steamer, is, in substance, confirmed; and thus all which Mr. Williams has stated is authenticated, on one hand or the other, except what occurred in the private interview. Here no one but themselves and God are witnesses. But, inasmuch as the letter from the Prince proves him not to be trustworthy in matters open and evident, there is no reason why we should give him credence in those which are secret. The reference to Beauchesne is unfortunate, and proves, to my mind, that there was a special necessity for the publication of such a work. It is curious that the very copy which I have reviewed, was left, by some person unknown, in the room of Mr. Williams, at Washington, with an anonymous note, begging his acceptance of it, "though the perusal might give him pain."

Let any one trace on a map the route of the Prince, and ask himself whether historical researches would be likely to take any man to a place like Green Bay, lying off the direct line of travel, leading nowhere, and having in its neighborhood no important memorials of the French. His natural course when at Mackinac, would have been either to go through the Saut Ste. Marie, to Lake Superior, the shores of which are crowded with mementoes of his countrymen, or to follow the track of La Salle and Hennepin down Lake Michigan to Chicago. Green Bay is a small town in the wilderness, having a palisade fort, and surrounded by a few Indian settlements. There is no historical attraction about it, and the Prince confesses as much by saying that a delay in procuring horses was the sole cause of his staying there even half a day, and declining an opportunity of meeting the neighboring Indians. It is true that Marquette was at Green Bay, but if the Prince had desired to follow his footsteps, he should have pursued the Fox River westerly, and not gone directly south to Galena.

invention, and there let it end." "Nay, but there is truth in it," suggested conscience, "and silence will be accounted equivalent to confession. I must say something." And then came the rub—puzzling as the horns of Hamlet's dilemma—"What shall I say?"

On the sixth of the next month he was at St. Louis, so that his historical researches on the Upper Mississippi could not have been very laborious or profound.

Again, the whole of his account is made to tally with the fundamental misrepresentation that the meeting with Mr. Williams was accidental. Now we know that it was not accidental; that it is an established fact that he went to Green Bay to see him, that he repeatedly and earnestly inquired after him, and can have no reasonable doubt that had Mr. Williams resided in any other place than Green Bay, he would equally have sought him out. But the account of the Prince contains nothing to meet the requirements of that fact. That fact demands that De Joinville should have had some object in seeking an interview with Mr. Williams. It is impossible to evade this. Now, no such object is apparent in the Prince's statement; nay, is studiously kept out of sight; and, though he solemnly declares that he states the whole truth, yet it is undeniable that he omits the most important portion of the history of the interview—and not only omits it, but precludes himself by the coloring which he has put on the transaction, from framing any substitute for the simple truth hereafter. But from Mr. Williams we learn why the Prince so particularly inquired after him, and so earnestly sought him out; and I assert and will maintain it, that herein he is entitled to the benefit of all the probabilities, physical, historical, and circumstantial, which tend to confirm the truth of his account. In other words, if there were no such evidence to sustain him, his cause would be by so much the weaker; but every iota of testimony which makes it probable that he is the Dauphin, increases the probability that he tells the truth concerning the facts of his interview with De Joinville; and yet some will say, the Prince denies the revelation asserted, and *therefore* Mr. Williams spoke untruly. I say there is no *therefore* about it, and defy any one to prove that there is. Why should there be? Because De Joinville is a prince—the descendant of the Regent Orleans, and of Philip Egalité? The opinion of the *New York Daily Times* is far more sensible; it predicted the course which the Prince would take, and the reasons which would actuate him. "If the story be true," it says, "neither the Bourbon nor the Orleans family have any justification before the world for the cruelty of suppressing the truth, always well known to them, for more than half a century, in order to enjoy the inheritance of the legitimate, but exiled king. They will be considered as usurpers, not of the property of a stranger, or of an enemy, but of one of their own household; one whose misfortunes, if not his rights, entitled him to consideration. It will prove to have been a conspiracy of a race against one of its members; a royal conspiracy to defraud. And it is scarcely likely that De Joinville will readily corroborate a tale which must sentence the Bourbons of either branch to infamy."

"Confess what you can't avoid," said the spirit of Machiavelli, "and call it the exact truth." Unfortunately, the execution of this project was left to the intellect of De Joinville, and the pen of M. Trognon.

To form a judgment of the Prince's letter, the reader must have the following testimony before him:

LETTER FROM CAPTAIN SHOOK.

"HURON, *February* 9, 1853.

"TO THE REV. J. H. HANSON:

"REV. AND DEAR SIR.—Yours of the 4th inst., together with the February number of 'Putnam's Monthly,' came duly to hand. It gives me great pleasure to communicate anything, and all I know, of what took place between the Prince de Joinville and the Rev. Eleazar Williams, upon the steamer Columbus, from Mackinac to Green Bay. I have carefully read your article in the Monthly, and so far as matters relating to me go, the Rev. gentleman has stated things truly. I have a very vivid and distinct recollection of the introduction of the Prince to the Rev. Mr. Williams, and of the apparent surprise manifested by the Prince on the occasion; and, furthermore, could not but wonder myself, why he should pay to the humble and unpretending Indian missionary such pointed and polite attention. I have long known the Rev. Mr. Williams, and seen much of him in our voyages up and down the Lakes, and have always found him an amiable, upright, and gentlemanly man, and to be relied upon in any statement he may make. I would again repeat, that what he has stated in relation to me is literally true. If I have not met your mind in this reply, please to write again, and put the matter to me in the form of questions. You say, 'I believe that the Prince gave to you a gold snuff-box upon the occasion.' He did, and I prize it highly.

"If you need an affidavit on the subject, I am willing and ready to give it.

"With sentiments of high regard I am yours,

"JOHN SHOOK."

The following is an extract from a letter of Mr. George S. Raymond—editor of the "Northern Light," Hallowell, Maine—dated March 1, 1853, and addressed to Mr. Putnam:

"I am acquainted with many of the circumstances connected with the Prince de Joinville's visit to Green Bay, his meeting with Mr. Williams, &c., having been myself a fellow-passenger with the Prince during the whole of his Lake tour. At that time I was an officer in the Brazilian service, and came home to the United States to visit a brother, then a resident at Fort Howard, near Green Bay. I joined the Joinville party in New York, travelled with it to Green Bay, and, during several conversations with the Prince, heard him express a most particular anxiety to find out this Mr. Williams, and have an interview with him."

The testimony of Mr. James O. Brayman, one of the Editors of the "Buffalo Courier." In an editorial he made the following statement:

"We remember the time of the visit of the Prince de Joinville well, having passed from Cleveland to Detroit on the same steamboat with him. He, in public conversation, spoke of the general object of his visit, and made inquiries in relation to the whereabouts of Mr. Williams. We recollect listening to a conversation between him and a Mr. Beaubien, of Detroit, in which the latter stated that it *was understood that Mr. Williams was of Indian blood.* The Prince, however, did not commit himself upon any point in regard to the specific purpose for which he sought Mr. Williams, but confined himself to generalities."

On seeing this, I addressed a letter of inquiry to the editors, and received, from Mr. Brayman, the following reply, dated, Buffalo, March 4, 1853:

"In the fall of 1841, I took steamboat at Cleveland for Detroit. The Prince de Joinville and company were on board, having come up from Buffalo. There were also several gentlemen of French descent from Detroit, aboard. In the evening, while sitting in the cabin, the Prince conversed freely—part of the time in French, and part in English. While conversing with the late Col. Beaubien, he made the inquiries concerning Mr

Williams, and spoke of his intention of visiting him at Green Bay. Col. B., who had, I believe, been an Indian trader, knew Mr. W. well, personally or by reputation, and replied to the Prince as to his whereabout and his occupation. The Prince *inquired as to his personal bearing*, and asked various general questions concerning him, and had the appearance of considerable earnestness in his inquiries. The conversation continued some minutes, and concluded by the Prince remarking, 'I shall see him before I return.' This matter has slept in my memory, and having been called up by the late discussions, is not very distinct as to particulars; the general features, however, are as fresh in my mind as an occurrence of yesterday. I have a relative who was some years a teacher in the Indian Mission School at Green Bay. I have heard her relate the circumstance of the visit of the Prince de Joinville to Mr. Williams as something involving much of mystery, and that it, for a while, produced a marked and observable change in Mr. W.'s conduct. He appeared abstracted at times, and excited as by some great emotion. She remarked that the Prince treated him with more than ordinary deference and consideration, for which she could not account at the time."

In a subsequent editorial, Mr. Brayman added:

"In regard to the matters that came under our own cognizance, in the fall of 1841, we derived no further impression from the conversation of the Prince de Joinville, which was public, than that the person for whom he inquired had been recommended to him as one who, from his familiarity with the west, was qualified to aid him in researches which he was prosecuting. Since the question of the Dauphinage has been raised, it is easy to connect the inquiries with it, although such a connection may never have entered the mind of the Prince."

Now let us lay out the facts before us for examination.

1. At the time of writing, the Prince had the narrative and journal of the Rev. Eleazar Williams before him. The letter of his secretary is a thoughtful and well considered reply to the statements contained therein—in proof of which the Prince has himself repeated almost verbally what M. Trognon has said. He

takes, then, his ground deliberately, and no one else has the right or power to change it for him, or to suggest modes of defence or explanation which he has not himself seen fit to adopt.

What then, let me ask, is the ground occupied by the Prince? Let him answer for himself. "Reflecting that a little truth is there mixed with much falsehood, the Prince has deemed right that I should, in his name, give a few lines in reply to show *the exact portion of truth* there is in this mass of fables"—and, lest there should be any mistake, M. Trognon adds, in conclusion, after having given the Prince's explanation in full, "There ends *all* which the article contains of truth."

Now, be it remembered, Mr. Williams had stated that the Prince had made inquiries for him almost from the time of arriving in this country, and had continued them up to the period of their meeting at Mackinac. And since, whatever does not fall within the scope of the Prince's admissions, is purposely excluded as false, it follows that *this* particular statement of Mr. Williams, must be ranked among them, and that the secretary's declaration is emphatic when he says, "It is very true, that in a voyage which he made towards the end of the year 1841, the Prince finding himself at Mackinac, met on board the steamboat a passenger whose face he thinks he recognises, but whose name has entirely escaped his memory." The design was evidently, to represent this meeting as the *beginning* of his acquaintance not only with the *person* but the *existence* of the man, and to discard as *fabulous* all pretences of having *known his name*, *expressed an interest in him*, *sought him*, *followed him*. The language of the letter bears the expression of accident upon its face; but, in the connexion in which it stands, accident is its essence. There is not the remotest hint given of anything lying back of the casual rencontre at Mackinac, and the secretary states the "exact" truth.

If, now, from the nature of the meeting, thus precisely stated by M. Trognon, we pass on to that of the conversation which arose between them, we find the same feature of accident. As fellow passengers on a steamboat, they began conversing, Mr. Williams related a crowd of anecdotes—told the Prince all about his family—the Prince got interested—asked him to put down in writing some details concerning the death of Montcalm; and promised in return to send him some historical documents; parted from him, and pursued his journey. Now, this is *all* which human ingenuity can make out of M. Trognon's letter. Beyond this must be "une œuvre d'imagination." Whoever attempts to make more of it, must supply it from another source, in direct contradiction to the repeated assurance that here is the "*exact*" *truth* and "*all*" the truth. You cannot by any process known to criticism, by any law or mode of interpretation, wring from the guarded and measured sentences anything which indicates or permits previous knowledge or set purpose. This construction of the letter is further required by the manner in which M. Trognon speaks of their detention at Green Bay, at which place they did not pause to visit unexistent historical sites, or inquire for information, but to get horses. I affirm, then, that the Prince does represent this meeting as *accidental and unsought.*

2. Now, then, compare with this, certain indubitable facts. Mr. Raymond, whose testimony was given unsolicited, accompanied the party of the Prince de Joinville, all the way from New York to Green Bay, conversed with the Prince, and heard him "*express a most particular anxiety to find out this Mr. Williams, and have an interview with him.*" I have seen another letter of Mr. Raymond's, in which he stated that these inquiries began almost from the time of leaving New York.

Captain Shook, also, heard the Prince make *repeated* inquiries for Mr. Williams, was employed by him to obtain a formal interview, introduced the gentlemen to each other, has "a most vivid and distinct recollection of the apparent surprise manifested by the Prince, on the occasion, and could not but wonder why he should pay to the humble missionary such pointed and polite attention"—attention not resolvable into common French politeness, because paid to no one else with whom the Prince conversed, but something marked and peculiar in its deference.

We now come to the testimony of Mr. Brayman, from a portion of which a meaning has been attempted to be wrested, which it cannot bear. A distinction must always be made between *the facts* stated by a witness, and his *impressions* concerning those facts. Once confound these, and you may shut up your courts of justice.

The facts stated by Mr. Brayman are these; that the Prince made inquiries concerning—1. The whereabouts. 2. The occupation. 3. The personal bearing of Mr. Williams, and that, besides, he asked various general questions concerning him, and had the appearance of considerable earnestness; that he remarked, "I shall see him before I return;" that Colonel Beaubien stated (doubtless, in reply to some questions of the Prince, as to his race), that it was understood Mr. Williams was of Indian blood, that the Prince did *not commit himself upon any point, in respect to the specific purpose* for which he sought Mr. Williams, and, consequently, did not say he wished to obtain aid from him in his historic investigations.

The impressions of Mr. Brayman, at the time, were natural enough, he heard the Prince speaking of the general objects of his mission, and inferred from thence that his inquiries respecting Mr. Williams, had some relation to his ostensible purpose, in going west, but it was only an inference, and one, too, which, however, superficially plausible, at the moment, would not, even then, have borne the test of comparison with the facts, for, if the Prince's design had been only what Mr. B. imagined, why be so earnest and particular about *personal bearing, race, occupation?* In all these repeated questionings of various persons, and in many places—questionings which would not be satisfied with an answer—there is clearly traceable the straining forward of the mind, towards an object which it was impatient to reach, and concerning which there was excited an insatiable curiosity.

Now, let any candid mind bring in juxta position, M. Trognon's letter, on the one hand, with its accidental meeting, and the statements of eye witnesses, as to what preceded, and what happened at that meeting, and there can be but one sound opinion, that the Prince is guilty of deliberate falsification.

But, look further at the internal evidence the letter bears against itself. The "name" of Mr. Williams "had entirely escaped his memory," says M. Trognon, and, in a subsequent place, not without affectation, he adds, "the Prince asked Mr. Williams, since such was the name of his interlocutor."

The memories of princes may be more treacherous than those of ordinary men; but that of the Prince de Joinville has something in it peculiar, an eclectic obliviousness truly extraordinary. He remembered a great deal about Mr. Williams, his appearance, his anecdotes, and many little circumstances connected with the interview, but entirely forgot his name. Now, let us see whether this was at all probable, or I may say possible. It is entirely in keeping with the theory of an accidental meeting, but how does it tally with the contrary, and with other facts?

There was an understanding between the gentlemen, at parting, that they should mutually interchange civilities, and Mr. Williams, a few days after, sent the Prince some historical memoranda, consisting, for the most part, of extracts from Hennepin and Charlevoix, which the Prince could have obtained without going to Green Bay for them, and in a brief accompanying note, he said he should be happy to transmit any similar information, adding, as a reason, "I am desirous to sustain the honor of the French name, in these ends of the earth." Now, what possible motive an American Indian should have to sustain the honor of the French name, I cannot understand. Explain this passage, by the facts related in the journal of Mr. Williams, and the whole is consistent. He received, in reply, the following letter from M. Touchard.

"Aide de Camp de Service,
"Auprès de Msr. le Prince de Joinville.

"*Frigate la Belle Poule à New York*,
"21 9bre (Novembre), 1841.

"MONSIEUR.—Je me suis empressé de mettre sous les yeux de Monseigneur le Prince de Joinville, votre lettre datée du 25 8bre, avec les notes qui l'accompagnaient sur les premiers établissements Français au bord des grand lacs.

"Son Altesse Royale me charge de vous remercier en son nom de votre obligeant et de votre aimable empressement. Il lira ces notes avec tout l'intérêt qui s'attache à vos recherches historiques, faites sur le théâtre même où nos Français ont laissé tant et d'honorable souvenirs.

"Je suis heureux, Monsieur, d'avoir à vous transmettre les remercimens de son Altesse Royale. Si jamais vous venez visiter notre France veuillez vous souvenir que S. A. R. vous reverrait avec plaisir.

"Recevez, Monsieur, toutes les assurances de mon considération la plus distinguée,

"Lieut. de Vaisseau V. TOUCHARD."

The hint here given, concerning the possibility of Mr. Williams visiting France, deserves notice. Some may explain it on the ground of compliment, but if so, it was empty to the verge of insult, as there was little probability that the poor Indian missionary would ever think of going as a guest to the French court, and nothing, certainly, had happened, according to the statement of the Prince, at the brief accidental interview, likely to turn his thoughts to Versailles and the Tuileries. But, taking Mr. Williams's version of the affair, and the invitation of the Prince, though couched in the phrase of ordinary civility has a meaning. The Prince, if he made such disclosures as Mr. Williams asserts, could scarcely think the latter would allow the matter to rest where it did, and he would seem here to intimate that the door of negotiation was still open.

After his return to France, the Prince, in accordance with his promise, sent Mr. Williams various books and documents.

In the spring of 1843, Mr. Williams was requested by an Iroquois chief, in the neighborhood of Green Bay, to forward to Louis Philippe, through the Prince de Joinville, a petition, which, as an act of neighborly kindness, he did, although the chief belonged to the Roman communion. In writing to the Prince, on the occasion, he alluded courteously to their interview. In this letter, it is remarkable that he speaks of himself to De Joinville, as a Frenchman, which would have been perfectly absurd in one who had confessed to the Prince he was an Indian, and had learned nothing to change his opinion. "To travel over the western lakes and country, as you did, which were formerly traversed *by the enterprising spirits of our forefathers*, whose names are celebrated in America to this day, must have been highly gratifying." Explain this allusion, also, by the journal of Mr. Williams, and all is consistent. M. Trognon, by the command of the Prince, replied to Mr. Williams in the following terms:—

"*Tuileries, Oct.* 14, 1843.

"Secretariat des Commandements
"de S. A. R. Mgr. le Prince de Joinville.

"SIR:—His Royal Highness the Prince de Joinville, who was abroad when you wrote to him, on the 31st March, has just now *ordered me to answer you*, that he has received with the greatest pleasure your letter, so full of *a friendly remembrance*. Receive then *the hearty thanks* of his Royal Highness, though expressed by me, so little acquainted as I am with the English language. *According to your desire, the Prince has presented the petition enclosed in your letter to his father, the King of the French, and earnestly recommended it* to the benevolence of his majesty. The good chief of the Iroquois and his people will be certainly satisfied to hear that our king, desirous to gratify their wishes, sends them a set of French books, the best appropriated to spread among them the religious principles of the Roman Catholic Church. These books, sir, I am ordered to send you, that they may be transmitted by your care to John Randarontye.

"I hope, when they are arrived at Green Bay, you will honor me, sir, with your answer, and meanwhile, I pray you to believe me,

"Your very humble and obt. sert.,
"AUG, TROGNON, Secretary for
"The commands of His Royal Highness,
"The Prince de Joinville."

From this letter, it appears, that De Joinville had the opportunity to refresh his memory, fully in regard to the name of Mr. Williams, spoke to his father respecting him, presented the petition, and had the whole circumstances of their interview recalled, in a manner which could not fail to imprint them with the name of Mr. Williams on any memory of ordinary tenacity. The books were sent, and accompanying them was a letter from Louis Philippe to Mr. Williams. This letter has unfortunately been destroyed, and its contents can only be collected from the statement of Mr. Williams, who says that, the king thanked him for the civilities he had shown to his son during his visit to the United States. The fact of the former existence of the letter is proved from the accompanying note from M. de La Forest, the French consul in New York.

"The Consul General of France, owing to the interruption of the communication between New York and Wisconsin Territory, was unable before to present to Mr. Eleazar Williams the enclosed letter, and the box of books sent by the King of the French. Mr. Williams will oblige M. de la Forest, by acknowledging reception of the whole, and accept his respectful compts.

"*New York*, 16*th April*, 1844."

Now, one would think that after having Mr. Williams's name on his lips all the way from New York to Green Bay, and making such repeated and particular inquiries about him; after all that is known to have transpired between them, and after the means for refreshing his memory which correspondence for years after afforded, the Prince would, at least, have remembered his name—but no it had "entièrement fui de sa mémoire," a thing, I repeat, consistent with a perfectly accidental meeting, but not harmonizing at all with facts which are incontrovertible. M. Trognon remembered him very well, and he certainly had not so much cause to do so as the Prince.

Taking all these facts together, the pretence of forgetfulness seems to be as untrue as the pretence of accident. The Prince could not have forgotten the name of Eleazar Williams. He started and trembled when he saw him. He recognized, in every lineament of his features, in every gesture of his hand, in every proportion of his form, the tokens of his race. Those who saw them meet, can swear to his agitation. But this, also, according to his statement, must be excluded from the exact truth. How would he wish the world to account for a fact which, though he may deny it, is proved. Again, a well-known gentleman, of the highest respectability in this country, Mr. George Sumner, brother to Mr. Charles Sumner, United States Senator from Massachusetts, met, in the year 1846, at Brest, one of the officers who accompanied the Prince to Green Bay, and, in the cabin of his vessel, looking cautiously round before he spoke, he said to Mr. Sumner, *that there was something very singular in the American trip of the Prince, who went out of his way to meet an old man among the Indians, who had very much of a Bourbon aspect, and who was spoken of as the son of Louis XVI.* Are we to exclude this also from the exact truth? Mr. Williams, at the time of the meeting with the Prince, at Mackinac, considered himself the son of an Indian woman. He could not, therefore, have spoken of himself as the son of Louis XVI. There was no such report concerning him current, to the knowledge of his most intimate friends, and the story must therefore have originated in the party of the Prince. This fact not only shows which way the thoughts of the Prince were tending, but establishes clearly that the meeting was not accidental, and that he went out of his way to see Mr. Williams, and thus confirms the statement of the latter, while it throws additional discredit on the account given by M. Trognon.

The whole subject, then, narrows itself to a single, simple, but stern issue—that of veracity between the only two witnesses who can testify concerning a contested fact. Dismiss from the mind the comparative rank of these two individuals: look at them merely as men. An interview has taken place between them. One asserts that it was *purely accidental* and *unsought*, and gave rise *to no secret communication* of a startling fact, and his account of the interview is made *to correspond* with the hypothesis of *a purely accidental meeting.* The other person affirms that the interview was *not accidental*, but *was sought* by the first individual, who communicated to him a *startling fact*, up to that moment unknown to him. Which shall we believe? The rule of law is, *falsum in uno, falsum in omnibus.* The first asserts an *accidental meeting*, and an *unimportant conversation*, its necessary consequence. *The accidental meeting is positively disproved.* The foundation goes and the superstructure goes with it. A *sought interview* requires a *specific object.* The second person, who has a fair character, and in whose story no misrepresentation can be proved, relates a *fact communicated* at the interview, adequate to explain the *proved solicitude* of the first person *in seeking him*, but which communication that person has the *highest earthly interest in denying.* If you believe the first, you must do so in the face of a *falsehood* and an *unexplained fact.* If you believe the second, the *fact is explained*, and *no falsehood on his part can be shown.* I leave the world to decide on which side *probability inclines.*

In defending, before the American people, the assailed reputation of an American citizen, I need scarcely ask whether, in this question of veracity, they will believe a person, who, out of his own mouth, stands convicted of the most glaring inconsistencies and misstatements, or one for whose truth there are so many vouchers, and who, as a minister of the Gospel, has labored, all his life, to do good to the most down-trodden and unbefriended denizens of this continent; and, I can scarcely doubt, that, should the subject of this volume attract attention to it in the country under whose flag I was born, the generous spirit of Englishmen will not allow mere nominal rank to outweigh the asseverations of manly worth.

Not content with charging Mr. Williams with falsehood, in the same breath that he furnished data to convict himself of the crime, the Prince, evidently afraid the world would not believe him, must bolster up his assertions with the corpulent volumes of M. de

Beauchesne. This very undignified proceeding, so entirely alien to the habits of men in his position, who generally affect to think their own word sufficient to ensure public credence, goes far in itself to discredit his assertions. Just imagine Prince Albert accused by some person in the wilds of Africa, of having made certain statements affecting his personal honor, writing a long, disingenuous, explanatory letter, and concluding by saying, "If the world won't believe me, I refer them to Mr. Macaulay's History." I beg the pardon of his royal highness for the supposition, but it illustrates the position of Ferdinand D'Orleans. Beauchesne, Beauchesne—here is the infallible specific, let everybody read Beauchesne. He will anathematize his own soul to convince them, and show them his album. It is of no avail—those lying volumes will never go down to posterity as history. But, those curious in the weakness and wickedness of deception, may deposit them on the same shelf with the memoirs of Naundorff, the Latin epitaph to the memory and ashes of Louis XVII., the letter of M. Trognon, and the forged affidavit of the Rev. M. Marcoux, of St. Regis, of which I shall shortly speak. If all were bound together, they would form what M. H. de Courcey calls "un Roman d'imagination."*

* The following items of unconnected information I here insert in a note, as they may at some time be of service.

I am informed by the Rev. Mr. Van Rensselaer, of Mount Morris, that he was acquainted with Mrs. Catherine Mancius, the daughter of Jacob Vanderheyden, the Indian trader, who, the reader of my previous article will remember, was present at the time that Mr. Williams was left among the Indians at the head of Lake George, and who, afterwards, in conversation with Thos. Williams, seemed anxious to pry into the subject. Mrs. Mancius mentioned to Mr. Van Rensselaer, that when Talleyrand was in this country, he made her father a visit. It is certainly singular to find Talleyrand in contact with old Jacob Vanderheyden. Again, Mr. Treadway, of Malone, informs me that on mentioning this subject to Mr. Brockway, a gentleman whose statements are to be relied on, he told him that in 1852 he was at the Sault Ste. Marie, when two Frenchmen, fresh from France, arrived there, and made earnest and particular inquiry for Mr. Williams, supposing that he was there, or in the neighborhood. Both were unable to speak English, and *one was a Romish Priest* On being informed where he lived, they immediately employed some Indians to paddle them in a canoe, through the lake to Mackinac, with a view to take a steamer for

On one point I must touch before dismissing consideration of the Prince de Joinville and his mission—viz. the motives of Louis Philippe in revealing to Mr. Williams the secret of his birth. The clue to these will be found in his political position. The régime of the citizen king had on it the stain, not only of illegitimacy, in the eyes of the royalists, but of treachery, ingratitude, and hypocrisy; "Ces D'Orleans sont de si honnêtes gens," was a compliment of contraries after the days of July. The world regarded Louis Philippe simply as a clever rogue, who could make good pen and ink sketches, and the problem concerning whom was whether he would die in his bed. Between Bonapartists, legitimists and ultra liberals, his chances of extreme unction were slender. Whatever would enable him to gain the confidence and affection of the world, to conciliate or crush opposing parties, while he united in himself the souvenirs of the past, would be esteemed by him a master-stroke of policy. Could he persuade France that he loved the memory of Louis XVI., and revered the Emperor, while himself the incarnation of liberalism, and thus twine his republican crown with wreaths from St. Helena and the Madeleine, that so the eagle, and the tri-color, and the drapeau blanc, might, in combination, ornament and defend his throne, he might yet have a sepulchre in St. Denis, and a list of successors like Hugh Capet.

From those who have been well termed "courtiers of all times, all dynasties, and all powers," he had doubtless learned those secrets which pursue a throne, and among them the existence of Louis XVII., a fact more clearly evinced by the Naundorff discussion. With a genius which would have shone in the neighborhood of the Astor, he seems to have designed converting France into a museum for monarchical and imperial relics, dead and living, and astonishing the world with the sight of the lusty embonpoint of the captive of

Green Bay. Here my information ends. But Mr. Williams has frequently told me that strangers from abroad have inquired for him, but seemed quite unsuspicious that their visits were of any meaning or moment, and has no particular recollection of the incident referred to.

the Temple, side by side with that of the sarcophagus of the mighty Napoleon. At the command of his father, De Joinville brought to Paris the coffined earthquake of St. Helena, and Louis Philippe reverently deposited it under his throne, while he despatched his son across the Atlantic, to bring over, with his abdication signed, the living monarch, whose quiescent simplicity might neutralize the explosive properties of the imperial corpse. With Williams in his hands, how boldly could he have confronted the Legitimists, and said, "You accuse me of plotting against Charles X., and usurping the throne of Henry V. Look at your own work and your own position. The wrongs of this man at once take from you all pretence of right, and consign you to historic damnation, as the blackest and foulest intriguers who ever swindled themselves into empire. I act a great, a noble, a generous part. I restore to France the consecrated dust of her heroic chief, and bring back from exile, to wealth, honor, and happiness, all that remains to the nation of her ancient kings. Between my royal cousin and myself there is no rivalry. My throne is based on the election of the people, but if he be deemed by any to have right, he surrenders to me. His religion, his profession, his language, his habits, his training, unfit him for political life in France. All parties are thus extinguished. I have shown I trust the nation; let the nation trust me. In me Bonapartist, Royalist, Liberal, find no opponent, but a friend and father."

Such, in brief, is my explanation of the conduct of Louis Philippe, and I deem it sufficient. You cannot say, there was any improbability he would reveal to Mr. Williams the secret of his birth, after bringing to France the ashes of Napoleon. The one is but the counterpoise of the other, requisite to prevent the other from being mischievous, while both together were calculated to extinguish parties, and make all souvenirs, all interests, all anticipations, centre in Louis Philippe.

## CHAPTER XX.

### THE BATTLE OF THE AFFIDAVITS.

My principal reason for urging Mr. Williams to consent to the publication of his story, in the imperfect form it was first presented, was to elicit evidence, I doubted not must exist, in various quarters. I was not mistaken. While General Cass was the only person who had attempted anything like argument against Mr. Williams, with a result certainly not unfavorable to the latter, confirmation of his statements grew up in all directions. Appendix M.

About the end of March, the Rev. Dr. Hawks received information from a friend in New Orleans, that a lady residing there was in possession of important facts relative to the preservation of the Dauphin, and I immediately determined to go there. The day before I left New York, I was introduced by a friend to M. H. De Courcey who had written several letters in the "Phare de New York," and more recently in the "Courrier des Etats Unis," in opposition to me. I consented to this introduction, because, I supposed Mr. De Courcey misapprehended my motives, and I wished to assure him, the investigation was conducted with the simple desire of obtaining historic truth. He replied, he had the same feelings; that the death of the Dauphin was a fact no well-informed Frenchman denied; admitted, however, there were some singular points in the evidence; said, the next day he was going to France; and, as he was well acquainted with M. de Beauchesne, would confer with him on the subject; and, in conclusion, assured me, as a Legitimist, Louis XVII., if alive, would have all his sympathies, notwithstanding any differences of religious faith, and expressed his firm conviction, the truth could not be hidden. Mr. A. Fleming, who introduced me to him, was present at our interview. The next day we set out for our respective destinations. M. de Courcey by the French, and I by the Charleston steamer. I left New York, April 9, arrived at Charleston in two days, and following the mail route across South Carolina, Georgia, and Alabama, reached New Orleans on the 18th of that month.

By the kindness of friends, I soon obtained an interview with the lady in question, and, after several conversations, in the presence of witnesses of the highest respectability, ascertained the exact amount of information she had, or was willing to communicate. I found her in a little wooden house in the Faubourg. It is a part of the town where everything remains as it was in old French times, and it seemed strange to make inquiries in such a spot respecting events which happened in Europe more than half a century ago. Mrs. Brown had resided in New Orleans since 1820. She bore the marks of extreme age, though only seventy-five years, and gave me the impression of one who had seen great vicissitudes. Her health was very infirm, as she was afflicted with a cancer in the breast, which threatened soon to put an end to her life; but her mind was clear and intelligent, and there was often much terse vigor in her language. She had read nothing which had been written in relation to Mr. Williams, did not even know there was any such person now living, and was entirely ignorant of the recent questions at issue. As the best means of arriving at the facts of the case, I requested her to tell me the story of her life. It was in substance, as follows: She was educated in Edinburgh, where she became acquainted with and married a man named Benjamin Oliver, a French republican, who took her to the continent. She obtained a divorce from him, and returned to Edinburgh; where, in 1804, she again married Joseph Deboit, secretary to the Count D'Artois, who then resided in Holyrood House. Deboit had previously been in the service of Louis XVI., and handed the Dauphin into the carriage on the night of the flight to Varennes, when the young Prince said they were going to the play. Soon after her marriage, the Count D'Artois left

Edinburgh, and went to the continent, she believed to Russia, to see the king, but at this distance of time could not speak with certainty concerning a thing in which she had no part. She remained in the palace at Holyrood, until after his return to England. In 1807, she joined her husband in London. Here, she first became acquainted with the Count de Lisle, as Louis XVIII. was then called, and with the Duke and Duchess D'Angoulême. As her husband occupied a confidential position in the royal family, she became very intimate with them, and especially with the Duchess D'Augoulême. There was much conversation among them at that time respecting the Dauphin, and Joseph Deboit told her, he was not dead, but carried away for safety. Being one day alone with the duchess, she mentioned what Deboit had said, and asked her if it was true, and if she knew what had become of him. The duchess replied, without any hesitation, and with an expression of pleasure, that she had assurance her brother was in America. Here, the conversation dropped, as the duchess did not seem inclined to enter into particulars. In the same year, however, she remembers having heard, either from the Duchess D'Angoulême, or from Deboit, but cannot, after so long a time, say which, that a royalist named Bellanger, was the chief agent in removing the Prince. As everything said to her was confidential, she spoke to no one except her husband of what she heard. " All the members of the royal family," she said, were well acquainted with the fact of the Dauphin's preservation," and, smiling at the idea of their ignorance, she continued, " they all knew it, sir, they all knew it."

She returned to Holyrood House with her husband, who died there in 1810, but, after his decease, she still continued her intimacy with the Bourbon family, and was employed by them, in various ways, until the Restoration.

Mrs. Brown, I heard, had for years mentioned to Mrs. Reid, of New Orleans, and others, that she had been employed to put into a convent some young woman connected, in some way, with the royal family, and I questioned her particularly about this, but could obtain no information. She did not think it had anything to do with the matter in hand, of which she would state all she knew, but she added, "there are some things, about which history had better be silent." This girl passed for her daughter, and is now living at a convent in France. This subject seemed to irritate her, and, being urged by those with whom she had previously, in unguarded moments, conversed, I often recurred to it, but could get no fuller information.

In 1809 she again went to France, and there, at a place called Morley, married an American gentleman, named George Brown, who led a wandering sea-faring life, in privateers and merchantmen. In 1812, Brown was sailing master, on board a privateer, called the True Blooded Yankee, which was bought by Mr. Henry Preble, a London merchant, brother to Commodore Preble. The vessel was commanded by Thomas Oxnard. She showed me Brown's portrait, which was that of a handsome, gentlemanly man.

In 1813, De Vaux, aide-de-camp to General Moreau, came to the convent, at Morley, in France, where she was staying, and said there was a crisis coming on, and she must cross the channel immediately, and carry despatches to the Count D'Artois, and the Count de Lisle, these, he sewed between the ticking and leather of her trunk. A badge, ornamented with fleurs de lis, which she still retains, was given her on the occasion, and she was told it would be useful to her, at several points she had to pass. Meeting a body of troops in one of these places, according to her instructions, she drew aside the folds of her dress, and exhibited the token, when every mark of respect was shown, and she was expedited on her journey. She arrived safely in England, and delivered the package into the hands of the Count D'Artois, in South Audley street, Grosvenor square, in the presence of M. de Belleville.

Before she relinquished her connection with the royal family, the *Duc D'Angoulême came to her, examined her papers, and removed everything relating to the private affairs of the Bourbons.*

Having executed her commission, she returned to France, and

went to sea with her husband; narrowly escaped death by wreck and mutiny, but; at least, arrived safely in the Brazils, and kept school in St. Salvador. Owing to misfortunes they were very poor, but, as soon as Brown could collect means, they embarked for New York, in the Tom Bowling, or Bolyn, but he died at sea on June 7, 1815, on the 4th July of which year, she arrived a widow in America. Her wanderings were yet far from being ended. A few months found her in the Havanna, where she was housekeeper to Grey and Fernandez.

Business once more drew her to Europe, and here she again became conversant with facts that bear upon the case. Thrown back among her old associates, she resided in Edinburgh, with Mrs. Chamberlaw, whose husband had been secretary to the Count de Coigny, one of the intimates, as well as the Prince de Condé, of the Count D'Artois, while at Holyrood. Mrs. Chamberlaw had accompanied the royal family to Paris, and was then fresh from the Tuileries. She told her she had recently heard in the palace, that the Dauphin was alive, and had been carried to America by one Bellanger, who took him to Philadelphia. "This," she said, "was no news to me, as I had heard the same years before, but Mrs. Chamberlaw added, the Prince was still living there, and was known as Williams, an Indian missionary."

The examination of Mrs. Brown, was conducted in the presence of an able and highly respectable lawyer, Mr. Bradford, and other persons. Having ascertained that she knew nothing of what had transpired at the north, and had not heard of the Rev. Eleazar Williams, she was asked, "Do you recollect whether Mrs. Chamberlaw mentioned the Christian name of the Indian missionary, said to be the Prince, by Mrs. Chamberlaw?" "It is so long ago, that I forget it now, but should probably recognise it, if I heard it." "Was it any Scripture name?" "I can't say." "Was it Joseph?" "No." "Was it Aaron?" "No." "Was it Eleazar?" "That was it, to the best of my recollection." Mr. Bradford smiled, as he wrote down the answer, perceiving, evidently, from her manner, that her recognition of the name was genuine. Mrs. Brown went on to say, that, according to Mrs. Chamberlaw's statement, the subject had been much discussed in the palace, and that the royal family said, Williams was incompetent to reign, and his elevation to the throne would only increase the difficulties of the times—that, a man had come out from America to confer with them on the subject, and she had seen him. When he first came to the palace, there was a report that Louis XVII. was himself there. Money. was given to this man, and he returned to America. Over and over again, I questioned Mrs. Brown, in the presence of many of the most respectable persons in New Orleans, if she was certain of these facts, and was assured, on the word of a dying Christian, that what she said was true. After this, I gave her my articles, in Putnam, to read, of which she previously knew nothing, and showed her a faithful crayon sketch of Mr. Williams, by Fagnani, in which she immediately recognised the Bourbon lineaments. When she had read the articles, she said, "I only wish I was as certain of salvation, as I am that he must be the man."

To test, in every possible way, Mrs. Brown's declarations, I applied to a lady who had known her intimately for many years, Mrs. Reid, sister-in-law of Commodore Patterson. She said she had known her for seventeen years, and was introduced to her as a person who had been intimate with the royal family of France, and that in conversation upon the events of her life, *as long ago as twelve or thirteen years*, she had told her all the particulars contained in her present affidavit, and especially that the Dauphin, supposed to have died in the Temple, *had been carried to Philadelphia, by a man named Bellanger, and was an Indian missionary, named Williams.* Up to a few weeks, Mrs. Reid had never heard of the existence of Eleazar Williams, and had not as yet seen my articles. All she knew on the subject was derived, simply, from conversations with Mrs. Brown, in former years. "But," she added, "that you may have more than my word for this, and that I may feel more secure in making an affidavit, inquire of the Rev.

Mr. Whitall. He knows well what I have said to him, for years, on the subject." I accordingly went to Mr. Whitall, a laborious and faithful missionary of the Protestant Episcopal Church, and applied to him for information. "All that Mrs. Reid states," he said, "is correct, and you can depend upon it. I have heard the story from her for seven or eight years or more. But, to be on the safe side, I can swear to five. I never paid much attention to the subject, but I am ready to attest to the facts."

This *triple chain* of testimony, thus standing secure, was drawn up, deliberately weighed, and sworn to by Mrs. Brown, Mrs. Reid, and Mr. Whitall, before G. Lugenbuhl, Esq., who himself added his testimony to the private worth and reliability of the witnesses. But, the city of New Orleans will stand voucher for that. Appendix N.

Besides obtaining this testimony, I endeavored to gain some information of Bellanger. One fact was testified to on all hands, by persons of highest respectability, that, in 1848, a paragraph did appear in the papers there, to the effect that, a person of that name, on his death-bed, had declared he brought the Dauphin to America. I diligently examined the files of the "Delta," "Picayune," "Bee," "Commercial," and other papers, but without success. Those who have ever attempted a similar research, can appreciate the difficulty it entails, and the time and patience it requires. In cases where the recovery of property depended on information, thus to be obtained, it has taken years to effect the object. In none of the papers were the files complete. The "Bee" was that which approached nearest to it. Sometimes half a paper was missing, just at the time most likely for the information to occur. I also examined the records of the courts, hoping to find some clue in the lists of successions, and also the registers of burials. The law respecting the registry of deaths is practically a dead letter. Scarcely one in a dozen is recorded, and, in times of epidemic, the dead are fortunate if they are numbered. In one of the courts, I found the papers of a person named Bellanger, a native of Paris, who married at St. Louis, in 1806 or 7, returned to France in 1816, and stayed there for several years—but, of him, whether dead or living, I could get no clue. The fact is, there have been Bellangers innumerable in New Orleans. Bellanger, a jeweller, Bellanger, a gambler, Bellanger, a cooper, Bellanger de Bouillé, a nobleman, and friend of Le Ray de Chaumont, and Colonel de Ferrière; and, to mention no more, one whose father was minister of Louis XVI. He died several years ago. I had an interview with his son, who said he expired in his arms, and made no such confession.

It has occurred to me, the report circulated in New Orleans, in 1848, and which reached Mr. Williams, through Mr. Kimball, may have originated in some distorted account of Mrs. Brown's conversations; and it may ultimately turn out, Bellanger was not in New Orleans so late as 1848, and may have died, if he is dead, which some reports deny, at some far distant place or time. This may be so; but, when I bear in mind, the efforts made to conceal and falsify testimony, in every shape and way, it is just as probable, means have been found to hush the matter up. The account which Mr. Williams received, is too particular to be altogether a dream. Meanwhile, thus much is certain that, years before Mr. Williams knew that Bellanger was a historic personage, or had any connection with the events in the Temple, he was informed that he was the chief agent in bringing him to this country, though, from his ignorance of events, he imagined the name must be an assumed one—that so long ago as 1807, a living witness heard in the royal household, the same fact respecting Bellanger, and that M. Beauchesne historically demonstrates, this agent of Louis XVIII. must have been the individual who removed the Prince. That he had his appropriate assistants is every way probable, and none seem more adapted to the purpose than those which Naundorff's statement, and Mrs. Dudley's letter, alike indicate, a girl to amuse the Prince, and a lady of the queen's household to take charge of them both.

My duties called me home, and I was compelled to relinquish the investigation. I came back by way of the Mississippi and the lakes, and as I was approaching New York, I read in a newspaper the following paragraph:

"The 'Courrier des Etats Unis' publishes the following affidavit of Mary Ann Williams, mother of the Rev. Eleazar Williams:

"*State of New York, Franklin County*, ss.

"Personally appeared before me, the undersigned, one of the Justices of the Peace in and for the said county, Mary Ann Williams, and being duly sworn deposeth and says, that she is upwards of eighty years of age, but does not know her exact age; that she is the widow of Thomas Williams, and that she is the natural mother of Rev. Eleazar Williams, and that she is aware of his pretensions to be the son of Louis XVI., and knows them to be false; that he was her fourth child, and born at Caughnawaga; that at the time of his birth her sister took him to the priest to be baptized, and that her sister gave the priest the name of the child's godfather, which was Lazar, from which the child took his name; that he was born in the spring, thinks in the month of June; says that when he was about nine years old some of his father's friends from the States came to Caughnawaga and took him and a younger brother away, to send them to school; that some time after he returned home and had a sore leg, which made him lame; that they doctored his leg; the sore was on his knee; that sometimes it would heal up and break out again, and that they were sometimes fearful it would never get well; that she has no recollection how the scar came on his face; that she never knew of his having any trunk or medals in his possession; and that her son Eleazar very strongly resembles his father, Thomas Williams; and says that no persons whatever, either clergymen or others, ever advised or influenced her in any manner to say that he was her son; that the first intimation she ever had of his pretensions to a royal birth, was from one William Woodman, an Oneida Indian, who came to her, about three years ago, and asked her if she would not be willing to go before a magistrate and swear that Eleazar was not her son, but was given her to bring up; she told him she would do no such thing, as she knew him to be her son; that Eleazar has since mentioned to her that some of his friends thought he was not an Indian, but descended from royal parentage; she told him it was no such thing, that he was her own son.

her
"MARY ANN + WILLIAMS.
mark

"Subscribed and sworn before me this 28th day of March, 1853.
"ALFRED FULTON, Justice of the Peace."

As I folded the paper, I could but smile at the folly of an act, which, I felt sure, would recoil on its contrivers. On my arrival in the city I learned something of the history of the affidavit. It travelled a long distance before it saw the light. M. de Courcey, with whom I parted on the eve of going to New Orleans, took the document with him to France, and thence transmitted it to America, for publication in the "Courrier des Etats Unis."

I felt sorrow for M. de Courcey, because I could not allow myself to imagine he was a party to this transparent forgery.

I felt sorry for M. de Courcey, because it is unpleasant, under any circumstances, to be made, however innocently, an instrument in assailing the reputation, and seeking to destroy the usefulness of another.

Though M. de Courcey has styled me a romancer, using the word in its most offensive sense, I will not retaliate.

The matter was assuming a serious form, and it was necessary to proceed with caution. In a western paper, the Rev. Mr. Marcoux, of St. Regis, was openly spoken of as the author of the affidavit, and I knew of no one excepting him, in St. Regis or Hogansburg, likely to correspond with M. de Courcey, whose initials only had been appended to his articles. But as the Roman priesthood have the reputation of being astute, it seemed difficult to imagine he would lend himself to the transaction, which, according to the maxims of Talleyrandic morality, was worse than a crime—a blunder. At my request, the Hon. Phineas Atwater, formerly Indian agent, undertook to discover the truth. He went to Hogansburg and made inquiries of Mr. A. Fulton, the magistrate before whom the affidavit was taken. and obtained the following certificate.

"I certify that the affidavit sworn to before me in March last, by Mrs. Mary Ann Williams, was in the English language. She came to my office, in Hogansburgh, either in company with, or met there, the Rev. Francis Marcoux, Roman Catholic priest at St. Regis. Two Indians were also present. Mr. Marcoux acted as interpreter, and put the questions to her in the Indian language, and interpreted them in English.

"*Hogansburg*, *July* 8, 1853." "A. FULTON, J. P.

Having learned the circumstances under which the affidavit was made, Mr. Atwater had an interview with Mr. Marcoux, and told him the object he had in view, when Mr. Marcoux acknowledged he had been agent in the matter, but said he was solicited, by letter, from Mr. de Courcey, to obtain the affidavit. How far he followed or outran the solicitations or instructions of M. de Courcey, he did not say, and this is a point these gentlemen must settle between themselves. I can only state facts. Mr. Atwater then proceeded to the residence of Mrs. Williams, whom he found two miles from Hogansburg, on the Racket river. He informed her of the object of his visit, when she consented to go to Hogansburg, and declare the truth. He had, however, great embarrassments to contend with, as there was no interpreter then in the village, with the exception of one entirely in the interest of Mr. Marcoux. But he had to make the best of circumstances, though, as Mrs. Williams was surrounded with Roman Catholic Indians, who have a bitter hostility to Mr. Williams, he could not obtain from her general and full statements. They thronged around her, and embarrassed the examination, and it was impossible to keep them from her. However, the old woman having heard the previous affidavit, to which she had put her mark, read to her, in Indian, determined to dispense with an interpreter, and express what she had to say, in her own language and manner, from which it was impossible to make her vary. Her declaration was taken down in Mohawk by an Indian, and *falsely* translated by Antoine Barron, the Romish interpreter, under cover of a written oath of fidelity. I give it in both languages as follows, having corrected the translation:—

Ii Mary Ann Williams, ne teiakeniterontakwe ne Thomas Williams, etho wakeriwaniraton tsi wakatati raonhake ne A. Fulton, Esq., etho Hogansburg, èh nonwe siwennitare ne March tkenne, tsi nikaririhoten wakatati, ne wahakeriwaneken tsinakiere ne Francis Marcoux, Akwesasne Ratsihenstatsi, nok raonha wahatewennakaratate, nok wahakeriwanontonnionse, ne kati tsi onen wahonkewennanotonse, etho wakeriwatshenri tsi iah ne tewaken nok iah oni tokenske teken tsini kaieren. Ne kati tewakatonwentsioni nonsaktakwarisionko tsi nonwe nisewatewatanion. Ken kati kaien enkeriwanirate ne tokenske tsi nenkiere, tsiniiore keiare; nok tsinikewennoten enwat-iaton, nok iah onka taiontewennakaratate;—wakiron kati, iah tokenske teken tsi waton ne kaiatonsera ia-onka ne ietsienstatsi, nok oni ne oiashonha nonkwe teionkenikonaraten; tsi wakeron *riienha* ne Eleazer, nok tsi wakatatsennaren ne kaiatonserake raonha-se ne Mr. Marcoux, ne Akwesasne ratsienstatsi wahakenaskwaien, nok oni, noiason nonkwe tsionatonwisen akatatsennaren nok raonha wahatewennakaratate. Ja-tokenske teken, tsi waton ne kaiatonsera rosinanonwakskwe ne *riienha tehotkohen* tiotierenten sonsasonkwaiatorenne neto tontahaientakwe tsi nonwe iehateweienstakwe. Keiare tsi roientakwe ne iontwistaniakta ne poseronni iakeniterontakwe; raonha ne rokstenha wahariwisa tsi wahatkaraientakwe ne roienha, oh-ki ok nahoten tehonekon tsi iontenninontha, sarokenha nok Tsiawiskenha.

"Kentho iesennaronnion ne keienhokonha, Peter, Catharine, Ignatius, Thomas (*Eleazer tehotkonhen*,) Louisa, John, Peter, Hannah, Rhoda, Charles, Jarvis; ok enskat wakewirense, onen tokat tsi wakateweton. Keiare tsi iakenenonne ne oseronni teiakeniterontakwe toha ioserake tsinae tsi tekiatonniarikon konwaiats; nok tsi keiaten hawe keienhokonha ne Eleazer, nok oni oiasonha, rakwanenne, nok oni tsi toha iateioserake etho ratoratskwe ne Oseronni teiakeniterontakwe.

her
"MARY ANN + WILLIAMS.
mark.

"Subscribed and sworn before me, this 8th day of July, 1853,

"A. FULTON, Justice of Peace."

TRANSLATION.

"I, Mary Ann Williams, widow of the late Thomas Williams, of Caughnawaga, made a declaration on oath, before A. Fulton, Esq., at

Hogansburg, in the month of March last, at the request of the Rev. Francis Marcoux, Priest of St. Regis, he acting as interpreter and putting the questions to me, which being read and explained to me, I found to contain what I did not intend to say and which is not true. I now wish to correct those errors, so far as my memory will allow, in my native language, without the intervention of any interpreter—that is to say—it is not true as stated in the affidavit, that no person, priest, or others, ever advised or influenced me to say, that Eleazar is *my own son.* It was Mr. Marcoux the priest, at St. Regis, who urged me with others, some women, to make the affidavit, and he acted as an interpreter on the occasion, as before stated. It is not true also, as stated in the affidavit, that *my adopted son* had a sore leg when he returned from school the first time to us. I remember that my husband had a medal which he ordered Charles and Jarvis to pawn to a merchant for him. The names of my children were Peter, Catherine, Ignatius, Thomas (Eleazar adopted), Louisa, John, Peter, Hannah, Rhoda, Charles, and Jarvis; I lost one child by miscarriage after the birth of several that lived. I recollect going with my husband to Lake George, a great many years ago, and took with me Eleazar and another older boy, and that my husband was in the habit of going there almost every year.*

her
"Signed, MARY ANN + WILLIAMS.
mark.

"Subscribed and sworn to before me, this 8th day of July, 1853,
"A. FULTON, Justice of the Peace."

Even without the affidavit, the facts recounted in the foregoing pages would be sufficient to show the utter falsehood of the state-

* The force of this document lies in the twice used word "tehotkonen," "adopted," the meaning of which Mr. Marcoux has acknowledged to Mr. Fulton. But Barron, the interpreter, at the time pretended he did not understand the word—and, where Mrs. Williams denies the statement concerning the sore leg, contrary to his oath of fidelity, substituted "Eleazar" for adopted son—"riienha tehotkonen" in order to render the translation of a most precise document, as indefinite as possible. He trusted to our failure in minute observation, and nearly succeeded, as his breach of faith, was only discovered in correcting the proofs. Twice, then, in this affidavit, Mary Ann Williams acknowledges that Eleazar is not her son. He is "riienha tehotkonen," "adopted son" in opposition to "riienha," which by itself, has the force of "own son." "Tehotkonen" is only applied to adopted persons of foreign

ments fabricated by Mr. Marcoux. That Eleazar Williams was nine years of age when he went to Massachusetts, that he was laid up on his return to Canada, with sores on his knees and ankles; that he resembled Thomas Williams in appearance, are stories so apocryphal that they could never have been hazarded, except under the idea that no farther inquiry would ever be made, but a lying affidavit be permitted to over ride the facts of history. But if such be the instrumentalities made use of against Mr. Williams, they will do him little injury. Nor does it require the confession of Mary Ann Williams to prove that Eleazar is only her adopted child. That he is her son may well be accounted a physical impossibility, and the mental characteristics, developed in the course of his history, are equally at variance with the supposition that he is an Indian, to say nothing of the testimony of Skenondogh. But the affidavit supplies the confirmation which some minds require.

That efforts may be again made to tamper with her, and frighten or force her to unsay what she has said, I have no doubt. Indeed, Marcoux had the impertinence, when he heard the nature of the affidavit she had voluntarily made, to carry her a second time to Mr. Fulton, who very properly declined, as he, doubtless, would have done in the first instance, if he could possibly have had the remotest conception of the iniquity intended to be perpetrated, to have anything to do with the affair. There stands the affidavit of Mrs. Williams. For once she has spoken freely, and were she now to make a thousand affidavits to the contrary, it could only be imputed to dark acts which shun the light.

The conduct of the Rev. Mr. Marcoux, of St. Regis, in this

blood. The word "iontatewerawi" is used in cases of adoption from one Indian family to another. To crown his rascality, Barron wished to make an affadavit in English implying by *indirect language* that the intention of Mrs. Williams was to assert that Eleazar is her own son. What are you to do with such men? Happily their deception recoils upon themselves.

transaction, is of such a nature, that I cannot trust myself to characterize it as it deserves. The simplest statement of the truth seems to savor of exaggeration. A Christian minister enters a foreign country, bringing with him an aged, and, I may say, dying woman, who stands to him in the sacred relation of a member of his flock—he carries her before a magistrate of that country, places in her hand the word of God, and voluntarily undertakes to act as interpreter of her sentiments, in a matter affecting vitally the reputation and welfare of a citizen of that country, who is, at the same time, her adopted child. It seems impossible to conceive a case in which more solemn demands could be made on a man for fidelity, or more pledges tacitly given by him of adherence to the truth. The office of the ministry, the pastoral relation, the responsible duty of interpreter, the sacred bond subsisting between the maker and the subject of the affidavit, and the delicate position of the citizen of one country availing himself of the magistracy of another, all seem so many guarantees, that if truth could be found anywhere, it would be here. Now, it must be remembered, this clergyman has previously tried in vain to induce this woman to make a certain statement, which she has peremptorily refused to make. She now appears before the magistrate, supposing that she is about to testify to the truth. Taking advantage of her ignorance of all languages but Indian, and relying upon the obscurity of a barbaric tongue to hide from the world his imposture, this clergyman falsely interprets her answers to the magistrate, substitutes wholesale statements, adapted to his own ends, for those which she, in reality makes, then, falsely interprets his interpretation to her, procures her oath to his fabrication, poisons the fountains of truth and justice at their primal and most sacred source, and seeks to send the poor woman into the grave with a sworn lie upon her lips, against the child of her adoption, that he might at once destroy his reputation, and deceive the whole world upon a grave question of history. I think all must admit that this is one of the most high-handed and gratuitous acts of imposition ever practised.

America, a free country! What is there left us of freedom, if foreigners may come into the United States, and, by the lips of others, swear away the characters of our most estimable citizens? There are noble and honorable men and women in the Roman communion. They are infinitely above treachery like this, and will as severely reprobate it as I can do. Nor do I think there will be wanting many persons who will consider the crime perpetrated by this priest, as too great and daring to have been undertaken on individual responsibility, and who will ask what is the natural inference from an act so strangely revolting? No persons would, to gain any ordinary point, run such risks, and the only cause to which it is reasonable to attribute so perfidious a transaction is, that it was felt necessary, at all hazards, to put a stop to investigation, and prevent the truth from flashing on the world. But in this case, as well as in every other in which attempts have been made to concel or pervert facts, the result has been precisely contrary to what was anticipated, and may serve as an additional confirmation of one of the homeliest maxims of proverbial philosophy.

---

## CHAPTER XXI.

### KIN AND KIND.

There remains for me only one unpleasant task, which is, briefly to criticise the remarks upon the history of Mr. Williams, in the Appendix and Notes to a recent edition of the "Redeemed Captive," edited by Dr. Stephen W. Williams. The authority of this gentleman has, by many, been deemed decisive, because a member of the Williams family, and, therefore, *ex naturâ*, acquainted with the subject on which he writes, and competent to give an authoritative opinion upon it. "In the year 1846," he says, "I prepared and wrote a 'Genealogy and History of the Williams Family in America,' which was published in a large-sized duodecimo volume, with plates, in the year 1847." Now, it appears that, in this volume, there is no mention made of the singular incidents relative to Mr. Williams's disputed parentage; although, while compiling it, Dr. Williams saw, conversed, and corresponded with, his supposed kinsman. He did not make, he complains, "the most distant allusion to his royal descent, or to his ever having had an interview with De Joinville. The reader can judge whether, if he believed himself of royal descent, he would not have alluded to the fact."

This is strange reasoning. Does a person always converse with strangers upon subjects nearest to his heart? It is not characteristic of Mr. Williams to obtrude his private concerns on others, and hundreds, within the last year, might have used the same argument, and said Mr. Williams never spoke on the subject—ergo, he has no faith in it. But the reader will say, Dr. Williams and Mr. Williams were not strangers, for, says the Dr., "I have known him since he was quite young,"—from which it is fair to infer an intimate acquaintance. The first time Mr. Williams remembers having seen Dr. Williams was in 1826, when he was not quite a child, and they have met four or five times since. The Dr. himself says, "I had but little knowledge [i. e. hearsay knowledge] of Eleazar's family, beyond his descent from Eunice Williams;" so that unless there be some mystic intuition in blood, I cannot see Dr. Williams has had any more personal advantages than others. But the Dr. is a man of observation, and "he has seen" the skin of Mr. Williams, and therefore "ought to know." "He showed me a scar on his side, which he said was in consequence of a wound he received in the late war with Great Britain. He requested me to examine that scar, for the purpose of determining whether I thought such a wound would be sufficient to entitle him to a pension from

Congress. I do not know how much the color of his skin may have altered since then, under his dress, but at that time it was more the color of an Indian than a white man." Now, inasmuch as the texture and color of the skin cannot change, I am compelled to say that, in this last assertion, Dr. Williams speaks untruly in fact, and refer the reader, who has not himself had an opportunity of personal examination, to the medical certificates. The opinion of a man is worth nothing whose mind is so warped by prejudice as to make such an assertion. The skin of Mr. Williams is peculiarly soft, delicate, and feminine. To the doctor's statement, on this head, I can only oppose a flat denial. But let all this pass.

Mr. Williams made, it seems, certain oral statements to Dr. Williams, which are entirely inconsistent with what he has since said; among them, that his mother was a Frenchwoman. This is an absurdity into which even Mr. Marcoux would not fall. It is well known that Mrs. Williams is almost entirely of Indian blood. Her descent is as follows. Her great-grandmother was a half-breed, and married a Frenchman; their daughter married an Onondaga Indian of full blood, and their child, her mother, did the same. Mr. Williams never could have said, on such a subject, what is here imputed to him. The doctor's memory is as much at fault as his observation.

We have, then, the following peculiarly strange statement, as coming from Mr. Williams: "He married Miss Mary Jourdan, a distant relative of the King of France, from whom he has been honored with many splendid gifts, among the rest a golden cross and star. He has one son by the name of John." All this, the reader must remember, was inserted by the Dr. in the genealogy of the Williams family, as having been told him, in conversation, by Mr. Williams. But there was another remarkable piece of intelligence, which, in the original text, follows the word John, and which our author had the prudence to omit in the Appendix and Notes, lest it should reveal the worth and character of his other reminiscences—"He has a son John, born ——, now (1846) on a visit to the King of France, by his request." Most veracious historian, and faithful chronicler of table-talk! And Mr. Williams told you, actually, his son was, in the year 1846, in France, on a visit to Louis Philippe? Yes, sir, he told it you in the same breath he told you his wife was a relative of the King of France, and the King had sent him a cross and star, but that breath never proceeded from his lips. John Williams has never been out of America. You knew so little of Mr. Williams's personal history, you could not tell when his son was born, but you were very sure that, then, when you were writing, 1846, he was in France.

But Dr. Williams contradicts himself in a manner which shows how little reliance can be placed on any of his recollections. On p. 174, we are told by him, Mr. Williams never made the "*most distant allusion*" to "his ever having had an interview with the Prince de Joinville;" and lo! on p. 177 we read, "*He frequently told me and my family that this visit from the Prince was in consequence of his relationship to his wife*, and that he received his presents from the same cause. His stories here were much at variance with those in the magazine." I wonder with what Dr. Williams's stories are at variance.

Still there remains another difficulty. Mr. Williams wrote to the Doctor several times, speaking of members of the Williams family as his relatives, and this, we are told, is conclusive evidence of the falsehood of all his statements respecting the Prince de Joinville. Here, I will let Mr. Williams speak for himself, in words with which you are already familiar.

"NEW YORK, *September* 12, 1853.

"TO DR. S. W. WILLIAMS.

"SIR:—Your recent edition of the Redeemed Captive was only yesterday put into my hands, by a friend. In it I perceive a note in especial relation to myself. I must express my astonishment, that before you took the liberty of thus using my name, you did not inform me of your intention, or, at any rate, that you did not have the courtesy to send me a copy of the work, on its publication, that I might have an opportunity of immediately defending myself against your assault on my reputation, and which I am constrained to say, exhibits as little of the feeling of a kinsman, as it does of the candor and truthfulness of a gentleman. Nothing on my part, that I am aware of, in our intercourse, can justify the malicious spirit displayed by you. You are pleased to call me "a distinguished gentleman," at the same time you stoop to every artifice which meanness can dictate to injure me in the public estimation. It is most true that in letters, as well as in conversation, I spoke of myself to you, as well as to others, after my interview with the Prince de Joinville, as a member of the Williams family—for the habits and feelings of a lifetime are not to be shaken off in an hour. I did so precisely in the same manner that I still continue to call myself Eleazar Williams, and to speak of Mrs. Mary Ann Williams, of St. Regis, as my mother, though she has given a solemn affidavit to the contrary. Besides which, at the time of which you speak, I had not had the opportunity of giving the subject the attention which I have since done. I had nothing but the revelation of the Prince de Joinville to depend on, and, as I had no intention of assuming the public position, in this affair, into which I have been forced through circumstances, I did not consider it necessary to thrust the question of my foreign extraction into a genealogical account of the Williams family. There were also feelings of delicacy towards that family, and an unwillingness to rupture ties which to me were so endearing, which kept me longer silent than I should otherwise have been. All generous and candid minds will, I think, appreciate the difficulties of my position, and not impute to deception what was the result of the uncertainty respecting my own history, and feelings of affection for those who had treated me so kindly, and for whom I can never cease to entertain the regard of a kinsman. In respect to other matters, you have grossly misunderstood and misrepresented me. The thought of my wife's being a relative of the King of France never entered into my mind. As her name indicates, I spoke of her, to you, as a supposed member of the family of Marshal Jourdan, which I believe to be the case. As to my mother, or rather, if I must be precise, Mrs. Mary Ann Williams, being a French woman, that I never could have said, for she is more, at least, than three-fourths an Indian, in blood, and has every outward indication of her race. She can speak no language but the Mohawk. As to the cross and star, there are such things in my possession, but I received them from the Indian family of which I supposed myself a member. You have, in these and other respects, utterly misconstrued what passed between us in conversation, and imputed your misconception to me. Unless I am greatly mistaken, you make me say, in your genealogical work, that my son had gone to France for an education, which is an absurdity of which I never could have been guilty. In short, my dear sir, it is not every person who is competent to report, truthfully, the substance of a familiar conversation, and you seem to be among those who cannot. What I have written, I am ready to acknowledge, but you must pardon me if I demur against pleading guilty to your confused recollections and misstatements. It is with deep regret that I have felt compelled to speak thus to one whom I formerly respected and esteemed, but you have, by your own misconduct, forced me to it.

"I am, sir, you obedient servant,

"ELEAZAR WILLIAMS.

"DR. STEPHEN W. WILLIAMS,

"Deerfield."

The statement of Dr. Lothrop I have elsewhere disposed of. The opinion of the late Gov. Williams, of Vermont, as to Mr. Williams's age, is to be estimated by his own account, "although I cannot fix upon any particular data, yet my impression is the same as yours, that he was born in 1790." The reader has had "particular data" enough to arrive at a very different opinion. Gov. Williams, in fact, knew nothing about the subject, he had not examined into it, nor thought upon it; and I cannot understand that the mere fact of a person's name being Williams renders him any more competent a judge on this point than others.

"Such," says Dr. Williams, "is some of the evidence to show that the Dauphin, if living, cannot be Eleazar Williams." I should rather say, such is some of the evidence to show that Dr. Stephen W. Williams has been writing on a subject he does not understand.

But the doctor next favors us with some of his historical

learning, and proceeds to show "by *direct* and *positive* evidence," that the Dauphin is actually dead. The italics are his own, and his idea of direct and positive evidence is illustrated by this list of authorities, which is as follows: "Thiers, Alison, Scott, the 'Debats,' a French Journal, devoted to the interest of the Orleans dynasty,' the 'Encyclopedia Americana,' 'Abbot's History of Marie Antoniette,' and *Putnam's Magazine*." Though in justice I will add, that he also brings in the 'Memoirs of the Duchess D'Angoulême,' which speaks of "three respectable surgeons testifying to his death." I trust the reader will not suppose that I have so long allowed "The Notes and Appendix" of Dr. Williams, to wander about the world, and be quoted, in discerning journals, as conclusive authority, because I felt any difficulty in answering his random assertions and inconclusive reasoning, but simply because I did not deem what he said deserving of notice, and was quite willing to bide the time when I could exhibit his facts and arguments in their proper light. If I have spoken with severity, it is because there is an evident desire throughout the whole of Dr. Williams's remarks, to injure his former acquaintance, and the manifestation, in a more unkind shape, of the feeling which prompted another member of the family to say he would never have shown him the attention he did, had he imagined he was not the descendant of Eunice Williams, but only the son of Louis XVI. Family pride and affection are things to be honored, but they become despicable, when they make us spiteful and unjust. Those members of the Williams family, who have known most of Mr. Williams, confide in, respect, and love him.

## CHAPTER XXII.

### CONCLUSION.

I HAVE now gone over the proposed ground, and presented everything in my possession, that can aid in the formation of opinion on the point discussed. It remains, briefly, to indicate the general bearing of facts and probabilities. But I have endeavored so to arrange my materials, that the reader, who has accompanied me through the preceding pages, will scarcely need any formal summing up of evidence.

There are before us two great bodies of fact and testimony—one proceeding from Europe, and, in a great measure, long since familiar to the public, who were, however, destitute of that clue to its meaning and connection, which a single fact alone can give—the other, recently rising to view, in this country.

The first proves that Louis XVII. did not die in the Temple, in the year 1795.

The second proves the exceedingly high probability, approaching, if it does not attain to moral certainty, that Louis XVII. now lives in the person of the Rev. Eleazar Williams.

I purposely assume a moderate position, in respect to my conclusion. My own belief in the identity is firm. But knowing the fallibility of human testimony and circumstantial evidence, I place myself on strong, because safe ground, and say, what all reasonable persons will, I think, concede, that the evidence adduced carries probability to nearly its highest extent. If any one shall say it makes the fact certain, he will find no opponent in me. I believe it does.

As the subject at first stood, there was a balance of probabilities against the identity. I met an entire stranger, who told me a marvellous story, hovering on the shadowy verge of possibility. He had the appearance of simple, unpretending sincerity, but had no means of substantiating his statements. He declared certain facts, of which he had been an eye and ear witness, but how these would tally with history he had no idea, or a vague one. According to the sage maxims of some, I should have dismissed my new acquaintance as a monomaniac or a fabricator. But I had been taught, since infancy, to regard faith in testimony as the principle of power, to prove all things, and to hold fast that which is good. Reserving in suspense, my ultimate judgment, I was willing to trust one who seemed trustworthy, till he proved himself the contrary; because, although it was more improbable that a person regarded by the world, for more than fifty years, as an Indian, should, in childhood, have been king of France, than that a clergyman should invent, there was a redeeming moral probability, in favor of his truthfulness, not lightly to be set aside. I remembered who had told me to judge not by the appearance, but to judge righteous judgment, and who was rejected by those who transgressed the rule. The very improbability of what Mr. Williams said, was, in one point of view a primâ facie argument in his favor, since it was not likely that a sane and sensible man, the member of an honorable profession, a minister of the Church of Christ, would risk all, in this life and the next, on untruths which would not bear a moment's serious examination. I believed in the power of a fact to vindicate its own truth, and reasoned, if this were a fact, it must have left a pathway all along, which, though obscured by ten thousand cross tracks, would become evident, on examination; and that opposition and discussion would only aid in the development of truth. The result is before the reader. I claim, in this volume, to have adduced evidence which reverses the first position of things, and to have thrown the overwhelming balance of probabilities in favor of the identity of Louis XVII. and the Rev. Eleazar Williams.

How far these probabilities fall short of historic certainty, a brief summary of the evidence will show. To repeat conclusions, in conjunction, which have already been stated separately is here inevitable.

I. The great fundamental fact that, Louis XVII. did not die in the Temple, on the 8th June, 1795, has been proved by an accumulation of evidence, which would compel the assent of any impartial jury. Those who assert the fact of death, deprive themselves of the benefit of any alternative. Their position is the strongest possible, if sustained, because it expresses no uncertainty; and, indeed, nothing short of this would have availed them. They say, he died at a particular time and place, and, pointing to a certain dead body, declare it was his. Disprove the last assertion—and they have nothing more to produce. The witnesses they cite, are, 1, four physicians, and, 2, two jailers. The physicians testify they know nothing about the matter. They saw a dead body, but were entirely ignorant whose it was. The jailers stand convicted of gross falsehood, in regard to an asserted fact necessary to the truth of their testimony, and no jury would, therefore, believe them on oath. There is, thus, no evidence to prove the death of Louis XVII., but that of two men convicted of falsehood.

On the other hand, it has been shown,

1. That it is physically impossible the body, described in the procès verbal, could be that of Louis XVII.: and,

2. That the police records of June, 1795, prove he was removed from prison before the 8th of that month.

So far the naked fact. In explanation of it, the history of France shows that, prior to the French Revolution, the Count de Provence was plotting to obtain the throne, and anxious to supplant his unfortunate brother; that to obtain this end, he fomented the troubles in the kingdom with the hope of forcing Louis XVI. to abdication; that, the king and queen distrusted him, on account of his unprincipled ambition, and abstained, at their death, from committing their children to his care; that, after usurping the nominal regency of the kingdom, the Count de

Provence attempted, by means of intriguing agents, to obtain the sovereign power, and corresponded with the most extreme of the revolutionary leaders; that having pledged himself, in a proclamation, to release Louis XVII. from the Temple, there is evidence he found means, through his agents, to surround the imprisoned Prince with persons devoted to his own interests, who, with the probable connivance of members of the Republican Government, took advantage of a treaty made by the Convention with Charette, the Vendéean leader, in which it was stipulated, Louis XVII. should be delivered to him, on the 13th June, 1795, to remove him from the Temple, and circulate the report of his death, having adroitly substituted a dying child in his stead.

II. The series of facts next in order are those which intimate, or prove, that the royal family of France were cognisant of the existence of the youthful king, viz.:—

1. The confession of the Duchess D'Angoulême, to the wife of the secretary of the Count D'Artois, in 1807, that she knew her brother was alive, and in America.

2. The contradictions and inconsistencies attending the funeral solemnities for the departed Bourbons, on the Restoration; the omission of any respect to the memory of Louis XVII., made only more glaringly evident by the decree to erect a monument to him, and the actual preparation of an epitaph, under the orders of Louis XVIII; and, also, the rejection by the royal family, of the asserted heart of Louis XVII., in the possession of Peletan.

3. The strange conduct of the Duchess D'Angoulême, in respect to the pretenders, and especially Herr Naundorff.

The list might be extended, but these are here sufficient.

III. We come, now, to the circumstances which, historically, project from the transactions in Europe to serve as means of future identification. These are often very trivial and minute, when viewed separately, but, in combination, they acquire an irresistible cogency, if it be found they all centre on some one individual, no matter in what part of the world he may be found.

1. The individual last known to have been with Louis XVII. in the Temple was named Bellanger, and was a confidant and creature of Louis XVIII.; and, it seems evident that, if the Prince were removed from the Temple, as it is proved he was, Bellanger, from his official position as acting commissary, which gave him, for the time being, supreme command in the prison, must have been the chief agent in the affair.

2. Louis XVII., at the time of his removal from the Tower, was in a state of imbecility, bordering on idiocy.

3. He had on his person the following marks, 1. A scar over the eyebrow, from a blow inflicted by Simon. 2. Tumors on both elbows. 3. Tumors on both wrists. 4. Tumors on both knees. 5. Inoculation marks on his arm, one of which was in the form of a crescent. Besides which, there were natural peculiarities not to be overlooked. 1. He strongly resembled the rest of his family in the general formation of the head, ear, jaw, chin, and mouth, but had hazel eyes, and a nose approaching to what is called the nez retroussé, which, as life advanced, would, probably, develope into a straighter shape, but could never acquire the aquiline form observable in the features of the Regent Orleans, Louis XVI., or even Louis XVIII.

4. It was intimated by Herr Naundorff that, besides Mr. B., probably M. Bellanger, there was engaged in the removal of the Prince from France, a lady of the court, formerly in the service of Marie Antoinette, and also that the destination of the Prince was America.

5. The time of action was 1795, when the Dauphin was ten years of age.

IV. And, now, let us examine the corresponding circumstances which tend to identify the Rev. Eleazar Williams with the royal child.

1. In the year 1795, a French lady and gentleman, the former of whom had been in the service of Marie Antoinette, came to Albany, having lately arrived from France, bringing with them a girl and a

little boy, the latter of whom was called Monsieur Louis, was about ten years of age, and was characterized by the same listlessness and lack of observation recorded of Louis XVII., and resembled, in the form of his head and face, the Rev. Eleazar Williams, and concerning whom much mystery was observed. The party suddenly disappeared.

2. In the year 1795, two Frenchmen, one of whom appeared to be a Romish priest, carried an imbecile French boy to Lake George, and left him with Thomas Williams, which boy, on the oath of a credible witness, present at the time, and who has known him in after life, is the Eleazar Williams.

3. His reputed mother acknowledges she adopted him.

4. Eleazar Williams recovered his mind by a fall into Lake George, since which his memory is perfect—but the images which come to him from his previous life, tally with the events of the Dauphin's history. His condition of mind, his absence of distinct memory of his childhood, are proved on respectable testimony.

5. He has *all* the natural characteristics, and *all* the accidental marks, necessary to identity with Louis XVII.

6. Money was sent from France to a merchant in Albany, and was expended on his behalf.

7. Nathaniel Ely, who had charge of his education, was acquainted with the fact, that he was of noble birth.

8. The rapid development of his mind indicates previous culture.

9. His condition of health, from boyhood to the present time, constantly wavering between robust vigor and excessive prostration, accompanied with pains in the head and side, indicate that a constitution originally strong, received, at some time, a great shock, but which is anterior to anything which happened to him in this country.

10. The mental and moral characteristics exhibited by him throughout life, the fertility of resource and military genius, which developed without culture and seemed innate, the generous ardor of his disposition, his religious feelings, his untiring labors for the

benefit of others, his absence of pecuniary tact and management, his ignorance even of his own powers, his gentle and forgiving character, and the very want of balance and symmetry in his mind, all agree, in combination with the best characteristics of the Bourbons, with what we know from history of the natural disposition of the Prince, and with what it is natural to expect would be the character, the power, and the weakness of one whose birth, sufferings, and entire history are such as those of Louis XVII. and Eleazar Williams in continuous unity of existence.

11. The wife of the secretary of the Count D'Artois, not only heard the confession of the Duchess D'Angoulême that her brother was alive in America, but also learned, in the Royal family, that Bellanger brought him to this country, and that he was known in America as Eleazar Williams, an Indian missionary; and it is on oath that she made, in substance these statements, in New Orleans, prior to the visit of the Prince de Joinville to this country in 1841.

12. The Rev. Eleazar Williams did become acquainted, in 1848, with the fact that Bellanger brought the Dauphin to this country, and that he was asserted by Bellanger to be the Dauphin four years before he, or any other man on the continent of America, not in the secret, knew there was an historic personage named Bellanger, who could be suspected of kidnapping the Dauphin, or was in any way connected with him in the Temple.

To these I might add other particulars, but those enumerated suffice for my purpose.

V. I proceed now to the series of facts connected with the intercourse between the Prince de Joinville and the Rev. Eleazar Williams.

1. The Prince de Joinville came to the United States in 1838, and leaving his ships at Newport, went on a secret expedition into the interior of the country.

2. Immediately after the return of the Prince to France, inquiries were made of the French vice-consul in Newport, concerning two servants of Marie Antoinette, who came to America during the French revolution.

3. The Prince de Joinville, on his return to America in 1841, inquired earnestly of many persons, and in divers places, concerning the Rev. Eleazar Williams, asking questions about him which cannot be resolved into anxiety to find one who could give him historic information, with which there is nothing in their intercourse that tallies, except what bears on its face the appearance of deception, a covert and blind to other designs; he caused word to be transmitted to him that he desired to see him; on meeting him he manifested agitation and surprise, and exhibited, in public, excessive deference beyond the requirements and the practice of ordinary politeness—even French politeness; he corresponded with him by name through his secretaries for several years, personally recommended to Louis Philippe a petition transmitted by Mr. Williams, from a Roman Catholic chief, and thus, *long before* and *long after* their interview, was well acquained with his name.

4. In the face of these facts, the Prince de Joinville represents his meeting with Mr. Williams to have been accidental, and denies he even remembered his name.

5. Mr. Williams, on the other hand, asserts that, at the interview, sought and solicited by the Prince, the latter communicated to him the secret of his birth, and demanded a resignation of right to the French throne in favor of Louis Philippe. In respect to this assertion, every syllable in this volume which renders it probable that he is Louis XVII., supports his credibility, while at the same time it discredits the affirmation of the Prince.

6. One of the officers of the Prince de Joinville confessed to Mr. Geo. Sumner the mystery attending the expedition to Green Bay, and that Mr. Williams was spoken of as the son of Louis XVI.

7. There is in the political circumstances of the times, the relative position of Louis Philippe to the Royalists and other parties in France, and his suicidal, albeit, compulsory folly in bringing the remains of Napoleon to France, everything to render it not improbable that, on the discovery of the secret of the existence of Louis XVII., he would adopt the course which Mr. Williams asserts he did.

VI. In the next place, let me group together some few of the reasons for confiding in the statements of Mr. Williams.

1. It is proved, that since the year 1803, or at the latest, 1804, he has been in the habit, with more or less regularity, of keeping a journal.

2. In his journal for 1841, occurs a full and minute account, which bears every mark of having been written at the time, of his interview with the Prince together with all that led to, and followed it—which account has not been made public by his instrumentality, although with his consent—and, in fact, has only been brought to light by a series of seeming accidents.

3. The history of his life exhibits him, as a man whose word can be depended on, if we are to depend on the word of any one. It will take much, I think, to make the world believe that the gallant soldier, and the laborious self-denying missionary, could, without aim or purpose, have contrived a story so foul and dishonorable, if false, and in the absence, too, of any knowledge how it could be sustained.

VII. A strong argument may also be drawn, in his favor, from the signal failure which has attended every effort to discredit his assertions. It matters not from what quarter the opposition has proceeded, or what have been the authorities cited. It is not difficult, we think, to dispose alike of Beauchesne, Lasne, Gomin, Naundorff, Richemont, the Prince de Joinville, General Cass, the Rev. Mr. Marcoux, and Dr. Stephen Williams, while there has not been, in all the pages of argument, ridicule, and abuse, heaped on Mr. Williams and his friends, one single word which has not fallen to the ground harmless, as it respects the issue really involved.

VIII. Nor is it unworthy of remark, in this brief resumé of the evidence, that the agency of some, at least, of the Romish priesthood, which may be traced from the beginning in this affair, comes in at last, with a puerile effort in the shape of forgery, to prevent the truth from coming to light, and thus, providentially, affords the crowning confirmation. I have spoken severely of this act of wickedness, but not one half as severely as it deserves, for if such things are tolerated in this country, religion is dishonored, law is a farce, liberty a name, and reputation the prey of every defamer.

No outline of the evidence, in this case, can do justice to it, as it stands in its living force and freshness, and if any one shall chance to open the volume at its termination, to see what has been accomplished, I must refer him to the foregoing pages for information. But rapid as has been the accumulation of evidence on this subject, I should not be surprised to find that it increases in every direction. The stores of Europe remain yet untouched. It is not too late to recover everything which relates to this transaction. I am much inclined to think that Talleyrand was fully conversant with the whole. We have seen that, when in this country, he was in communication with old Jacob Vanderheyden, an Indian trader, who was present at the time that Mr. Williams was left among the Indians; and it is not too much to hope that, when the period comes, for the opening of his Memoirs, the whole facts relative to the removal of Louis XVII. may come to light.

The saddest thought, to my mind, connected with the whole of this dark historic drama, which convicts of crime and perfidy so many who have stood high in name and power, is that the sister knew the brother's doom. And yet, I would not speak or think harshly of the Duchess of Angoulême. She was the victim of the unnatural and abhorrent villainy of Louis XVIII, and was entrapped, ere she was aware, in the meshes of a dark web of subtle fraud, from which she could not, throughout life, escape. At first, she was taught to believe her brother dead, and, before she knew the contrary, found herself the wife of him to whom the crown would, in all human probability, ultimately fall, in consequence of the removal of Louis XVII. from France. And when the fact did come to her knowledge, she, doubtless, had no idea of the ultimate designs of her uncle, but regarded the exiled child as placed in security till the political storm was entirely over. In this frame of mind she could speak to one who enjoyed her confidence with pleasure of her conviction of his safety, and cherish the hope that in brighter days they would be again united. It is not difficult to picture the conflict of feeling which would rise in her mind, when the overthrow of Napoleon brought again the crown of France within reach of the House of Bourbon, nor the subtle arguments used by the uncle, who had the authority of a father, to prove how expedient it was for the welfare of all, for the happiness of France, for the repose of Europe, for the prevention of such scenes of blood as 1793 exhibited, that the Gallic crown should be placed on the brow of one competent to govern. What a contrast could be drawn between the mature statesman, educated in the midst of courts, acquainted with every avenue of diplomacy, and all the reciprocally balancing powers of which Europe is composed, and the half-barbaric boy, ignorant of French language and habits, ignorant of political life, ministering to savages in a western wilderness, and above all, a Protestant. It would be said, and said, too, with much appearance of reason, that to place such an individual on the throne of France, in 1814, would be to ensure a relapse into anarchy; that he could only be a mere tool of others; that he could, for a long time, have no opinion of his own; and, in the old cant phrase of the proclamation, of 1795, "France needed a father," and not a monarch in leading-strings. The heir presumptive to the throne stood by her side as a husband; and could she for so dubious a benefit as a crown, which had proved to her father an instrument of death, recall from rustic happiness and security, one who *suffered* no wrong, because not *conscious* of any, while she endangered the welfare, and sacrificed the interests of all she loved, and prepared for France and Europe, just resting after their long convulsion, an endless succession of those evils which accompany weakness and misrule? All this she could understand and submit to—but conceive her feelings and her indignation when requested to receive the dried heart of her wronged and exiled brother; or admire the chaste harmony of the epitaph, which, in strains of Augustan elegance, spoke of the forlorn boy as travelling starlike in the heavens, and from his pathway of eternal light, gazing with calm eye of angel love, on the affectionate uncle who had swindled him out of empire, and, in return, would exalt, while living, into the paper paradise of Rome, the Protestant who would certainly be excluded from it when dead.

It is said, the duchess never smiled, but went through life and to the tomb, bowed down by some deep-seated and mysterious sorrow. Many a night may she have spent, like that so graphically described by the Viscountess Chateaubriand, pacing her apartment in restless agony, unable to lay her perturbed spirit, and writhing, amid the splendors of royalty, in inward humiliation and self-upbraiding sorrow. Yes, the sister was the victim of the ambition of others and more to be pitied in her titled desolation than the hardy man, toiling on a far strand in the dusty thoroughfare of common life, but still able to breast with honest heart the crush and variation of the crowd, and lift to heaven a trusting eye. As for those whose ambition demanded of a weak woman's heart this costly sacrifice, verily they had their reward. On no page of history are the stern retributive workings of Providence more legibly inscribed than on that which chronicles the history of the Bourbons since the first French Revolution. The curse of impotence has rested on all they essayed to do. No sooner were they lifted, on the tide of events, towards an apparently stable throne, than they were dashed back again, and engulfed in the abyss from which they had emerged. Reiterated exiles, agitations, assassinations, tracked their career. Life, with them, was all unreal. In their proudest days they were but crowned brigands. Distrust, suspicion, felon fear, pursued them till the last. In vain was the cry of legitimacy raised to support that which was illegitimate. In vain did monarchical Europe rally, to ensure to them a throne, which they had neither wisdom to preserve, nor courage to defend. Their's was "a barren sceptre,"

> "Wrenched from their grasp by an unlineal hand
> No son of theirs succeeding,"

and be it fiction or be it fact, the prophecy of the letter read by the midnight lamp, shall be fulfilled to its final punctuation, and on their dynasty, their name, their lineage, and their memory shall be stamped with livid hand—"Death!!!"

A word before I conclude, with respect to the position of Mr. Williams. On his part there is no claim and no pretension. The last thought in his mind is that of political elevation. Educated in a republican country, he is himself a republican in sentiment and feeling. A minister of the Protestant Episcopal Church, he has no wish but to labor in her fold and worship at her altar until death. Devoted to the regeneration of the Indian, his chief earthly hope is to rear among those formerly reputed his countrymen, a temple to the name of the Almighty God, which shall be at once a means in future years of recalling them from their ignorance and vice, and a monument of his love and sacrifices for them. He is now rapidly approaching that period of life when the ambitions and the interests of earth are of little avail. Had he known all he now does, thirty or even twenty years earlier, the case might have been different. If at times thoughts and aspirations of a different character have entered his mind, he has now dismissed them; and to go down to a Christian's grave in peace, usefulness, and honor, is all he wishes for himself, and all his friends wish for him.

His late years have been embittered by many sorrows, and especially by the knowledge of his early history, and having been myself the means of dragging him into an unpleasant notoriety, I have deemed it my duty to do what lay within the power of an unpractised pen, to vindicate him from assaults.

To the eye of a cold philosophy, kings and the sons of kings, are much like other men—but few of us are philosophers, and God forbid we should be, if it would deprive of sympathy for the fallen. If I read any truth in history it is, that the hand of God is there, guiding the motions of the vast machine of human destiny, and making kings and rulers, and great men, statesmen, orators and poets, the agents for accomplishing his all-wise designs, nor can I, from the loop-holes of republican retreat, gaze with cynical eye upon the centuries that are fled, nor on the realms that are afar. The blood of a Bourbon or a Guelph may be composed of much the same ingredients as my own—but I recognise in it a something which the Providence of God has sanctified through many generations, and I confess to the weakness of dropping a tear at the thought of the forlorn descendant of European kings, ministering, on the desolate outskirts of civilization, to the scanty remnant of a race, once the barbaric sovereigns of this continent. But God, who deals equally with all, has, doubtless, granted to him as much happiness in the toils of missionary life, as to those who have successively occupied the throne of his fathers.

"Stemmata quid faciunt? quid prodest, Pontice, longo
Sanguine censeri, pictosque ostendere vultus
Majorum, et stantes in curribus Æmilianos,
* * * * Nulla aconita bibuntur
Fictilibus: tunc illa time, quum pocula sumes
Gemmata et lato Setinum ardebit in auro.'

What boots it to be deemed of regal birth
And reckon ancestors in endless line,
Warriors enthroned, bright damės and steel clad knights?
* * * * * *
No aconite is drank in cups of earth;
Then may you fear it when your fingers clasp,
A jewelled goblet and the Setine wine,
Sparkles in ample gold.

# APPENDIX.

[Appendix A.—*Page* 31.]

*Asserted Correspondence of the Count de Provence.*

Note by the Hon. and Rev. G. C. Percival, accompanying the asserted letters of Louis XVIII. to the Duke Fitz-James, and the Count D'Artois.

The letters professedly written by the Count de Provence, afterwards Louis XVIII., are of so atrociously wicked a character, so calculated to blacken his memory for ever, and, what is more startling, that of Charles X., that the editor would gladly have avoided being the instrument of increasing their publicity. The French editor is not only perfectly satisfied of their authenticity, but maintains that he could prove it incontestibly in a court of justice. Unfortunately, there was a time when the princes of the blood royal were not the best friends of Louis XVI. and his queen; and the Count de Provence, at the beginning of the Revolution, proved himself anything but what he ought to have been.

---

LETTERS FROM THE COUNT DE PROVENCE.

*To the Duke Fitz-James.*

Versailles, *May* 13, 1787.

Here is, my dear duke, the Assembly of Notables drawing to its close, and yet the great question has not been touched upon. You cannot doubt that the Notables will not hesitate to believe, from the documents which you sent them, more than six weeks ago, that the king's children are not his own. These papers give the clearest proofs of the queen's guilty conduct. You are a subject too much attached to the blood of your sovereign, not to blush at bowing before these adulterous fruits. I shall be absent, but my brother, D'Artois, whose committee does not hold its sitting, will preside in my place. The fact in question once averred, it is easy to infer the consequences. The parliament, which dislikes the queen, will not make any great difficulty; but, if it should have the fancy to raise any, we have the means of bringing it to reason. In short, we must attempt the blow.

LOUIS STANISLAUS XAVIER.

---

*To the Count D'Artois.*

It is done, my brother, *the blow is struck.* I hold in my hand the official news of the death of the unfortunate Louis XVI., and have only time to forward it to you. I am informed, also, that his son is dying. You will not forget how useful to the state their death will be. Let this reflection console you, and remember that the Grand Prior, your son, is, after me, the hope and heir of the monarchy.

LOUIS STANISLAUS XAVIER.—

*Percival, page* 147.

---

[APPENDIX B.—*Page* 120.]

A new and most extraordinary interest has begun to invest his tragical story in this very month of April, 1853; at least, it is now first brought before universal christendom. In the monthly journal of Putnam (published in New York), the number for April contains a most interesting memoir upon the subject, signed J. H. HANSON. Naturally, it indisposed most readers to put faith in any fresh pretensions of this nature, that, at least, one false Dauphin had been pronounced such, by so undeniable a judge as the Duchesse D'Angoulême. Meantime, it is made probable enough, by Mr. Hanson, that the true Dauphin did not die, in the year 1795, at the Temple, but was personated by a boy unknown; that two separate parties had an equal interest in sustaining this fraud, and did sustain it; but one would hesitate to believe whether, at the price of murdering a celebrated physician; that they had the Prince conveyed secretly to an Indian settlement in Lower Canada, as a situation in which French, being the prevailing language, would attract no attention, as it must have done in most parts of North America; that the boy was educated and trained as a missionary clergyman; and, finally, that he is now acting in that capacity, under the name of Eleazar Williams, perfectly aware of the royal pretensions put forward on his behalf, but equally, through age (being about sixty-nine) and through absorption in spiritual views, indifferent to these pretensions. It is admitted, on all hands, that the Prince de Joinville had an interview with Eleazar Williams, a dozen years since; the Prince alleges, through mere accident, but this seems improbable; and Mr. Hanson is likely to be right in supposing this visit to have been a preconcerted one, growing out of some anxiety to test the reports current, so far as they were grounded upon resemblances in Mr. Williams's features to those of the Bourbon and Austrian families. The most pathetic fact is that of the idiocy common to the Dauphin and Mr. Eleazar Williams. It is clear, from all the most authentic accounts of the young prince, that idiocy was, in reality, stealing over him; due, doubtless, to the *stunning* nature of the calamities that overwhelmed his family; to the removal from him, by tragical deaths, in so rapid a succession, of the Princess de Lamballe, of his aunt, of his father, of his mother, and others whom he most had loved; to his cruel separation from his sister; and to the astounding (for him naturally incomprehensible) change that had come over the demeanor and the language of nearly all the people placed about the persons of himself and his family. An idiocy resulting from what must have seemed a causeless and demoniac conspiracy, would be more likely to melt away under the sudden transfer to kindness, and the gaiety of forest life, than any idiocy belonging to original organic imbecility. Mr. Williams describes his own confusion of mind as continuing up to his fourteenth year, and all things which had happened, in earlier years, as gleaming through clouds of oblivion, and as painfully perplexing; but, otherwise, he shows no desire to strengthen the pretensions made for himself, by any reminiscences piercing these clouds, that could point specially to France, or to royal experiences.—*Thomas de Quincey's Autobiographical Sketches*, vol. i. p. 330.

---

[APPENDIX C.—*Page* 120.]

*Declaration of the Death of Louis XVII.*

Section of the Temple, year 3 of the French Republic, 22d Prairial, decease of Louis Charles Capet, aged ten years and two months, profession ——, resident at Paris, in the Tower of the Temple, son of Louis Capet, last King of the French, and of Marie Antoinette, of Austria. The deceased was born at Versailles, and died the day before yesterday, at three o'clock in the afternoon. On the requisition made to us, within the twenty-four hours, by Etienne Lasne, aged thirty-nine, profession ——, resident at Paris, Rue et Maison des Droits de l'homme, No. 41, such declarant calling himself keeper of the children of Capet, and by Baptiste Gomin, thirty-five, profession, French citizen, resident at Paris, Rue de la Fraternité, No. 39, such declarant calling himself Commissary of the Convention for the Guard of the Temple, the present declaration has been received in presence of the citizens Nicola Lawrence Arnoult, and Dominique Goddet, Civic Commissaries of the Section du Temple, in terms of the decree of the Committee of General Safety, and who have signed with us.

LASNE, ARNOULT,
GODDET, GOMIN,
*Commissaries.*

Verified according to the Law of the 10th December, by me, commissary of police of the said section. DUSSER.

As Beauchesne has produced nothing more pertinent in the way of proof than this, he might have spared himself the trouble of twenty years composition, and printed the original certificate of Lasne and Gomin on a thousand consecutive pages.

---

APPENDIX D.—*Page* 176.

*Albany*, 7 *Oct.*, 1853.

SIR.—If the following remarks are considered of importance in the investigation you are prosecuting respecting the history of Monsieur Eleazar Williams, you are at perfect liberty to make use of them as you please.

Among the reminiscences of early days, I have always recollected with much interest being taken by my mother to visit a family who arrived here in 1795, direct from France, consisting of four individuals. There was a gentleman and lady, called Monsieur and Madame de Jardin. They had with them two children, a girl and a boy—the girl was the eldest—the boy about nine or ten. He apparently did not notice us.

Their arrival caused considerable excitement in our city, and those ladies who could converse in the French language felt it their duty to call on Madame. They were but few in number, and as far as I can recollect are now registered as inhabitants of that world where the events and cares of this cannot interest us any more.

On my first visit I was much struck with the appearance of the family. A gentleman was in the hall. He showed us into the parlor, but did not enter with us. His dress was very plain, and as I never saw him except at that time, I could never realize how he was connected with the family.

We were received with politeness by Madame. She was imposing and agreeable in her language and appearance, had large dark-colored eyes, and every way evinced a great desire to welcome us. After a short interview, she took me to a room up-stairs with shelves on one side of the wall, and containing a number of handsome books, many of which had elegant prints. On a table were jointed cards and other articles for amusement, and there were in the room two pussey cats full of frolic.

I was here introduced to Mademoiselle Louisa and Monsieur Louis.

Mademoise e and I played together, but Monsieur Louis did not join us. He was dressed in shorts, and amused himself, at some distance from us, in balancing himself over a cane or something in that way. Madame told my mother that she was maid of honor to the Queen Marie Antoinette, and was separated from her on the terrace at the palace. She appeared very much agitated, and mentioned many things which I was too young to understand, but all in allusion to the difficulties then agitating France, and her friends. She played with great skill on the piano forte, and was much excited singing the Marseilles Hymn, floods of tears chasing each other down her cheeks. My mother thought the children were those belonging to the crown, but I do not now recollect that she said Madame told her so. After some time, Madame called and said they were obliged to leave us, and had many useful and handsome articles to dispose of, and wished my mother to have the first choice out of them.

There were several large plates of mirror glass, a time-piece, a pair of gilt andirons representing lions, and a bowl, said to be gold, on which were engraven the arms of France. I have heard it spoken of some time after; and it was said to belong to some gentleman near Albany, and was recognised at a dinner party, with celery on the table.

The andirons were purchased by Gen. Peter Gansevoort's lady, and are still belonging to a member of that family.

We never heard of this family after they left Albany. In looking at the features of Eleazar Williams I think I can discover considerable likeness to those of the young Monsieur Louis in charge of Madame de Jardin.

Blendusia Dudley.

Rev. J. H. Hanson.

---

[Appendix E. No. 1.—*Page* 177.]

*Affidavit of John O'Brien.*

John O'Brien, a half-breed Indian, otherwise known as Skenondough, deposes and says, that he resides in the town of Salina, Onondaga county, State of New York, that he is known to the Hon. P. Sken Smith, of Philadelphia, and to Gerrit Smith, Squire Johnson, Mayor Baldwin, and Lawyer Wood, of Syracuse; that he is now directly from Philadelphia, where he was taken sick, on his way to Washington, and is returning to Salina; that he is now very aged, having been born in Stockbridge, Mass., in 1752; that his father was an Irishman, of the name of William O'Brien, and his mother an Indian woman, of the Oneida tribe, named Mary Skenondough; that, at the age of twelve years, he was sent from America to France, for his education, and remained there until during the War of the Revolution, when he returned, in the same ship with Lafayette, to America. After his return, this deponent went among the Oneida Indians in the State of New York, and, in the year 1795, was at Ticonderoga, on Lake George. At that time two Frenchmen came to the Indians on Lake George, and this deponent conversed with them in their own language. Their names deponent does not remember. They had with them a boy, which this deponent supposed to be between ten and twelve years of age. This boy the deponent talked with in the French language. The two Frenchmen told this deponent that the boy was French, by birth. The boy seemed weak and sickly, and his mind was wandering, so that he seemed rather silly. This child, after the Frenchmen had departed, this deponent saw in the family of Thomas Williams, an Indian, where the child lived. This deponent further recollects that he was at Lake George some time after this, when this boy, playing with the other children, fell, or threw himself from a rock into the lake, and was taken out with a wound, he thinks upon the head, and was carried into the hut of Thomas Williams. After this he, from time to time, saw the boy, and that boy is the person now known as the Rev. Eleazar Williams. Deponent further declares that, in 1815, when Mr. Williams first came to Oneida Castle, to preach to the Indians, deponent was there, and asked Mr. Williams if he remembered his fall into the lake, which he did not. Deponent also further declares, that one of the two Frenchmen who brought the child to Lake George seemed to have the appearance of a priest of the church of Rome. Deponent recollects Colonel Lewis, Captain Peters, Captain Jacob Francis, chiefs of the St. Regis tribe, who always believed Mr. Williams to be a Frenchman. This deponent also declares that he was acquainted with Thomas Williams, and Mary Ann, his wife, and that there is no resemblance between the Rev. Eleazar Williams and the said Thomas Williams or his wife, or any of the children of the said Thomas Williams and his wife Mary Ann, who were known also to this deponent. This deponent also further declares that Captain Jasper Parish, of Canandaigua, was appointed by the General or State Government, agent for the Six Nations, some time before the war of 1812, and after the war was over, in the year 1815, he took the census of each family, for the purpose of distributing the presents from the government. Eleazar Williams was set down by Captain Parish on the record as a Frenchman, adopted by the St. Regis tribe, and transferred to the Oneidas. This deponent was, at the time, a member of the general council of the nation, serving in the capacity of Marshal, and gave, himself, the returns to Captain Parish; and this deponent has seen the record of the census, which record may probably be found at Canandaigua, by writing to Mr. Edward Parish aforesaid. This deponent further says, that he remembers the spot at which the child now known as

Eleazar fell into the water, and that it was at the south end of Lake George, on the west side, not far from the Old Fort.

JOHN O'BRIEN.

Sworn before me, this 14th day of June, 1853.

RICHARD BUSTEED,
*Commissioner of Deeds*,
45 William Street, New York.

At my request, the Rev. Francis Vinton, D.D., of Brooklyn, who was present at the examination of O'Brien, and aided to take down his statement, wrote to the Hon. B. Sken Smith, of Philadelphia, brother of Gerrit Smith, and obtained the following answer :

"MY DEAR SIR,

"I have been much indisposed, and not able to answer your letter of the 18th ult. till now, and am still weak. I have known John O'Brien Skenondough, a half-breed Indian of the Oneida tribe, for thirty years and upwards. I suspect the 'important testimony' from him, which you refer to, relates to the Rev. Mr. Williams. I hesitate not to say, Skenondough can be relied on. I also know much of Mr. Williams.

"In much haste, very truly and respectfully yours,

"B. SKEN SMITH."

I opened, myself, a correspondence with the Rev. Mr. Ashley, of Syracuse, in order to obtain information from the other gentlemen referred to by Skenondough, but the letters in reply, of that gentleman, never reached me, like many others, which appear to have been intercepted. I would say that Skenondough is nephew of the old war chief Skenondough, who died some years ago, at the age of 112, and also that, as assistant surgeon, he dressed the wounds of Lafayette, at the battle of Brandywine.

---

[APPENDIX E. No. 2.—*Page* 177.]

*Writing of E. Williams, while insane, preserved.*

I will mention here a fact, which, however interesting, I have not stated in the text, because the evidence on which it rests is, unfortunately, only that of the testimony of Mr. Williams ; and, though I believe his word is as good as that of any one in the world, certain persons are perpetually harping on the chord, "Oh, Mr. Williams says so." There is now before me an Indian mass book, in MS., which, from the color of the paper, the faded, writing, and its dilapidated condition, seems at least two centuries old. It was given Mr. Williams in 1836, by an Indian woman, now dead, who told him that, while in an insane condition, he one day snatched a pen, and wrote in it a number of figures and letters. There is, on one of the covers, on the inside, in French characters, the numerals from 1 to 30, and from 1 to 19 ; a letter c, precisely like that element in the handwriting of the Dauphin while under the care of Simon ; and, in a less distinct form, but still quite legible, the word duc, and the letters Loui. One thing is evident, the numerals and letters are the random scribbling of a child, and they are many years old.

---

[Appendix F.—*Page* 183.]

*Baptismal Record.*

Extracts des registres de la Mission du Sault St. Louis.

1779, du 7 Janvier, Thomas Tehora Kwanekeu à épousé Marie Anne, fille de Haronhumanen. Leurs enfants sont

| | | | |
|---|---|---|---|
| Jean Baptiste, | né le | 7 Sept. | 1780. |
| Catherine, | née le | 4 Sept. | 1781. |
| Thomas, | né le | 28 Avr. | 1786. |
| Louise, | née le | 18 Mai, | 1791. |
| Jeanne Baptiste, | " | 21 Avr. | 1793. |
| Pierre, | né le | 25 Août, | 1795. |
| Pierre, | " | 4 Sept. | 1796. |
| Anne, | née le | 30 Janv. | 1799. |
| Dorothée, | " | 2 Août, | 1801. |
| Charles, | né | 8 Sept. | 1804. |
| Jervais, | " | 22 Juil. | 1807. |

*Marcoux, Prête.*

---

[Appendix G.—*Page* 189.]

*Ely MSS.*

These MSS. were obtained in 1851, from Col. Mack, of Amherst, Mass., who married the eldest daghter of Deacon Ely.

---

[Appendix H.—*Page* 190.]

*First coming to Long Meadow.*

We are assured by one of their schoolmates, who remembers their entrance into the village, in their Indian costume, that a distinction was at once perceived between Eleazar and John. John was evidently of Indian blood. He showed no fondness for study, always kept his bows and arrows hid away, and on any excuse or occasion would make use of them. Eleazar although entirely illiterate when he came there, soon became fond of his books. John learned little or nothing, and soon returned home. Eleazar made satisfactory progress and remained. His affable manners were such as to excite unusual attention in a quiet village, not much used to exaggerations of the graces of life, so that he was always called a plausible boy. He was thought by his schoolmates somewhat haughty, despised the Indian games of his supposed brother, and yet was led by those who had learned his character, without much difficulty. These peculiarities we have heard spoken of quite independently of any presumption that Mr. Williams was other than a son of Thomas Williams.

The only considerations of importance which those who knew Mr. Williams at West Hampton can contribute to the inquiry respecting his birth is the fact that he showed none of *the traits of the Indian race, and although spoken of as an Indian, was not really regarded as of Indian blood.—Boston Daily Advertiser, February* 17, 1853.

---

[APPENDIX I.— No 1.—*Page* 190.]

*Affidavit of Urania Smith.*

Declaration of Urania Smith, Point Washington, Ozaukee County, Wisconsin.

I, Urania Smith, do hereby declare that my maiden name was Urania Stebbings, that I was born on March 22d, in the year 1786, in Long Meadow, Massachusetts, that I was deprived of my parents when young, and was brought up by Ethan Ely, of Long Meadow, Massachusetts, who was my uncle, and lived next door to Deacon Nathaniel Ely. In the beginning of the year 1800, two boys were brought from Canada to Long Meadow, to receive an education, and lived with Nathaniel Ely, who had charge of them. They were said by the said Nathaniel Ely to be called Eleazar or Lazau Williams and John Williams, and were represented as the descendants of the Rev. John Williams, who was captured by the Indians in the year 1704, at Deerfield. They were entirely unlike each other in complexion, appearance, form and disposition, John having the look of an Indian, and Eleazar that of an European. I distinctly remember that when the said Nathaniel Ely was remonstrated with for calling Eleazar and John brothers, as there was no similarity between them, he said there was something about it which he should probably never reveal; that Eleazar Williams was born for a great man, and that he intended to give him an education to prepare him for the station. Eleazar was very rapid in his acquisitions of learning, and wrote at an early period. Much notice was taken of him by everybody, and Mr. Ely was very fond of exhibiting him to strangers.

URANIA SMITH.

Sworn to and subscribed before me, October 8, 1853, at Point Washington.

LAFAYETTE FORSLEY, I. P.
*Clerk Ozaukee District Court.*

---

[APPENDIX I.—No 2.—*Page* 190.]

*Expenses of Eleazar Williams paid from France. From the Albany Morning Epxress, Oct.* 10. 1853.

As we remarked the other day, there are strong circumstances in favor of the assumption set up by Mr. Hanson. One of the strongest to our mind is the fact, that certain gentlemen of this city for many years received regularly a sum of money from France, to be applied to the clothing and education of this same Williams. How is this fact to be accounted for, except upon the supposition that Williams is indeed the Dauphin.

---

[APPENDIX K.—*Page* 324.—*Page* 190.]

*Title Deed of Mrs. Williams's Estate.*

Know all men by these presents, that we, the chiefs, warriors, and head men of the Menominie nation of Indians, living and residing on the banks of Fox River and Green Bay, for and in consideration of the love and friendship we entertain for Magdeline Williams, and her heirs, of the Menominie Nation, and, also, in consideration of the sum of fifty dollars, to us in hand paid, the receipt whereof is hereby acknowledged, have given, granted, bargained, sold, and quit claimed to the said Magdeline Williams and her heirs for ever, all that certain piece or parcel of land situated, lying, and being on the north-west side of Fox River, at a place usually called Little Cacalin, bounded and described as follows:—Commencing at low water mark on Fox River, opposite to the lower end of "Black Bird Island," so called, and running thence up said river three hundred and fifty chains, thence north-west, two hundred and fifty chains, thence north-east, three hundred and fifty chains, thence south east, two hundred and fifty chains, to the place of beginning, be the same more or less, together with all, and singular, the appurtenances and hereditaments in any manner thereto appertaining or belonging to her, the said Magdeline Williams and her heirs, for ever, provided, nevertheless, that the said Magdeline Williams shall not, in any manner hereafter, for ever sell or dispose of the same, or any part thereof. In testimony whereof, we hereunto put our hands and seals, this 22d day of August, eighteen hundred and twenty-five.

SARKSTOK, his + mark. [Seal.]

PINONTO-OH, alias BLANDED, his + mark. [Seal.]

SHO-MIN, his + mark. [Seal.]

MATSI KI NEAOH, his + mark. [Seal.]

KESHA SHIK, his + mark. [Seal.]

OTA TSI A KIAOH, his + mark [Seal.]

Signed, sealed, and delivered in presence of A. S. ELLIS.

---

[APPENDIX L.—*Page* 324.]

*Certificate of Mr. J. F. Schermerhorn.*

[COPY.]

I hereby certify that the following provision, in the 3d Article of the Treaty concluded by me with the New York Indians, in Council at Duck Creek, on 16th day of September, 1836, in behalf of the St. Regis Indians, in the following words, viz: "Out of the above sum of $340,000, shall be allowed and paid the sum of $5000 to the St. Regis tribe, as a remuneration for the money laid out and expended by the said tribe and parties, and for services rendered by their chiefs and agents, in securing the title to these lands (viz. Green Bay, W. T.) and removal to the same, to be apportioned and paid out to the several claimants, by the chiefs and commissioners of the United States, as may be deemed by them equitable and just," and which said provision was inserted and made in the treaty finally concluded at the Buffalo Creek Reservation, January 15, 1838, in the language as above recited, understood when the treaty was made and concluded to be $1000, if paid to the St. Regis Tribe for their claims for advances made by them, and the balance, being $4000, was intended to remunerate the Rev. Eleazar Williams, as one of the Chiefs of the St. Regis Indians, and their agent, for his services for years, for securing the title to the Green Bay land, and for removing thither, and by whose exertions and persevering efforts these lands were finally attained for the New York Indians from the Menominies and Winnebago Indians, as is evident from the document on this subject, on file at the Indian Department at Washington. These facts being known to me personally, I deem it my duty, in justice to Mr. Williams, to make the above statement.

J. F. SCHERMERHORN,
Commissioner to treat with New York Indians, 1837.

*Washington City, June* 21, 1838.

The foregoing, enclosed to the President, July 10, 1838. Package of papers, &c., marked W. 572, Indian Office Files, Green Bay, 1838.

---

[APPENDIX M.—*Page* 424.]

*General Cass.*

The following is the pith of General Cass's letter, and of my reply:—

*St. Clair.*

His color, his features, and the conformation of his (Mr. Williams) face testify to his origin. They present the very appearance which everywhere marks the half-breed Indian.

I have seen persons partaking of the Bourbon blood, and I endeavor in vain to recall any decisive traits of resemblance between them and Mr. Williams.

*Reply.*

There are no traces of the aboriginal or Indian in him. Ethnology gives no countenance to such a conclusion. This fact is verified by anotomical examination by Drs. Francis and Kissam.

In painting the portrait of Mr. Williams, I noticed many of the peculiar characteristics which are developed, in a greater or less degree in most of the Princes of the House of Bourbon, whose portraits I have taken. I was particularly impressed with his resemblance to the portraits of Louis XVI. and

| *Clair.* | *Reply.* |
| --- | --- |
| | XVIII., and the general Bourbonic outline of his face. Had I met Mr. Williams, unconscious that he was in any way other than his name would indicate, I should immediately have spoken of his likeness to the Bourbon family.—Vide letter of Chevalier Fagnani, in "Putnam," for April. |
| The death of the Dauphin is a fact as well established as any incident of that kind can be. | I have myself shown, I consider, conclusively, that the fact *is not* and *cannot* be established. It is mere ignorance to assert that it is. |
| If I am not in error, there was a procès verbal, a kind of French legal narrative, which recorded the circumstances of his illness and his decease. | St. Clair's historic knowledge is of that peculiar kind which is proverbially dangerous. |
| The Dauphin was attended, towards the close of his life, by Desault, a physician of the highest personal professional character, and who could neither be guilty of imposition, nor suffer it in relation to the true condition of his interesting patient. | True, but the close of Desault's life was prior to the asserted close of the Dauphin's, and the high moral and professional character of this eminent physician forms an adamantine link in the evidence which disproves the death of the royal child. |
| I have no belief that such a diary as that which purports to recount the interview between the French Prince and the French pretender was ever kept by Williams. I can see no reason for it. His usual uneventful life furnished neither motive nor material for such a daily recurring labor. | It is vain to theorize against facts. Mr. Williams has kept a journal, and if St. Clair wishes, he can read in it the record of certain proceedings between General Cass and the Indians at Butte des Morts, in 1827, together with other not uneventful occurrences, with which St. Clair may be familiar, and to the publication even of which Mr. Williams can have no objection, provided St. Clair can obtain the consent of "the distinguished western statesman," above mentioned. |

| *St. Clair.* | *Reply.* |
|---|---|
| The Count de Chambord, the son of Charles X. the youngest brother of Louis XVI. | Another proof of the accuracy of St. Clair's historic knowledge. The Count de Chambord is son to the Duc de Berri. |
| It is further stated that Mr. Williams received letters from Lcuis Philippe and from the private Secretary of Louis Napoleon, &c. These were all burned, says the memoir. They never existed, says common sense. | No such statement was made. It is stated that Mr. Williams received a letter from Louis Philippe, and another purporting to be from the secretary of Louis Napoleon. As I mentioned that the note of the French consul-general, stating that it enclosed the letter of the French king, was before me at the time of writing, it is to be hoped that St. Clair alludes to his own common sense. |
| The Prince de Joinville inquired after Mr. Williams. So says Mr. Williams. | And so also say Captain Shook, Mr. Brayman, and Mr. Raymond. |
| Louis Philippe wrote him a letter. So says Mr. Williams. | And so says M. de la Forest, the then consul-general. |
| Bellanger confessed that he brought the Dauphin to this country. So says Mr. Williams. | And so said the southern newspapers of the time, from which Mr. Kimball, the informant of Mr. Williams, derived his knowledge. Respectable living gentlemen remember reading those newspaper statements. |
| I am sorry to be obliged to consider as apocryphal, the account of the magnificent brocade dress "against whose silken folds Mr. Williams had fondly rested, when the living loveliness of Marie Antoinette was within it," and it taxes my imagination beyond its capacity, when I am asked to picture to myself my old Indian acquaintance fondled in the arms of that beautiful queen. | That a trifle may tax the imagination, or any other mental quality of St. Clair, I can readily conceive. The dress was not adduced as evidence; but the following note from the donor may explain the position of Mr. Williams in regard to it, and the probabilities that it is what it is said to be:— "Presented to the Rev. Mr. Williams, with the respectful regards of Mrs. Edward Clarke, of North- |

| *St. Clair.* | *Reply.* |
| --- | --- |
| | ampton. Being in England some years since, I had an opportunity there to purchase this dress, once worn by Marie Antoinette, of France. It had been bought at the court by a gentlemen attached, at that time, to our embassy.—Round Hill, Northampton, Jan. 3, 1851." |
| That Mr. Williams is a respectable clergyman. Mr. Williams has voluntarily placed himself in no enviable position. He must stand or fall not by his character, but by his proofs. The Romans said of the departed, "He has lived." I am afraid we shall have to say of Mr. Williams, "He has been a respectable clergyman." | That St. Clair is a distinguished statesman. St. Clair has voluntarily placed himself in no enviable position. He must fall or stand, not by his character but by his proofs. The Romans said of the departed, "He has lived." I am afraid, if the letter of St. Clair be the criterion of his claim to the title of a distinguished statesman, we shall have to say, "He has been distinguished." |

---

[APPENDIX N.—*Page* 430.]

*Affidavit of Margaret Brown, of New Orleans.*

My name is Margaret Brown. I live in the city of New Orleans. I was born in the year 1779, but whether in Scotland or France is uncertain. I was educated in Scotland. The name of my first husband was Benjamin Olivier. He was a French Republican. I was married to him in Edinburgh and went with him to France. After the birth of my first child, I accompanied him to Normandy. I was married a second time in 1804, to Joseph Deboit, then Secretary to the Count D'Artois, who was at that period residing at Holyrood House, in Edinburgh. The Count d'Artois left Scotland shortly after my marriage with Deboit, who accompanied him. During the absence of the Count d'Artois from Edinburgh, I lived in the vicinity of the palace, except a portion of the time when I joined my husband in London. The Count de Provence and the Duchesse d'Angoulême arrived in England, and I first saw them with the Count d'Artois in South Audley street, Grosvenor Square. In consequence of the situation held by my husband, I became very intimate with the Duchesse d'Angoulême and the rest of the royal family, with whom I resided. Shortly after the arrival of the Duchesse d'Angoulême in England, in 1806 or 7, my curiosity having been excited by my husband, who had told me that the Dauphin was not dead, I asked the Duchesse her opinion respecting her brother's fate. The Duchesse d'Angoulême replied to me, that she knew he was alive and safe in America. At this period I first heard that a man named Bellanger, had carried the Dauphin to America, but whether it was from the Duchesse d'Angoulême or from Joseph Deboit I cannot now certainly say. But it was from one of the two, and my impression is that it was from the Duchesse. I distinctly remember that I heard the fact at that time from one of them, as they were the only persons with whom I spoke on the subject, and also that the Duchesse d'Angoulême told me that she knew the Dauphin was then safe in America. Joseph Deboit died in 1810. Until his death I resided with him in Holyrood, in intimate acquaintance with the royal family. I went to France in 1811, to look after some property. I there married George Brown, an American, at Morley in France. Brown was sailing master to the True Blooded Yankee, under Commodore Preble's brother. In 1813, the aide-de-camp of General Moreau gave me dispatches to carry to the Bourbon family in England. His name was, I think, De Vaux. He put them between the ticking and the leather of the trunk. I took them in this way across the channel, and gave them into the hands of the Count d'Artois, in South Audley street, in the presence of M. de Belleville. Shortly after this I again went to France, and after remaining there a short time went to sea with my husband. There was a dangerous mutiny on board. We arrived in the Brazils, and I kept school in St. Salvador. From St. Salvador I set out for New York with my husband in the Tom Bowling, Capt. Carleton.

Mr. Brown died at sea on the 7th June, 1815. The Tom Bowling arrived in New York on or about July 4th, 1815. From New York I went to the Havana, and was housekeeper to Grey and Fernandez. I then returned to Scotland. In the year 1817, I was living in the same house with Mrs. Chamberlaw, wife to the Secretary of the Count de Coigny, who had lived with the Count de Provence during his residence in Edinburgh. I was familiar both with the Count and Mrs. Chamberlaw while I lived with Deboit in the palace of Holyrood. Mrs. Chamberlaw told me, that some time before, she had heard in the Tuileries that the Dauphin was alive, that a man named Bellanger had carried him to Philadelphia, and that he was then known by the name of Williams. She mentioned his christian name, and I think I should remember it if I heard it. It was not Joseph. It was not Aaron. It seems to me that it was Eleazar. She said that Williams was a missionary among the Indians, and that the royal family said he was incompetent to reign. She also told me that a person came over from America to France on this business, who was supposed in the palace to be Williams himself. She saw him—money was given to him, and he returned to America. Such was Mrs Chamberlaw's statement to me in 1817. I have the most distinct remembrance of it. The name of Bellanger has been kept in my memory by seeing it on shops. That of Williams, the Indian Missionary, who was said by Mrs. Chamberlaw to be the Dauphin, was impressed on my mind of itself and I have never forgotten it. I again came to New York in 1819. I settled in Louisiana in 1820, where I have since lived in great retirement. I have spoken to several people on this subject for many years, and especially to Mrs. Catherine Read. I do not expect to live long, and have no wish in this matter to say one word, but what I have always said, and which as a person soon to appear before God, I solemnly declare to be true.

Signed MARGARET BROWN.

Sworn to and subscribed before me the 28th day of April, 1853, at the city of New Orleans.

Signed G. LUGENBAHL,
*5th Justice of the Peace.*

*Affidavit of Mrs. Catherine Read, made in New Orleans.*

My name is Catherine Read. I am a native of the state of New York. I have resided in New Orleans since 1805. I have known Mrs. Margaret Brown for many years, and I believe her to be a person whose veracity can be depended on. She is poor, but a religious, conscientious woman. My attention was first called to her about sixteen or seventeen years ago, by the Rev. Mr. Fox, a minister of the Episcopal church in this city. He told me that she was a person who had seen great vicissitudes, and had been intimately acquainted with the royal family of France. I have for years been in the habit of conversing with Mrs. Brown respecting the events of her life and have repeated to others and especially to the Rev. Mr. Whitall much that she had said, in the hope of exciting sympathy for her reverses. She mentioned to me long before I heard anything of the publications which I am now informed have been made in late years respecting the identity of the Rev. Eleazar Williams with the Dauphin, and before she could have heard anything on the subject derived from American sources, and evidently without any object but to communicate facts of interest, or any idea that the information was of importance, or that I should repeat it, that her second husband was named Joseph Deboit, and was Secretary to the Count D'Artois, that she had been personally acquainted with the Count de Provence and the Duchesse d'Angoulême, and had been employed previous to the accession of Louis XVIII. to carry dispatches to members of the royal family of France, then resident in England, in proof of which she showed me the secret badge, ornamented with fleur-de-lis, which she had used on the occasion. She also stated that when she was living in Edinburgh she had been informed that a person named Bellanger had carried the Dauphin, Louis Charles, son of Louis XVI. and Marie Antoinette, from France to America, and had taken him at first to Philadelphia, and that he was a missionary among the Indians, and was known by the name of Williams. She also mentioned that a man went from America to France on this business about 1815. She has been in the habit to my certain remembrance of telling this story for twelve or thirteen years past, but few persons would pay any attention to her, and imagined her to be insane, and I have listened to her out respect to her character, and because what she said amused me, but without any idea that the information she gave me could ever be of any practical importance. It is just to add that Mrs. Brown is not only a good and conscientious woman, but that she is in all human probability very near the hour of death from cancer in the breast, and that I can conceive no possible reason why she should state anything but the simple truth. She never spoke to me respecting the Dauphin, except when questioned concerning her history, and then mentioned these circumstances as forming part of the events of her life.

Signed, C. Read.

Sworn to, and subscribed before me, on the 28th day of April, 1853, at the city of New Orleans.

Signed G. Lugenbahl,
*5th Justice of the Peace.*

*Affidavit of the Rev. Charles Whitall, of New Orleans.*

I am a native of New Jersey, and have resided eleven years in the city of New Orleans, as a minister of the gospel. Mrs. Catherine Read is a lady of the highest respectability, and is a communicant of my parish, and a person in whose statements the most implicit confidence can be placed. I am also acquainted with Mrs. Margaret Brown, and know her to be a very respectable, pious old lady, of whom nothing but what is creditable can be spoken. I first became acquainted with her through Mrs. Read. I have read both their affidavits, and am perfectly familiar with the statements made in them, from hearing Mrs. Read speak of them for many years past. With Mrs. Brown I have never conversed in reference to the Dauphin, because I did not think the matter of any moment, and felt rather inclined to ridicule the affair—but for five or six years past, I have heard Mrs Read say, that she had been acquainted with the royal family of France, and that a man named Bellanger, brought the Dauphin to this country. I can add my testimony not only to the good character but to the infirm health of Mrs. Margaret Brown, and regard it as to the last degree improbable that she should state anything but the truth,

Signed CHARLES WHITALL.

Sworn and subscribed before me, this 28th day of April, 1853, at the city of New Orleans.

Signed G. LUGENBAHL.

I am myself personally acquainted with the parties whose affidavits are before given, and can cheerfully vouch for their respectability, and the entire reliability of their testimony. I have known Mrs. Margaret Brown for thirteen years, and believe her to be a religious, good woman.

Signed G. LUGENBAHL, *5th Justice.*

---

[APPENDIX O.—*Page* 436.]

*Names of the Children of Thomas Williams*

There are some striking discrepancies between the list of names, as given by Mrs. Williams, and the baptismal register at Caughnawaga. I do not pretend to account for this, except it can be ascribed to failure or confusion of memory on the part of the old woman, who appears to know little about Eleazar, except that he was "adopted," and brought to her by Thomas Williams. One great reason, I learn, why she has been hitherto unwilling to acknowledge boldly that Eleazar was her adopted child, was, that the idea was hinted to her that, being now without husband or children, and only Eleazar left, if she confessed he was not her child, he would think himself no more bound to take care of her.

THE END.

www.ingramcontent.com/pod-product-compliance
Lightning Source LLC
LaVergne TN
LVHW020931110826
845150LV00004B/829
* 9 7 8 1 4 2 5 5 5 4 4 7 7 *